ABERDEEN UNIVERSITY STUDIES
NUMBER 146

THE FUSION OF 1860

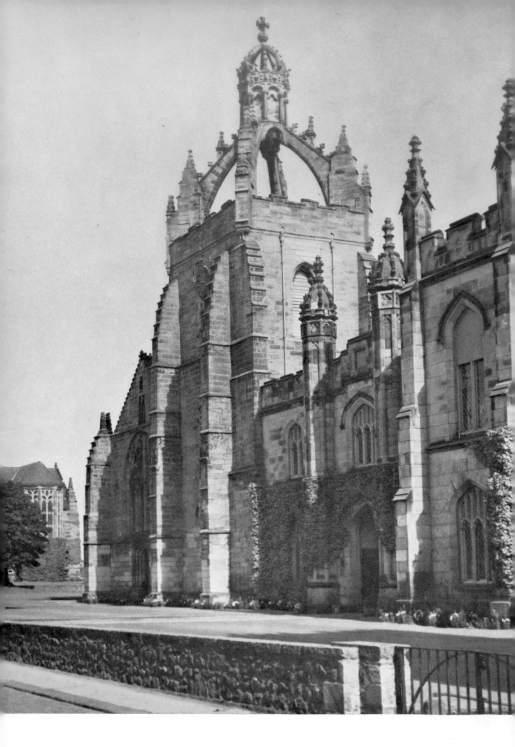

THE UNIVERSITY OF KING'S COLLEGE

Founded 1494
Under the Bulla of Pope Alexander VI
by Bishop Elphinstone

THE FUSION OF 1860

A Record of the Centenary
Celebrations and a History
of the United University of
Aberdeen 1860-1960

EDITED BY

W. DOUGLAS SIMPSON

C.B.E., D.Litt., LL.D.

Published for the University of Aberdeen

OLIVER AND BOYD

EDINBURGH: TWEEDDALE COURT
LONDON: 39A WELBECK STREET, W.I.

FIRST PUBLISHED . . . 1963

© 1963, THE UNIVERSITY OF ABERDEEN

PRINTED IN GREAT BRITAIN AT THE UNIVERSITY PRESS, ABERDEEN
FOR OLIVER AND BOYD LTD., EDINBURGH

PREFACE

THIS VOLUME contains (1) the official Record of the Centenary Celebrations of the " Fusion"; (2) a History of the United University during the first century of its existence, written by Dr. Douglas Simpson; (3) a History of the General Council during the same period, written by Mrs. Louise Donald; and (4) a reprint, *in toto*, of the Centenary issue of the *Aberdeen University Review*, containing much information of fascinating interest about the internal life of the University during the past hundred years, with vivid pen-portraits and reminiscences of the leading personalities who have served it.

The Business Committee are grateful to the University Studies Committee for including it in their series, and to the Committee of Management of the *University Review* for permitting the inclusion of their Centenary Number.

The late Principal Sir Thomas Taylor, Dr. H. J. Butchart, the former Secretary of the University, and his successor Mr. W. S. Angus, were good enough to read through the History of the University. As Mrs. Donald is meantime in Rhodesia, the typescript of her contribution, with her full approval, was adjusted for the press by Dr. Simpson and myself. The index to the volume has been prepared by Dr. Simpson.

In their respective contributions, Dr. Simpson and Mrs. Donald inevitably to some extent traverse the same ground: but their points of view are different, and no attempt has been made to achieve a synthesis of their narratives.

As more than two years have now elapsed since the Centenary I think it desirable briefly to enumerate the more important happenings in the history of the University that have taken place in the interval.

This volume is published under the shadow of the heavy loss which the University has sustained by the sudden death on 19 July 1962, of Principal Sir Thomas Taylor. His interest in the General Council was constant and unflagging; and no one did more than he to ensure the success of the Centenary Celebrations, and to forward the project of the present book. As is fully set forth both by Dr. Simpson and Mrs. Donald, no cause lay nearer his heart than the preservation of Old Aberdeen: and two of his greatest achievements were the persuading of the Town Council to make a generous gift to the University of land at Seaton to compensate for the sacrifice of the northern playing field at King's College required for building expansion; and the obtaining from the McRobert Trustees of a munificent grant towards the reconditioning of the old houses in the Aulton.

Since this book was in type the restoration of a working arrangement with the North of Scotland College of Agriculture has been achieved, and plans made for a joint building on the northern playing field. The new building in the High Street, designed to accommodate the Faculties of Arts and Law, approaches completion. So also does the new Natural Philosophy Department on the Market lands; and beside it will arise a large new Science Library, work on which has now commenced.

Tarradale House has been reconditioned, under the direction of the Department of Geography, and has already proved its worth as a centre of Field Studies, not only for Aberdeen but also for other British Universities. So our University continues to develop, strong in the zealous service of its members and confident of its ability to face the many and serious problems of a rapidly changing world and an unprecedented programme of expansion.

JOHN N. MILNE
Convener of the Business Committee
of the General Council

April, 1963

CONTENTS

ILLUSTRATIONS

I

THE CENTENARY CELEBRATIONS
14-16 September 1960

I T was on 28 October 1955 that the Clerk of the General Council, Dr. W. Douglas Simpson, called the attention of the Business Committee to the fact that the centenary of the " Fusion " of the old Universities of King's and Marischal Colleges would fall due on 15 September 1960. He suggested that this unique event in academic history should be celebrated in a manner worthy of the occasion. The Business Committee welcomed the suggestion; and it was agreed to recommend accordingly to the forthcoming Statutory Meeting of the General Council.

This meeting, held on 17 December 1955, accepted the proposal with acclamation. It was pointed out, in the Business Committee's Report for that occasion, that the centenary of the General Council itself fell due in the same year—the first Statutory Meeting of Council having taken place on 10 October 1860. The Council accordingly agreed to recommend to the University Court that the forthcoming centenary of the Fusion of 1860 should be suitably celebrated, and that the celebrations should include also the centenary of the General Council.

These proposals were warmly received by the University Court and the Senatus Academicus; and in due course a Joint Committee of the three bodies concerned was set up.

During the deliberations that followed it was pointed out that the year 1960 would also mark the centenary of the University Court; and it was decided that this event should likewise be recognized in the forthcoming celebrations.

At a Meeting of the Business Committee on 23 January 1957, the Convener Mr. John N. Milne, made the proposal, which was immediately approved, that the occasion should be utilized to compile and distribute a short history of the General Council.

It was further suggested that the opportunity should be taken of compiling and publishing a further instalment of the Roll of Graduates covering the period 1926-55; and Mr. John Mackintosh, M.A., accepted an invitation from the Convener, to act as editor of this volume.

The Joint Committee expressed the opinion that there should also be compiled a history of the united University during the first hundred years of its existence. Dr. Douglas Simpson undertook this work, and Mrs. Louise Donald, M.A., was invited to compile the history of the General Council for the same period.

Out of the deliberations of the Joint Committee the following programme of events finally emerged:

Wednesday, 14 September 1960, 8 p.m.: General Council Dinner for Graduates in the Elphinstone Hall.

Thursday, 15 September 1960, 10 a.m.: Special Graduation Ceremony in the Mitchell Hall.

Thursday, 15 September 1960, 12 noon: Commemoration Service in King's College Chapel.

Thursday, 15 September 1960, 1 p.m.: Graduation Lunch in the Elphinstone Hall.

Thursday, 15 September 1960, 8 p.m.: University Reception in the Mitchell Hall.

Friday, 16 September 1960, 1 p.m.: Lunch by the University Court in the Elphinstone Hall.

Friday, 16 September 1960, 8 p.m.: Civic Reception in the Beach Ballroom.

It was further decided that an Exhibition illustrating the history of the University should be arranged in the Court Room, and that there should be another Exhibition of suitable items at King's College Library.

On 22 April 1959, Mr. Norman J. Logie, T.D., M.B., suggested to the Business Committee that the General Council should be invited to mark the centenary by providing a gift to the University. After discussion it was decided that this gift could best take the form of the provision of a service of silver plate for use on ceremonial occasions. This proposal was adopted by the General Council at its meeting on 19 December 1959.

Favoured by excellent weather the programme of events as set forth above was carried out with complete success.

The General Council Dinner on the 14 September was attended by 408 ladies and gentlemen, including twelve guests and three representatives of the press. After the Loyal Toast the health of the University was proposed by the Convener of the Business Committee and replied to by Principal Sir Thomas Taylor. Mr. Norman Logie, on behalf of the subscribers, presented to the University the first instalment of the silver table furnishings, and the gift was acknowledged by the Principal.

A souvenir of the Dinner which will long be treasured by those who were present was the Toast List which included the University's Coat of Arms in full heraldic colours, and fine pictures of King's College and Marischal College, with an explanation of the heraldic bearings, and short notes on the two Colleges.

At the Graduation Ceremony on the 15th, in addition to those academic and civic dignitaries usually invited on such occasions, the

Provosts of Stonehaven, Inverbervie, Inverurie, Dornoch, Cullen, Nairn, Banff, Elgin and Inverness, took part in the procession, as well as representatives of other British Universities, and the Chairman and Secretary of the Carnegie Trust of the Universities of Scotland. The following seven honorary degrees were conferred:

Doctors of Divinity: Marc Boegner, D.THEOL. (Paris), President of the French Academy of Moral and Political Sciences.

The Rev. Ronald Hugh Wilson Falconer, M.A., B.D. (Aberdeen), Organizer of Religious Broadcasting for Scotland.

Doctors of Law: Sir Robert Stevenson Aitken, M.D. (N.Z.), D.PHIL. (Oxon.), LL.D. (Dalh., Melb., Panj., McGill and Penn.), D.SC. (Syd.), F.R.C.P. (Lond., Edin.), F.R.A.C.P., Vice-Chancellor of the University of Birmingham and Chairman of the Committee of Vice-Chancellors and Principals.

The Right Honourable Lord Clyde (James Latham McDiarmid Clyde), P.C., B.A. (Oxon.), LL.D. (Edin., St. And.), Lord Justice-General of Scotland.

Edmund Langley Hirst, C.B.E., M.A., B.SC., PH.D., LL.D. (St. And.), D.SC. (Birm.), M.SC. (Manc.), F.R.I.C., F.R.S., F.R.S. (Edin.), Forbes Professor of Organic Chemistry in the University of Edinburgh and President of the Royal Society of Edinburgh.

John Nelson Milne, M.A., LL.B., B.COM. (Aberdeen), Convener of the Business Committee of the General Council of the University of Aberdeen.

William Douglas Simpson, O.B.E., M.A., D.LITT. (Aberdeen), F.S.A., F.S.A. Scot., Librarian, Clerk and Registrar of the General Council of the University of Aberdeen.

These honorary degrees were conferred by the Chancellor of the University, the Rt. Hon. Thomas Johnston, P.C., C.H., LL.D. The Honorary Graduands in Divinity were promoted by the Dean of that Faculty, the Rev. Professor John Macleod, M.A., D.D., and those in law by the Dean of the Faculty of Law, Professor Farquhar MacRitchie, M.A., LL.B.

The Graduation Address was delivered by the Principal.

The Commemoration Service, immediately thereafter in King's College Chapel, was attended by a crowded and distinguished congregation, and was relayed to an equally large audience in an adjoining classroom. The Service was conducted by the Rev. Alan O. Robertson, B.D., S.T.M., Chaplain to the University, and the Address was given by the Very Rev. John A. Fraser, M.B.E., T.D., B.D.

Thereafter the Graduation Lunch took place in the Elphinstone Hall. It was attended by a gathering representative of Town and Gown in Aberdeen, delegates from other Universities at home and abroad, and other guests of distinction, the company present numbering in all 230.

After the Loyal Toast had been given by the Principal, the health of the University was proposed by Principal Sir Hector Hetherington, K.B.E., LL.D., D.LITT., M.A. and replied to by our own Principal. Thereafter

Sir Thomas Taylor proposed the health of the University's guests and this was replied to by Dr. Marc Boegner.

Since the texts of all the speeches delivered on the various occasions during the centenary celebrations are not available, it has been decided not to print any of these. It should, however, be recorded that none of those present at the Lunch on the 15th will ever forget the impromptu speech delivered, in the most beautiful French, by Professor Boegner.

It deserves also to be placed on record that the senior guest on this occasion was Mrs. Gilroy, widow of the late Professor James Gilroy, D.D., who held the Chair of Semitic Languages and Literature from 1895 till his death in 1931. Mrs. Gilroy was in her 99th year and was thus, almost in her own person, a link spanning the hundred years of the existence of the united University. She completed her own centenary on 23 November 1961 and died on 9 December 1961. To the end she retained an unrivalled memory of life in the University and, particularly in Old Aberdeen, for the past sixty-five years.

The Graduation Reception held in the Mitchell Hall that evening followed the pattern of such functions, but was marked by the unusual size of the gathering. It is estimated that it was attended by between 800 and 900 persons, including many of the University's guests and graduates and alumni from near and far.

On Friday, 16 September, the University Court entertained a large and distinguished gathering to lunch in the Elphinstone Hall. This lunch was specially intended to mark the University Court's own centenary. It was attended by a company of 155 ladies and gentlemen. On this occasion the only toast proposed was that of Her Majesty the Queen.

The Evening Reception given by the City Corporation in the Beach Ballroom was another very brilliant occasion, when a large company of graduates and friends of the University were received and entertained by the Lord Provost and members of the Town Council.

With this function a strenuous and most enjoyable programme was successfully brought to a close. It should be added, however, that various class reunions were arranged to take place coincidentally with the official functions. In particular, a most successful reunion of graduates between the years 1917 and 1924 was organized by a special committee, of which Mrs. Louise Donald, M.A., acted as secretary.

During the period also, all the University premises were open for inspection by graduates and their friends; while visits were arranged to the out-stations at Tillycorthie and Culterty.

The general impression left by all those who were privileged to take part in this memorable occasion may be best summarized in the reference made to it by our Principal in his address to the General Council at the Statutory Meeting on 17 December following. The Principal referred to the celebrations in the following terms: "I think it may be fairly claimed that what we did then was not unworthy of the occasion. For the vital thirty-six hours we were favoured with a spell of fine weather sandwiched between two downpours of rain. These were strenuous but memorable days. In retrospect the nicest thing about them was the appreciation of our guests and visitors, and the obvious pleasure which the occasion gave to great numbers of our own graduates gathered from far and wide. Among the many who contributed to the success of the centenary I must make reference to Miss Nan Shepherd, whose special number of the *University Review* was immensely and deservedly appreciated. I should also acknowledge the fine work which was done by the University secretariat in making the detailed and very complicated arrangements for these celebrations."

It remains to be added that up to date (January 1962) there has been received for the Centenary Silver Fund, from all sources, a sum amounting to £2151 5s. From this Fund the following articles have been purchased: 2 crystal and silver wine decanters, 4 flat dishes, 3 mustard pots, 3 salt cellars, 3 pepper pots, 1 sugar caster, 1 cream jug, 6 small spoons, 1 rose bowl, 2 dozen table forks, 2 dozen dessert forks, 2 dozen dessert spoons, 2 dozen coffee spoons, 2 dozen soup spoons, 2 dozen pairs hors d'oeuvre eaters, 1 dozen pairs serving spoons and forks, 2 dozen grapefruit spoons, 2 dozen ice/fruit spoons, 2 dozen table knives, 2 dozen cheese knives, 2 dozen pairs fish eaters.

Furthermore the General Council has used part of the money to present to the University a replica of the original King's College Mace, which has become too frail for regular use. This replica was formally handed over by the Convener of the Business Committee at the Statutory Meeting of Council held on 1 July 1961.

The Graduates' Roll for the period 1926-55 was published early in 1961. The speed with which this volume was completed and passed through the press reflects the utmost credit on the editor, Mr. John Mackintosh, M.A. No higher compliment to him can be paid than the bare statement that the volume is fully worthy of its predecessor, the Graduates' Roll for 1901-25 with supplement 1869-1900.

W. D. S.

THE UNIVERSITY OF MARISCHAL COLLEGE

Founded 1593
By the fifth Earl Marischal of Scotland
George Keith

2

THE UNIVERSITY OF ABERDEEN
1860 - 1960

BY

W. DOUGLAS SIMPSON

ON 15 September 1860, in accordance with the Universities (Scotland) Act, 1858, the University and King's College in Old Aberdeen, and Marischal College and University in the New Town, were united to form the University of Aberdeen as we know her today. By this enactment, referred to at the time as " the Fusion ", an end was put to a chapter of academic history unique in Britain.

For the greater part of a period of 267 years, Aberdeen—or rather, " both Aberdeens ", to borrow the phrase so beloved of its old-time chronicler, honest John Spalding—had possessed as many universities as all England: for, after Oxford and Cambridge, Durham University dates only from 1832, and London from 1836.

The two Universities of Aberdeen originated thus-wise. There was first the University in the Old Town, founded by the Papal Bull granted, at the instigation of the wise and good Bishop William Elphinstone, by Pope Alexander VI (Rodrigo Borgia) on 10 February 1494—that is, 1495 according to our reckoning, for in the Middle Ages the calendar year began on 1 March. By this Bull—still preserved in the University Library—a *Studium Generale*, or University, was founded in " the renowned City of Old Aberdeen "—a University complete in all its Faculties: Theology, Law, Medicine and Arts. Pursuant to the Papal Bull, the College of St. Mary of the Nativity, known almost from its foundation as King's College in honour of its patron, James IV, was formally constituted on 17 September 1505. Then, on 2 April 1593—almost exactly a century after the establishment of the University in Old Aberdeen— George Keith, fifth Earl Marischal, scholar, traveller, soldier and statesman, founded in the New Town a second University, known ever since as Marischal College. This was by no means merely another College within the University of Aberdeen, like the Colleges of Oxford and Cambridge. It was nothing less than a separate University, likewise complete in all its Faculties, and with the power to grant a degree in any of them. The circumstances of its foundation have been investigated, with his usual scholarly thoroughness, by the late Professor G. D. Henderson;[1] and while it cannot be maintained that Marischal College was set up deliberately as a Protestant rival to her elder sister in the Aulton, nevertheless it is certain that much crypto-Catholicism hung around King's, and that Marischal College was founded, strictly and expressly, as an organ of the Reformed Church.

The provision of two Universities within little more than a long mile of each other, in a region sparsely populated and poor in natural resources, and competing with each other for staff, students[2] and endowments, was bound to result in a rivalry seldom generous and too often downright hostile. For long, indeed, King's College refused to recognize her younger sister as a University at all. She, King's College, was " the University "; the Earl Marischal's foundation was " the New Town College ". This painful matter was not finally settled until a decision of the House of Lords was obtained in favour of Marischal College, on 11 April 1745. Repeated attempts were made to negotiate a union: first in the " Caroline University " of 1641, an enlightened project unfortunately brought to ruin by the Civil War; then, on no less than four occasions in the course of the eighteenth century; again between 1818 and 1839, with partial success in the establishing of a joint and thriving Medical School at Marischal College—terminated, alas! by a resolution of the Senatus Academicus at King's College that it was " inexpedient, and even dangerous, to maintain further intercourse with Marischal College "; yet again in 1826 and 1836 by the emphatic yet unregarded recommendations of Royal Commissions; and finally by a third Royal Commission in 1857, whose findings were embodied in the Act of Parliament of 1858, as a result whereof the " Fusion " was duly effected, two years later.

Although the necessity of this measure was evident to the wisest heads at that time, the union was not achieved without strong opposition and bitter heartburn, particularly among the teachers, graduates, alumni, and students of Marischal College, not to speak of the inhabitants of the New Town, who felt that it was being deprived of its status as a University city:[3]

> 'Twas not that Don should run to Dee,
>   Or Dee fall into Don;
> But that their Colleges should be
>   United into one.

---

[1] G. D. Henderson, *The Founding of Marischal College* (Aberdeen University Studies, No. 123), 1947.

[2] For example, in 1669 it is recorded that the regents of both Universities spent their vacations in " goeing throw the cuntrie and intysing the scholleres from the one Colledge to the other "!

[3] It must be remembered that Old Aberdeen and New Aberdeen were then separate Corporations, and remained so until 1891, when the latter absorbed the former.

So still the old prophetic dream
Explains its mystic course,
And learning's long-divided stream
Shall run with double force.

At the " Fusion " it was decided that in the united University the Faculties of Arts and Divinity should be located at King's College, and those of Law and Medicine, with the classes in Science, at Marischal College.[1] It was provided that there shall not be more than one Professor in any one branch of instruction in the Faculty of Arts.[2] The consequent redundancy of existing Principalships and Chairs was solved, for the most part, by retiring, on full salary during life, the senior of the two Professors in each case; but in one notable instance this was departed from, and so the University of Aberdeen lost the greatest scientist who has ever graced her walls—James Clerk Maxwell.[3] The existing Chairs, amalgamated in this fashion, were those of Humanity (Latin), Greek, Mathematics, Moral Philosophy, Natural Philosophy, Oriental languages, and Natural History; the sole existing Chair of Chemistry (at Marischal College) was of course retained; the Chair of Church History was formed by conjoining the Professorship of Divinity and Church History in King's College, the Professorship of Divinity in Marischal College, and the Professorship of Church History in Marischal College; and new Chairs were created in Logic and English Literature[4] (replacing the old separate Chairs of Logic), Biblical Criticism, Systematic Theology (representing the former King's College Chair of Divinity), Botany, Institutes of Medicine (now represented by the Chair of Physiology), Materia Medica and Midwifery.

For the united University a coat of arms was devised quartering the heraldic bearings of Elphinstone, Keith, Old Aberdeen and New Aberdeen, with the motto (from Psalm lxi. 10): *Initium Sapientiae Timor Domini*. To the red gown carried by the students of both Colleges was added the

[1] Ordinance of 1858 Commissioners, No. 2 (Aberdeen No. 1), Section 2. It is interesting to note that this was precisely the arrangement proposed by the wise mind of Cosmo Innes, when in 1854 he published his splendid edition of the King's College muniments: " The greatest and most evident of all academic reforms in Aberdeen is the union of the sister Colleges. The trifling inconvenience that may be felt by some of the citizens is hardly to be named in comparison with the great advantages that would result from such a measure. If the law and medical lectures were carried on in the Town building, in the neighbourhood of the courts and hospitals; if the education in languages, philosophy and theology were conducted in the venerable rural retreat, Aberdeen would afford a specimen of as convenient arrangements for teaching as any University can boast of. An end would be put for ever to the petty jars which have sometimes disturbed the neighbouring schools; and by uniting classes and salaries, a respectable maintenance would be secured for the masters, and consequently the means of obtaining the best masters " (*Fasti Aberdonenses*, Preface, pp. lxvi-vii).

[2] Section 1 of above Ordinance.

[3] A memorial to him was placed in 1956 in the Picture Gallery at Marischal College.

[4] The existing Chair of English was founded in 1894 by Ordinance No. 36 (Aberdeen No. 4) under the Trust Disposition and Settlement of John Hay Chalmers.

2

velvet collar—hitherto a distinctive feature of the Marischal College " toga ".

At Marischal College, what remained of the ancient conventual buildings of the Greyfriars, as enlarged by the elder Adam in 1731-41, had been recently (1836-44) swept away to make room for a new quad-rangle, designed by Archibald Simpson.   At King's the position was different.   On the east side of the quadrangle the medieval common hall still survived; the south side was occupied by the picturesque neo-classical piazza and lodgings built in 1725 by the generosity of a graduate, James Fraser, first Secretary of Chelsea Hospital, and a munificent donor to the Library; while the west front was closed by the existing range, a creditable specimen of " Abbotsford Gothic " erected in 1825 by the " town's architect ", Simpson's great rival, John Smith—familiarly known as " Tudor Johnnie " from his affection for his own particular version of that architectural style.   Fraser's buildings had been designed partly for residential purposes: indeed, a solitary old bachelor Professor, *ultimus Romanorum*, was still " living in " at the time of the " Fusion ". New buildings, devised purely as classrooms, were therefore requisite; and these were in due course provided by the Board of Works.   The University Library contains a series of plans, sections and elevations for a horrific scheme in florid neo-Gothic, somewhat after the manner of Fettes College.   Mercifully, considerations of parsimony intervened, and between 1862 and 1865 the present east and south ranges, dull yet inoffensive, were built, followed in 1870 by the Library.   Previous to then the books had been housed in the ante-chapel.   The total cost of these new buildings was £20,000.   In 1884 an eastward extension to the Library was made to house the Melvin Bequest.   As a result of these sweeping changes, the only ancient buildings now surviving at King's College are the Chapel with its Crown Tower (1500-5); the Round Tower (*circa* 1525); and the " New Wark "—now known as the Cromwell Tower—built in 1658.

The Act of 1858 created two new administrative bodies in the Scottish Universities—the University Court and the General Council, or assembly of graduates.   Both these bodies therefore, as well as the united University, celebrated their centenary in 1960.   Of the General Council Mrs. Louise Donald tells the story later in this volume.   In Aberdeen the University Court, as constituted in 1858, consisted of the Rector (ap-pointed by the matriculated students), the Principal, and four Assessors, nominated personally by the Chancellor, the Rector, the Senatus Academicus, and the General Council.   To the General Council was given the right to appoint the Chancellor.   The first Chancellor of the new University was the fifth Duke of Richmond and Gordon; the first Rector, Edward Francis Maitland, Solicitor-General for Scotland, later Lord Barcaple ; and the first Principal, Dr. Peter Colin Campbell, formerly Principal of Marischal College.   To the University Court was given power to revise all decisions of the Senatus and to be a Court of

Appeal from the Senatus and to appoint Professors. The Senatus retained the power of superintending and regulating the teaching and discipline and also of administering its properties and revenues subject to the control and review of the University Court. The Court was further given power to censure or suspend or deprive from office the Principal or Professors, this to take effect only after approval by Her Majesty in Council.

It is interesting to note that power was given to the Commissioners under the 1858 Act to found a National University for Scotland, and for converting the existing Universities into Colleges of the National University, subject to the consent of the existing Universities.

By the Representation of the People Act, 1868, the Scottish Universities were given the right to elect two Members of Parliament, one for St. Andrews and Edinburgh, the other for Glasgow and Aberdeen. In 1881 enrolment on the Register of the General Council was made compulsory upon all graduates.

The organization thus set up for the united University remained unchanged until the passing of the Universities (Scotland) Act, 1889. By this measure, the University Court was enlarged to its present number of fourteen, by the addition of the Lord Provost and the Town Council's Assessor, and by the increase from one each to four each of the Assessors appointed respectively by the Senatus Academicus and the General Council. The introduction of a municipal element in the government of the Scottish Universities was doubtless a recognition of historic fact: for both Marischal College in Aberdeen and Edinburgh University had from the outset been very much " the Town's Colleges ", over which the municipality had exerted a strict, indeed at times a highly irksome control. Most fortunately, the importation of a municipal interest in the governance of the University was not accompanied by any obligation upon the City Corporation to contribute to its finances. Had it been otherwise, the consequences today, when Town Councils are controlled by party politics, would have been disastrous.

It is curious to note that, in the early stages of preparing the Parliamentary Bill which ultimately became the Act of 1889, it was at one time proposed to have Assessors on the University Court nominated by the Crown. The Act of 1889 greatly strengthened the powers of the University Court, at the expense of the Senatus Academicus. The powers of the Court were not only strengthened but very much enlarged. It was created a corporate body with perpetual succession and a Common Seal. All property heritable and moveable forming part of the University, irrespective of who then held the title of such property, was vested in the University Court. It was also given power to administer and manage the whole revenue and property of the University and Colleges thereof, to act as a Court of Appeal from the Senatus, to appoint Professors, Lecturers and Examiners, to recognize teaching by Colleges or individuals for graduation purposes, to define Professors' duties, to take proceedings against teachers and examiners, under Section 12 (5) of the 1858 Act, and to found new Professorships. The Act further established the Universities Committee of the Privy Council, and gave the Court the power to appoint a representative of the University upon the General Medical Council. The Act also provided for the establishment of the two Standing Joint Committees of the Court and the Senatus, namely the Library Committee and the Museums Committee. Previously, the Library had been administered by a Senatorial Committee appointed first in 1862. At the time same the powers of the General Council were enlarged. Likewise, the Act of 1889 established the Students' Representative Council (in existence, informally, at Aberdeen since 1884), and gave the Rector power to consult it in choosing his Assessor on the University Court. And finally, except for Divinity Chairs, it abolished the Test Act of 1690.

The constitution of the University, as adjusted by the Act of 1889, remains in force at the present day: except that by the Universities (Scotland) Act of 1922 Readers and Lecturers who have served for one year become members of the General Council, and by Ordinance No. CXV (Aberdeen No. 16), enacted in the same year, were made eligible for admission to the Senatus. By University Court Ordinances CXXVII (Aberdeen No. 18); CXCI (Aberdeen No. 34); CCI (Aberdeen No. 31) Lecturers were made eligible for admission to the Faculties. By Ordinance No. CXXVIII, enacted in 1924, such Readers and Lecturers were made eligible for membership of the Senatorial Committees for Honorary Degrees. To the existing higher degrees of D.LITT. and D.SC. the Doctorate of Philosophy (PH.D.), for which a somewhat lower standard is exacted, was added in Aberdeen by Ordinance No. LXXXIX (Aberdeen No. 10), enacted in 1921: the other three Scottish Universities had taken this step two years earlier.

In these modern times, when our Universities have become so dependent on public moneys, it is amusing to find that, under the Act of 1858, the united University of Aberdeen received a yearly grant from the Treasury of £4,000! Under the Act of 1889, supplemented by the Education and Local Taxation (Scotland) Act, 1892, the grant to Aberdeen University was increased to an annual sum of £14,400. Since 1709 the four Scottish Universities had enjoyed the privilege of obtaining a free copy of every book entered at Stationers' Hall. King's College claimed the sole right to the Aberdeen share of this grant: but Marischal College vindicated her claim to a share in this right by a decision of the Court of Session in 1738. In 1836, however, under the Compensation Act, Aberdeen lost this valuable privilege in exchange for a paltry Treasury grant of £320 a year. Under the 1889 Act this sum was doubled—yet it remains a poor recompense for a privilege that today would be worth many times that amount.

One of the most important Ordinances promulgated by the Crown Commissioners appointed under the Act of 1889 was No. 11, approved in June 1892, establishing the Scottish Universities Entrance Board and the Preliminary Examination, and reorganizing the curriculum for the ordinary degree of Master of Arts. In place of the old rigid course of eight prescribed subjects—Humanity, Greek, English, Mathematics, Natural Philosophy, Logic, Moral Philosophy and Natural History— there was substituted an elaborate series of groups of options, which, while retaining a minimal core, resulted in producing a degree to which there were no less than 617 avenues of approach! The way was thus laid wide open for those students of inferior calibre who are prone to seek the path of least resistance.

In the same year, on 12 July 1892, under Ordinance No. 18, women were admitted to graduation.

Another step of vast importance was taken by Ordinances Nos. 31 and 48, issued in 1893 and 1894. These Ordinances established in the Scottish Universities a Faculty of Science.[1] In Aberdeen it consisted of the Professors of Botany, Chemistry, Mathematics, Natural History (Geology and Zoology), Natural Philosophy and Physiology. The provision for this new Faculty, and the increase in the medical curriculum from four to five years, raised in an acute form the inadequacy of the accommodation at Marischal College. Looking back with facile hind- sight across a span of more than sixty years, it is easy now to say that the opportunity ought to have been seized to abandon Marischal College and concentrate the entire University in Old Aberdeen.[2] But in the nineties there were yet many graduates of the old Marischal College and University in whose heart still burned fierce loyalty to their *Alma Mater*. Moreover until 1891 Old Aberdeen was still a separate burgh; and the pride of the citizens of Bon-Accord once again, as in the fifties, was roused by the thought that their good town might no longer count as a University City.

Already at Marischal College, with the aid of a Treasury grant of £6,000, the south wing of Archie Simpson's quadrangle had been doubled in width, so as to provide for the Departments of Natural History, Physiology, Materia Medica, Medical Jurisprudence and Midwifery. But the Department of Pathology—a Chair founded in 1882—was hopelessly crowded, and Surgery, Practice of Medicine, Chemistry, Botany and Law were all equally straitened. Nor was there any Administrative Office: this work was done for the University by a private firm of lawyers.

No useful purpose would be served, in a brief sketch such as the

---

[1] By an Ordinance of the 1858 Commission it had been possible to obtain an M.A. Degree with Honours in Natural Science. Candidates had to pass on a higher standard in Botany and Zoology and Chemistry than was required from those taking these subjects for an Ordinary Degree in Arts or Medicine. The first prize earmarked for Natural Science was established by the Senatus Academicus in 1868.

[2] This radical solution had in fact been advocated by the Royal Commission of 1826: " the large area now belonging to Marischal College, which is nearly in the centre of the Town of New Aberdeen, may be very advantageously disposed of ".

present, by setting forth the complicated and at times acrimonious discussions and negotiations between Town and Gown and Presbytery and other interested parties. Already in these days the University possessed eight acres of open ground in Old Aberdeen. Yet the idea of transferring the Faculty of Medicine thither was abandoned because the distance was deemed too great from the Royal Infirmary in Woolmanhill and the Dispensary, Lying-in and Vaccine Institutions in the Guestrow. The open question therefore was: where to site the Faculty of Science? In view of current developments, it is interesting to note that, so far back as October 1892, the Court approved the erection of a Natural Philosophy Department in Old Aberdeen. Yet within sixteen months the fateful decision was taken to retain the Faculties of Medicine, Science and Law at Marischal College, and to seek ways and means of carrying out an immense enlargement of the buildings there.

Now came forward the Treasury with the promise of a grant equal to what the University Court could raise itself, but not exceeding £40,000. A scheme was drawn up by the architect, Mr. Alexander Marshall Mackenzie, which secured the retention in the new *ensemble* of the historic Greyfriars Church, built by Bishop Gavin Dunbar, and in a sense the germ-cell of Marischal College. How in the end faith was broken by the Town Council, and the resultant costly litigation, culminating in the destruction of the church, is a sorry tale that need not here be told anew. In the end, thanks largely to munificent donations from Mr. Charles Mitchell, his son Mr. Charles W. Mitchell, and the Chancellor of the University, Lord Strathcona and Mount Royal, the " Marischal College Extension Scheme " was completed in 1906, at a total cost of £250,000. Its principal features are the " show front ", extending to a length of some 400 feet; the noble Mitchell Hall; and the raising of Archie Simpson's tower to a height of 235 feet. The work is carried out in white Kemnay granite, and the style chosen was English Perpendicular Gothic. It is now the fashion, in certain quarters, to deride Dr. Marshall Mackenzie's great achievement. But if its premises, as a *tour-de-force* in scenic architecture, be conceded, Marischal College is undoubtedly a notable achievement. Of course it was designed for a narrow street, and is therefore meant to be seen from either flank in steep perspective, with the tall shadowed buttresses standing forth in strong relief. Whatever may have been the merits of the town planning scheme (now abandoned) to create in front of it a large square or open space, the silliest argument in favour of that project was that it would have " opened up a vista of Marischal College ". Nevertheless, the imprisonment of scientific teaching and research behind a rigidly holocrystalline Gothic façade, on a site offering scant room for expansion, has in practice proved a serious incumbrance. In the last fifty years many thousands of pounds, and ingenuity almost incredible, have been expended in endeavouring to adapt Marischal College to ever changing, ever growing modern requirements. And the end is not yet.

It was about the crystalline beauty of Marischal College that Thomas Hardy, when he came to it on 7 April 1905, to receive the honorary degree of Doctor of Laws, penned the following lines:

> I looked and thought: she is too grey and cold
> To wake the warm enthusiasms of old.
> I looked again, and saw the radiant form
> Of her who stays in stress, who guides in storm,
> On the grave influence of whose eyes sublime
> Men count for the stability of the time.[1]

The Marischal College Extension Scheme was opened on 27 September 1906, by King Edward VII, accompanied by Queen Alexandra. The great occasion was combined with the Quatercentenary of the University—reckoned from the first academic year of King's College as a corporate institution, 1505-6. The festivities, which lasted several days (25-28 September) were attended by a large and distinguished gathering from all the world over. From first to last over 4,000 people took part in the various functions. It was the high noontide of Edwardian prosperity and ostentation: and the Quatercentenary Celebrations were conducted with a lavish exuberance not likely to be repeated on any academic occasion in this century.

During these years of strenuous achievement, the University Court had not been unmindful of the needs of King's College. In 1891 the Chapel was restored, and richly adorned, under the driving force of Principal Sir William Geddes. At the same time a playing ground and changing room and refectory were provided, and a common room for women students fitted up on the first floor of the Cromwell Tower. On the top storey of this Tower an observatory was installed. After the death of Principal Geddes in 1900, the south-east transept of the Library was fitted up as a Classical Reading Room in his memory.

No account, however brief, of the recent history of our University would be complete without some acknowledgment of the benefits which she has received, in common with the other Scottish Universities, through the munificence of Andrew Carnegie, who established his famous Trust in 1902. Class fees, buildings, endowment of Chairs and Lectureships, research and teaching fellowships—all have gained from this memorable benefaction. Mr. Carnegie was Rector of the University in 1911-14.

Great as had been the effort involved in bringing the " Marischal College Extension Scheme " to fruition, the Quatercentenary Celebrations of 1906 ushered in no pause in the steady expansion of the University—least of all in the two principal Faculties, Science and Medicine, housed in the new buildings. In both, development since 1906 has been nothing short of astounding, and has far outrun the capacity of the premises then provided for them.

---

[1] Isaiah xxxiii. 6: " Wisdom and knowledge shall be the stability of thy times." Hardy's holograph of this poem is in the University Library.

Let us look first at the Faculty of Science. At the " Fusion " in 1860, Chairs existed, or were then created, in Natural History, Natural Philosophy, Chemistry, and Botany. The Faculty of Science, as we have seen, was established in 1894. At first the Chair of Natural History included Zoology and Geology. Theoretically, it included even more; for the full style of the Professorship, inherited from the Marischal College arrangements of 1753, was the " Chair of Civil and Natural History ". But since the days of Professor William MacGillivray, the distinguished naturalist who held this Chair at Marischal College from 1841 till 1852, Civil History had been omitted from the course—doubtless much to the comfort of the Professor! MacGillivray's successor, who continued to occupy the Chair in the united University, was the famous geologist, James Nicol, who was the first, in opposition to Sir Roderick Murchison, to unravel the complex metamorphic structure of the North-West Highlands of Scotland. Lectures in Geology had been given both at Marischal College and at King's College since the latter part of the eighteenth century; but its systematic teaching, upon modern lines, dates from the time of MacGillivray. When Nicol resigned in 1878, he was succeeded by the distinguished zoologist, Cossar Ewart, upon whose transference to Edinburgh in 1882 the Aberdeen Chair was given to Henry Alleyne Nicholson, one of the foremost palaeontologists of his time. In his lectures Nicholson devoted more and more time to Geology. He was an accomplished artist and some of his large-scale drawings of geological scenery and phenomena, made for display on the walls of his lecture room, are still in use in the Department of Geology. Owing to Nicholson's preoccupation with matters geological, a Lecturer in Zoology was appointed to relieve him of much of the burden of teaching the latter subject. When Nicholson died in 1899 the separation between the two sciences became final and complete. To the Chair of Natural History, now in practice restricted to Zoology, was appointed Professor J. Arthur Thomson, while a full-time independent Lectureship in Geology was established, the post being given to Dr. Alfred W. Gibb. A Department of Geology, with its own Museum, was established in the front wing of the new buildings at Marischal College. In 1922 the Lectureship was elevated into a Chair, Dr. Gibb being appointed Professor.

Sir John Arthur Thomson, who held the Chair of Natural History until his death in 1933, will always be remembered as one of the most brilliant popularizers of his subject that Britain has ever known. To him, more than to any other single person, is due the wide measure of understanding and sympathy that Natural History enjoys in this country today. Of Professor Gibb it may be said that, in the recollection of former students, he shares with his colleague of the Chair of Greek, Professor John Harrower, the reputation of the two Professors who, for sheer teaching power and ability to inspire their students with their own enthusiasm for their subjects, were probably unsurpassed on the academic staff of Aberdeen University during the first half of the present century.

Our Natural History Department has always been famed for initiative and enterprise. Since 1909 it has conducted a valuable bird migration inquiry, and at different times has undertaken research projects into matters of public importance, such as the food of birds, the habits of beetles in the Aberdeen area, and the causes of disease amongst bees. The Department's capacity to undertake such field work has recently been much increased by the establishment of an outstation at Culterty, near Newburgh on the Ythan.

The Chair of Botany, founded in 1860, was rendered illustrious by the long tenure, from 1877 until 1919, of Professor James W. H. Trail, a graduate both of Arts and Medicine in the University of Aberdeen. His career is an interesting commentary upon the fact that, earlier than any other natural science, Botany was taught in Aberdeen as part of the medical curriculum. Trail's work as a field botanist has perhaps never been surpassed in this country. The outstanding event in the history of his tenure was the establishment of the Cruickshank Botanical Gardens in Old Aberdeen in 1898. Previous to that time, the sole provision for growing plants were a greenhouse and a roof garden on top of the North Tower of Marischal College! The Cruickshank Botanical Garden was made possible through a Trust established in 1898 by Miss Anne H. Cruickshank in memory of her brother, Dr. Alexander Cruickshank (M.A., Mar. Coll., 1840), a keen naturalist and a loyal and generous son of the University. Her munificence enabled the trustees to acquire the grounds of the Gymnasium, formerly a private school of great repute in the Chanonry. Here in due course the gardens were laid out. These were run by special trustees. In 1946 the University Court suggested that the trustees might hand over the Trust to the University Court. The trustees, however, in a letter dated 4 June 1946, stated that " they have come to the conclusion that it would be *ultra vires* either to hand over the Trust property to the University or to divest themselves of the management of the Trust ". The trustees, however, agreed to pay over the full free income of the Trust, after meeting the expenditure on and connected with the property, on condition that the University paid the wages of the staff employed at the garden and the cost of the garden supplies. They further agreed to leave the actual work of the garden to the University subject to the right of the trustees to be consulted from time to time as they considered necessary, to ensure that the conditions of the Trust were being complied with. Although the income from the Trust was then short by at least £120 of the cost of the upkeep of the gardens, the University agreed to take over the management of the gardens on the above conditions as from 1 November 1946 on the terms stated above. Thereafter the layout and contents were re-constituted. In its summer glory, the Cruickshank Botanical Garden is now one of the sights of Old Aberdeen.

The establishment of the Botanical Garden deserves to rank as a moment in the history of the University. It represented the first step in the eventual transference of Science teaching to the Aulton—a development never lost sight of by some of the ablest minds in the University, even at the height of the hectic enthusiasms of the Marischal College Extension and the Quatercentenary Celebrations. In due course this first step was followed by the transference in 1922 of the Department of Botany itself, from its overcrowded quarters in the north wing of Marischal College, to a purposeful new building adjoining the Cruickshank Garden. This was the first occasion in which the University Court deserted the Gothic tradition and provided a scientific department devised upon practical or functional lines. Such a building can be adapted, altered or extended in a way impossible within the rigid Perpendicular framework of Marischal College.

Next door to Botany was established in 1925 the Department of Forestry, a Chair in which subject, of so great significance for the neighbourhood of Aberdeen, was founded in that year. Hitherto teaching of Forestry had been a joint responsibility, shared between the University and the North of Scotland College of Agriculture, under whose combined patronage lectures in this subject had been delivered since the session 1908-9. The degree of B.SC. in Forestry was established in 1913. It is worth remembering that recognition of Forestry as an academic subject in Great Britain is in large measure due to the efforts of Mr. J. Crombie Brown, who had been King's College Lecturer in Botany before the " Fusion ". It was chiefly owing to his persistence that the House of Commons appointed a Select Committee, from whose report in 1887 has stemmed the whole modern conception and apparatus of State Forestry. The special interest of Aberdeen University in Forestry, due to its geographical situation, has been recognized by the Forestry Commission, who have charged our Forestry Department with the duty of investigating the best methods of conducting the afforestation of peatlands.

Due to the physical environment of Aberdeen, scientific research in its practical application, at the University and at kindred institutions in or near the city, has tended to concentrate upon the biological sciences—agriculture, fisheries, forestry. At Marischal College a Lectureship in Agriculture, comprising a course of twelve lectures each year, had been in existence since 1840, under the foundation of Sir William Fordyce, a London physician, graduate and later Rector of Marischal College. The first professional agriculturist to be appointed was Dr. Thomas F. Jamieson, well known in his day as a glacial geologist, farmer, and breeder of short-horn cattle. He held the Lectureship from 1812 until 1874. The degree of B.SC. (Agric.) was first conferred in 1898. Upon the establishment in 1904 of the North of Scotland College of Agriculture in Aberdeen—the University being represented on its Board of Governors—a joint arrangement was worked out, whereby the Governors appointed the Lecturers in the University to be licensed Lecturers in the College, while providing their own arrangements for other subjects as well as for extension work. In 1911, through the munificence of Lord Strathcona, a Chair of Agriculture was established in the University. Its first occupant, Professor James Hendrick, who held it until his retirement in 1942, did much to place the teaching of the subject, so far as the University was concerned, upon a satisfactory footing. His own special subject was agricultural chemistry, and he made important contributions in the then new field of soil science. But the link with the College of Agriculture has not in practice proved wholly satisfactory, and in 1951 it was terminated by the University. Relations between the two bodies are now once again under review. In the meantime, certain College courses in Agriculture are conducted at Marischal College, and all College of Agriculture students attending these are matriculated students of the University. The experimental farm at Craibstone is run in close association with the laboratories at Marischal College; while the University is also represented on the governing bodies of the Rowett Institute for Research in Animal Nutrition and the Macaulay Institute for Soil Research, located respectively at Bucksburn and at Craigiebuckler.

An important development in the agricultural facilities available to the University was marked by the purchase in 1953 of the estate of Tillycorthie, 11 miles north of Aberdeen. It comprises three farms totalling about 500 acres, with a mansion house. The usefulness of this acquisition, alike for the purposes of teaching, research and experiment, has already to become abundantly evident.

The next great scientific department to move out to Old Aberdeen was Chemistry. In the Marischal College Extension Scheme it was given the entire westward projection, three storeys high, of the north wing of the enlarged quadrangle. Yet even at that time, provision had to be made for the teaching of students in relays; and already in 1919, when Professor Alexander Findlay was appointed to the Chair, consideration was being given to the eventual provision of a new Department in Old Aberdeen. The advent of the Second World War for the time being put a stop to the project; and it was not until 1952 that a large new Chemistry Department was opened in Old Aberdeen, by Sir Robert Robinson, O.M., F.R.S. Early in the nineteenth century Chemistry had been taught at King's College in a single room with a table " not three feet in length ". Our new Chemistry Department contains in its five storeys and garrets a main lecture theatre with accommodation for 220 students: smaller theatres for tutorial purposes; an elementary teaching laboratory with 108 student places; inorganic and organic laboratories each for 50 students; physical laboratory for 40 students; besides research rooms (including a special room for noxious experiments), photo-chemical rooms, library, store rooms and workshops. The Departments of Agricultural Chemistry and Soil Science are also housed in this building.

When the new Chemistry Department was a-building it aroused some criticism in University and public circles. The main grounds of offence alleged against it were its enormous bulk and size, and its unimaginative fenestration.   So far as the last-mentioned matter is concerned, it may at once be conceded that there was warrant for the strictures: in this respect, certainly, the Chemistry building does remind one somewhat of Blake's " dark Satanic mills ".   But the sheer height and mass of the buildings are not in themselves fit subject for cavil.   They are in full accordance with its modern purpose and functional requirements.   Moreover the use of granite of varying colours and shades from a number of different quarries creates an effect which tones in with the freestone of King's College and the granite of the houses in Old Aberdeen.   It is possible, when in 1658 the authorities of King's College built their " New Work ", a tower-house six storeys high, cheek by jowl against the apse of the venerable chapel, that contemporaries in the Aulton held up their hands in horror. Yet I cannot believe that anyone did: for in olden days men built always to suit their requirements and in the current style of their times.   Ground being scarce and costly to acquire, it is certain that, if the University in the next ten or twenty years is really destined to expand to twice its present size, more than one lofty building will have to be put up on the perimeter of the Aulton.   So long as College Bounds, the High Street, the Chanonry and Don Street are retained, as far as practicable in their original homely character as the pattern of an old-time Scottish burgh, no one will have the right to cast stones at the University because, in the altered requirements of the twentieth century, she continues to regard, as her Founder did in 1494, the " famous City of Old Aberdeen " as a meet place where " there should flourish a University in every lawful Faculty ".

After the Union in 1920, St. Mary's, the former U. F. Church in Old Aberdeen, became surplus to requirements, the congregation merging with that of St. Machar's Cathedral.   In due course the abandoned building was acquired by the University.   For some years it served as a book-store for the University Library; but after the Second World War it was remodelled and fitted up to house the Departments of Geography, Psychology and Law.   The last two are now about to move into new accommodation in the Old Town, and St. Mary's will then become the sole quarters of the Geography Department.

The development of the teaching of Chemistry in Aberdeen University is characteristic of the evolution of British science during the past two centuries.   At first it was taught as an ancillary subject, " found to be of great use in different arts "—that is to say, as a means of widening the basis of student culture.   In its second phase, it came to be wholly subordinate to the requirements of the medical curriculum.   Finally it achieved the status of a great and living—and highly humane—branch of science, to be cultivated in its own right and for its own sake: in the words of the real founder of the School of Chemistry in Aberdeen, Professor Thomas Carnelley—despite his brief tenure of the Chair (1888-90)— " an effective means for training the faculty of observation and the reasoning powers ", an important branch of general knowledge " that enables a man to understand those things which are ever present with him, which contribute so much to his daily comforts, and which, in the hands of a beneficent Creator, are the very means of life itself and in the midst of which we live and move and have our being ".[1]

Another great and kindred Department of Science that has expanded enormously in recent years, and indeed has become of crucial, not to say agonizing importance to each and all of us, is that of Physics—or, to give it the ancient term, still happily in use at Aberdeen University, Natural Philosophy. From the Fusion until the Quatercentenary only two Professors presided over this Department—David Thomson, who after serving in the old Chair at King's College since 1845, occupied its successor in the united University until his death in 1880, when he was succeeded by Charles Niven, who retired in 1922 and died next year. To Professor Niven it fell to devise the accommodation allotted to his Department in the Marischal College Extension Scheme. As completed in 1898, the Department of Natural Philosophy ranked among the most up-to-date of its time, and was equipped to deal with a maximum of 150 students. It has since been greatly enlarged, but has long been inadequate for the vast modern demands of the science. So a new Department, north of the Chemistry building in Old Aberdeen, is now in course of erection. It will be even larger in area than the Chemistry Department; but it will be less likely to invite criticism upon aesthetic grounds.

It is worth mentioning, *en passant*, that the Natural Philosophy Department possesses one of the very few ancient scientific instruments still owned by the University: an Atwood's Machine, used for unifying the accelerative action of gravity, which formerly belonged to Professor Patrick Copeland, who held the Chair of Natural Philosophy at Marischal College from 1775 until 1823.

Biochemistry, as defined in Professor Carnelley's notable inaugural lecture from which I have already quoted, " treats in brief of the action of dead matter on life, and of the mutual action of life on dead matter ". Even in 1888 he could claim that this branch of Chemistry, today a major discipline in its own right, " now excites more popular and almost more scientific interest than almost any other branch of science ". From a mere segment of chemical study, Biochemistry has now burgeoned forth into a great and fascinating science of itself, fraught with cardinal importance to physicians, agriculturists, foresters and fruit-growers, to all those concerned with food storage and preservation, and to a whole array of industrial processes. A Chair in this subject was, belatedly, founded in 1947; and the Department is now, for the time being, adequately housed on the north side of the Marischal College quadrangle.

[1] The modern advocates (or victims) of blinkered specialization and the purely utilitarian or " applied " approach to science should all be made to study Professor Carnelley's remarkable inaugural lecture, " The True Place of Chemistry in the University Curriculum ", delivered on 23 October 1888, and published next year by the Aberdeen University Press.

The Jackson Chair of Engineering was established in 1923. This Department occupies buildings specially designed for it at the external north-eastern corner of Marischal College quadrangle. It contains laboratories fully equipped for Materials Testing, Hydraulics and Heat Engines. The courses in Mechanical and Electrical Engineering are conducted, by arrangement with the University Court, at Robert Gordon's Technical College.

But it is in the noble Faculty of Medicine that progress in Aberdeen University has been, perhaps, most astonishing during the hundred years of our review. At the Fusion, Chairs existed, or at that time were founded, only in Anatomy, Physiology, Materia Medica, Surgery, Forensic Medicine, and Midwifery. Only Anatomy was taught in a practical manner. Broadly speaking, instruction in the other branches of medicine was given by means of lectures, aided by diagrams and an occasional peep through a microscope. The remaining Chairs, completing the Faculty as we have it today, were established respectively in the following years: Pathology, 1882; Bacteriology, 1925; Mental Health, 1945; Child Health, 1947; Social Medicine, 1951. The Chair of Forensic Medicine was unhappily reduced to a Lectureship in 1933, despite strong protests from the General Council and from other quarters. At the Fusion, the number of medical students was no more than 145; by the Quatercentenary, it had risen to 299. In 1860, the total number of teachers of medicine on the academic side was 9; by 1906, Professors and Lecturers and Assistants all included, the figure had reached 21. Generally speaking, the last half of the nineteenth century was an epoch of rapid development and expansion in the Aberdeen School of Medicine. Above all things, the lesson had been fully digested that academic teaching must move out from the ivory towers of the University into the practical arena of the hospitals, whose staffs of surgeons and physicians form an integral part of an academic Medical School. So in due course working arrangements were built up with the Royal Infirmary, the Maternity Hospital, the Sick Children's Hospital, the City Hospital for Infectious Diseases, the Dispensary, and kindred institutions in the City.

For this Faculty, at once so venerable and so perennially young, accommodation was provided, ample beyond the wildest dreams of the men of 1860, within the Marischal College Extension Scheme. Thus to take a single instance only, prior to 1896 the Department of Materia Medica was housed in one moderate-sized room with a second room, not more than 6 feet square, adjoining it! When the first instalment of the Extension Scheme was completed in that year, Materia Medica found itself in premises proudly acclaimed as more ample than those provided for any parallel Department in this country, with the sole exception of Edinburgh University. Yet, ten short years later, the Professor complains that " this statement has ceased to be valid "; and extra accommodation had to be sought for research and practical laboratories. Thus it was in all the other Departments of Medicine. " Under the rapid development in every department of medical science ", so it was reported even at the Quatercentenary, the new premises at Marischal College " do no more than barely meet the requirements of the University ". By the outbreak of the First World War in 1914, their utter inadequacy had become patent to all.

Meantime the urgent need for greatly increased hospital accommodation in Aberdeen had become equally obvious; and the advisability of moving all the facilities for the care of the sick out of the congested, soot-laden heart of the town was enforcing itself, to an increasing extent, upon enlightened opinion. The credit for welding these two kindred needs—those of the City Health Services and those of the University Medical School—into what emerged as the Joint Hospitals Scheme, is due, more than to any other single man, to Professor Matthew Hay, who from 1883 until 1926 held the Chair of Forensic Medicine in the University, and undoubtedly was one of the most far-seeing medical statesmen that Aberdeen has ever known. It was in February 1920 that Professor Hay, at two special meetings of the Aberdeen Medico-Chirurgical Society—that remarkable fraternity from which so many major developments in medical facilities in the City have stemmed—set forth his bold proposals for a concentration of all the public medical services in the City, including the teaching departments of the University, and a hostel for resident officers and senior students, upon a site of about 111 acres at Burnside, Rosehill and Foresterhill, on the western outskirts of the town:

" The conjunction of the needs of these two hospitals "—i.e. the Royal Infirmary and the Sick Children's Hospital—" renders this a specially opportune time for the consideration of a common site of such extent as to provide for these hospitals, and eventually, it is hoped, for almost the whole hospital system of the City. It is felt that the advantages of the concentration of the hospitals on such a common site would be incalculable in the interest of patients, as well as of the training of medical students and nurses. Such a concentration would render it practicable to transfer to the same site the University departments most closely associated with clinical work, such as those of medicine, surgery, pathology, bacteriology and biochemistry. The transfer would be of inestimable advantage to the clinical work of the hospital, to medical education, and to the scientific investigation of disease."

No time was lost in pressing forward with this majestic project. On 20 April following, a conference of all interested bodies took place in the Town House, at which the proposals received unanimous and hearty approval. It was helped by the spirit of optimism, the eager forward-looking to a brave new world—" a land fit for heroes to live in "—that marked the years immediately following the Armistice of 1918. By 1935 the new Sick Children's Hospital and Royal Infirmary had been built, and the Maternity Hospital almost completed—at a total cost of nearly £550,000, all raised by the generosity of countless donors, great and small, throughout the north-east and north of Scotland, and far beyond! It was indeed a proud occasion for Aberdeen, when the Joint Hospitals Scheme was formally opened, on 23 September 1935, by Their Royal

Highnesses the Duke and Duchess of York (afterwards King George VI and Queen Elizabeth). Alas! the ordainer and deviser of the whole magnificent achievement was not spared to be with us on that memorable day. Professor Matthew Hay had died on 30 July 1932.

Throughout all this vast and complex undertaking the University had manfully played her part: and the culmination of the Joint Hospitals Scheme was duly reached when, on 28 September 1938, the new University Medical School was opened, on a site over against the Royal Infirmary. No one who was present will ever forget that occasion. It was the day before the Munich Agreement was signed. All Europe trembled on the brink of war. In London, shelter trenches were being dug feverishly in the public parks. The brave new world of which the promoters of the Joint Hospitals Scheme had fondly dreamed was crumbling into dust and ashes. Yet it was with a spirit of undaunted hopefulness that Viscount Dawson of Penn, in performing the opening ceremony, looked forward to the immense opportunity for pioneering progress offered by the Aberdeen achievement:

Where you stand in the forefront and point the way is in this lay-out of 111 acres— this assemblage of hospitals and clinics—this gathering together of diverse paths of knowledge, with a great centre, under the aegis of the University which inspires and serves this region of the country, the hospital services of which, in their turn, look towards your leadership and help. And maybe your regional scheme could be a pattern for the mapping of Great Britain into similar areas. This Foresterhill site offers a unique opportunity for giving reality to that wider comprehension of medicine which is necessary to the progress of the nation. . . . . Curative and preventive medicine are separated too much into compartments. They should be brought together, taught together, practised side by side. At present preventive medicine is inadequately taught and is too often but a postscript to the student's career. The contact between the two branches is at present fitful—too much a matter of phrases—and never will be effective until it comprises organised cooperation. If here, on this site, the golden opportunity is seized, curative and preventive medicine can be taught side by side, and a new unity in medicine secured.

It was characteristic of the pioneering spirit which inspired the Joint Hospitals Scheme that the University, in designing its Medical Building, for the first time broke loose from traditional modes of architecture. Built in ferro-concrete, and proclaiming its structure in its form, the four-storeyed building with its " battle-ship front " contrasts forcibly, and by no means to its own disadvantage, with the cubic granite echelons of the Royal Infirmary opposite. Internally, the building typifies in its arrangement the concentration or merging of forces embodied in the new Medical School. Previously, each great Department of Medicine at Marischal College had its own lecture rooms, laboratories and museums: but here now are common lecture rooms and laboratories and one single museum. The Ground Floor, in addition to cloakrooms for men and women in the Basement, provides Departments for Bacteriology, Clinical Chemistry, Library, also Entrance Hall and Caretaker's House. On the First Mezzanine Floor there is a large Practical Laboratory for the use of all Departments. On the First Floor proper are the

Departments of Medicine and Pathology, with a small common Lecture Room and Side Rooms, with, on the Second Mezzanine Floor, a large Lecture Theatre, common to all Departments, and Workshop. On the Second Floor proper are the Departments of Surgery, Photography, Child Health, Midwifery, and Demonstration Room common to all Departments, with on the Third Mezzanine Floor a common Museum, and part of the Department of Mental Health. The Third Floor proper provides a Staff Room and Roof Garden, with a noble outlook over the silver city and the wine-dark sea; here also are the Departments of Social Medicine, Mental Health, and Materia Medica. The Attic is occupied by the Animal House, etc.

Before the Hospitals were taken over under the Health Scheme the University Court along with the Governors of the Hospital acquired jointly the Estate of Woodhill adjacent to Foresterhill, and bounded on the south by Westburn Road, on the west by Anderson Drive, and on the north by Ashgrove Road West. This provides very ample land for the extension of the Hospital Services and for University Buildings for many years to come.

" Great reforms ", as Principal Fyfe remarked on that occasion, " like great qualities of character, have their concomitant defects." One defect of removing the Medical School to Foresterhill has been that the University is now, like Gaul in Caesar's book, divided into three parts: King's College, Marischal College, and Foresterhill. This separation is the more regrettable because, by the nature of their studies and by the fact that during part of their course they are segregated in a hostel, it is precisely the medical students among whom a corporate sense is most developed. Recognizing this disadvantage, the University has striven to counter it by various measures: by the enlargement and re-equipment of the Student's Union opposite Marischal College; by the provision of a handsomely appointed Students' Common Room in what used to be the gallery of the Elphinstone Hall: and, most recently, by a large Hall of Residence in Old Aberdeen, to be noticed later. Fortunately, the distances between the three teaching centres are not so great as they are elsewhere—for example, in Edinburgh. Nor has the total number of students, so far, been large enough to prevent a remarkable degree of solidarity in the student body.

Among the many famous names that have been associated with the Aberdeen Medical School during the past century, it may seem invidious to pick out a few for mention in such a brief sketch as the present. Yet it appears to me that this little history would be incomplete without some reference to such great personalities as Sir Alexander Ogston, Professor of Surgery from 1892 till 1909—the discoverer of *staphylococcus*; his successor, Sir John Marnoch (1909-32); Sir Ashley Mackintosh, Professor of Medicine from 1912 to 1928—in very truth " the beloved physician "; Professor John A. McWilliam, who held the Chair of Physiology during the long period 1886-1927, and whose researches into the structure and working of the human heart are classic; and his successor, John J. R. Macleod (1928-35) who will always be remembered for his share in the discovery of insulin—though it should likewise never be forgotten how much preliminary work had been done in Aberdeen by two more of our own graduates, Dr. Thomas Fraser, a well-known city physician, and Dr. John Rennie of the Natural History Department. To Dr. Fraser fell the high honour of occupying the presidential chair when the British Medical Association met in Aberdeen in 1939.

At the conclusion of our brief survey of the great scientific and medical departments, this seems the best place to say something about the University Museums. As already stated, the former departmental medical museums are now all combined into a single unit at Foresterhill, with the exception of the Anatomy Department, which, still housed in Marischal College, retains its own teaching museum, with a large collection of specimens illustrating the anatomy of man and the higher animals. At Marischal College is also the fine Geological Museum, including the Harry Gordon Collection of precious stones and minerals. This contains some 3,700 specimens, and is particularly strong in minerals and rocks from Switzerland. The donor, Rev. J. M. Gordon, was an English country vicar, whose grandfather, Harry Gordon, had been a student at Aberdeen University, and was a descendant of the ancient Gordons of Beldornie. The Botany and Forestry Departments in Old Aberdeen each possess teaching museums. But the two most important museums, those open to the public, are the Natural History Museum and the Anthropological Museum, on either side of the vestibule of the Picture Gallery and Mitchell Hall in Marischal College. The Natural History Museum is largely the creation of Sir John Arthur Thomson, but has been reorganized, and in its layout greatly improved, by Professor Wynne-Edwards and his staff. As now displayed, its contents are arranged to illustrate the evolution of animal life. Perhaps its most notable feature is the superb collection of birds' eggs presented by the late Mr. R. Hay Fenton. This contains over 7,000 specimens, all in clutches, and representing more than 300 species of birds. Among them is an egg of the Great Auk. Only seventy-four eggs of this extinct bird are known to exist: the specimen in the Fenton Collection was bought in 1908 for 190 guineas.

Perhaps of wider general interest is the Anthropological Museum. This owes its origin to the initiative of Professor Robert W. Reid, who held the Anatomy Chair in the University from 1889 till 1925, and was no less distinguished in his day as an anthropologist than as an anatomist. In 1907, after the contents of Marischal College Library had been transferred from the galleried room on the north side of the Picture Gallery vestibule, Professor Reid assembled in the vacated room all the ethnographical collections hitherto dispersed throughout the University buildings, both at King's and at Marischal Colleges. Thus originated the Anthropological Museum, now one of the most notable of its kind in

Scotland. The ethnological collections are arranged by geographical regions, and in each region are grouped thus: (1) prehistoric objects; (2) historic objects, under the following heads—(a) religion; (b) dress and ornament; (c) home; (d) arts and crafts; (e) music and games; (f) agriculture; (g) fishing and hunting; and (h) warfare.

Perhaps the most important section of the Museum is the large local collection. This includes a splendid assemblage of the contents of pre-historic burials in the north-east and north of Scotland, and a fine collection of " byegones ". Then there are the Wilson Collection of classical and oriental antiquities made by Robert Wilson, M.D. (King's College) 1815, who for some time was private secretary to the Marquis of Hastings; the Egyptological Collection presented in 1897 by Grant Bey (James A. S. Grant, M.D. (1864), LL.D. (1882)); and the Henderson Collection of Greek vases bequeathed in 1863 by William Henderson of Caskieben, M.A. (Mar. Coll.) 1813. The Museum also includes a valuable collection of ancient and modern coins and Church tokens, and an extensive series of objects from Melanesia, Africa and North America, bequeathed in 1919 by Sir William Macgregor (M.D., 1874, LL.D., 1895), Governor of Queensland.

In 1912 Professor Reid published an illustrated catalogue of the Museum, and followed this up in 1924 with a catalogue, likewise illustrated, of prehistoric interments found in the north-east of Scotland. His great work is fittingly commemorated by the granite bust, the work of Sir William Reid Dick, which now stands in the main hall of the Museum. The link between the Anthropological Museum and the Anatomy Department has been happily maintained by his successors, Professor Alexander Low (1925-38) and Professor Robert D. Lockhart, the present Curator. A notable addition, at present sub judice, to the contents of the Museum is the magnificent Celtic silver treasure hoard, dating from about A.D. 800, discovered in 1958 by a party of Aberdeen University students excavating the old church site on St. Ninian's Isle, Dunrossness, Shetland, under the direction of Professor Andrew C. O'Dell of the Chair of Geography.

Both these Museums, the Natural History and the Anthropological, are now seriously overcrowded, and can do no more than display a portion of their contents. It is hoped to find extra accommodation for them when other scientific or medical departments move out from Marischal College.

The " Fusion " of 1860 found the Faculty of Law in poor case. It is not too much to say that but for the existence of the Society of Advocates, incorporated by Royal Charter in 1774, the Faculty might have died out in Aberdeen, as it did in St. Andrews, and for a time in Glasgow. An opinion was widely prevalent that Edinburgh University provided sufficiently for all academic instruction in law required for Scotland. So at Aberdeen in 1860 the Marischal College Lectureship in Conveyancing (founded by the Society of Advocates) was suppressed, and a single Chair of Law provided for the united University. The 1858 Commission had established the degree of Bachelor of Laws (LL.B.) which could only be taken sequent to a degree in Arts. The course for the new degree was to cover three academic years, and to comprise six subjects: Civil Law, Scotch Law, Conveyancing, Public Law, Constitutional Law and History, and Medical Jurisprudence. Since all these subjects were taught only in the University of Edinburgh, those of Glasgow and Aberdeen were empowered to confer the degree provided classes were attended in them for ten sessions and for one session in another University. The degree of Doctor of Laws (LL.D.) was retained as a distinction granted *honoris causa*.

At the " Fusion " in 1860 the Civilist in King's College, Patrick Davidson, was appointed Professor of Law in the united University. He never taught, but appointed as active head of the Department George Grub, who since 1843 had been Lecturer in Scotch Law at Marischal College. In 1881 Grub succeeded to the Chair, which he held until 1891. Though an alumnus of King's College, which he entered at the age of thirteen and a half, he did not graduate M.A. until 1856. A distinguished teacher of Scotch Law, he is now remembered chiefly for one of the most notable historical works that has ever been produced by an Aberdonian— his massive four volumes on the *Ecclesiastical History of Scotland*, published in 1861. Written from the Episcopalian standpoint, but distinguished by a scrupulous impartiality and a tranquillity of judgment rare indeed in works upon this theme, it still remains, after the lapse of a century, the greatest and the most satisfactory work on the subject. It earned the author the degree of LL.D. from his *Alma Mater* in 1864.

The Commissioners appointed under the 1889 Act broadened the curriculum for the degree in Law (LL.B.) and introduced the principle of options. Eight subjects instead of six were now required, as follows: Jurisprudence; Public International Law; Civil Law; Scotch Law or English Law; Constitutional Law and History; Conveyancing, or Political Economy, or Mercantile Law; and two of the following— Private International Law, Political Economy, Administrative Law, Forensic Medicine. By an Amendment in 1874 the University of Glasgow was empowered to grant the degree of Bachelor of Law (B.L.) which could be taken if an applicant held either a degree of Arts or had passed the Arts examination in Law and in three Arts subjects listed in the Amendment. The Law subjects required for the degree were Civil Law, the Law of Scotland, Conveyancing and one other Law subject. A similar Amendment permitted the University of Edinburgh to grant the degree of Bachelor of Law (B.L.) on the same conditions. The Commissioners, in 1893, opened the degree of Bachelor of Law (B.L.) to candidates of any of the four Scottish Universities. They were required to pass the Preliminary Examination, be a graduate in Arts or have passed the Arts Degree examination in Logic and Metaphysics or Moral Philosophy; Latin; and one other Arts subject. The Law course was to comprise a minimum of four subjects: Civil Law, Scotch Law, Conveyancing, and Forensic Medicine. Its duration was fixed at two academic years.

It was not until 1909 that the University was able to provide full training for the LL.B. Degree. The improvement in the status of the Faculty of Law was mainly due to Professor Dove Wilson (1891-1911), who reintroduced the teaching of Roman Law and restored the Lectureship in Conveyancing. Nevertheless, at the Quatercentenary it was complained that " while the number of students of law now attending the University is somewhat greater than the number of students entered in all the Faculties for many years after 1494, our teaching staff and equipment are less than when the Faculty of Law was first founded ". All this is now utterly transformed. In the Faculty of Law today there are Chairs in Conveyancing (1927), Jurisprudence, including Roman Law (1951) and Scots Law (1958), besides lectureships in Evidence, Pleading and Procedure; Mercantile Law, International Private Law and Comparative Law; Public Law; and Forensic Medicine.

Alone among the Faculties Law until recently possessed no higher degree. This defect has now been removed by Scottish Universities Ordinance No. 1, whereby the four Scottish Universities in 1957 instituted a non-honorary doctorate, entitled " Doctor of Laws (LL.D.) ", while retaining the long-established LL.D. *honoris causa*. The new higher degree in Law can be taken only seven years after graduation, or, in the case of teaching members of the Law Faculty, four years after appointment, providing that not less than seven years have elapsed from the date of first graduation. Many in Aberdeen University and elsewhere would have preferred a different title for the research degree, having regard to the long established prestige of the Doctorate of Laws as the highest honorary distinction in the gift of a Scottish University.

In the new Marischal College buildings the Faculty of Law was allotted two classrooms, a tutorial room and a library, which was made available for evening study, since most of the Law students were apprentices engaged all day in some legal firm. Since 1950 the Faculty of Law has been housed in the former St. Mary's (U.F.) Church in Old Aberdeen, and here also the Law books of the University Library are kept. Thanks very largely to the vigorous policy initiated by Professor Thomas B. Smith, who held the Chair of Scots Law from 1949 till 1958, the Law Library has become one of the most notable in Scotland. In 1952 it was enriched with a splendid collection of some 1,000 books and 2,000 pamphlets, mostly in Roman Law, acquired on extremely favourable terms from the late Professor Francis de Zulueta, M.A. (Oxon.), D.C.L., who held the Regius Chair of Civil Law in the University of Oxford from 1919 until 1948. In 1953 Professor Zulueta received the Honorary Degree of Aberdeen University. Both the Law Library and the Law lecture rooms are now too small, and a shift to new and ample premises in Old Aberdeen is imminent.

3*

No academic discipline in the Scottish Universities has passed through greater vicissitudes than the Faculty of Divinity, once acclaimed as the Queen of the Sciences. This is due to the fact that, for several centuries, theological training provided in the Universities had to accommodate itself to the dogmatic requirements of the Church party for the time being in power; so that, inevitably, the Divinity Faculty found itself caught up in the politico-religious conflicts of the time. The results for sound theological training were of course disastrous. " Theology ", it has been remarked, " cannot, any more than science, flourish in an atmosphere of strife. . . . Scottish religion has been too controversial to develop theology."

From their foundation until the Reformation in 1560, the primary aim of the Scottish Universities was the training of ecclesiastics, and therefore the fostering of Theology as the Church of Rome understood it. Equally severe, until the Revolution of 1689, was the control exercised by the Reformed Church over theological training in the Universities— and indeed over all academic studies.[1] Not until after this date did the concept begin to emerge that the Universities were national institutions and that, as such, the final word in their management should not rest with the Church, but with Parliament. It was the Commissioners of 1828 who first boldly propounded the novel thesis that the function of the Divinity Faculty was to provide a course of theological study as a science, without reference to the conditions which the General Assembly of the Established Church might lay down from time to time to suit its own requirements. The great difficulty in providing such a scientific Faculty of Divinity was the delicacy felt in making public money available for the endowment or support of Theological Chairs: for in practice the courses in Divinity were designed to prepare students for entry into the Church of Scotland. Hence the Commissioners appointed pursuant to the Act of 1858 made no attempt to devise an Ordinance for degrees in Divinity. They left it to the separate Universities " to take such steps as, after careful inquiry, they may consider most likely to promote the advancement of theological learning ". The Act of 1889 laid down, in stringent terms, that no Government grants should be applied to the endowment or augmentation of Theological Chairs, except in the case of Chairs of Hebrew or Oriental Languages. Accordingly the Commissioners appointed under that Act felt themselves precluded from taking any steps to bring the Faculties of Divinity in the Scottish Universities abreast of modern requirements. They did, however, promote an Ordinance regarding the requirements for the degree of Bachelor of Divinity, which was to be conferred upon graduates in Arts who thereafter had completed a course in Theology. The Doctorate of Divinity continued, as it is now, to be awarded purely *honoris causa*.

---

[1] *Primarius studiorum finis esse debet pura religio Dei optimi maximi divinorumque operum et beneficiorum cognitio*—from the King's College regulations of 1641; see *Fasti Aberdonenses*, p. 226.

By the end of the First World War the desirability had become patent of promoting a General Ordinance for the degree of B.D., common to all four Scottish Universities. This was duly enacted in 1924 (Ordinance No. CXXIX). It provided for courses in a quadrilateral of subjects: Old Testament Language and Literature; New Testament Language and Literature; Ecclesiastical History; and Systematic Theology. The Course now includes at least three years in Arts and three in Divinity. This great step forward was followed by a still more radical change, arising from the Union in 1929 between the Established Church and the United Free Church. Under the Universities (Scotland) Act of 1932 the Faculties of Divinity in the Universities of Glasgow, Aberdeen and Edinburgh were amalgamated respectively with the former United Free Church Colleges in these three cities. Incumbents of Chairs in the Colleges were to be admitted to the respective University Senates and Divinity Faculties, provided that the requisite emoluments were guaranteed by the Church of Scotland. Appointments to Divinity Chairs were to be made by the University Courts, with the assistance in each case of a Board of Nomination consisting of ten members, half appointed by the University and half by the Church. All religious tests were abolished. Permission was given for the foundation of Divinity Chairs by Churches other than the Church of Scotland. So far, no advantage has been taken of this provision in any Scottish University.

As a result of this important Act, the Divinity Faculty in the University of Aberdeen now comprises five Professors and three Lecturers. A change regretted by not a few was the abolition of the time-honoured practice of awarding the Chair of Systematic Theology as the result of an open competition. Beyond doubt the old procedure had enriched the Chair with a succession of distinguished incumbents.

Instruction in Divinity is at present shared between premises at King's College and the former United Free Church College—now known as Christ's College—at Holburn Junction. Broadly speaking, the principle governing the division of classes is that all instruction that is academic, in the sense that it can be offered by the University, is given at King's College, while such further teaching as is required by the Church of Scotland alone for the training of her ministers is provided at Christ's College. Under the energetic leadership of the late Professor George D. Henderson, who held the Chair of Ecclesiastical History in the University from 1924 until his death in 1957, and from 1947 was Master of Christ's College, the accommodation in the College was greatly improved, its fine Library reorganized and brought up to date, and a Chapel provided. No account of our University would be complete if it failed to include a tribute to Professor Henderson, one of the most profound ecclesiastical historians and accomplished clerical statesmen that Scotland has produced in our century. In 1956 he was Moderator of the General Assembly; and the news of his sudden death on 28 May 1957, while attending the Assembly, evoked dismay throughout the nation.

A highly successful development in the life of the University has been the appointment of a Chaplain, rendered possible by a handsome endowment made in 1945 by Mrs. Duthie Webster. In addition to conducting the Chapel services and playing a part in the religious life and work of the University, the Chaplain carries out pastoral and welfare work among the students. Very wisely, the appointment in each case is limited to a term of five years. By this arrangement a constant succession of young ministers is secured, familiar with the problems that beset our undergraduates in these difficult times. That the Chaplaincy has abundantly justified itself in the fifteen years of its existence is obvious to all who take an interest in the higher values of academic life.

Somewhat curiously, it might be contended that the great Faculty of Arts—" the foundation, mother and nurse of all the others ", as it is called in an account of Paris University published in 1517—has to some extent been the Cinderella of the University amid the crowded record of material expansion which we have chronicled for the other Faculties. So far back as 12 December 1891, the General Council was informed by its Committee on the Buildings Extension Scheme that " it is impossible to continue Arts teaching in King's College without some additions, not inconsiderable, to its present buildings ". Yet it was not until 1912 that a large new building, providing classrooms for the Departments of English, History, French and German, was built on a site to the north-west of King's College. This site had previously been occupied by the Old Aberdeen Brewery; and the change of use led to a remarkable spate of Greek and Latin verse in the academic publications of the time! After the opening of the Elphinstone Hall in 1931, the temporary examination hall which had been fitted up in what remained of the quondam brewery buildings was reconstructed to provide sorely needed extra accommodation for Arts Lecturers and Assistants: and much internal remodelling has been carried out since the last war in the old Quadrangle at King's College. But the accommodation available for the large and ever-growing Faculty of Arts remains at the moment utterly inadequate for modern requirements. Perhaps the reason may be partly due to the overlong persistence, in the Faculty of Arts possibly more than others, of the old, deeply ingrained Scottish practice of formal lecturing and note-taking. This is a grievance of long standing. So far back as 1642 a Commission of Visitation of the four Universities, set up by the General Assembly, criticised the " unprofitable and noxious paines in writeing " involved in dictating notes, and added the astringent comment that " the dyteing of long notes hath in tymes past proven ane hindrance, not only to other necessar studies but also to the knawledge of the text itselfe ". Two hundred and sixty years later it was alleged that in Aberdeen University classes represented to the students " a professorial monologue ". Nowadays, the tendency is more and more towards the provision of " seminars " or tutorial teaching; and to meet this need a new and well devised Arts

Building, including a large reading-room for students, is now about to be erected in Old Aberdeen. Thus in the near future an old reproach should be removed.

Something has already been said (see above, p. 13) about the substitution in 1892 of a course with multiple options for the old inflexible Arts curriculum with its eight prescribed courses. While the reaction against over-rigidity was understandable, there remained much truth in the dictum of a report issued in 1878 by a Royal Commission appointed two years earlier to inquire into the state of the Scottish Universities. Referring to the Arts curriculum, the Commissioners observed:

> We think it of great importance that the field of study should be so enlarged as to make it more suitable and attractive to different classes of students than at present, and this object can, in our opinion, be best attained by allowing, after a certain foundation of general culture, a tolerably free choice along certain distinct lines of study adapted to various bents of mind, and having relation to different professional pursuits. We believe that, by the opportunities which such a freedom of selection would present, many students would be induced to take a larger share than they do now in University study, and the advantages of the culture which the University affords would be extended.

No better statement has ever been put out of the proper purpose of a degree in Arts. Within little more than a decade, experience had shown how far short the 1892 curriculum fell of providing the balanced course, with its " foundation of general culture " which the 1876 Commissioners had envisaged. In 1907, therefore, the four Universities agreed each to devise their own scheme for the degree of M.A. The Aberdeen Ordinance (No. XXIV, Aberdeen No. 2, 4 July 1908) provided for the Ordinary degree a course of five subjects, two of which must be studied for two academic years, and passed on a higher standard than the other three. Some twenty-five subjects were prescribed from which the curriculum could be selected; and these were grouped into four classes: Language and Literature; Mental Philosophy; Science; and History and Law. For the Honours degree, it was enacted that each candidate should take up at least two subjects outside his Honours group, and must attend seven classes, taking a minimum of four classes (two of which at least must be Honours classes under separate Professors and Lecturers) in his Honours group. Bound up with this remodelling of the Arts curriculum was the extension of the academic teaching year, which had been under discussion between the four Universities since 1905. It was claimed that the existing twenty weeks' session of two terms, Winter and Spring, resulted in over-compression: " lecture succeeds to lecture with startling rapidity, and such spare time that there is has to be largely given up to exercises, essays and examinations." In Aberdeen a Summer session did exist, but it was mainly devoted to classes for Honours students. The controversy over the proposed three-term session was fought out in the most lively fashion. The protagonists in favour of the traditional practice were Professors Harrower (Greek), Davidson (Logic), Macdonald (Mathematics) and Thomson (Natural History), while in favour of the new proposals were arrayed Professors Terry (History) and Baillie (Moral

Philosophy). With such academic titans embattled against each other, the war of memorandum and counter-memorandum, as recorded in the minutes of the General Council, is still well worth reading. In the event, the University Court, falling into line with the other Scottish Universities, embodied a three-term course of twenty-five teaching weeks in the new Ordinance.

The general principle involved in the new Arts curriculum of 1908 was more specialization of study, and concentration upon a smaller range of subjects. Yet the field of selection still appeared too wide; and from time to time efforts were made, by new regulations, to approach more closely to the spirit of the Arts curriculum envisaged by the 1876 Commissioners. The Second World War threw everything academic into the melting pot; and, after much travail, finally in 1956 the existing regulations came into force, whereby every candidate for the Ordinary degree is required to include in his curriculum (i) Logic or Moral Philosophy; (ii) a language other than English; (iii) either (a) (1) an advanced course in any one subject and (2) Mathematics or Natural Philosophy or Chemistry or Botany or Zoology or Geology; or (b) two subjects chosen from one of the following groups and the other from another: (1) Mathematics; (2) Natural Philosophy, Chemistry, Botany, Zoology, Geology, Biology; (3) a second language other than English. The Honours degree is conferred upon a candidate after examination in his Honours group and two subjects outside it. An Honours degree may now be taken in ten different subjects: Classics, Economics, English, Geography, History, Mathematics and Physics, Modern Languages, Music, Philosophy, and Semitic Languages. Within these broad departments there are no less than forty-one possible groups.

In the Arts curriculum of 1892 at least one classical language (Latin or Greek) was compulsory. In practice this amounted to a compulsion in the former subject. At Aberdeen this remained in force until 1956, when, by a revision of Regulation No. 10 (as set forth in the preceding paragraph) the linguistic requirement was altered to " a language other than English ". Many friends of the Classics will feel that the change was in the best interest of Latin studies. It will be noticed that, following ancient Scottish tradition, a compulsion is retained in what used to be called Mental Philosophy. One is reminded of Rashdall's well-known observations on the Scottish insistence upon Philosophy as an academic discipline:

The consequences of the retention of the old medieval curriculum in the Scottish Universities, and the subsequent evolution of distinct Chairs of Philosophy out of it, have been of the utmost importance, not only in the history of Scotch education, but in the history of British and even European thought. Scotland gained from it an education at once stimulating and practical, however grave its disadvantages on the score of sound preparation and classical discipline; while to the seemingly accidental circumstance that the Scotch Universities provided philosophers not only with Chairs, but with classes to teach, Europe probably owes in no small measure the development of an important and influential School of Philosophy.

In spite of the fact that Aberdeen University was specifically founded in 1494 to serve the educational needs of the Highlands and Islands (*insulae boreales et montes*), and that the three Celtic Counties of Inverness, Ross and Sutherland were included in its " province " by Act of Parliament in 1863, it was not until 1916 that the University Court, after years of prodding by the General Council, instituted a Lectureship in Celtic. This was promoted to a Readership in 1925. Other subjects in which degrees may be taken, successively added, with teaching facilities, to the Faculty of Arts have been Education (1918)—now about to be raised to the status of a Chair; Commerce (1919); and Spanish (1920). In 1919, through the munificence of Sir Thomas Jaffrey, a Chair was established in the subject of Political Economy. In 1926 followed a Chair in French, and in 1951 a Chair in German; in 1947 a Chair in Psychology; and in 1950, a Chair in Geography. A most interesting innovation was the creation in 1950, in the Faculty of Arts, of a lectureship (now a readership) in the History and Philosophy of Science.

In 1922 the Scottish Universities under Ordinance No. 104 (Aberdeen No. 14) acquired the right of conferring Ordinary degrees upon nongraduate members of their staffs. This power has been sparingly exercised. The first two recipients were Mr. Harry Townend (M.A. 1924), Curator of the Aberdeen Art Gallery and University Lecturer on Painting, in the course in Fine Art; and Mr. William Brown (B.SC. [Agric.] 1924), who since 1913 had been Lecturer in Veterinary Hygiene. Such degrees are not properly designated as Honorary degrees, since the recipients are required to register as members of the General Council, and enjoy the full privileges of membership thereof.

In 1923, with the aid of a bequest from Miss A. H. Cruickshank, the University established a Lectureship in Astronomy and Meteorology, associated with the Observatory which since 1868 had existed on top of the Cromwell Tower at King's College. Unfortunately since the war it has not been found possible to obtain a suitable person for the post. Astronomers are a scarce commodity; and most of them are picked up by the National Observatories.

In 1919 a degree of Bachelor of Commerce was instituted by the University; but it failed to answer expectations, and in 1949 the degree was abolished. A much more important and successful development has been the establishment, in 1955, of a Department of Statistics, housed in a large addition to the Chemistry Building in Old Aberdeen. At present the Department is staffed by a reader, who is also Director of the Agricultural Research Council Unit of Statistics; two Lecturers; two Research Fellows; and one Assistant. The University grants a Diploma in Statistics to Honours graduates of any University recognized by the Senatus, after a course of whole-time study extending normally to six terms.

We have noted above the steady transference, since the Second World War, of teaching departments to Old Aberdeen. But this process by no means sums up the impact of a highly modernized and dynamic University *in inclita civitate Veteri Aberdonensi*—to borrow the language of our Papal Bull of Foundation. Some time after the First World War the University, partly with a view to safeguarding the amenities of King's College, and likewise to provide housing for its ever-increasing staff, embarked upon a systematic policy of buying and reconditioning properties in Old Aberdeen. Out of this, and in most harmonious co-operation with the Town Council as Planning Authority, has emerged the idea of a University Precinct in Old Aberdeen, which already has gone far towards converting the Aulton into a *ville universitaire* not unworthy to rank alongside of St. Andrews. In this connection it may not be amiss to recall the words used by our Principal in his address to the General Council on 17 December 1949:

> One thing however ought to be made clear for the reassurance of the inhabitants of the Aulton. The University does not desire to create there a homogeneous academic community. It is one of the attractive features of the present community that all types and classes live there. The University has no intention whatever of destroying this community in order to replace it by a suburb of academes.

Unfortunately, the inflation of post-war years, with its consequent rise in costs, has prevented the University, for the time being, from realizing to the full extent her programme for reconditioning the quaint and venerable houses in Old Aberdeen. That, in spite of all difficulties, so much has been accomplished must be a source of deep satisfaction to all lovers of the Aulton.

The history of the successive arrangements which the united University has adopted for the conduct of her central business is interesting. At first the secretarial work of the Senatus Academicus and of the Faculties was attended to by different Professors. The University Court had its own Secretary, while the General Council had its Clerk and Registrar. The strictly legal business of the University, in particular the management of its property and lands, was in the hands of the Factor, a post held by a city lawyer. In 1894 Mr. Donaldson Rose Thom was appointed Secretary of the Senatus and Faculties; and in 1905 the offices of Secretary of the Court, Secretary of the Senatus and Faculties, Factor and Treasurer were all combined, Mr. Thom being appointed to the new post. This he held with great distinction until his death on 23 January 1920. He had been born in 1860, the year of the Fusion, and for almost the whole of his working life had been associated, in one form or another, with the service of his *Alma Mater*. Many will recall his unfailing patience, courtesy and self-effacement. Mr. Thom's successor was Colonel H. J. Butchart, who held the post until his retirement at the close of the academic year 1951-52. When Colonel Butchart vacated the post which he had held for the long period of three and thirty years, an epoch in the history of the University may be said to have closed. It had been a period of unexampled expansion in buildings, equipment, teaching and research staffs, students, and curricula. When be became Secretary, the teaching staff numbered 108, of whom 25 were Professors. In 1952 there were 39 Professors, 12 Readers, 159 Lecturers, and 97 Assistants, besides 10 Research Fellows. In the same period the number of students rose from 1239 to 1956, and the annual expenditure from £62,000 to £523,000. Many details of this enormous expansion have been chronicled in the foregoing paragraphs. All of them owe much to Colonel Butchart's imagination, initiative and driving power. No academic distinction in our whole long history was more amply deserved than the honorary degree of Doctor of Laws which the Chancellor conferred upon him at the graduation ceremony of 4 July 1952. Dr. Butchart's successor was the present Secretary, Mr. William Stephenson Angus, M.A., LL.B., a grandson of Professor William Stephenson, who held our Chair of Midwifery from 1875 until his retirement in 1912.

The united University has been fortunate in her Principals. The Principal of the Fusion, Dr. Peter Colin Campbell, was succeeded in 1876 by William Robertson Pirie, previously Professor of Divinity, first at Marischal College and thereafter in the united University. A theological scholar of distinction, he was likewise a sound practical administrator. Perhaps for the first time among our Principals since the foundation of the University, he was not a graduate: his first degree was the honorary Doctorate of Divinity, conferred upon him simultaneously by King's College and Marischal College in 1844. In Scottish Church history he will always be remembered as the successful protagonist of the Act of 1874 which abolished patronage. On his death in 1885 he was succeeded by Sir William Duguid Geddes, who since 1855 had been Professor of Greek at King's College, and afterwards in the united University. " Old Homer ", as he was affectionately called by his students, was a man of high scholarly and academic worth, who guided the University with sureness and skill through the tangled and sometimes acrimonious negotiations of the Marischal College Extension Scheme, the fulfilment of which he was not spared to witness. His successor in 1900 was John Marshall Lang, a Glasgow divine who had earned himself a great name in the Church of Scotland for the vigour and idealism with which he had championed social service and improvements in public worship. He was no stranger to Aberdeen, for he had served as minister of the East Church of St. Nicholas from 1856 until 1858, and thereafter had been minister at Fyvie. Like Principal Pirie, he was not a graduate. Principal Lang will always be remembered for the dignity and grace with which, as resident head of the University, he presided over the Quatercentenary Celebrations. Older *alumni* will likewise recall that the students, both individually and as a body, never had a truer or a more understanding friend.

On his death in 1909 the tradition of appointing a divine, broken so far only in the case of Sir William Geddes, was resumed. The new

Principal was Dr. George Adam Smith, who came to us from the Chair of Old Testament Language and Literature in the Free Church College, Glasgow—but as one well knowing Aberdeen, in which his brilliant ministry at Queen's Cross Free Church (1882-92) is by no means yet forgotten. It is in no sense a disparagement of his two distinguished successors when I write that, to the members of Aberdeen University belonging to my generation, he stands forth luminously as the Principal of our time. One of the greatest Old Testament scholars whom Britain has ever produced, he combined vast learning with a firm Christian faith that survived, unshaken and unsoured, a more than ordinary burden of public and private worry and sorrow. His matchless pulpit eloquence, and the organ voice in which it was expressed, can never be forgotten by those who listened to him so often in our ancient University Chapel. What is not always equally remembered, and about which the account of him in the *Dictionary of National Biography* is strangely silent, is the vision, grasp of detail, patience and tenacity that he showed in the conduct of academic business during a fruitful period of progress, and the influence which the University derived, in her dealings with H.M. Government, and with outside bodies generally, from his acknowledged eminence and weight of character. In 1916 he was knighted, and in 1931 he received the Freedom of the City, being the only Principal of our University thus to be honoured. Sir George Adam Smith retired in 1935, and died in 1942. His wife, who played a great part in the life of the University, and, like her husband, received our honorary degree, died in 1949.

His successor, Sir William Hamilton Fyfe, came to us from Queen's University, Ontario, but with a pleasant Aberdeen connection through his wife, a daughter of John Forbes White (M.A., Mar. Coll., 1848, LL.D., 1886)—a scholar and art critic, and sometime an Assessor of the General Council on the University Court. To Sir William Fyfe fell the task of guiding the University, with wit, wisdom and good humour, through the long trying years of the Second World War, when no major development was possible, and all that could be done was to maintain the essentials of teaching, and of academic life, amid every conceivable hardship, distraction and danger. In recalling these sombre years of strain and stress, I must not omit to mention 12 July 1940, when King's College had the narrowest escape in all its long history. A German aircraft, hotly pursued, unloaded nine bombs upon the playing fields. Fortunately the buildings, though badly shaken, escaped serious damage. But the Melvin window in the Library was destroyed, and the Library, " New King's " and the Elphinstone Hall retain some honourable scars.[1] From the far heavier night raid of 21 April 1943, the University buildings escaped unscathed.

[1] The smoke of the explosions was still drifting over the playing fields when the late Mr. Alexander Webster, the University's splendid groundsman—" Webbie " to all his many friends—was seen running about, anxiously collecting every dislodged divot of his beloved turf!

Principal Fyfe's term of office lasted long enough for him to be able to guide the University through the initial stages of the difficult period of rehabilitation.   On his retiral in 1948, he was succeeded by a graduate of our own, the present Principal, Sir Thomas Murray Taylor, c.b.e., q.c., d.d., ll.d.—a native of Keith and, at the time of his appointment as Principal, our Professor of Law.   In him, for the first time, the Faculty of Law gave a Principal to the University.   Lady Taylor is likewise one of our own graduates (m.b., 1920; m.d., 1937).

If the united University has been well served by her Principals, she has been equally fortunate in her Chancellors.   But as the office of Chancellor—the titular head of the University—is in the gift of the General Council, I propose to leave this matter to be dealt with by Mrs. Donald, my collaborator in this historical survey of the last hundred years in our academic record.

As to the third great historic office, that of the Rector, who ranks next in dignity to the Chancellor, and is appointed for a term of three years by the student body, it is perhaps necessary to write with some degree of circumspection: for unhappily in the Scottish Universities the Rectorship seems to be in a condition of decline, and neither the choice of candidates, nor the circumstances connected with the installation of the Rector, have always been such as to enhance the prestige of the office. It is perhaps sufficient to note here, with pride, that Aberdeen University, alone in all the world, preserves intact the medieval method of electing the Rector by the indirect votes of the students grouped in their four " Nations ".   Each Nation choses a procurator, and by the four pro-curators the Rector is elected.[1]   And among the long succession of Rectors so elected during the past hundred years will be found many names of high lustre, including some who have given yeoman service to the University.   Undoubtedly the most famous of all our Rectors has been Sir Winston Churchill, who was elected in 1914, in the early days of the First World War.   For this reason, alone among our Rectors he has never delivered his Rectorial Address.   But for that omission he made handsome amends in the impromptu and deeply moving speech which he gave to a packed audience in the Mitchell Hall when he received our honorary degree on 27 April 1946.   Certainly one plea that he then made has lost nothing of its relevancy in this present age of materialism and the hectic pursuit of quick and cheap and short-term satisfactions:

I hope that we shall realize that Universities are centres from which wide thoughts spread, and that these thoughts should never exclude a study of the past.   For what is it that we can tell of the future except we have gathered from meditating upon all the triumphs, the glories, and miseries, the crimes and follies and the disappointments, but

[1] " The procurators must be regarded as the oldest of all academic offices of any kind. In the long perspective they are older than all university senates, councils and courts; than any principal, or head of a college; then any professoriate, or university staff. There is only one office which can make any claim to be coeval with theirs, namely the Chancellorship "—W. M. Alexander, *The Four Nations of Aberdeen University and their European Background*, p. 46.

still in the end the great achievements of those toiling, suffering generations which have gone before us? Those who do not look back to their ancestors will not look forward to their posterity. This is a time when we are entitled, nay bound, to look forward, and I trust that from the University of Aberdeen there will always be a broad and liberal light shining, which will comprise within its radiance and its beams a full proportion of the knowledge and study of the Humanities and the Classics.

It will long remain a symbol of the University's faith in the future, during our nation's darkest hour, that the rhones of the Pavilion at King's College bear the date 1940. This building, completed in that *année terrible*, represented a second and salutary departure from the Gothic tradition in academic architecture. The handsome and " serviceable " pavilion—to quote the adjective used about it by Sir William Fyfe— includes common rooms for men and women members of the students' Athletic Association, as well as a " common common room " for both— naturally the most popular of the three!—a fine freshwater swimming pool, and two squash courts, as well as the requisite accommodation— changing rooms, wash basins, showers, and so forth—for all who play games on the King's College playing fields. Another building completed in the early years of the war is the Hall of Residence for final year medical students, opened for use in October 1941.

For long it had been counted as a reproach against the University of Aberdeen that she provided no residential facilities for students. In this way it is certain that we have lost many students from the north-east and north of Scotland, who for lack of a hostel here have been forced to by-pass Aberdeen. Since the last war, the problem has become much more urgent owing to the influx of English, Commonwealth, and foreign students. Ever since 1869 the General Council had been periodically urging the need for a hostel upon the University Court; and now, after the lapse of a century all but a decade, the idea has burgeoned into fruition. A large and handsome Hall of Residence, with provision for 46 men and 64 women, has been provided opposite King's College and on 13 August 1960, was formally opened by Her Majesty the Queen, who was accompanied by His Royal Highness the Duke of Edinburgh.[1] Built partly of Triassic sandstone from Elgin, with other walls harled white or timber-boarded, and red tiled roofs, it marks a welcome departure from the grey or drab tradition of Aberdeen University architecture. Including its residents, the Hall can accommodate some 240 persons for lunch or dinner. Quite apart from the University's natural desire to

---

[1] On this occasion our Royal visitors also inspected King's College Chapel and the Library, where the St. Ninian's Isle Treasure was on view. It is interesting to note that, in the course of its long history, King's College has been visited only four times by a reigning monarch: in the summer of 1541 by James V and his queen; on 2 November 1562 by Queen Mary; on 20 June 1953, by Queen Salote Tupou of the Friendly Islands; and in 1960, as above mentioned, by our present queen. It is remarkable that Queen Victoria, for all her regular and prolonged sojourning at Balmoral, never visited the University.

offer a welcome to students not only from her own " province " but also from " a' the airts ", it is hoped that a common life of residence, with all its spontaneous activities and social stimulus, will be of benefit to many, particularly among our rural entrants. Yet the north-eastern student has always preferred the relative independence of " digs "; and the experiment of providing a hall of residence will certainly be watched with sympathic interest. And if the University of Aberdeen is to play her part in catering for the large expansion in the student population which the national interest appears to require, it is certain that an increasing number of our undergraduates will be drawn from further afield; and for some at least of this extraneous intake our new hall of residence ought surely to provide living quarters—indeed it has already done so. Nay further, if the proposed expansion of the University to cope with a student population of over 4,000 materializes, then Crombie Hall, as our new hall of residence has been christened, will be only the first of several.

Most appropriately the building has been named Crombie Hall, in memory of the late Dr. James Edward Crombie of Parkhill, one of the University's most munificent benefactors, who died in 1932. He graduated M.A. in 1882, and in 1907 was awarded the honorary degree of LL.D., mainly in recognition of his devoted work in connection with the Quatercentenary Celebrations. From 1900 until 1908 he served as Rector's Assessor on the University Court, and from 1913 until his resignation, owing to ill-health, shortly before his death, as Chancellor's Assessor. As Rector's Assessor he displayed an intense personal interest in the welfare of the undergraduate, and his solicitude for them continued unabated during the later years of his membership of the Court. He would have been delighted to have seen the University's hall of residence in being; and, for all his innate modesty, would have been pleased that it should bear his name. Dr. Crombie will remain in the grateful memory of his contemporaries as an outstanding example of the busy man of affairs who gives unstintingly of his time and skill in serving his *Alma Mater*. With his manifold and often anonymous generosity, he may well serve as a pattern of those " rich men furnished with ability, dwelling peaceably in their habitations " whom we have high authority to praise. His mantle was worthily borne by his business associate, and successor as Chancellor's Assessor, Dr. John A. Ross, whose resignation in 1955 deprived the University of one who will long be remembered for his vigorous and fruitful Convenership of the Edilis and Lands Committee. In this branch of University work, perhaps his most notable memorials are the new Medical Building at Foresterhill and the new Students' Union in Broad Street, which was opened in 1939, and has recently (1960) received a large extension. Our University has indeed been lucky in being able to command the voluntary services of business men of such capacity and distinction as Dr. Crombie and Dr. Ross. Their names are happily linked in the title of the Crombie-Ross Fund, which has proved itself of such benefit to many good causes connected with the University.

4

It is well here to remember that Dr. Crombie and Dr. Ross are only the most recent among a succession of public-spirited men who, whether members of the academic staff or not, have given unstintingly of their time and ability in furthering the interests of the University. The University Court is a small body, charged with responsibilities at once weighty and formidable. It has been able to measure up to these only by reason of the extraordinary amount of time, energy and skill which, at all periods since its constitution a century ago, some of its members have been prepared voluntarily to devote to the work of the Court. Mention has already been made of Professor Matthew Hay and Sir Thomas Jaffrey: and this little history would be sadly incomplete if it failed to acknowledge the debt which the University Court, and thereby the *tota Universitas*, have owed to the untiring labours of Professor Hector Macdonald, who held our Chair of Mathematics from 1904 until 1935, who served on the University Court for the long period of twenty-eight years, and whose masterful chairmanship of the Edilis Committee was marked successively by the building of " New King's " in 1912; the Botany Department in 1924; the Engineering Department in 1926; notable extensions and improvements to King's College Library; the building of the Elphinstone Hall in 1932; the provision of the upper playing field in Old Aberdeen, and the restoration of the Chapel, carried out under the supervision of the late Dr. William Kelly. All these undertakings owed much to Professor Macdonald's foresight, judgment, and driving power, as well as to his close and watchful personal superintendence. Nor must we forget to acknowledge the University's debt to Dr. George Duncan, who died in 1949. As an Assessor of the General Council on the University Court, from 1921 until his death, he made his sound judgment and grasp of business felt in every branch of academic life. Of his services to the General Council, as the Convener of its Business Committee from 1941 till 1946, Mrs. Donald will speak later in this volume. Professor Macdonald and Dr. Duncan, the one an academe and the other a business man, will serve as types of not a few others, past and present, who have served, and are serving, our University with unfaltering loyalty, self-sacrifice and zeal.

The history of the teaching and study of Music in the united University has been an interesting one. It may be said to have taken its origin, as a serious pursuit, with the advent of Professor Sanford Terry to the staff of the University, as Lecturer in History, in 1898. Himself a musician and a musical scholar of high distinction, gifted moreover with phenomenal and highly infectious enthusiasm, driving power and organizing capacity, Terry at once took in hand the revival of the moribund, or at least merely *dilettante*, University Choral Society. Against strong opposition, and by dint of six years' persistent effort, he forced through in 1905 the admission of women students to the Society. Thereafter he set himself to form an orchestra " which should be capable of studying the works of the great musicians: his aim was to give the student performers an education in good music and a standard of musical taste, and at the same time to submit to their audience not an entertainment but a serious performance of an educative type, thus making the University a real centre of musical culture ". In all his efforts he was ably seconded by Miss Elisabeth Christie (afterwards Mrs. Christie Brown), the first organist of King's College Chapel—indeed the first woman to hold office in the University. Her brilliant handling of the Chapel choir forms a landmark in the development of Music in the University. In 1909 Professor Terry organized the first Musical Competition Festival in Scotland, thereby inaugurating a movement which has since spread all over the country, with incalculable benefit to our national culture. When he retired from the post of conductor in 1914 he had securely established Music as an honoured element in the life of the University, and had paved the way for its establishment as a taught subject in 1927. At first it formed part of a course of public lectures in Fine Art, embracing Architecture, Sculpture, Painting, Music, and the Theory of Art. Very soon this course was included as one of the seven required for a minimum curriculum for the Ordinary M.A. degree. During the war years the course in Fine Art lapsed; but a part-time Lectureship in Music was instituted in 1943, and was held by Mr. Willan Swainson. In 1948 the Lectureship became full-time. In 1951 Mr. Swainson retired, having done yeoman service in furthering the cause of Music in Aberdeen. In 1955 Music was added to the subjects which may be taken both for the Ordinary and for the Honours M.A. degree. The Department of Music now has two Lecturers and two Assistants. Its concerts and lunch-hour recitals have become an established and valued element in the corporate life of the University.

The laggard recognition of Music in the united University is all the more remarkable because, first of all the Scottish Universities, King's College was provided, by Elphinstone's *Fundatio* of 1506, with a master of music, to be known as the *Cantor*, to whom was assigned a yearly stipend of 20 merks.

In 1920 Aberdeen University broke new ground in academic history by being the first British University to appoint a Director of Physical Training.[1] This important step was followed next year by the institution of a Student Health Service, and in 1938 by the appointment of an Adviser to Women Students.

Since 1914, the life and work of the University have been chronicled, year by year, in the pages of the *Aberdeen University Review*, which, like so many other valuable developments, is a child of the General Council.

---

[1] " No University," wrote Sir Ernest Barker in his book on *Universities in Great Britain*, published in 1931, " would think of assigning any member of its staff to organise or even to encourage the sports of its students." He was ignorant of what Aberdeen had been doing for eleven years before his book appeared.

It is now under the management of the Alumnus Association.   At first three numbers were published annually: now, with the rise in printing costs, the number is reduced to two, a spring and an autumn issue.   The *Review* has been fortunate in a succession of devoted and capable editors. It circulates far and wide among graduates—though by no means as wide or as far as it should—and it is sent on an exchange basis to a long list of Universities at home and overseas.   In addition to providing a full service of University news, topics and personalia, the *Review* has afforded a means of publication to many distinguished scholars, writers and poets. In a Foreword to the first issue, Principal Sir George Adam Smith portrayed the *ethos* and achievement of our University in language whose lustre the lapse of time has in no wise dimmed, and which remains as relevant to the conditions of today as it was to those of well-nigh half a century ago:

> Our University today has a history second to no other of the land in the weight of its traditions and the brilliant variety of its examples. Her founders planned her on more liberal lines than any other Scottish school of the time, and if the realisation of their ideals was delayed for centuries by the comparative scantiness of her resources, she found a moral compensation for this in the close touch which she has always maintained with the popular life about her, and in those energies and habits of hard work, which were fostered alike by the poverty of her students, and by the invigorating climate in which she is set. We are not more proud of the eminent benefactors who have judged our University worthy of the use of their wealth, than we are of the longer list of humble men and women whose devotion to her of the thrift of their laborious and unselfish lives has been by far the noblest tribute to her power and will to serve the common people of this part of the Kingdom.   How she has discharged her trust is to be measured by that unceasing supply of recruits whom she has trained for the services of the Commonwealth and Empire, and by the large proportion of those who, from the lowliest origins, have risen by the help of her hand to the first places in their professions: who have governed provinces, administered the national justice and led armies, who have explored new territories and widened the bounds of science, who have been the leaders in the practice of medicine and surgery, who have been pioneers in education and founders or presidents of colleges and universities, or who have influenced philosophy and inspired religion.

Every great department in a modern university must be a centre of research as well as instruction.   It is not merely that the one function is as important as the other, or even that the two are complementary. They are mutually interdependent.   No university teacher who is not himself actively engaged in promoting the advancement of knowledge and discovery in his subject can fail to escape stagnation on his own part and loss of interest on the part of his students.   Moreover, it is the duty of a Professor, not only himself to engage in research, but to train his staff and his post-graduate students in the difficult art of research.   It is primarily as a stimulus to post-graduate research that the degree of PH.D. has proved its value.   Nevertheless, research can all too easily become an end in itself, instead of what it ought to be, a means to the advancement of knowledge: and every university is painfully aware of the grisly phenomenon of the graduate who embarks on " research " primarily as a device to postpone the day when he must place his neck in the collar and accept the drudgery of earning his living.   To administer grants for purposes of research, the University has appointed a joint Standing Committee for Research, consisting of representatives from the Court and the Senatus, the latter including members from each Faculty.   Since Ordinance No. 61 was passed, in 1895, by the Commissioners appointed under the Act of 1889, the Scottish Universities have enjoyed the power of appointing Research Fellows;   and this department of academic activity has been powerfully aided by the liberal policy of the Carnegie Trust, which awards Research Fellows and Scholarships, grants in aid of publication, and financial help in other forms.   There are now (1960) Research Fellows or Officers in the following subjects: Bacteriology (2); Biological Chemistry (2);   Chemistry (2);   Child Health;   Crop Physiology;   Engineering;   Fish Technology;   Fisheries and Oceanography; Food Technology;   Jurisprudence;   Medical Physics;   Mental Health; Midwifery (5);   Natural History;   Natural Philosophy;   Physiology of Nutrition;   Scottish Arts and Crafts;   Scottish Language (3);   Social Medicine (2);   Soil Science (2);   and Statistics.   The Research Fellowship in Scottish Arts and Crafts is held in connection with the Curatorship of the University's pictures, silver, and glass, and of *Am Fasgadh*, the Highland Folk Museum created by Dr. I. F. Grant at Kingussie, for the maintenance of which the four Scottish Universities have made themselves jointly responsible.

Most University researchers prefer to publish their work either in book form through a commercial firm, or as contributions to the transactions of a learned or scientific society.   There remains, however, a class of work which is too large for acceptance by such a journal, and too specialized to attract a commercial publisher.   As a vehicle for publishing works of this class, the University has for many years conducted a series of University Studies.   At first these consisted of collected papers by members of the staff, the requisite number of offprints being secured, with altered pagination, etc., so as in due course to build up a volume.   But this kind of University Study has now been superseded by individual works of the category indicated above, and issued by a publishing firm, the cost being guaranteed by the University.   Including both categories, the series of *University Studies* issued up to date (1960) amounts to 141 volumes. In a class by itself stands *Scottish Gaelic Studies*, a periodical issued since 1926 by the Celtic Department of the University.   The series of *University Studies*, together with the *Review* and *Scottish Gaelic Studies*, are used by the Library as exchange material (by no means adequate) for the enormous mass of publications received from other universities at home and abroad.

Finally, a word must be said about Further Education.   It is now everywhere agreed that part of the duties incumbent upon a university— and by no means the least important part—is to offer instruction in the higher branches of learning to those who have not had the benefit of attending a university, or who in adult life may desire to extend their

4*

acquaintance with fields of knowledge which in their youth they had no opportunity or leisure to cultivate. As the late Sir Michael Sadler put it, a university ought to contribute towards the work of training " those who cannot give years of their life to residence in a University, but whose minds are of the quality which rewards careful cultivation, and who have a love of study, and the perseverance to pursue it ". In this noble work our University has played a worthy part. In 1928 a joint Adult Education Committee of the University and the Workers' Educational Association was set up, and this in due course was enlarged into the Aberdeen and District Adult Education Committee. The Principal of the University is chairman, and the membership includes representatives of the University Court and Senatus Academicus, as well as of the Education Committees of Aberdeen, Aberdeenshire, and Kincardineshire, the Workers' Educational Association, and kindred bodies. The University herself has set up a Department of Extra-Mural Studies, which, in co-operation with the Education Committees within the University's area, provides for a large number of classes and lectures in a great variety of subjects. Some idea of the scope of the University's Department of Extra-Mural Studies may be obtained from the following statistics for the year 1958-59. During this academic year, the University conducted extra-mural classes, week-end and one-day schools in the following places: Aberchirder, Aberdeen, Aberlour, Banff, Balmacara, Brora, Buckie, Cullen, Dingwall, Forres, Gairloch, Grantown-on-Spey, Huntly, Inverness, Keith, Kingussie, Kirkwall, Kyle of Lochalsh, Lerwick, Lossiemouth, Nairn, Peterhead, Plockton, Portsoy, Thurso, Tolsta, Tomintoul, Stornoway, and Wick. The total number of students enrolled was 1,286. In addition, lectures were given to members of H.M. Forces in the Aberdeen area, and University Weeks were held in Ross and Cromarty, Lewis, Orkney, and Shetland.

The University now has on her staff a whole-time Tutor-Organiser in Extra-Mural Studies, with headquarters at Elgin. It would be wrong to imagine that, by conducting all this work in Further Education, our University was merely acting in the role of public benefactor. The University herself gains incalculably by the effort. As the late Sir Ernest Barker once said, " one of the great duties of the University teacher is to remain a man in becoming a scholar, and to keep a rich humanity at the same time that he acquires a large erudition ". And there is no better way by which an academic teacher can realize this aim than by seeking the contacts with outside life that Further Education offers him. His own teaching in the University will be vastly enriched by the experience. Some of the greatest teachers in our own University, like Sir John Arthur Thomson, have been remembered among those who did most to spread knowledge of their subjects among the community at large.

No account of Further Education in the University would be acceptable without including a tribute to the devoted work in this high cause of Dr. Norman Walker, Reader in Education, who retired in 1960, but happily retains his post as Director of Adult Education.

The service which students and staff of our University rendered in two world wars, and the greatness of their sacrifice, will always remain poignant memories with the present generation. A salute is surely due to the splendid work, in preparing so many for the ordeal, and in helping to safeguard our country against any such further trial, which has been performed by the University's Officers' Training Corps, Air Squadron, and branch of the Women's Royal Auxiliary Corps—all belonging to the Territorial Army. In their relationships with the University, these Service formations are looked after by a Military Education Committee. The Convener is the Principal, and the Committee consists of representatives of Court and Senatus, as well as the Commanding Officers of the three Service units.

Our University has been fortunate in her historians. Of these the earliest was our first Principal, Hector Boece, who in his *Murthlacensium et Aberdonensium Episcoporum Vitae*, published in 1522—the greater part of which is a biography of Elphinstone has given us a charming picture, couched in elegant Renaissance Latin, of the beginnings of King's College, and of the happy band of distinguished humanists whom our Founder gathered round about himself in the Aulton. A long standing reproach against the University, that she has published no adequate life of her Founder—one of the greatest of Scottish ecclesiastics, statesmen and scholars—is now about to be rectified by Dr. Leslie J. Macfarlane of our History Department; a forestaste of whose remarkable discoveries, in the Vatican, at Paris, Orleans and elsewhere, was given to a fascinated audience in his P. J. Anderson Memorial Lecture on 1 November 1960. The advent of the Quatercentenary Celebrations produced what are still the two standard histories of the University, both published in the same year, 1895; one by J. M. Bulloch, afterwards the well-known editor of *The Graphic*, and the other by Robert S. Rait, who later became Principal of Glasgow University and Historiographer-Royal for Scotland. In the *Quatercentenary Handbook*, published in 1906, a quite excellent summary of the history of the University was contributed by Dr. Robert Walker, who at that time was Secretary of the University Court and Registrar of the General Council.[1]

The fundamental stuff of history of course is documents. Aberdeen University is fortunate in the completeness and amplitude of her records; and still more fortunate in the way in which they have been published. So far back as 1854, on the eve of the Fusion, a beginning was made in the fine volume of selections from the muniments of King's College, *Fasti Aberdonenses*, published by the Spalding Club under the editorship of Cosmo Innes. But the major credit for the arranging, investigating,

[1] Some account of " Functions " Walker—one of the most remarkable personalities in the modern history of the University—will be given by Mrs. Donald later in this volume.

editing and publishing of the records of both the former Universities must surely be accorded to Mr. P. J. Anderson, Librarian of the University from 1894 until his death in 1926. " Our incomparable Librarian ", Principal Sir George Adam Smith very truly called him at the time when the University mourned his passing: and indeed the University Library owes an undying debt to his devoted stewardship—a debt of which nobody is more conscious than the present writer. But it may be questioned whether, in the long perspective, P. J. Anderson's greatest service to his *Alma Mater* was not rendered rather in the compilation of the four stately volumes which he edited for the New Spalding Club: *King's College, Officers and Graduates* (1893), and *Fasti Academiae Mariscallanae* (3 vols., 1889-98). No one except those who have used these works almost from day to day can have the faintest conception of the magnitude of the task to which Anderson consecrated the leisure hours of a busy life, or of the accuracy, skill and sheer downright love of the self-imposed task which he brought to bear on its fulfilment. On his memorial panel in King's College Library is carved the classic quotation, *Si monumentum quaeris, circumspice*; and certainly its complete appropriateness to that setting will never be called in question. Yet the four massive green bound volumes may all be deemed to form a memorial, even more permanent, of one whose passionate loyalty to his *Alma Mater* was equalled only by the self-effacement with which he served her during one of the most fruitful generations in her whole long history.

To a large extent, the history of the University is the history of her graduates. One advantage of the old rigid Arts curriculum, in which all the undergraduates took more or less the same course, sat on the same benches and listened to the same Professors, was the development of an intense class spirit and sense of solidarity. Many classes therefore, particularly in the Faculty of Arts, thus formed their own Associations, with an annual re-union, dinner and perhaps other functions. The secretaries of these Class Associations kept careful records of their members, and not a few of these have been published. In addition to these class records, Aberdeen University has been notably distinguished for the three successive Rolls of Graduates which she has published: the first, covering the period 1860-1900, edited by Colonel William Johnston; the second, 1900-25, edited by Theodore Watt; and the third, prepared in connection with the Fusion Centenary, and covering the period 1926-55, edited by Mr. John Mackintosh. Only those who have had occasion to consult these three Rolls can be qualified to estimate the devoted and arduous labour which has been put into their compilation by the three successive editors. Their names are enrolled with honour among the long list of our alumni whose voluntary service of their *Alma Mater* knows neither stint nor bounds.

It may be of interest to mention that the current (1960) Register of the General Council of the University includes the names of 12,939 graduates, as well as those of 153 *ex officio* members.

In 1932 Mr. R. W. Davies of Aldroughty, Elgin, an ex-Indian Civil Servant, presented to the University the Estate of Aldroughty, which included a mansion house, fully furnished, a farm of 164 acres, a home farm of 69 acres, and 164 acres of woodlands. The mansion house is used as a holiday residence for members of the staff and their families.

Perhaps the last event of general interest in the hundred years of our history that we have chronicled has been the acquirement by the University, in 1960, of the historic property of Tarradale in Ross-shire—the seat of a royal castle in the thirteenth century, and famous in modern times as the birthplace, in 1792 of Sir Roderick Murchison, one of the founders of geological science. Subsequently the house was an occasional home of Field Marshal Lord Napier of Magdala and of Sir Henry Yule, the orientalist. It contained a fine library of some 20,000 books, including many valuable works on oriental studies, military history, and Italian history and literature. Latterly the mansion house had been run as a study retreat for Scottish university students: but the funds being no longer sufficient for this purpose a scheme was devised under the Education (Scotland) Acts 1939-50, whereby the property and endowment were vested in the University of Aberdeen. The house has been reconditioned and is to be run as a field studies centre under the supervision of the Geography Department of the University.

It may be added that Aberdeen University shares an interest in The Burn, a fine country house amid lovely surroundings near Edzell. It is administered by the Dominion Students' Hall Trust, and is available for the use of men and women students from the British Commonwealth, the United States of America, and the Home universities, either for holidays or for study, particularly by reading parties. It has also become a favourite venue for conferences of the four Scottish University Courts.

And so we bring to a close this brief chronicle history of the hundred years of our existence as a united University. However imperfectly my task has been achieved, it will surely be apparent to all my readers that the record has been one of continuous and astonishing progress and expansion, sustained by pulsating energy and directed, one may fairly claim, by wisdom, vision and enterprise.[1] What of the future? In common with all the British universities, Aberdeen faces a programme of unprecedented enlargement, dictated by the Government. This is not the place to discuss, or even to set forth, the formidable problems posed by such an expansion: but one point at least may be referred to here. Aberdeen University has always claimed, not without justification, to be the most Scottish of the Scottish universities. Certainly she possesses a " province ", or natural reservoir from which hitherto the majority of her

[1] The expansion of the University has been most graphically portrayed in the series of diagrams prepared for the Centenary Celebrations by Mrs. Muriel J. F. Barnett, Cartographer in the Geography Department. These fascinating drawings are unfortunately too large for reproduction here.

students have been drawn, more compact and more defined, by its physical and human characteristics, than is perhaps the case with any of her sister universities.   Now if we are in truth to expand until we have a student population of 4,500, it is obvious that these are not going to come from our own " province ".   Young men and women of the requisite calibre are simply not there in anything like the prescribed numbers. No, our huge new intake of students will be drawn from south of the Mounth, from the members of the British Commonwealth, from foreign countries, from " a' the airts " in east and west.   The danger thereby involved in our own native, deeply rooted and highly cherished traditions and standards, to the essential Scottishness of our University, is too obvious to need labouring.   Nevertheless, experience shows that national character, particularly Scottish national character, is one of the toughest and hardiest of growths.   Upon the whole, there is perhaps no need for undue alarm: and we may conclude by expressing the hope, indeed the firm belief, that the same enterprise, vision and wisdom which have guided our *Alma Mater* in the past, will be manifest in grappling with the problems of the future—problems likely to be far vaster in scope and more complex in nature than anything in the long centuries of our previous history.

3

THE HISTORY OF THE GENERAL COUNCIL

OF THE

UNIVERSITY OF ABERDEEN

1860 - 1960

BY

LOUISE DONALD

I. EARLY YEARS

The Watchdog of the University! That is how Colonel Butchart once described the General Council. Consisting mainly of the whole body of graduates—13,000 of them in 1960—the General Council in itself has no legislative power within the University but by its resolutions and recommendations it can help to shape and guide University policy and action. The supreme ruling body is the University Court on which the General Council now has four Assessors. The Senatus Academicus, as its name implies, considers the curricula and the academic standards of the various Faculties and makes recommendations to the University Court. Conversely, the Court submits to both Senatus Academicus and General Council matters for their comment and criticism; and a notable and interesting feature of the life of the University over the past hundred years has been the influence on the Court ruling of the opinion of the General Council. Representing as it does the rank and file of the University, the General Council can often blow a wind of everyday commonsense into the more rarefied atmosphere of the cloisters.

1860 is a notable year in the history of all four Scottish Universities for by Ordinance of the Commissioners under Act 21 and 22 Victoria, Chapter 83 of 9 January of that year, the Ordinance being approved by Her Majesty in Council on 30 June, a General Council was established in each of the four Universities. Particularly in the history of the University of Aberdeen, however, is 1860 a landmark, for the same body of Commissioners authorized the Fusion of the two Universities in our city and the " University of Aberdeen and King's College " and " Marischal College and University of Aberdeen " were united and incorporated under the style and title of the " University of Aberdeen ".

The 1860 Ordinance is the direct outcome of the Universities (Scotland) Act 1858—" an Act to make provision for the better Government and discipline of the Universities of Scotland and improving and regulating the Course of study therein; and for the Union of the two Universities and Colleges of Aberdeen ". By this Act both the University Courts and the General Councils of all four Universities were constituted, while the powers of the already existing Senatus Academicus in each University were defined. The General Council in each University was to consist of the Chancellor, the members of the University Court, the Professors, all graduates and certain alumni;[1] no one could be a member " until he has attained the age of twenty-one years complete and has the name registered in a book to be kept for the purpose by each University "; an annual fee of 2s. 6d. after the initial payment of 5s. could by 1862 be compounded into a single payment of £1—one item in the cost of living which has not altered in a century! It was not until 22 August 1881, that registration in the General Council became a necessary preliminary to graduation. The General Council, to assemble twice a year under the Chairmanship of the Chancellor, were to " take into their consideration all questions affecting the well-being and prosperity of the University and to make representations from time to time on such questions to the University Court ".

In the Act special mention has to be made of the General Council of the University of Aberdeen which was to consist of " the Chancellors or Chancellor, of the members of the University Court, of the professors and of such graduates and students as are herein above provided in regard to the other Universities, whether they be graduates and students of the University of King's College or of Marischal College and University ". No doubt the meeting together in this way of the products of the two rival establishments whose fusion at long last settled a decades-old controversy was an important factor in the unification of the two Universities.

The Commissioners of the 1860 Ordinance set down regulations for the conduct of the meetings of the General Council. Failing the presence of the Chancellor, the Rector would preside, whom failing, the Principal; in the absence of Chancellor, Rector and Principal, the Professor longest in office would take the Chair. The twice-yearly meeting of the General

---

[1] " all persons who within three years from and after the passing of this Act shall establish to the satisfaction of the Commissioners herein after appointed that they have, as matriculated students, given regular attendance on the course of study in the University for four complete sessions, or such regular attendance for three complete sessions in the University, and regular attendance for one such complete session in any other Scottish University, the attendance for at least two of such sessions having been on the course of study in the faculty of Arts ".

Council could not be adjourned to a later day; but proceedings could be adjourned to a later hour of the same day. The General Council had power to appoint a committee or committees at one meeting to arrange or prepare business for a future meeting; but at this stage none of the power of the General Council could be delegated to a committee.

One of the most cherished privileges of the General Council was conferred on it at the very beginning of its existence. The Council has in its power the election of the Chancellor—the holder of the highest office in the University. In the event of a vacancy, the election of a successor takes place at the first Ordinary Meeting of the General Council after the lapse of two months from the occurrence of the vacancy. Such an election—as also an election of the Council's Assessor on the University Court—one only in these early days—takes place before any other of the Council's business is transacted.

In the elections both of Chancellor and Assessor the vote in the first instance is taken at the Council's Statutory Meeting by a show of hands; but a poll by postal vote of all the available members of the General Council can be demanded by the proposer or seconder of a candidate. In this year of 1960 the full machinery of a postal vote to settle the filling of two vacant Assessorships has been in action—proof, if any were needed, of the vitality of the century-old General Council and of the interest of its members in the legislation of the University.

The General Council having been thus set up by Act and Ordinance, the first meeting was held on 10 October 1860, in the Hall of the University, now the Picture Gallery of Marischal College.

Since December 1956, the twice-yearly meeting of the General Council has been held in the Lecture Theatre at Marischal College—the old Debater with a new look—and it has proved excellent from the point of view of both accommodation and acoustics. The change from the Picture Gallery was made as a result of protest about difficulty of hearing and here even in this small matter of the meeting-place we see in action the whirligig of time. A similar protest in April 1871 resulted in the end-of-the-year meeting's being held not in the Hall of the University but in the Natural History classroom. A classroom, however, proved unsuitable and H.M. Board of Works were asked, evidently with little effect, to remedy " the state of the Hall ".

In 1860, this year of fusion, the two Chancellors were the Earl of Aberdeen and the Duke of Richmond. Both were absent from this meeting and the office of Rector having been declared vacant, the Principal, the Rev. Peter Colin Campbell, formerly King's College Principal and now Principal of the new University, took the Chair and for this meeting the Registrar of the University, the Rev. John Fyfe, A.M., was appointed Clerk. The pattern of the meeting set up at this initial gathering has been followed ever since. After the mace and procession comes the opening prayer and the proceedings are always closed by the apostolic benediction.

This historic first meeting of the General Council began with the reading of the Ordinance of the Commissioners, dated 2 July 1860 and approved by Her Majesty, Queen Victoria, by Orders in Council dated 27 August 1860, regulating the order of procedure in the General Councils of the Universities of Scotland. And the first importance piece of business was the election of an Assessor to represent, for the ensuing four years, the Council in the University Court. After three nominees had been voted on by a show of hands, the proposers of the two losers each demanded a poll and so at this very first meeting the machinery for the postal vote of all graduates—at that time 815 in number—was set in motion. As a result of this poll Dr. Alex. Kilgour of Aberdeen was elected the Council's first Assessor on the University Court, the decision of the meeting arrived at by a show of hands that the Rev. James Bisset, minister at Bourtie, be the Assessor, having been overturned by the postal vote. Four years later, Dr. Kilgour, have been voted in again by a show of hands at the Statutory Meeting, was unseated as a result of the poll asked for by the proposer of his opponent and from 1864 to 1868 the Rev. Wm. Mearns, A.M., minister at Kinneff, represented the General Council in the University Court. Were Church and Medicine the two strongest elements in this first decade of the life of the General Council? At the end of Mr. Mearns's four-year period of office, Dr. Kilgour was again proposed and, unopposed, was appointed Assessor, to be succeeded in 1872 by Wm. F. Ogg, A.M., the proposer in this case being the retiring member, Dr. Kilgour. Similarly in 1876, Mr. Ogg, now the retiring member, proposed as his successor, the Rev. John Christie, who, unopposed, was unanimously elected. Not until 1880 was there again a contest and a subsequent demand for a poll for the General Council's one and only seat on the University Court.

A resolution that no money deposit be required from members of the Council for borrowing from the Library was the only other outcome of this meeting and the Minute thereanent was the first to be submitted to the newly-constituted University Court.

Early in the first session of the united University, 1860-61, the Duke of Richmond, one of the Chancellors, died and within two months the remaining Chancellor, the Earl of Aberdeen, also died. Accordingly, the first business of the General Council at its second meeting was the election of a Chancellor, the unanimous choice being the new Duke of Richmond. An so began a long reign of more than forty-two years.

Not so happily settled would appear to be the method of election of the Rector. Edward Francis Maitland, H.M. Solicitor-General for Scotland, had by this date been elected by the students as Rector, but the General Council joined Court and students in protesting against the clause in the Ordinance of the Commissioners by which a casting vote in the election of Rector was conferred, in certain events, upon the Chancellor and the Principal. Three years later the Council renewed their protest but it was not until 1891 that the desired change in the Act was made.

At this second meeting too the first Business Committee—of twenty-one members—of the General Council was elected—" to arrange and prepare business for the next meeting "—with Aberdeen's Provost, Alexander Anderson, as its Convener.

It is understandable that the early years of the combined University and of the newly-constituted governing bodies should be a time of adjustment. The records would suggest that the General Council, easing itself into the saddle, rather self-consciously concerned itself with trivialities—the borrowing of Library books, the publication of marks in the Bursary Competition—and anxious to give weight and purpose to its deliberations, kept passing to the University Court suggestions, not, however, very practicable or worthwhile. The University Court, its mantle of authority still new upon it, would be equally self-conscious and somewhat aloof; and the variety of phrase with which during the first five years its Deliverances rejected the Council's advances is admirable.

On matters such as admission of reporters to meetings, the publications of University accounts, the amount of class fees, University Court pronouncements read—" there is no reason to enter upon the renewed consideration . . . at present "; " they have not the power of dealing with the question "; " considers it to be premature "; " cannot at present interfere "; " the Court disapprove "; " the Court do not concur ". The restrained replies suggest exasperated elders dealing with a precocious and irrepressible child!

It is interesting to see too how often matters concerning the University Library crop up in the Minutes of those first five years—the question of a Library deposit, rules about numbers of books to be borrowed, a Library catalogue and, perhaps most significant of all, a suggestion, well-supported and hotly debated in the Council and seriously considered before rejected by the Court, that the whole Library be removed " to the University Buildings at Aberdeen " as " much more accessible to readers resident at the seat of the University, as well as to readers resident at a distance ". This would appear to indicate a trend for the life of the University to be concentrated at Marischal College—a trend reversed only within the last quarter of a century with the development of a University precinct in Old Aberdeen and the tremendous amount of new University building in the Old Town.

Some concern with academic standards within the University, combined with attempts to give University recognition to teaching outside the University, is reflected too in those early Minutes. Apart from recurring questions about Bursary Competitions and Preliminary Examinations, a move was on foot for the introduction of a degree of Bachelor of Arts, "a scheme of Examination for those who are not of the University", Middle-Class Examinations as at Oxford and Cambridge, Classes for Persons in Business and a motion—" to adopt measures for preventing young men from attending any class in the Curriculum of Arts as Public or Gown Students, who are incapable, from deficiency in their previous education of deriving due advantage from the instruction communicated in that class ". Indeed, after October 1863, meeting a Representation from the General Council to the Court asked rather sweepingly for a review of the whole Regulations of the University "with a view to ascertain the effect which these Regulations have . . . upon the discipline of the individual classes of the University, upon the efficiency of teaching in the classes and upon the cost of a University Education at Aberdeen ". The Court's " retort courteous " expressed dignified disapproval, with more than a hint that the General Council was over-reaching itself. " The University Court are unable to agree " . . . " are of opinion that it is at least premature to ask them to enter on so wide a field and that greatly more experience is needed before a trustworthy judgment can be formed on the workings of the present system."

Court and Council came together, however, over the matter of Representation in Parliament for the Scottish Universities. As early as April 1861, Charles F. Runcy, Advocate in Aberdeen, had moved " that the Scottish Universities should be put on a similar footing with those of England and Ireland, with regard to Representation in Parliament " and he was the seconder of Professor Nicol's motion in April 1867: " That the Council petition Parliament, that in any Reform Bill for Scotland provision be made for the due Representation of the Scottish Universities." Although the Principal, presiding at this meeting of the Council, reserved his opinion as to the power of the Council to petition, there was sent, duly signed by him and by authority of the Meeting, a Petition to the House of Commons which the Rector of the University, Mountstuart Elphinstone Grant Duff, M.P., was requested to present, the Members of Parliament for City and County being asked to give the Petition their support.

Proceedings were regularized, however, by a later representation from the General Council whereby they requested the University Court to petition Parliament " that provision be made for the representation of the Scottish Universities by the allotment to them of not less than two Members ".

Further petitions to both Houses of Parliament went directly from the General Council; and again the University Court were asked by the Council not only to petition but to " press the matter, by Deputation and otherwise, on the Government and Members of Parliament ". The Court acted in full harmony with the Council in this and in their name forwarded copies of the Petition to the Rector for presentation to the Chancellor, to Members of Parliament representing the area and to Clerks of the other University Courts, with the intimation that the University Court of Aberdeen concurred in any similar representation being made in this connection by the other Universities.

Success crowned these efforts: for by the Representation of the People (Scotland) Act, 1868, the Scottish Universities were given two members in the House of Commons, one to represent the Universities of

Glasgow and Aberdeen, the other the Universities of Edinburgh and St. Andrews. The first Member of Parliament to represent the Universities of Glasgow and Aberdeen, the Right Hon. James Alexander Campbell, LL.D., took his seat in 1868; and from that date until the abolition of the Universities Constituencies in 1948 most male graduates had this direct voice in Government affairs. From 1918 women graduates shared in the privilege if they were over thirty, an age restriction removed in 1928 when women were fully enfranchised.

But at this stage, most of the General Council's activities were on a domestic level; and a pretty piece of comedy, revealing the nice adjustment of relations between Council, Court and Senatus, would appear to have been enacted over the paying of a printer's bill. By the end of these first ten years steps had been taken for the printing of the Minutes of the General Council. The Clerk of the Council was instructed to transmit to the Senatus—who then evidently held the purse-strings—" the Printer's Account for the Collected Minutes ". The Senatus returned the account " with instruction that the Senatus can receive communications from the General Council only through the University Court ". Discretion evidently prevailed over outraged dignity and hurt pride on the part of the General Council for, after amendments suggesting defiance, the motion that the University Court be asked to transmit to the Senatus Academicus the printer's account was carried.

It is small wonder then that at the close of this first decade the General Council could feel little satisfaction in its achievement and suffered a sense of frustration. At the meeting which completed the first ten years of its life a motion unanimously agreed to ask for amendments of the Universities Act which called the Council into being, so that the members might have " greater power ", this to be achieved mainly by more adequate representation in the University Court; and a Committee was set up to consider the whole question. This sense of irritation arising from limited responsibility was evidently general to all the Scottish University Councils and from this point investigation proceeded so that concerted action could be taken.

Another motion of this period has very special significance for us in 1960. In this year the Crombie Hall of Residence—the first in the kingdom to be designed for a mixed population of both men and women students, 110 in all—was opened on 13 August by H.M. Queen Elizabeth. Fully in action in the Winter Term of 1960, Crombie Hall first opened its doors in the preceding Summer Term with a pilot scheme whereby sixty men and women students lived and worked there. Ninety years ago the General Council set up a Committee to consider ways and means whereby students could be " provided with Rooms within the College for board, lodging and common study ". The first Report of this Committee is of great interest. Twentieth-century social and economic revolution has changed material values but the unalterables remain and many a statement in this ninety-year old Report rings as true today as in

5

1870. But how different are prices! The estimated cost of building and furnishing a Hall to accommodate fifty students—" with bedrooms sufficiently commodious, large dining-room, library for common study, a few parlours for those who might wish for them, kitchen accommodation, etc., and suitable residence for the Head or Master " was £6,000!—about the cost of setting up and equipping a modern tabloid home! A plea was made for appealing for subscriptions so that capital cost could be defrayed, " so that the building could be erected and furnished free ", and " good board and lodging could then be offered to the students at such a rate as to be within the means of any of them who might choose to take advantage of it, and not much above what is ordinarily paid by them at present for private lodging ". The Report went on to express what is still the held belief: " But if such a hall is to produce all the benefits desired from it, it must be done well, with everything comfortable and good, else it had better not be done at all." With subscriptions to defray building and furnishing costs, the rate of board and lodging could be much reduced from the " £50 for the five months of the college session " which would be required if the workings of the residence had to show a profit to shareholders. The institution of " such a Collegiate Hall . . . would be attended with the greatest possible advantage to the health of the students. It would give, in short, a fresh start to University life in Aberdeen and to higher education in the north of Scotland."

The planners of this ewer-and-basin, pre-gaslight era could not possibly have foreseen the wonderful interpretation the Age of Science would in Crombie Hall give to their ninety-years old dream—nor would they in their highest flights of fancy have pictured a community of inter-racial men and women students—but the ideals of those Victorian visionaries command our respect for they had the root of the matter in them and in imagination and foresight they builded better than they knew. There stands Crombie Hall today at last " done well, with everything comfortable and good " but it has cost £298,000 to build!

Another theme that recurs like a *leitmotif* throughout the records of the time is the concern over the lack of medical bursaries. The Faculties of Arts and Divinity—the only other Faculties then in being—were well endowed; but there was only one bursary—founded sixty-five years earlier by Dr. John Milne of Bombay—to be competed for in the Faculty of Medicine. The poverty of endowment is explained by the fact that until well into the nineteenth century the method of medical training had not been by means of University classes and clinics but by individual apprenticeship to a medical practitioner.

This matter presented for the consideration of the University Court is notable on this point, if for nothing else, in that it brought full measure of agreement remarkable in its cordiality of expression—" The Court will gladly go along with the other authorities of the University in any measures to be taken for accomplishing the desired object."

Thus encouraged, the Committee appointed in April 1870, to consider

Medical Bursaries, reported the results of their investigations at each meeting of the parent body over the next few years and finally in 1874 published a full and detailed report which was printed and circulated among the members of the General Council. The Committee's hope that their scheme might be " regarded with favour by intending benefactors of the University " had one immediate happy result in the institution of a Bursary for the students of Medicine of the University of Aberdeen by the Glasgow Aberdeenshire Association.

II. THE STRUGGLE FOR FULLER RECOGNITION

Throughout the eighteen-seventies the Committee of the General Council, appointed first in April 1870, to consider means of greater representation of the General Councils on the University Courts, later considerably increased in membership and with its remit widened " to include all changes desirable in the Universities' Act of 1858 ", continued its work and many meetings were held along with the representatives of the General Councils of the other three Scottish Universities. As no change could be made in the Universities Act without the sanction of Parliament, it was necessary that the several Universities should be agreed on the desired alterations so that any representation to Parliament should be " unanimous and complete ". Each of the four General Councils concurred in the need for change in the Constitution of the Scottish Universities and, while there was general agreement in certain matters, the circumstances in the four Universities varied so that the needs of one did not exactly coincide with the needs of any other. It became obvious that it was impossible to reach complete unanimity. In 1874, the Committee of the General Council of the University of Glasgow circulated to the other General Councils a draft of " A Bill to Amend the Scottish Universities Act, 1858 ". The Joint Committee representing the four Universities agreed, in spite of some demur, to revise the Bill with a view to its being brought before Parliament. Even amended and adjusted, however, it could not be regarded as other than a " partial remedy " and the matter of the need for setting up a Royal Commission became urgent. At this point the Aberdeen Committee asked successfully that their General Council would reappoint them with " power to approach and urge on the Government the appointment of a Royal Commission on the Universities and to communicate with the General Councils of the other Universities, to induce these Committees to co-operate with them, with a view to these objects ".

Consequently a deputation of representatives from the Councils of the Universities of St. Andrews, Glasgow and Aberdeen—Edinburgh not being represented—accompanied by several members of both Houses of Parliament who were " warmly interested in the Scottish Universities ", waited personally on the Lord Advocate who along with the Home Secretary met them in the Home Office on 12 July 1875. The deputation was introduced by Dr. Lyon Playfair, M.P., and it was the Convener of the Aberdeen Committee, the Rev. Robert Stephen, who presented to the Home Secretary the Memorial asking for the appointment of a Royal Commission to consider the amendment of the Scottish Universities Act of 1858 " particularly with regard to the composition and function of the University Courts and the enlargement of the range of study for the honours which the University confer ".

In presenting this Memorial, Mr. Stephen brought before the Home Secretary four points representing the fully considered findings of Aberdeen General Council, while members of the deputation from the Universities of Glasgow and St. Andrews and the Marquis of Huntly, Rector of Aberdeen University, spoke on other matters which they considered necessitated the appointment of a Commission. The report goes on to say that " the Home Secretary listened most attentively and courteously with evident interest and promised a careful consideration of the whole subject ".

Early in 1876 the Scottish Universities' Commission was set up and the work of this Commission, the evidence presented to it and the framing of the Universities' (Scotland) Bill which eventually became the Universities' (Scotland) Act in 1889 provided the dominating interests for the rest of this and for almost the whole of the next decade.

The four points presented by Mr. Stephen as a tailpiece to the Joint Committee's Memorial have both significance and interest. The first pointed out the need for larger representation of the Council in the University Court. The second asked that the Council might have the opportunity, before such new measures were carried into effect, of considering and commenting upon, without power of veto, all improvements and alterations in the internal arrangements of the Universities, devised by Court and Senatus and sanctioned by the Chancellor. The third stressed the need for modification, alteration and widening of the curriculum of study and the fourth asked for some measure of autonomy within each of the four Universities, whose different circumstances made uniformity in courses of study, manner of examinations, conditions under which degrees were conferred both undesirable and unworkable. These prove on the part of the General Council no mere power-seeking or involvement with petty concerns but a real desire to give in time and skill and interest for the betterment of the whole University. The other Committees set up by the General Council and working through these years of development reflect this growing maturity. Of particular note in this respect are the Committees on the curricula for Arts and Medicine.

At the meeting in October 1871, on the motion of the Rev. Dr. John Christie, a Committee had been appointed to consider the question of the Arts curriculum and the Regulations for granting degrees in Arts; and in April 1873, a Committee on the Medical curriculum and Faculty was constituted on the motion of Dr. Alex. Ogston. By April 1874, the latter Committee had circulated a printed report in which under five heads they suggested improvements in the four years course then leading to a Medical degree. These were—some uniformity, without compulsory Greek, in the Preliminary Examination for the medical course throughout the Scottish Universities; more practical work and certain additional courses, these to be made room for by the reduction of time spent on other subjects; the need for a Chair of Anatomy within the University as well as courses in Insanity and in Diseases of the Eye, the Ear, the Teeth; some changes in the Examination system and improvement and extension of Medical Library facilities. Evidently the Senatus had also prepared a Report on the Medical curriculum and, when the Representation of the General Council on the subject was sent in 1874 to the University Court, it drew forth a Deliverance expressed in chilly terms in which the Council is referred to the Court's views on the Report of the Senatus, concluding " and therefore it appears to be unnecessary to go over the same ground again by a separate reply to the Report of the Council's Committee ". The Council had to accept this reproof, but it had at least the satisfaction of knowing that its report probably reinforced that of the Senatus.

The findings of the Committee on the Arts course met with more acceptance by the Court, however.

The main point at issue in regard to the Arts curriculum was the question of compulsory Greek. Coming events here cast a long shadow before them and with a quarter of the old century still to go there already appeared signs of the decline in influence of the Classics, their giving way to the modern humanities of English and French and German and the coming ascendancy of scientific studies. Much heated discussion must have taken place in Committee and in Council, die-hard opinion evidently regarding the new proposals as both revolutionary and retrograde.

Amid counter-motions, amendments, recorded dissent, it was finally decided to recommend that a new degree other than the classically-based M.A.—probably a revival of the B.A.—be instituted. The University Court in its Deliverance on this Representation by the General Council said, " The Court thoroughly sympathize with the main design and object proposed by the Council " and in a draft Deliverance prepared by the Rector, Mountstuart Elphinstone Grant Duff, M.P., it is said that " to enlarge the present Curriculum and to introduce other and optional branches of instruction is a thing right in itself and called for by the community ". But " a new and inferior degree " did not seem to the Court to provide the solution and they set about revising the curriculum for the M.A. degree with the idea of " lightening the load of Classics which at present overweights these students who have no special turn for ancient literature ". The Court's suggestions for the widening of the Arts curriculum were duly considered by the Council's Committee. In 1874 this Committee reported " that there is a growing body of opinion in various quarters and in the different Universities in favour of the revival of the degree of B.A. as affording the most flexible machinery for adaptations

to the varied requirements of different classes of the community ".
By 1875, however, the Committee is convinced " that a satisfactory
solution of the questions involved in this subject will only be reached
through a Royal Commission on the whole subject of Scottish University
Education ".

The Commission having been set up, the two Committees of the
Council, that on Changes Desirable in the Universities Acts and Ordinances and that on the Arts Curriculum, met together on 3 October 1876,
to draw up a joint report on subjects to be brought before the Royal Commission.   While recommendations already agreed to by the Council
were to be laid as such before the Commission, individual opinions on
controversial points strongly held by those appointed to give evidence
could be freely stated before the Commissioners.

These two Committees continued in being until after a joint meeting
in March 1878, they decided to recommend their discharge at the April
meeting of the Council, so that they might be replaced by " a new Committee appointed to draw up a statement of the principal changes con-
templated by the Royal Universities' Commissioners in their recent
Report and to indicate their bearing on Scottish education generally,
and particularly their effect on this University ".

The Universities Commission having published their Report, this
new Committee of the Council, having formed two open Sub-Committees,
one on the Arts curriculum and degree, the other on constitutional
questions, considered it and made their report to the Council.   The
Commissioners had recommended the introduction of alternatives in the
Arts curriculum and correspondingly " in the competition and pass
examination for bursaries and scholarships and in any entrance or preliminary examination that may be instituted ".   Both in Committee
and in Council there was again, along with acceptance of the general
principle, considerable discussion on the proposed alternatives.

On constitutional matters, the Commissioners had approved the
Council's suggestion that the Council should have three Assessors on the
Court and had also followed the Council's recommendation that the
election of the Rector should be by general poll rather than by voting
by nations—a suggestion that happily has never been accepted!

Following discussion of this second report, both reports " lay on the
table " until a year later it was decided " that in the absence of any
immediate prospect of definite legislation upon the subject of University
education in Scotland, the Council do not find it necessary to commit
itself to approval of abstract resolutions ".   And so for a time the whole
matter which had exercised the Council for the best part of ten years
rested.   Throughout the eighteen-eighties, however, the Council kept
a watching brief over the framing of the Universities Bill.

Library affairs which had been the pre-occupation of the General
Council in its early years have, apart from some reference to the Library
Catalogue, little part in the records of the seventies.   From a Minute

of April 1875, however, we gather that the distance between the New Town and King's College Library in the Old Town still presented difficulties to Council borrowers. A motion unanimously agreed to ask the University Court " to sanction an arrangement whereby Members of Council, and others entitled to the use of the University Library, may be able to take out and return books through an agency to be established in the buildings formerly belonging to Marischal College at least twice a week, subject to such regulations as the Court may make thereanent ". This has a delightful follow-up in a Report by the Senatus to the University Court dated 2 October 1877, which had been sent to the Council by the University Court on 9 October 1877.

" The scheme of interchange referred to has now been in operation for two summers and one winter, having been commenced after the annual inspection which took place in April 1876. Readers living in Aberdeen may have books belonging to the General Library delivered to them at Marischal College Buildings, by sending a certain preliminary notice and are not under the necessity of applying at the Old Town, and similarly regarding readers in the Old Town, who may wish to receive books located only in the New Town.

" The arrangement has to a considerable extent been taken advantage of in winter and the journey of the cab with its freight of books has taken place twice a week, as was first projected. In summer the requirements have not been so extensive, and it has been found practicable to make one journey a week suffice."

" The expense has not come to a great amount, and the whole arrangement, though still provisional, and though chiefly employed for returning books which have been taken out in the ordinary way, is one that affords facilities for the exchange of books, is advantageous to the readers, and ought in the opinion of the Senatus, to be further continued." A happy outcome of a Council suggestion and a delightful picture of " the cab with its freight of books " jingling its way along the Spital!

Another matter of note of these years is the resignation on 11 April 1877, of the Clerk to the Council, the Rev. John Fyfe, A.M., who had held that office since his appointment at the Council's first meeting on 10 October 1860. Now he had been appointed to the Chair of Moral Philosophy in the University. The cordial thanks of the Council were presented to Mr. Fyfe for the " able, painstaking and impartial manner " in which he had performed his duties. He was succeeded in the office of Clerk by Mr. Robert Walker, Registrar and Librarian of the University, and almost continuously since that date the two offices of Clerk to the General Council and Librarian of the University have been linked.

In the lull which followed the years of activity on matters of constitution and curriculum which led to the setting up of the Royal Commission the question of the University pictures was raised. The Council represented to the University Court in October 1878, that " many of the Pictures belonging to the University are in an unsatisfactory state and that a re-arrangement of the collection is desirable ". Not until March 1880, however, was a Deliverance by the Court sent to the Council. In the interval the Court had referred the matter to the Senatus who now recommended that a catalogue be made, the pictures be cleaned and a " Henderson Bequest " be formed and that the Hall and Public School be repainted to be suitable for the proper exhibition of the pictures belonging to the University. Is this the beginning of the Picture Gallery as we know it?

In 1880, the election of the holder of the single, coveted General Council seat on the University Court again fell due, Dr. Christie, now Professor of Divinity and Church History in the University, not again standing. The election of John F. White, A.M., by a show of hands at the General Council meeting in October was upheld by the postal vote and four years later, in 1884, he was unanimously re-elected. In 1888, however, Mr. White had as opponent the Rev. James Smith of Newhills, who was elected both by a show of hands at the meeting and as a result of the poll that was demanded.

The state of suspended animation in which the General Council seems to have existed while the matters that had previously so exercised them were being considered on Parliamentary level came to an end in 1883 when a Committee was formed which considered the first Universities Bill and later the amended versions of that Bill. It is noteworthy that the Council's representation to the Court on the Bills met with the Court's " cordial approval " and the Court further in 1886 " desired to inform the Council that it is entirely in harmony with them ". The Council's Committee on the Universities' Bills became later a Committee to watch over University legislation and the Report of this Committee on the later amended Bill again called forth the Court's commendation for the Court declared in its Deliverance of April 1885, that it had been " pleased to find that the views of the Council were so largely in harmony with its own ".

There is no doubt that the Council's close interest and watchfulness over these long negotiations and the good sense of their criticisms won the respect of the University Court and had their share in shaping the all-important Universities (Scotland) Act, 1889, which came into force on 1 January 1890.

Two other items of the later eighteen-eighties capture our interest. The first is that Principal Geddes and Dr. Bain presented on behalf of the Council " a loyal and dutiful Address to Her Majesty the Queen on the occasion . . . of the Jubilee of her reign " and that Queen Victoria was graciously pleased to receive the Address at Windsor on the 27 June 1887.

The second is an interesting pointer to the shape of things to come. In 1889 the Council represented to the Court " that it is desirable that the University of Aberdeen, without further delay, confer Degrees in Science ". To this the Court returned " a favourable answer ". And on this happy note, the third decade in the life of the General Council closed. After a precocious infancy, an adolescence alternately turbulent and lethargic, the General Council had grown up.

III. YEARS OF DEVELOPMENT

For the General Council the most important single enactment of the 1889 Universities (Scotland) Act was the granting to it of four Assessors— one more than the Council originally asked—on the University Court. On 27 November 1889, a special meeting of the Council was held " for the purpose of electing three additional Assessors for the Council on the University Court ". Mr. Alexander Edmond, Dr. Angus Fraser and Dr. William Dey, being the only three nominated, were duly elected and along with the Rev. James Smith, in office since the previous year, represented with this much-increased strength, the body of graduates— by this time about 3,000 in number—on the all-important University Court, almost a third of the total composition of that body.

Later, it was fixed by an appropriate Ordinance that of these four Assessors two should retire in 1891, the remaining two continuing in office until 1893. From that time until the present this rota has been maintained. Every two years, two of the Council's Assessors complete a four years' term of office. They are eligible for re-election but, as recent experience has shown, the continuance in office is by no means automatic and graduates at home and away cherish their right to elect their representatives on the University Court.

In those early years of fuller representation, however, the tendency was for the sitting members to be re-elected and from 1889 until 1905 there was no contest. In 1891, the Rev. James Smith and Dr. Angus Fraser were re-elected and Mr. C. B. Davidson was elected to fill the vacancy caused by the death of Mr. Alexander Edmond. Thereafter there was no change in the Assessors until in 1900 Mr. David Littlejohn replaced Mr. C. B. Davidson who had resigned. In 1903 Dr. S. D. F. Salmond replaced the Rev. James Smith, again without contest, but in 1905, when the death of Dr. Salmond created a casual vacancy in addition to the two vacancies occurring in rota, seven nominations were made for the three seats and there would appear to have been considerable interest in the contest which was finally resolved by a postal vote.

The Commission brought into being by the 1889 Act had the task of working out the detail of the new Constitution to be set up for the Scottish Universities and the next few years were filled with great activity and revolutionary change. A new Committee was appointed by the General Council " to investigate and report upon the changes desirable for increasing the efficiency of the University, in as far as the Universities' Commission has the power to carry into effect such changes ". Sub-Committees of this larger Committee considered respectively matters relating to the Faculties of Arts, Medicine and Law and points of interest

in their conclusions, reported to a special meeting of the Council in
June 1890—all transmitted in representations to the University Court
and by this means to the Commission—indicate the academic trend of the
times.   The " new teaching " in Arts, Greek no longer to be compulsory,
required a Chair in English Language and Literature.   (It was 1894
before the Chalmers Chair in English Language and Literature was
inaugurated.)   Next in importance came a Chair in Modern Languages,
Chairs of History and of Education also being considered " likewise
desirable ".   The Chairs of History, French and German were established
respectively in 1903, 1925 and 1951; but the last of these, a Chair in
Education has only now, in 1960, been approved in principle.   The
Bursary Competition provided the passport of able students to the
University but it was considered desirable to institute a preliminary
examination to fix a minimum standard; a Leaving Certificate of the
Scottish Education Department, provided it was of a " proper standard ",
would also be acceptable for University extrance.   " The new conditions
of the University " also made it " expedient while retaining the present
curriculum of four Winter Sessions as the normal curriculum, to institute
a Summer Session in Arts as in Medicine, and so to allow Graduation
after three Winter and three Summer Sessions ".

The Committee's recommendation that " in accordance with the
terms of the Universities' (Scotland) Act of 1889, women be admitted to
Graduation in all Faculties and, that suitable provision be made for
their instruction " was adopted unanimously by the Council, one dis-
sentient voice asking that this clause be " struck out " happily finding no
seconder!   It was 1893 before women were admitted to the Universities
of Scotland.

The Medical Sub-Committee recommended a more exacting preliminary examination, Greek to be no longer compulsory for the M.D.
degree, fewer lectures and more practical work and an extension of the
four years' curriculum to five years.

The Law Sub-Committee asked for enlargement of the Faculty by
Chairs and Lectureships, additional to the two existing Chairs, and so to
" allow of degrees being granted to which every man claiming to belong
to the profession might reasonably aspire ".   The degrees both of LL.B.
and B.L. should be instituted.

The implication of these suggested changes make us realize how very
different the University of even seventy years ago must have been.

This Committee, moving with the times, became later the Committee
on University Changes and Draft Ordinances and continued its work until
its discharge in April 1896, the Business Committee of the Council then
dealing with any further references from the Commissioners, who had by
this time all but discharged their long task, their powers expiring at the
end of the year 1897.

In all 168 Ordinances, some dealing with the Scottish Universities
generally, others dealing particularly with the individual Universities,

came under the scrutiny of this Committee and the consequent consideration of the Council.

At this time of retrenchment it was appropriate that the General Council should seek to set its own internal affairs in order. In 1891 Standing Orders were revised and by these a more efficient method of calling meetings was devised. Apart from the newspaper notices twenty-one days before every statutory meeting, specifying day, hour, place, and requiring notice of intended motions, and a notice seven days before the meeting specifying day, hour, place and stating business to be transacted, notices of the meeting and relevant printed papers were to be despatched to every member of Council resident within the Counties of Aberdeen, Banff and Kincardine and to such other members as asked to be so provided. Nowadays this print is sent to all graduates at home and abroad.

A welcome diversion from the consideration of Ordinances occurs in the Minutes of the special meeting of 5 March 1892, when there was recorded " an expression of the general feeling of pleasure and satisfaction with which the members had heard that Her Majesty the Queen had been pleased to honour the Principal of the University by conferring on him the dignity of Knighthood ". Sir William Geddes was the third Principal of the joint Colleges, having succeeded in 1885 Principal Pirie who in 1876 became successor to the first Principal the Rev. Peter Colin Campbell. Three of the four Principals who have held office since this time—Principals Lang, Sir George Adam Smith, Sir Wm. Hamilton Fyfe, and our present Principal, Sir Thomas Taylor—have been similarly honoured.

In passing it may be noted that, while the University Commissioners recognized the need for " the new teaching " in Arts, they still paid greater due to the older disciplines; for while the salaries attached to the Chairs of Latin, Greek, Mathematics and Natural Philosophy rose to a maximum of £800 per annum, those of the Professors of Logic, Moral Philosophy, English and History were to achieve their maximum at £700 per annum. The Council's Committee, finding nothing in the " comparative laboriousness " of the two sets to justify this distinction, made a protest accordingly and suggested a uniform maximum of £750 per annum and a minimum of £500. The outcome of this suggestion is not recorded in the Council's Minutes. It is a sobering thought that in those days a Professor of Hebrew and Oriental Languages could be paid as little as £350 per annum!

This season of celebration in 1960 gives particular interest to earlier occasions of a similar nature. The year 1894 marked the Quater-Centenary of the Founding of the University in 1494, and a Committee of five of the General Council were appointed at the invitation of the University Court to confer with them regarding arrangements for a " celebration adequate to the occasion ". No further mention is made in the records of the Council's share in these celebrations but it is otherwise with later events.

In 1895, extensions to Marischal College—made necessary by the expansion of these years and largely financed by Dr. C. D. Mitchell of Jesmond Towers, Newcastle-on-Tyne—having been completed, the inauguration of the Mitchell Graduation Hall and the Students' Union called for some ceremonial and again the Council contributed five members to the Joint Committee that made the arrangements.

The planned programme is delightfully Victorian in flavour. On Tuesday, 22 October 1895, the celebrations were to begin with a " Grand Reception . . . and Conversazione ". When the following day the Mitchell Tower was to be inaugurated, the occasion was to be marked by a " Response of bells in the city ". Thursday was to begin by the giving of the Freedom of the City to the benefactor, Dr. Mitchell, and the day was to end with a Torchlight Procession of Students. Friday's Graduation Ceremony was to be preceded by " Presentation of Address and Commemorative Medal " to Dr. C. Mitchell.

The sudden death of Dr. Mitchell on 22 August 1895, meant a curtailment of the elaborate programme and the modified arrangements were confined to two days, Thursday and Friday, 24 and 25 October, but the Conversazione and the Response of bells still had their place in the programme.

In the Marischal College of today the Administrative Block occupies a considerable part of the accommodation and a large staff of officials, working under the Secretary to the University, take care of the ever expanding business affairs of the University. It is difficult to realize that only in August 1893, did the University Court—as part of the setting of their house in order—consider placing the whole business of the University " under the direction of one competent official ". The Court suggested further that in existing circumstances such " an official should be appointed temporarily to act as Secretary of the University Court, Secretary and Treasurer of the General Council, with the concurrence of the General Council, and Registrar of the General Council, the salary of the official to be £200 yearly including the Statutory Fees for preparing the Register of the General Council ". The Council, however, strongly objected " to any appointment of a Clerk to the General Council being made by the Court " and so retained the right to appoint its own Clerk to " receive for his services in that capacity a salary of £50 a year ". When Mr. Walker, Clerk to the Council since 1877 became the first Secretary of the University Court and Registrar of the University, he retained his office as Clerk to the General Council, but as a separate appointment as it has been ever since. The University Court fixed the salary for the three combined offices at £250 with an additional sum of £10 towards the cost of clerical assistance.

Even today the University Bursary Competition is an event of some importance in the academic life of the north-east of Scotland. Although the social revolution of the twentieth century has made the needy student's subsistence allowance now a national responsibility and no Shon Campbell need try to exist on " a mean and scanty fare ", a good place in the Bursary Competition still carries with it considerable kudos. But success was a matter of real urgency in the old days. The humble lad o' pairts, coached by his scholarly country dominie, needed that bursary which made his University education possible. Matters touching on the Bursary Competition figure over and over again in the Minutes of the General Council and when in 1894 the " Draft Ordinance Dealing with Bursaries in Arts ", in order to create more valuable scholarships, made proposals which would mean the loss of thirty-three Bursaries and the alienation of £585 in all from the Bursary funds, the Council's Committee was roused to a fine frenzy and in their strongly expressed disapproval declared such Scholarships would be bought at " too dear a price if they cannot be obtained except by sacrificing these Bursaries, which have done so much good in the past, and, as part of a system, have given an immense impetus to the Secondary—as well as to the best Elementary Schools in the N.E. of Scotland ". This heated protest went on: " It is no exaggeration to say that the Bursary Competition has for more than a hundred years been the chief educational event in this district and the interest in it is not waning but is still on the increase." As a result of the Council's representation to the Commissioners, the Ordinance was considerably altered and it was with satisfaction that the Committee reported in 1895 that " the threatened sacrifice of so many valuable and useful bursaries has not been carried out but the number of small and practically inoperative bursaries has been reduced ".

Another matter of finance features in the deliberations of the General Council towards the end of the century. In January 1896, at the adjournment of the Statutory meeting of the previous October, Mr. Patrick Cooper's motion that the Business Committee consider " what steps should be taken to associate the Alumni and other friends of this University in a scheme for its further Extension and better Endowment " was carried. The Business Committee enlarged by the additions of the Deans of the five Faculties and seven others, reported in April of that year: " If the University of Aberdeen is to hold its proper place among the Universities of this country, and fitly to discharge its duty to the community of the North and North-east of Scotland, extensive additions must be made to its equipment ". Enumerated among the " more pressing wants " were Additional Library, Laboratory and Museum accommodation, a Botanic Garden, Residential Halls for male and female students, seven new Professorships (of those considered desirable by the Arts Sub-Committee of 1889 only the Chair of English Literature had been founded), fifteen new Lectureships, new Bursaries in Science, Law and Medicine and Scholarships in all Faculties. The need for a " vigorous movement " pressed by the Committee led to the appointment of the University Extension and Endowment Committee who proceeded to create the Aberdeen University Endowment Association, the inaugural meeting being held on 14 April 1897. Membership of this Association could be secured on the annual payment of half a guinea or by the donation of five guineas or for an Executor or Nominee in respect of a bequest of £50. The application of the funds of this Association was to be subject to the consent of the University Court after consultation with the Senatus Academicus. When in 1903, the Burnett-Fletcher Chair of History and Archaeology came to be founded, the Association formed by the General Council was able to contribute the sum of £1000 to the endowment.

Two other matters not unconnected with each other engage the attention of the General Council in these closing years of the nineteenth century. Both are related to the spread of popular education, so important a feature of the social legislation of the late Victorian era. By the 1895 Code of the Scottish Education Department, changes in the training of teachers had been introduced. On the motion of Dr. James Moir a Committee was appointed to consider the whole question of the University training of teachers. The University Court had appointed a similar Committee which had conferred with representatives of the Senatus, the local School Board and the Committee of the two Training Colleges in Aberdeen, these being under the control of the Church. This joint body proposed in 1896 that a local committee of all interested bodies be constituted and the General Council was invited to appoint two representatives. The Council's Committee on this matter now discharged, Dr. Moir and Mr. P. J. Anderson were appointed to represent the General Council on this local committee. Two years later these two were re-elected to this Committee to hold office as from 1 May 1898, and again in 1902, their appointment was renewed.

Associated with the rising standard of general education is the matter of qualification for university entrance. One provision of the 1889 Universities (Scotland) Act was that the Secretary for Scotland should lay before the General Councils Annual Reports of their respective Universities with regard to statistics and finance. The Preliminary Examinations under the new Ordinances began in the academic year 1892-93 and the consequent drop in the number of students is significant in the statistics for all four Universities. In 1896 the General Council of the University of Glasgow asked the co-operation of the other General Councils in obtaining from the various University Courts the numbers in the 1895-96 classes of Latin, Greek and Mathematics—staple subjects for the Arts Course—of those who had passed the Preliminary Examination and those who had not. The object in view, apart from assessing the suitability of the standard of the new Preliminary Examination, was to see how far the recent Act had " tended to raise the standard of University education and how far the University is still competing with secondary schools ". The hope was that with " a well-organised system of secondary education " the non-qualifying—that is, not qualifying for graduation—classes in the University would disappear.

When the General Council of Aberdeen approached the University Court on the matter, the Court was entirely in agreement with the Council in regard to the value of obtaining these figures. By the end of 1897 a Joint Memorial by the University Court and the General Council had been prepared and presented to the Scottish Universities Commissioners, asking that included in the Annual Report of Statistics laid before the Secretary for Scotland should be a statement of the number of students attending the classes of Latin, Greek and Mathematics, with distinction between those qualifying for a degree and non-qualifying students and the relation of these numbers to passes in the Preliminary Examination. The figures thus obtained, supplied by the Senatus for the Sessions between 1895 and 1898, reveal the fluctuations of this transition period.

In Aberdeen, after the introduction of the Preliminary Examination, the total number of students dropped by one hundred to 812 in the Session 1893-94. This downward trend continued, as it did in the other Universities, for the new few years—even though from 1894, when twenty-one women attended, the number of women students steadily increased. It was not until the academic year, 1898-99, that the total number of students reached the 800 mark again and by then the figures included ninety-three women who were attending the University.

Nowadays with our well-established senior secondary schools in Scotland and the very well-defined regulations for University Entrance either by the Preliminary Examination of the Scottish Universities Entrance Board or by the Leaving Certificate of the Scottish Education Department, it is difficult to get into focus this picture of the educational set-up in the late nineteenth century. Ill-equipped as we may consider some University entrants today, how much greater must have been the range of attainment of the students seventy years ago and how difficult it must have been for Professors and Lecturers to cater for both " qualifying " and " non-qualifying " students!

The variations in the numbers of degrees granted each year over this transition period would seem to indicate either that there was a tightening up of graduation standards corresponding to more difficult entry, or that previously many non-qualifying students qualified during their course and so became eligible for degrees. By the beginning of the new century numbers both of the student population and of graduates had steadied and a consistent upward trend was established.

The year 1897 marks the publication of the first volume of the printed Minutes of the General Council. As far back as October 1868, it had been agreed that the Minutes from the date of the Council's first meeting in October 1860, should be printed and circulated among members. (It was the expense so incurred that led to a brush with the Senatus). A motion of the following year added the recommendation that subsequent prints as well as the Collected Minutes should also be transmitted to the other official bodies of the University of Aberdeen and to the Library as well as to the official bodies and the libraries of the other three Scottish Universities. In October 1892, a suggestion, that, as the volume containing the Council's Minutes in manuscript was nearly filled, the written

Minute-book might be dispensed with, was not accepted because of difficulties in the way of " due authentication " of the Minutes. Consequently, as well as the issue of twice-yearly prints, the Minutes in manuscript were continued until a second volume in handwriting, begun in 1893, was completed by the Minute for October 1906. The same Minute was the last to be included in the second volume of printed Minutes and thereafter the " authenticated printed Minutes " began with " a new pagination ".

Of the first volume of printed Minutes, made up to include the October Meeting of 1897 and duly bound with an index prepared by the Clerk, Mr. Robert Walker, only about 170 copies were available. After the presentation of one copy to each of the General Councils of the other Scottish Universities, 100 copies were given to the Librarian " to be by him exchanged for the printed papers issued by other Universities " and the remainder were to be disposed of at the price of 2s. per copy, to any interested members of the General Council!

Besides the first volume of the Minutes, another publication, prepared by a member of the General Council and of great interest to the Council, appeared in the closing years of the century. Lieutenant-Colonel William Johnston, M.A., M.D., compiled and had printed at the University Press at his own expense *A Calendar of the University of Aberdeen for the Sessions 1860-61 to 1863-64.* As the first Aberdeen University Calendar did not appear until 1864, Colonel Johnston's Calendar filled the gap between the Records of King's and Marischal College and the first issue by the joint University. The General Council was especially indebted to Colonel Johnston as he had included in his work " a carefully annotated list of the Council as originally constituted in 1860 with identification of all the non-graduate members who subsequently joined ".

The General Council's appreciation of Colonel Johnston's valuable work led them to suggest " as a fitting task for the end of this century the publication of an annotated Roll of the Graduates of Aberdeen University" 1860-1900, and to express the hope that Colonel Johnston " might see his way to edit such a Roll ". Colonel Johnston on duty at the War Office—the country was at war in South Africa at this time—could not then immediately consider the work but, when leisure came, he did so and the first Roll of Graduates (1860-1900) was published by subscription as part of the Quatercentenary Celebrations of 1906.

Queen Victoria was still on the throne at the close of the nineteenth century. The Diamond Jubilee of her reign had been fittingly celebrated in 1897 and at the time the General Council had again as in 1887, presented a " loyal and dutiful Address ". The Queen's death in the first month of the twentieth century marked the end of an era. A corresponding chapter in the life of the University of Aberdeen had ended in the last year of the century with the death of Sir William Geddes, Principal since 1885 and before that Professor of Greek from the year 1855 (at King's College). His is a name that even now, two generations later, still commands veneration.

The momentum with which the last decade of the old century had begun had now eased. With the new legislation arising from the 1889 Act now mainly established, the General Council had had leisure enough to consider its own affairs; so the publication of the first volume of the Minutes and the proposed Roll of Graduates would suggest. If the list of names—a list comprising places from Chile to Japan—of " Academic Institutions " to which sixty-two of the hundred copies of the Minutes left in the hands of the Librarian were sent is any pointer, one would like to think that the end of the century marked a decline in the less admirable aspects of parochialism both in the University and in the General Council and the dawn of an era of widened horizons.

IV. THE NEW CENTURY

The Rev. John Marshall Lang succeeded the late Sir William Geddes as Principal and Vice-Chancellor of the University and he was in the Chair at the first meeting of the General Council in the new century. The first business of the meeting was the decision to send a " humble address " to the new King, Edward VII, offering deepest sympathy on the death of the Queen and " respectful congratulation " on his accession to the throne. The era we now call Edwardian seems in retrospect a halcyon period and there is nothing in the records of the General Council to disturb this view.

The statistics reveal a steady growth in numbers largely due to the increasing proportion of women undergraduates. Of the thousand students in attendance at University classes by 1910 more than a quarter were women. No doubt this factor in university life made even more urgent the need for better provision in Modern Languages, somehow considered a more proper medium of feminine education than the ancient disciplines. As early as 1889 the General Council's Arts Sub-Committee had indicated the desirability of endowing a Chair in Modern Languages and this need was again urged as one of the more " pressing wants " by their Committee on University Extension and Endowment in 1896. The University Commissioners, however, unwilling to break too abruptly with tradition, had in the Ordinance dealing with the Bursary Competition allowed, for bursaries endowed before August 1864, for a paper in Modern Languages only half the marks allotted to papers in English, Latin, Greek and Mathematics so that the classical scholar had an initial advantage over the Modern Languages student.

Communications to the General Council from various interested bodies among school and university teachers led to a special remit on the subject of Modern Languages in the Bursary Competition being given to the Business Committee. In April 1902, this Committee adopted a resolution that the total number of marks attainable in the Bursary Competition should be the same for all candidates. In 1904 a Joint Committee of the

Councils of the four Universities—four members from each Council—was formed to confer on the whole matter of the Bursary Competition. Further, the Students' Representative Council adopted in May 1905 a motion which expressed the hope that the Council's Committee on the reform of the Bursary Competition would recommend the removal of " certain anomalies in the marking of papers " whereby " inequitable results " were obtained.

Finally in 1906 this Committee considering the position of Modern Languages in the Bursary Competition produced a seven-points report which was submitted to the University Court as a representation from the General Council. It was not until 1908, however, that a special Ordinance anent Bursaries made by the University Court of Aberdeen— each University Court having been so empowered after the dissolution at the end of the year 1897 of the 1889 Commission—received the Royal Assent. Under this provision the Senatus Academicus of the University of Aberdeen could frame its own regulations subject to the approval of the University Court who would take into account any representation made by the General Council. Regulations so framed in 1909 proposed eight subjects of examination from which the candidate chose four, the maximum number of marks assigned to each subject to be the same; the possible combinations of subjects open to the candidate were sixty-five of which twelve were wholly linguistic. The Council's Committee on Bursary Regulations, while approving generally of the scheme, suggested some further adjustments, many of which were later incorporated. As Appendix to their Report they added a most interesting short history of the Bursary Competition, tracing up to 1909 its evolution from 1549, when and for 300 years thereafter the test applied was the ability " to make a congruous theame in Latine ", through the changes of 1861, 1871 and 1895. In the last half-century there have been further alterations in Bursary Regulations to meet the changing pattern of our national and academic life but none so revolutionary as those of 1909 which after years of controversy at last gave recognition to the twentieth-century growth of modern studies, both linguistic and scientific.

During the years of these protracted negotiations events of considerable moment in the life of the General Council had been taking place. In September 1903, occurred the deaths of two men each of whom had long served the University and the General Council. On the 18th of that month Dr. Alexander Bain, Professor of Logic and English in the University since 1860, died. Almost from the creation in 1860 of the General Council he had been a member of its Business Committee and had acted on almost every other committee of note. On behalf of the General Council he gave evidence before the Commission in 1876 and in 1887 he was one of the deputation of three who presented the Council's loyal address to the Queen on the occasion of her Diamond Jubilee. The Minute of October 1903, puts on record " the loss which has been sustained by the University and the cause of Education " by the death of one

" whose labours during more than sixty years as a teacher, as a thinker and as a man of letters, have shed lustre on this University ".

On 27 September 1903, the Chancellor of the University, the Duke of Richmond and Gordon, K.G., full of years and honour, died at the age of eighty-five. For more than forty-two years he had held the highest office in the University.

The Chancellor's death having occurred less than twenty-one days before the date of the October statutory half-yearly meeting of the Council, it was necessary, according to the 1889 Act, to call an adjourned meeting within twenty-one days thereafter to consider the election of a successor. The date chosen was 3 November 1903, and in the interval of time before that adjourned meeting a representative Committee was formed to arrange for the nomination of " a suitable person or persons ". For this purpose the Business Committee of the General Council was augmented by Council members in the University Court and the Deans of the Faculties of Arts, Science, Divinity, Law and Medicine, with the Principal as Convener. The unanimous recommendation of this Committee was the nomination to the office of Chancellor of the Rt. Hon. Lord Strathcona and Mount Royal, G.C.M.G. who had been Rector of the University since 1899. A special meeting of the General Council was held on 20 July 1904, for the Installation of the Chancellor with the Principal in the Chair and members of the University Court, the Senatus Academicus, the Students' Representative Council and others present. The Rector introduced the Chancellor-elect to whom the Principal administered the impressive oath:

" Ego, tactis sacris Dei Evangeliis, juramentum praesto corporale, me officio Cancellarii hujus Universitatis fideliter functurum, omnia statuta et constitutiones inviolabiliter observaturum, singula dictae Universitatis jura ac privilegia defensurum, ejusque commodum et utilitatem in omnibus juxta posse meum procuraturum. Ita me Deus adjuvet."

The Principal then having vacated the Chair, the Chancellor took his place and returned thanks for his appointment.

This ceremonial, the first recorded in the annals of the General Council, was followed by the Summer Graduation, the Chancellor conferring the degrees on the Graduands presented to him. Thereafter the Chancellor delivered an address.

In the evening of that day a dinner was given in honour of the Chancellor in the Town and County Hall " and there were in all 110 gentlemen present including fifteen guests ".

By this time plans for another University celebration had been mooted. The year 1905 would mark the 400th anniversary of the foundation of the College of St. Mary (later King's College) under the University Constitution sanctioned by the Papal Bull of 1494-95. In the spring of 1904, a large Committee consisting of representatives of the

University Court, the Senatus Academicus, the General Council and the Town Council was formed to make arrangements " to celebrate the 400th year of the University as a Teaching Institution sometime in the year 1905 ". Six months later it was decided, however, that because of " the state of the work on the new buildings ", the celebrations should be deferred until 1906 by which time the extensions at Marischal College might be completed. In September 1906, H.M. King Edward VII and Queen Alexandra came to Aberdeen to open the new buildings and from the 26th to the 28th of that month—" eventful days "—celebrations were held, tales of the magnitude and magnificence of which have now passed into legend!

An official Quatercentenary Memorial Record of the occasion was prepared, but, in addition, the Business Committee on the instruction of the General Council made a record of the Quatercentenary celebrations of the University and of the opening of the new buildings of Marischal College. This account " brief " because of the official Memorial Record, makes a lively contribution to the Minutes of April 1907, which opened the third printed volume, and which also record the first meeting of the General Council in the Mitchell Hall.

A General Committee of forty-five members, under the Convenership of the Principal and consisting of representatives of University Court, Senatus Academicus, General Council and of the Town Council of Aberdeen, was divided into sub-committees on academic invitations, on hospitality and on publications and it is recorded that the General Council through its Business Committee had a " direct voice in all the arrangements ". Responses to invitations were received from about " 200 learned bodies who either sent delegates or forwarded addresses or both and from about 150 invited guests ". In addition to the " very generous hospitality shown by the City, the Chairman of the Art Gallery Committee and by others, 230 private citizens received and entertained University guests to the number of about 320 ". The publication of no fewer than six Quatercentenary volumes also marked the occasion.

It was not until August 1906, that it was finally known that H.M. King Edward VII accompanied by H.M. Queen Alexandra would " grace the occasion " and that the actual date was fixed. The invitations which had gone out in the beginning of the year had contained only an approximate date—" medio mense Septembri "—and now all who had accepted had to be further communicated with. The record stresses the " incessant " labours of those involved in " so many months of preparation ".

Lord Strathcona, the Chancellor of the University, announced in the month of June that not only did he intend himself to be present at and share in the celebrations, but he wished to give a Dinner for all the invited guests of the University and for all graduates and other members of the University taking part in the celebrations. This proposal, " gigantic as it was generous ", implied a banquet to upwards of 2,400 guests. To make this possible a special building was erected for the occasion in an empty space in the Gallowgate north of Marischal College. " This huge temporary structure with a floor space of upwards of 3/5ths of an acre, being more than quadruple that of any hall in the City " was also used for the reception of delegates. The Strathcona Banquet, unparalleled in its lavishness of scale in the annals of either City or University, was held on the evening of the day of the royal inauguration of the New Buildings, Thursday, 27 September 1906, and provided, along with, for the populace, a display of fireworks on the Broad Hill, the culmination of an unforgettable day of rejoicing for both Town and Gown.

The Council's lively record of this great three-day celebration and the impressive programme of procession, receptions, banquet, torchlight procession, graduation, sports, inauguration ceremony, fireworks display, University At Home and Students' Symposium involving in all " about 4,000 persons " and suggesting the spaciousness of Edwardian days, comes to a fine peroration:

It might perhaps be deemed out of place for the Business Committee, of whose members so many were intimately associated with all the arrangements, to add an expression of its opinion regarding the result of the arduous labours of so many months of preparation. Undoubtedly, however, the general estimate was favourable in the highest degree. The opening religious service in the University Chapel, crowded in every part, was most solemn and impressive; the Procession through the gaily-decorated streets from Marischal College Buildings to the Strathcona Hall, and the Reception there (it occupied nearly three hours) of such a galaxy of distinguished men from all parts of the world were singularly imposing; the conferring of Honorary Degrees in the Mitchell Hall was academic and dignified; and the scene in the densely-crowded quadrangle of Marischal College, with the thousands assembled in well-ordered ranks before their Majesties, our gracious King and Queen, was one never to be forgotten. The hospitality shown publicly by the City and by the citizens privately in their houses was unbounded; and the weather, had the season been the height of summer instead of late in September, could not have been more propitious throughout. The University, the Committee thinks, may be congratulated that on every hand one was met by the assurance that our distinguished visitors must have carried away the most pleasant impressions of all their experiences.

A film made on the occasion was some years ago found and refurbished for the archives of the Town Council of Aberdeen, and it too serves to keep alive the memory of a most notable occasion in the history of the University.

Between these two periods of celebration, two elections of interest had taken place. In April 1905, the Rev. Stewart D. F. Salmond, D.D., Principal of the U.F. Church College, Aberdeen, and one of the General Council's Assessors on the University Court, died. The occurrence of this casual vacancy along with the fact that two of the Assessors were due to retire in October 1905, meant that three places had to be filled at the statutory half-yearly meeting of the Council. Seven nominations— one of these was withdrawn at a later stage—were made for the three vacancies. The result of the vote by a show of hands at the meeting was upheld by the postal vote that followed the demand for a poll and Dr. Dey and Dr. Littlejohn, the two sitting members, were returned

6*

along with Dr. Westland to fill the place of the late Dr. Salmond.   The
generous number of nominations and the evidently largely-attended
meeting, as revealed by the show of hands, and the ample return to the
postal vote suggest lively interest in the election.   A letter written by
Dr. Bain at the time of the first election of Assessors under the Statute of
1889 was quoted in the Business Committee's report which preceded the
election.   In this letter Dr. Bain had expressed the view that the General
Council's four Assessors on the University Court should represent the
four " sections or interests " that compose the Council—the clergy, the
doctors, the legal and business men and the teachers.   This principle,
generally accepted by the Council in 1889, would appear to have been
followed until this 1905 election when a medical man was voted to the
vacancy caused by the death of Dr. Salmond.

Early in the year 1906, the Rt. Hon. James Alexander Campbell, LL.D.,
Parliamentary Representative of the Universities of Glasgow and Aberdeen
since 1868-69 retired from office, and at the subsequent Parliamentary
Election, Sir Henry Craik, late Secretary of the Scotch Education
Department, was returned by a large majority.   Until his death in
March 1927, he represented Scottish Universities' interests at West-
minster, first as member for the Universities of Aberdeen and Glasgow
and then, after the Representation of the People Act of 1918 gave three
Parliamentary seats to the Scottish Universities, as a member of the
combined constituency.

These more spectacular events of the early years of the new century
tend to throw into shadow matters more limited in compass.   It is
interesting to note that the General Council in spite of its more assured
position in the life of the University—or perhaps because of it—still cast
a supervisory eye on the affairs of the Library.   In October 1901, the
General Council formed a Committee " to consider how the supply of
new books to the University Library may be increased ".   This Committee, among other comments on the Library's spending, reported that
they were of opinion that " the Expenditure on Periodicals should be
reduced ".   This Report, submitted to the University Court, was sent
by them to the Library Committee and to the Senatus.   The Library
Committee justified its position at some length but, in spite of the fact
that both Court and Senatus approved of the Library's Report, the Council
would not be silenced, and, asking the Library Committee directly for a
further report, " accompanied by the printed list of current serials
purchased by the Library with the prices of each annexed ", urged on
them " the necessity of thoroughly overhauling their expenditure ".
The Library Committee, roused to anger, forwarded a copy of the Council's
resolution to the University Court and pointed out that, " while such a
list of serials as is requested can easily be supplied, as it happens to be in
type, the Committee is not prepared to take instructions as to reporting
from the General Council ".   Acting as mediator, the Court reminded
the Library Committee that the General Council at its inception had been

empowered " to take into their consideration all questions affecting the well-being and prosperity of the University " and asked them to consider the Council's request. Still protesting angrily that the General Council had " assumed powers not belonging to it " and " was in error " in sending a resolution directly instead of making a representation to the University Court and that they adhered to the views expressed in their earlier report, the Library Committee supplied the requested list, stating amidst other dignified comment that anxiety over the " miserably inadequate provision for the purchase of new books " had been " greatly relieved " through the action of the Carnegie Trustees. This is only one of the ways by which the Carnegie Trust, founded in 1901 as a result of the munificence and foresight of Mr. Andrew Carnegie, has greatly enriched the life of the Scottish Universities in the present century. This wrangle evidently ended peaceably by the Council's conveying through the Principal to the Court and through the Court to the Library Committee " the cordial thanks of the Council for the great amount of trouble taken in the compilation of the statement ".

Further evidence of the sturdy independence of the General Council and its determination to preserve its identity and to fulfil its function was provided in the matter of the Administration of the University which came up again for consideration when in 1905 Mr. Robert Walker, Secretary to the University Court, intimated to the Court that he could no longer satisfactorily perform the duties of his various offices " under existing arrangements ". Mr. Walker also held as a separate office—in accordance with the finding of 1893-94—the Clerkship of the General Council.

The whole matter of the Official Administration of the University was considered at a Joint Conference of representatives of Court, Senatus and Council. In the discussion on the principle of unification of the Administration of the University, the Council's representatives put forward the view that, while the Clerk of the Council should be appointed by the Council and should also be its Registrar, he should not hold office as Secretary of the Court or of the Senatus. This decision was accepted by the University Court who, with the Senatus, agreed that a Secretary might jointly serve these two bodies, while the General Council appointed its own official, the Court reserving the right of appointment of the Registrar. Mr. Robert Walker, who had been appointed Clerk to the General Council in April 1877, continued in this office until on the completion of thirty years of service, he resigned in April 1907. He retained, however, the office of Registrar. As his successor to the Clerkship of the Council, Mr. P. J. Anderson, University Librarian, was appointed and the association between Clerk of Council and Librarian, temporarily in abeyance during part of Mr. Walker's tenure of office, was restored. The salary attached to this office was fixed at £25 per annum, " this sum to include outlays for clerical assistance ".

The general feeling emanating from the records of these first seven

years of the century is one of vigour and growth.   There would appear to
have been a great upsurge of life in the University, a vitality that both
generated the lively celebrations of September 1906, and was in turn
regenerated by them.   As the jubilee of the fused University approached,
the growth of years having obliterated the memory of old inter-collegiate
feuds, and the spread of popular education and the consequent development of secondary education having more clearly defined the place of the
University, there was proof of the success of the union.   The rapid
increase in the number of women students gave too a new flavour and
direction to University life.   Along with the impetus towards change
and adaptation to meet new needs, always in Universities, however,
because of their deep rooting in the past, is the tendency to cling to tradition; and it is this pull which made an arduous battle of a matter to be
considered in the next section.

V.   EDWARDIAN TO GEORGIAN

Accustomed as we are to a University Session extending over nine months
of the year and comprising three terms each of ten weeks, it is difficult
to realize that not much more than half a century ago many students—
like the boatmen and his father in Barrie's " Mary Rose "—attended
classes during the winter only and that the University academic year was
contained in five months.   Summer classes in some departments of
study, instituted by the Ordinances of 1889, had been intended not as
supplementary classes but as substituting for one half of the Winter
Session.

It is in the Minute of April 1907, that the question of " an Extended
Session of Three Terms " first appears in the business of the General
Council.   A committee of twelve, including five professors in the Faculty
of Arts, was formed to consider the proposal.   Later Professor J. Arthur
Thomson as representing the biological sciences was associated with this
Committee.   In 1905, representatives of the four University Courts,
met in conference " to consider the advisability of instituting a three-
term session and the further question of the reconstruction of the Curriculum in Arts ", had declared for the Extended Session.   Indeed,
since 1901, when the Arts Faculty in Glasgow first raised the matter, it
had been carefully considered " by Conferences, Committees, Faculties of
Arts, Senates and Courts " of the four Scottish Universities.   By 1905,
Aberdeen alone through its Arts Faculty persisted in an " attitude of
antagonism ".   A Committee of the University Court deplored this and
declared itself " in thorough sympathy " with the Report of the Conference of the four Scottish Universities.   But the Chairman of the
Committee, Professor Harrower of the Chair of Greek, dissented from
this finding and his Dissent is recorded in six " closely-printed " pages of
strongly-worded protest.   He argued that " the proposal to make the
Summer Term an extension of the Ordinary Graduation Class Teaching

of the Winter " would mean " the deterioration of the Honours degree without securing any certain improvement in the attainments of the Passman, would prevent the attendance of Arts students at Summer Classes and of Medical Students at Arts Classes ". Professor Harrower extended in ringing words his arguments in a memorandum of equal length laid before the General Council Committee and his opposition to the proposed change in the academic year was supported in a joint memorandum by Professor Davidson of the Chair of Logic and Professor Macdonald of the Chair of Mathematics and in a further joint memorandum by Professor Thomson of the Chair of Zoology and Professor Macdonald; while Professor Terry of the Chair of History and Professor Baillie of the Chair of Moral Philosophy favoured the Extended Session. War indeed among the dons! And both sides turned to the General Council for a sympathetic hearing.

It is not surprising, considering the length and complexity of the documents submitted on 9 October 1907, by the Business Committee to the General Council and embodying all these controversial memoranda, that consideration of their Report was postponed till an adjourned meeting of the Council held on Saturday, 23 November 1907. Then the Council " in view of the keen conflict of expert evidence and the need for moving cautiously in such an important matter " deferred making a decision and appointed a Committee " to make exhaustive inquiry into the whole subject of the Arts Curriculum, in all its bearings ".

But before the General Council's next Statutory meeting, a special meeting was convened on 14 March 1908, to which was submitted a Draft Ordinance by the University Court fixing the " Academic year " as being divided into three periods and comprising at least twenty-five teaching weeks. Concession to die-hard opinion was made, however, in that it was to be in the power of the Senatus with the approval of the University Court " to accept attendance on at least one course of study in each of two of the periods aforesaid, as completing an Academical year ".

This establishment of the Extended Session was only one feature of this lengthy Ordinance which made important changes in the requirements of the Preliminary Examination, now divorced from the Bursary Competition, and a thorough revision of the Arts curriculum for both Ordinary and Honours degrees. An accompanying Ordinance dealing with the Bursary Competition has already been referred to.

Commenting on the various provisions of the new Ordinances, the Committee of the General Council remarked that it " views with satisfaction the renewed recognition of the right of the General Council to be consulted in all important University changes and the extension to two months of the period during which its opinion may be expressed ". It was by the 1889 Act that the period of one month had been allowed for the General Council to express any opinion of proposed alterations of an old Ordinance or of the suggested enactments of a new one. This extension of time was welcomed not only for its practical convenience but as an indication of the growth in status of the General Council.

In the course of its investigations on the related subjects of Preliminary Examination, Bursary Competition and Arts curriculum—the " exhaustive inquiry " that was its remit—the Council's Committee had gone into the matter with great thoroughness and the documents prepared for the Report included accounts of the Arts curricula of such different Universities as those of Manchester, Birmingham and New York. Perhaps the most interesting of all, prepared by the Clerk of the Committee was the outline of the evolution of the Arts curriculum in Aberdeen from Pope Alexander VI's Bull of 1494-95 and Bishop Elphinstone's Foundation in 1505 of the College of St. Mary through Reformation changes, eighteenth-century stagnation, nineteenth-century reform and eventually to the Ordinance of 1892 which " swept away " the old Arts curriculum and introduced new regulations of great length and complexity; they in their turn were now to be altered and adapted and extended to suit the needs of the rapidly-expanding University and the changing world of the twentieth century. The Ordinance approved by Parliament in July 1908, outlined the general shape of the new Arts curriculum and empowered the Senatus of each Scottish university with the approval of its University Court to make its regulations for the grouping of the subjects. The proposals of the Aberdeen Senatus in this respect were put before a Special Meeting of the General Council on 6 February 1909, and carefully considered and commented upon. By the time later in the year that these regulations came into force the Edwardian era was all but over. The University with a student population of over 1,000 and a General Council of over 4,000 members, had nearly doubled its size in less than half a century of vigorous growth.

A further matter of investigation and controversy among all the General Councils of Scotland at this time was the question of University autonomy. The method of University legislation by Ordinances which required Parliamentary sanction was proving " cumbrous and tedious ". This process had been established by the 1858 Act which made provision for the " better government and discipline of the Scottish Universities " and which with this end in view had established in each University, a Court, a Senatus Academicus and a General Council. Again Aberdeen through its representatives at the Conference of General Councils attacked the matter with assiduity but, none of the suggested alternative methods of legislation meeting with acceptance, the conclusion was reached that the subject was not " ripe for decision ". The Autonomy Committee continued in being, however, and their watchfulness was in line with the alert spirit of the times. The Minutes of the General Council over these years are very full and the work of the Business Committee shows a steady increase in volume. Amidst such long-term considerations as the major reconstruction of the Arts curriculum and of the Bursary Competition, appear for the first time in 1908 an Obituary of the General Council, a record of University Staff changes, a reference to measures taken to bring up to date with regard to addresses the Register of the General Council, in May 1909, a plea to the University, repeated in October 1914, to establish a Lectureship in Celtic, and in April 1910, the Report by the Carnegie Trust with the list of Research grants to Members of the Council. Apart from war years, the Obituary, the record of Staff changes, the Carnegie Trust Report were to reappear along with the Reports as to Statistics and Finances of the University as annual features of the Business Committee's Report.

In 1907, the two retiring Assessors in the University Court, Dr. Angus Fraser and Dr. Albert Westland, renominated without opposition, had been re-elected, but in 1909, when Dr. David Littlejohn did not seek re-election, three candidates were nominated for two vacancies. Of these the retiring member, Dr. Dey, was along with Mr. Patrick Cooper, elected by a show of hands at the statutory meeting, which decision was upheld by the demanded poll. Again in 1911 there were three nominations for the two seats, this time Dr. Angus Fraser not seeking re-election. In this case the decision of the meeting was partly overturned by the postal vote, the successful candidates being Colonel Wm. Johnston and Dr. Westland. In 1913 the election was uneventful, Mr. Cooper and Dr. Dey being re-elected unopposed; but it is noteworthy as the last normal election of Assessors until after the 1914-18 war.

On 2 May 1909, the Principal, the Very Rev. John Marshall Lang, c.v.o., d.d., ll.d. died. At an adjourned meeting of the General Council on 29 May, it was " resolved to place on record an expression of the Council's appreciation of the signal services which the late Principal rendered to the University, of the dignity and eloquence with which he presided over its assemblies, and the ability and wisdom with which he guided its affairs ".

The new Principal, the Very Rev. Dr. George Adam Smith, presided over the General Council for the first time at its meeting on 16 April 1910—the Principal who was to lead the University through the poignant and distressful years of the First World War. His period in office was largely to coincide with the reign of George V, who succeeded to the throne on the death of his father, Edward VII, in May 1910.

It is interesting to note that the Business Committee elected at the October 1910, meeting included for the first time a woman, Miss Jessie Elliot Murdoch.

Earlier in 1910, in the Parliamentary Election, the joint University seat of Aberdeen and Glasgow had been contested for, the sitting member, Sir Henry Craik, having been challenged by Sir Frederick Pollock. The poll resulted in the return of Sir Henry Craik by a majority in each of the two Universities.

One direct result of the 1909 Election of Assessors and the 1910 Parliamentary Election was a change in the Standing Orders of the General Council. Notices of meetings had been sent regularly only to members in the three North-Eastern Counties of Aberdeen, Banff and Kincardine, these representing but one-third of the members resident in the United Kingdom and the Channel Islands. Graduates at a distance complained that, not having been kept in touch with University politics, they were " unable to form satisfactory judgments when called on to vote in contested elections ". The Business Committee recommended that prints should be sent to every member of the Council having a known address and accordingly an appropriate alteration was made in the Standing Orders. This alteration was further amended after the adjourned meeting of 8 July 1914, held for the sole purpose of installing the new Chancellor. Many graduates abroad could not have received the notice until after the event. To avoid such waste of labour and expense, the Standing Order, after six months' notice of motion given by the Convener of the Business Committee, was altered in April 1915, so as to read: " Before every adjourned or Special Meeting of Council, such intimation shall be given as the Business Committee may deem expedient ". This greatly increased distribution of General Council notices involving extra outlay for clerical assistance, the expense of which would fall on the Clerk of the Council, led to a reconsideration of his remuneration. In the light of his much increased work—the Minute of a single meeting of the Council now running to an average of sixty printed pages and the prints now having to be sent to 4,300 members of the Council—the Business Committee recommended that the General Council should represent to the University Court that the Clerk's remuneration (still to include the cost of clerical assistance) should be raised to £50. The change met with the approval of the University Court. And in 1960—fifty years, two world wars and a social revolution later—the remuneration of the Clerk to the General Council remains at the same figure!

A further re-wording of the Standing Orders arose out of the fact that the second volume of the Minutes of the General Council, 13 October 1897 to 10 October 1906, had been printed off. Volumes I and II, bound together in cloth, would now be forwarded to any member " paying the sum of two shillings and sixpence to the Clerk ".

The first years of the new reign, both royal and academical, comprise a period of continued revision in the teaching within the University. The Arts degree and the Bursary Competition having been overhauled, the University Court had turned its attention next to the Medical course and now issued a Draft Ordinance regulating degrees in Medicine. A sub-committee of the Council's Business Committee, consisting of medical members, studied in detail the Ordinance and recommendations based on their findings were transmitted as a representation from the Council to the Court. Similarly, later in the same year, 1910, when a Draft Ordinance issued jointly by the University Courts of St. Andrews, Glasgow, Aberdeen and Edinburgh made suggested alterations in the courses leading to the two Law degrees, B.L., and LL.B., the General

Council could again supply from its ranks, appointed by the Business Committee, a sub-committee of experts to consider and report on the terms of the Ordinance.

In April 1911, a Draft Ordinance was before the General Council setting forth the terms of the Foundation of the Strathcona-Fordyce Chair of Agriculture. The endowment of the new Chair had largely been made possible, as the Business Committee noted with the " liveliest satisfaction ", by the munificent gift of £10,000 made by the Chancellor, Lord Strathcona. The Council put on record " its deep sense of gratitude to the Chancellor for the further proof of his great interest in the welfare of the University ".

Further extension of opportunity in Science education came in 1913 when an Ordinance instituting a degree in Forestry was prepared by the Court. Again an appropriately selected sub-committee of the Business Committee considered the terms of this Ordinance and, when their suggested adjustments were reported to the General Council, the Business Committee added that " in view of the natural opportunities for scientific and practical training in Forestry which Aberdeen by its situation in the North East of Scotland so conspicuously possesses, the Business Committee heartily welcomes the prospect of the institution by the University of a special Degree in Forestry ". The General Council, in transmitting to the Court the proposed amendments to the Forestry Ordinance, gave " cordial support to the University Court in its application for a Grant from the Development Fund for the extension and proper equipment of the Forestry Department ". Later it recorded that " the Business Committee learns with satisfaction that the University Court has given effect to the greater part of the alterations in the Forestry Ordinance recommended by the General Council ". This growth of mutual respect and helpfulness between Court and Council is a noticeable feature of the many activities of these busy years.

While these new Ordinances were being shaped, considerable investigation had been going on into the working of the Arts Regulations of 1909. As early as April 1910, the Council had resolved to ask the University Court " to supply the Council with a classified return of the different Curricula in the Faculty of Arts submitted by students and approved by the Faculty ". The Court readily granted the request and the Return proved most interesting, 325 students availing themselves of the privileges of the new Ordinance, selecting no fewer than 245 different curricula, " no proposed curriculum within the strict letter of the Ordinance " having been rejected.

The General Council, troubled because of the unsatisfactory grouping of subjects in many courses and aware of the need for " curricula with more backbone ", remitted to a sub-committee of the Business Committee to consider the advisability of the appointment of an official Adviser of Studies. Having enquired fully into the practice in the other Scottish Universities, this sub-committee came to the conclusion that the University

Court of Aberdeen should appoint an Adviser of Studies who would not be a member of the Senatus. This report was transmitted to the Court as a Representation of the Council in April 1911, but more than a decade had to pass before the recommendation became a reality.

Simultaneously and in association with these investigations into the workings of the Arts curriculum, another sub-committee, on which sat many distinguished heads of schools in the north-east, had been considering the whole question of the Preliminary Examinations. This matter had become all the more urgent because of the development of the Scottish Education Department and the growth of secondary schools and more especially by the institution of Intermediate and Leaving Certificates.

The Report of this Committee on the Preliminary Examination, presented to the General Council in 1910, makes most interesting reading. In a scholarly way the whole history of the Preliminary Examination had been enquired into from the first record of an Entrance Examination in Aberdeen in 1593 when it must have been a test of the entrant's " ability to follow a discourse in Latin and to write and speak in that Language ". Along with this interesting history, the Report provided a " History of the Development of Secondary Schools and of the Leaving Certificates of the Scottish Education Department " and a statement as to the nature and practical working of the Preliminary Examination or Equivalents in Oxford, Cambridge, London, Birmingham, North of England Universities, the University of Wales, the National University of Ireland, Harvard, Chicago, Germany, France. Having asserted that a Preliminary Examination must be maintained, whatever the direction of the development of the Leaving Certificate, and making suggestions as to suitable preliminary requirements for each faculty, the Report concluded with " Recommendations as to Examining Board ", advocating, instead of the peripatetic Board then in existence, a Scottish Universities Entrance Board with considerable power and at some fixed place. This Report with some emendations was transmitted as a Council Representation to the University Court in October 1910. The Court at its November meeting directed that the Report on the Preliminary Examination " be sent to the Senatus for any observation it may have to offer " and that the thanks of the Court be conveyed to the Council " for its trouble in compiling this valuable Report ".

This Aberdeen Report was one of the documents before a Conference of Representatives of the General Councils of the four Universities held at Perth in January 1911, to consider Preliminary Examinations. It was two years later before the University Courts issued a Draft Ordinance on the subject, by which time the Scottish Leaving Certificate had achieved new status and the General Council was not so sure of the position of the Preliminary Examination. A further Conference of University Courts led to the drawing-up of an amended Draft Ordinance but by this time the graver issue of the First World War had altered the whole situation. It was not until 1918 that the Scottish Universities Entrance

Board—the body whose foundation the Aberdeen Council's sub-committee had advocated in 1910—was set up and made responsible for all regulations as to university entrance.

Further adjustment of Bursary Regulations and of curricula for the M.A. degree, the matter of Inclusive Fees and of Carnegie Grants, the proposed new degree in Education—in all these additional concerns of the pre-war years the Council continued to take an active and informed part, more and more responsibility developing on the Business Committee as the volume of work accumulated.

Several other matters peculiarly the affairs of the General Council are recorded in the Minutes of these years. For instance, when in 1911, St. Andrews University celebrated its Quincentenary, Aberdeen General Council was invited to send a delegate. The Clerk of the Council, Mr. P. J. Anderson, was appointed to attend the Celebrations and it was thought proper that he should present an address of congratulation. Accordingly, a dignified address in Latin, headed " Commune Concilium Universitatis Aberdonensis Universitati Sancti Andreae " composed by Mr. Wm. Keith Leask and Dr. H. F. Morland Simpson, engrossed in vellum by Mr. Arthur E. Payne and signed by the Chancellor, Lord Strathcona, was duly presented by Mr. Anderson at St. Andrews on Wednesday, 13 September 1911.

In the Minute of October 1910, there first appears a list of " University Studies ", a series of publications, the authors or editors of which were almost exclusively members of the General Council. The object of the series was " to stimulate original research in all branches of study, to prove a bond of union between alumni such as is much required after they leave the University and to provide a means of effecting exchanges with other Universities and learned institutions at home and abroad ". Under the general editorship of the Clerk of the General Council, the Publications Committee with the co-operation of the New Spalding Club and the help of a grant of £50 from the Library Committee published forty-five such volumes between 1900 and 1910 and a further twenty-five between 1910 and 1941.

Another publication that has been an important feature of University life—and never more so than in this centenary year of 1960 when, with Miss Nan Shepherd as Editor, the excellent Fusion Centenary Number of the *University Review* has been issued—had its beginning about this time. At the Council's Meeting of 13 April 1912, Mr. Wm. Stewart Thomson seconded by Mr. Alexander Mackie proposed " that, with a view to fostering among graduates an interest in the affairs of the University, and drawing closer the ties binding them thereto, it be remitted to a small Committee to collect information and to furnish suggestions as to the feasibility of establishing an Aberdeen University Magazine ".

After due exploration of the idea and the testing of response amongst graduates, 950 of whom promised subscriptions, a Committee of Management consisting of twelve representatives of the General Council, six representatives each of Court and Senatus, one undergraduate representative and four co-opted members, was set up under the Chairmanship of the Principal. The first number of *The Aberdeen University Review*, with Mr. Mackie as Editor, was published in November 1913, and was " in the hands of its most distant subscriber before Christmas " of that year.

Reporting in April 1914, after the first two numbers of the *Review* had been issued, the Committee put on record that subscribers, resident in all parts of the world, now totalled nearly 1,050, more than a fifth of the number of graduates. An anonymous donor had made it possible " to send nearly 100 copies free of charge to Libraries and Universities in many parts of the world " and there had been a " very considerable demand " by the general public. According to the notice of " an important English paper " the *Review* spoke " well for the talent connected with the University ".

A fascinating story—" tragical-comical-historical "—that runs in serial form through several volumes of the Council's Minutes had its beginnings as far back as 1909. At the October meeting of that year, the Rev. Dr. John Milne seconded by Professor John Harrower moved: " That a Committee be appointed to consider the propriety and feasibility of reconstructing the tomb of Bishop Elphinstone in the University Chapel, King's College, in its original form ". A Committee of thirty-five, later augumented, was immediately elected. Keeping two conditions " steadily in view ", first, " that the reconstruction should adhere as closely as possible in all essential particulars to the original tomb as it must be conjecturally restored from the account in the King's College ' Fasti '," and, second, " that it should not be out of harmony with, or an obstruction to, the present arrangements and use of the chapel ", the Committee proceeded to consider various sketches and models and made recommendations which were approved by the University Court. A preliminary appeal resulted in subscriptions totalling £1,018 10s. 6d.; the list headed by a donation of £10 from H.M. King George V. The Advisory Sub-Committee and the Executive Sub-Committee of the larger Committee met Mr. Henry Wilson of Borough Green, Kent, at King's College on 4 August 1910, as a result of which Mr. Wilson prepared a sketch which received the " hearty approval " of the Advisory Committee of Artists to whom it was submitted. " A reduced reproduction, in collotype " of this sketch was sent out with the General Appeal " to graduates, alumni and friends of the University generally ". So gratifying was the response to this appeal that the Committee felt justified in approaching the University Court to ask its approval of Mr. Wilson's design. The Court asked that a model of the reconstructed Tomb be created in the Chapel " sufficient to show the height and general features ". Accordingly a rough model was erected and inspected by members of the Court on 3 August 1911. At the further request of the Court a model " more closely resembling the sketch of the monument submitted " was later erected. The Court desired particularly " to see whether the base represented on Mr. Wilson's sketch would not demand a total height for the Tomb greater than the four feet mentioned as the maximum in the Committee's report of 26th March ". A Committee of the Court met in the Chapel on 21 August, inspected this second model and met the artist, Mr. Henry Wilson, who explained his design after which they reported to the Elphinstone Committee their approval " of the model as shown, with a total height from the Chapel floor of four feet four inches ". By this time 630 subscribers had paid £1,349 2s. which with promises brought the total sum well beyond the required £1,600.

The Committee was now ready " to make the necessary arrangements with Mr. Wilson and to adjust all minor details, such as the position of the effigy and the terms of the inscriptions on the tomb ". Accordingly, on 21 March 1912, an agreement was entered into with Mr. Henry Wilson, Sculptor, Borough Green, Kent, " whereby he bound himself, in consideration of the sum of £1,500, to execute in accordance with a sketch-design prepared by the Sculptor and approved by the Committee of General Council, a recumbent figure in bronze of Bishop Elphinstone on a marble die surrounded by eight figures of the Graces and Virtues; Faith, Hope, Love and Contemplation on one side, and Prudence, Justice, Fortitude and Temperance on the other, having at the head the Bishop's arms with Angels as supporters; at the feet the epitaphium panel with servitors as supporters, all in bronze, the whole to be erected in the Chapel of King's College, Old Aberdeen ".

All was set fair. The first third of Mr. Wilson's fee, £500, was paid to him on 26 March 1912. The whole reconstruction was to be completed on or before 31 December 1913—but it was over twenty years later before the end of the story was reached!

The consideration and expense being devoted to the tomb of one Founder evidently stirred thoughts about the other. For at the Statutory Meeting of 13 April 1912, the General Council resolved, on the motion of Professor Cowan, seconded by Professor Davidson, that " in view of the partially-ruined condition of the Tomb of the Founder of Marischal College in Dunnottar Churchyard " a committee should be appointed to consider " the restoration of the Tomb in a suitable and worthy manner ". Court and Senatus had already appointed Committees now joined by the Council's Committee. The Joint Committee, convened by the Principal, appointed Mr. G. P. K. Young, Perth, as architect for the restoration. By October 1912, a sum of £320 had been contributed or promised, including £100 from the Chancellor of the University, £100 from the Senatus and £50 from the University Court. Graduates and others interested were to be circularized and invited to contribute. From the fact that no further reference is made in the Council's Minutes to Earl Marischal's Tomb, we can only assume that this enterprise was more speedily concluded than that of Bishop Elphinstone's Tomb.

Lord Strathcona and Mount Royal, Rector of the University, 1899-1902, and Chancellor since 1903 died on 21 January 1914. At the

7

Council's Meeting of 18 April 1914, it was remitted to the Principal, the Convener of the Business Committee (Mr. David Milligan) and the Clerk (Mr. P. J. Anderson) to frame a suitable Minute regarding the late Chancellor. This is recorded in the following terms:

> The Council would place on record their sense of the loss which not only the University but the whole Empire has sustained through the death on 21st January last of the Right Honourable Lord Strathcona and Mount Royal, G.C.M.G., G.C.V.O., P.C., F.R.S., LL.D., High Commissioner for Canada, who for ten years held the office of Chancellor of the University. Lord Strathcona discharged the duties of the high positions to which he was called with a constant faithfulness to the trust reposed on him and adorned them by the sagacity, the courage and the integrity for which he was ever distinguished. During his tenure of the Chancellorship the University has enjoyed large additions to her buildings and other resources, to which he himself most liberally contributed. He has left a deep influence on the generation which he served; and his country and this University in particular, are rich in possession of his memory and inspiring example.

Acting on the precedent created at the election of Lord Strathcona as Chancellor, the Business Committee of the General Council, for the purpose of arranging for the nomination of a suitable person for the office of Chancellor, formed an augmented committee of thirty-nine. Members of the University Court who were also members of the General Council, representatives of the Senatus, the Deans of the Faculties of Arts, Science, Divinity, Law and Medicine, joined the twenty-one members of the Business Committee. This enlarged Committee, having met five times, resolved " after very careful consideration " on the unanimous nomination of the Earl of Elgin and Kincardine, K.G., G.C.S.I., G.C.I.E., M.A., D.C.L. (Oxon.), LL.D. (Cambridge, St. Andrews, Glasgow, Aberdeen and Edinburgh). At the Statutory meeting of the General Council on 18 April 1914, the Convener of the Business Committee, Mr. D. M. M. Milligan, seconded by Professor Grierson of the Chair of English in the University, proposed the election of the Earl of Elgin as Chancellor.

On Wednesday, 8 July 1914, the Installation of the Chancellor took place according to the usual ritual in the Mitchell Hall, Marischal College. Within a month of this important occasion in the life of the General Council and of the whole University, the country was at war. Many of the young men capped that July day were soon to be in mud-filled trenches in Flanders. The only indication in the General Council's records at this point that the lights had gone out all over Europe is that the first item on the business of the Statutory Meeting of 17 October 1914, is entitled " Roll of Honour " and consists of the formal words:

> The President (the Principal) submitted a statement regarding the number of graduates, alumni, and students of the University known to him as at present serving their country in various capacities.

The tabulated list shows that over 1,000 men, students, graduates, and members of staff, were even thus early in the Services, and that the 368 students represented half the male students at the University.

In the hundred years of recorded history of the life of the General Council some names stand out as those of members of the Council who have given unusually devoted service to it. One such is that of Colonel William Johnston, C.B., M.A., M.D., LL.D. His death on 26 December 1914, was a great loss to the University and severed an interesting link with pre-Fusion days.

For twenty-six years Colonel Johnston had been a member of the Business Committee of the General Council and for three years one of the Assessors in the University Court. In 1900 he was appointed by the University Court a member of the Library Committee; and when he became one of the Council's Assessors on the Court, he served on the Edilis, Finance and Lands Committees, "interesting himself in all academic activities ".

Six months after the death of Colonel Johnston, University and Council suffered another great loss by the death on 25 June 1915, of Mr. Alexander Mackie, M.A., Principal of the Albyn Place School. Since 1901 Mr. Mackie had been a member of the Business Committee and had given in that capacity fourteen years' active and devoted service through the period of educational reforms. The life of our University has been much enriched by the devoted service graduates like Colonel Johnston and Mr. Mackie so willingly gave. Fortunately such men have their successors in the Council's story.

By the end of 1915 the Business Committee had suffered two further losses in the death on 14 November of Dr. William Dey and on 31 December of Dr. Albert Westland, both Assessors on the University Court. Both men had served long and well.

Colonel Johnston's death created among the General Council Assessor-ships of the University Court, a vacancy which had to be filled " by a show of hands " at the meeting of the General Council on 17 April 1915. Colonel the Rev. James Smith, Minister of St. George's-in-the-West Parish, was elected to serve for the remainder of Colonel Johnston's tenure of office—till the following October. By that time, however, the General Council, in view of the War Emergency, agreed to refrain from exercising its power of electing Assessors and empowered the Court to deal with casual vacancies. Accordingly, the University Court in February 1916, appointed Dr. George Smith, Director of Studies, Aberdeen Training Centre, to succeed Dr. Dey and Dr. John Scott Riddell to succeed Dr. Westland. These two, with Mr. Cooper and the Rev. James Smith represented the General Council on the University Court until the election of Assessors held on 18 October 1919—the first normal election since 1913. Four nominations were made for four vacancies, three of the four Assessors seeking re-election with Mr. David M. M. Milligan in place of Mr. Cooper who did not seek re-election.

Just before the outbreak of war in August 1914, one of the great themes of debate in the Universities, both within and without the General Councils, had been the Administration of the Carnegie Trust. By his Trust Deed of 7 June 1901, Mr. Andrew Carnegie gave the capital sum of £2,000,000, the income of which at 5 per cent, was to be used in two ways, first, " applied towards the improvement and expansion of the Universities of Scotland " (Clause A) and, second, " devoted to the payment of the whole of the ordinary fees exigible by the Universities from students of Scottish birth and extraction " (Clause B). Even with £50,000 per annum at its disposal, the fund for the payment of students' fees showed strain as the years went on. In an endeavour to restrict the demand, the Carnegie Trustees imposed the condition that applicants from Scottish schools for the grant must qualify by means of a Leaving Certificate of the Scottish Education Department. This apparent denigration of the Universities Preliminary Examination brought a storm of protest and the whole situation was further complicated by the raising of class fees. In Aberdeen in 1903 the fee for each class in Science, Medicine and Law was raised to 4 guineas and in Divinity to 3 guineas; in 1907 the fee for each class in Arts became 4 guineas. The Trust, now unable to pay in full the fees of any applicant, favoured the proposed system of an inclusive fee. The University Court, their hands forced by the fact that the payment of the increased Treasury Grant of 1910 was conditional on the establishment of such a system, agreed in 1911 to institute an inclusive fee, this arrangement to begin in the Session, 1912-13. The new fees ranged from 30 guineas for a three years course in Arts or Law to 90 guineas for the five years course in Medicine. For the Trust the question turned on how best Mr. Carnegie's desire that " no capable student should be debarred from attending the University on account of the payment of fees " could be met. Was it to be by restricting the payment to all students or by reserving the funds for the really needy although Mr. Carnegie obviously wanted to avoid any kind of " means test "? The Trust's decision was to pay a proportion of the fee—£27 towards the 30 guineas, £75 towards the 90 guineas and similar proportionate sums for the fees in Science and Divinity.

Professor Matthew Hay, Aberdeen's representative on the Carnegie Trust, in a speech to the University Court on 11 March 1913, deprecated the Trust's action, deploring the fact that " the poor applicant has suffered equally with the well-to-do applicant ". A sub-committee of the Business Committee of the General Council agreed with the view that by a proper bestowal of the income of the Trust the needs of every poor student would be fully met and recommended a Conference of General Councils on the Administration of the Carnegie Trust.

A Joint Conference of Councils met at Perth in June 1914, to consider the policy of the Carnegie Trustees, both in regard to Clause A and Clause B of the Trust Deed. The resolutions of the Conference deplored " the payment of only part of the fees of all students irrespective of their necessities, as injurious to the interests of the poorer students " and suggested " drawing the attention of all applicants and their parents or guardians to the terms of the Carnegie Trust Deed and relative letter; and making parents and guardians parties to applications for fee grants, and asking them to declare that assistance from the Trust is necessary to enable applicants to attend the University ". While the General Councils of the Universities of St. Andrews, Glasgow and Edinburgh decided to take no action, the Aberdeen Council adopted the resolutions which were communicated to the Secretary of the Trust.

No change was made in the decision to pay a proportion of fees, but Professor Matthew Hay was able to report to the University Court in March 1915, that the Executive Committee of the Trust had decided to give " further pecuniary assistance, if thought desirable and necessary " to students showing " exceptional merit " and had arranged " to increase restraint on applications for the ordinary assistance " from " students whose circumstances do not properly justify their application ".

By July 1915, the Carnegie Trustees had prepared a new form of application for assistance in the payment of class fees. It quoted the whole of the letter which Mr. Carnegie had in 1901 sent to the Chairman of the Trust and which explained the purpose of his benefaction. Further, the applicant was now required to name parent or guardian to whom intimation of the grant would be sent. These measures evidently provided the necessary restraints and the consequent fairer distribution of the available money.

All over the world today there are Scottish graduates, who, born too soon to claim a student's grant, were the recipients of either the whole or part of their fees and who bless Mr. Carnegie's inspired generosity which for them made University education possible.

An academic matter to which the General Council was giving particular attention before the outbreak of the First World War, another evidence of the educational expansion of the early twentieth century, was the question of a degree in Education. At an adjourned meeting of January 1913, Mr. Charles MacGregor, Master of Method in the Training Centre, seconded by Dr. Charles McLeod, Mathematics Master in the Grammar School, proposed that it be remitted to the Business Committe " to consider the desirability and practicality of establishing a Degree in Education ".

A sub-committee of eight, later doubled in size by the addition of co-opted members, presented to the October meeting of the Council, memoranda on the subject, embodying three proposals—an independent degree which, while embodying some Arts courses, would have a strong teacher-training bias, a post-graduate degree or an Arts degree with Honours in Education. The Honours degree proposal was strongly supported by a memorandum from Professor Baillie of the Chair of Moral Philosophy and one of the co-opted members of the sub-committee. After a further remit, the sub-committee having based its deliberations

7*

on a memorandum by Mr. Macgregor, its Convener, and Professor Baillie's memorandum, unanimously agreed to ask the Business Committee to recommend the establishment of a post-graduate degree in Education. This recommendation was adopted by the General Council at its meeting in April 1914, and a Representation accordingly made to the University Court.

The Representation was not acknowledged by the Court. Instead, in March 1915, the Court sent to the Council as a counter-proposal a scheme, approved by the Senatus, for the institution of an Arts degree with Honours in Education. One is tempted to suspect that the professorial representatives, defeated in the General Council, had turned for a more sympathetic hearing to their brother Professors on the Senatus. Outraged, the Business Committee expressed their opinion that this scheme " should not be received by the General Council without protest ".

The General Council at its meeting in April 1915, on the motion of Dr. James Wattie, H.M.I.S., seconded by the Director of Studies of the Training Centre, Dr. George Smith, reiterated approval of a post-graduate degree in Education and asked the Business Committee to draw up a statement of objections to the proposed scheme for Honours in Education, one of the grounds of such objection being that " the proposed scheme is apparently not to apply to students in Science ".

A five-points objection was submitted to the University Court before its May meeting in 1915 and was followed by a report of the findings of a Conference held at Perth in October of that year, when, at the suggestion of the Glasgow General Council, representatives of the Councils of Glasgow, Aberdeen and Edinburgh met to consider the question of degrees in Education. While recommending further the institution of a Doctorate in Education and the establishment of a Faculty of Education in each of the four Universities, the Conference decided against an M.A. Honours Degree in Education and for a Post-Graduate Professional Degree of Bachelor of Education. In this stand the General Council of Aberdeen had the declared support of the Students' Representative Council at their meeting in December 1915.

The University Court must have recognized the cogency of the General Council's arguments for a Committee was appointed by the Court to consider the question of a degree in Education. In November 1916, the Principal wrote to Mr. P. J. Anderson, Clerk to the General Council, saying that the University Court had resolved to institute a post-graduate degree in Education and inviting the Council to appoint three representatives who with three representatives of the Senatus would meet the Court's Committee to draft an Ordinance accordingly. " We felt it right," said the Principal's letter, " that since the General Council moved first in this matter of a post-graduate degree in Education, it would expedite the preparation of the Ordinance, on which the Court have resolved, if we had from the beginning the assistance of the Council as well as of the Senatus in our deliberations ".

The General Council, rejoiced to find that their efforts between the years 1913 and 1915 had now been successful, received this invitation " with pleasure ", pleasure that must have been tempered by sadness at the thought that Mr. Charles MacGregor, the first promoter of this degree, convener of the sub-committee on the matter, had in May 1916, died of wounds received in action in France.

It was fully a year later—in December 1917—before an Ordinance to institute a Degree of Master of Education was prepared, approved by the Court and submitted to Senatus and General Council for their opinion. Final adjustments, involving a change of designation from " Master " to " Bachelor " occupied a further year and the First World War was well over before the course leading to such a degree was finally established.

The third volume of the printed Minutes of the General Council is concluded with the Minute of the meeting of April 1915. Even if we had no other reminder of the very great activity in all University matters in the years before the First World War we could have it in this volume which, similar in size to the combined first and second volumes which recorded ninety-three meetings covering the years from 1860 to 1906, comprise the Minutes of only sixteen meetings held between 1907 and 1915. Like the preceding combined publication, this third volume, bound in cloth, was to be bought for the sum of 2s. 6d.

The only other mention of the war in those concluding Minutes of Volume III beyond the Principal's Roll of Service is a reference to a request from Canada, from the Montreal Graduates Society, for the names of our graduates there so that they could be kept informed of the true state of matters in Britain. Although there is no later indication of how these were used, a list of eighty-three names and addresses was sent.

The opening Minute of Volume IV, however, carries a stark reminder of the first terrible months of the war. The obituary of General Council members, an annual feature of the Minutes since Ocotober 1908, included the names of those who died in action up to August 1915. For the next five years these lists continued to be swollen by names in heavy black type with the poignant addition of " killed in action " or " died of wounds" or " reported missing, now believed killed " or some similar brief descrip-tion of untimely death. As many of us who were students years later can testify, the Principal never offered public prayer without including some testimony to the heroic dead of these terrible years. By September 1915, the number of names on the Roll of Service was over 1,430. In a statement made at the General Council Meeting of April 1917, the Principal said that the total number of graduates, alumni and students in service was 2,250 and that 144 had fallen in action or died of wounds. The last number was to be more than doubled before the signing of the Armistice in November 1918.

Though sadly depleted in both students and staff, University life had to go on but it could do so only in a limping, limited way. The life of the General Council was correspondingly circumscribed; much of the business of those years was routine and, generally, an atmosphere of dreariness and delay emanates from the records. The matters of the Carnegie Trust and the Degree in Education had been carried by their own momentum into the early years of the war. Another issue which after long delay reached a settlement in 1917 yet did not become effective until peace came was the matter of a Lectureship in Celtic, a project sponsored over many years by the General Council. But even before the General Council had come into existence, the Society for the Propagation of Christian Knowledge in the Highlands and Islands of Scotland had set before the House of Commons as an accompaniment to a Bill presented by Alex. Bannerman, M.P., in June 1835, proposing the uniting of King's College and Marischal College into one University, a Petition urging the establishment of a Professorship of Gaelic. Mr. Bannerman's withdrawal of his Bill nullified the Petition.

In 1896, when the General Council brought to the notice of the University Court, " pressing wants " of the University, the Establishment of a Lectureship in Celtic was included, but again without effect. The General Council renewed its representation in 1909, again in October 1914, and yet again in October 1915. Yielding at last to importunity, the University Court early in 1916 instituted a Lectureship in Celtic and Philology and appointed as Lecturer, Mr. John Fraser, Lecturer in Latin and Comparative Philology and University Assistant in Humanity. The initiation of the Course, however, had to be postponed till 1919 as Mr. Fraser just after his appointment was required for work at the War Office.

The Business Committee recorded the " great satisfaction " with which it learned that the Court had by this appointment " at last removed what had been so long a reproach to the University ", commenting further that the late Dr. Dey's endowment of a Celtic Department in the University Library would make more effective the study of Celtic.

Perhaps it is part of the general malaise of the times that relations between Court and Council appear to have deteriorated between 1914 and 1918. A feature of the very active early years of the century had been the co-operation of the two bodies. Here and there in the wartime Minutes of the Council, an aggrieved remark would suggest less happy relations. Perhaps the long wrangle over Preliminary Examinations exacerbated feelings and jangled war-frayed nerves. The Joint Draft Ordinance on Preliminary Examinations, drawn up by the Courts in 1913 and reframed in 1914, met with steady opposition from the Aberdeen Council who took their stand on the necessity for conference with the Scottish Education Department, so that the rapidly-developed and now fully-recognized Leaving Certificate should have due place as providing a ticket of entry to University study. The Council argued that " it would be more reasonable to discuss with the Scottish Education Department the need for a Preliminary Examination before setting up the machinery for such an Examination ". They maintained this attitude when in 1916 a third Draft Ordinance on the matter was issued by the four Courts and duly laid before Parliament in June. A petition to Parliament to present an address to His Majesty praying that assent to this Ordinance be withheld was sent by Aberdeen General Council. The arguments used were that this Ordinance, drafted before the war, took no account of altered educational outlook; that it entailed unnecessary new expenditure; and that it stereotyped an examination rapidly being superseded by the Schools Leaving Certificate examination. Further, the petition argued, that prior to such an Ordinance the University Court should confer with the Scottish Education Department so that " a common system of examination " to serve the purposes of a Leaving Certificate and a University Entrance Examination might be evolved.

The petition was presented to the House of Lords by the Chancellor, the Earl of Elgin, and to the House of Commons by Sir Henry Craik, M.P., a similar petition being presented on behalf of the General Council of Glasgow University. At the same time the Scottish Education Department also lodged a series of " Observations " with regard to the proposed Ordinance, requesting the Privy Council to withhold assent. To these " Observations " the four University Courts replied in July 1917, in a series of " Representations ", which in turn were criticized in a series of " Remarks " by the Business Committees of Glasgow and Aberdeen General Councils. This Gilbertian situation was resolved by the holding of a Preliminary Conference of the Universities Committee of the Privy Council, the Scottish Education Department and the Principals of the four Universities followed by a regular Conference between the Committee, the Department and duly elected representatives of the four University Courts. In January 1918, a redrafted Ordinance constituted a Scottish Universities Entrance Board of sixteen members whose duty it would be to act as intermediary between Universities and the Education Department and schools and to frame regulations for Admission to the University, taking full account of the Leaving Certificate which about this time became a " group " Certificate. The operations of this body were to make much more intimate the connection between secondary schools and the Universities.

The Business Committee now reported that it was glad to recognize that the principles for which the Council had contended were embodied in the new Draft Ordinance and rejoiced that the three points emphasized in the Report on Preliminary Examinations drawn up in 1910 by a Committee presided over by Emeritus Professor McKendrick had been recognized and that the hope that unnecessary duplication of examinations would be done away with had been fulfilled.

Midway through the war years, on 19 January 1917, Lord Elgin, Chancellor of the University, died after less than three years' office— the three years that coincided with Mr. Churchill's Rectorship of the University. As the Minute recording the Council's sense of loss goes on to say of Lord Elgin, " Appointed just before the storm of War broke on Europe, he had to see many of the University schemes for improvement and enlargement laid aside for the time being; but his interest never flagged and he only awaited the coming of peace to turn his energies to their development and completion. His position as Chairman of the Carnegie Trust had already given him wide insight into the needs and aspirations of the Scottish Universities and, when the General Council invited him to become Head of the University, it was with the consciousness that they were thereby ensuring sympathy and understanding in all academic difficulties that might arise ".

In spite of a war-time régime, the procedure now established by both regulation and precedent was repeated for the election of a new Chancellor. The unanimous recommendation of the augmented Committee of forty-one was the nomination of the Duke of Richmond and Gordon, K.G., G.C.V.O., C.B. Here was a return to an old tradition, for the seventh Duke was the third in line of Aberdeen Chancellors, his grandfather having been one of the two Chancellors at the time of the Fusion, and his father having held the office for the best part of half a century. Again following precedent, the Duke was installed at the Summer Graduation Ceremony of 6 May 1917.

VII. PLANNING FOR PEACE

By the end of 1917 new stirrings in University life reflected the spirit abroad in the nation. Perhaps with the thought that after three years of war the end could not be long delayed, tentative efforts towards creating the " land fit for heroes " were made. Plans had been afoot for some time for Electoral Reform. The Universities noted with satisfaction that not only was recommended the retention of University representation but also an increase in the amount of representation assigned to the Scottish Universities. The First World War increased university representation in Parliament, the Second World War abolished it! The proposal was that instead of the combined constituency of Glasgow and Aberdeen sending one member and the combined constituency of Edinburgh and St. Andrews another, the four Scottish Universities should be regarded as a single constituency returning three members under the system of a single transferable vote.

The General Council of Aberdeen presented to both Houses of Parliament a Petition expressing approval of the proposals made by the Speaker's Conference on the subject and also of the measures in the consequent Bill before the House which, in addition, proposed recognizing the right to vote in a parliamentary election of a woman graduate who had attained the age of thirty. The Representation of the People Act of 1918, notable as giving women the vote for the first time, became law on 6 February of that year. Accordingly a Register was required of those members of the General Council entitled to a Parliamentary vote. As no General Council Register had been prepared since 1914, it was necessary to prepare a new register on which would be indicated by a special mark the name of an under-thirty woman graduate who would not have a parliamentary vote. The Registrar prepared a revised Register to come into force in October 1918, and remain in force till 15 March 1919, containing 5,105 names of which 497 were those of women under the age of thirty on 15 April 1918. This register was authenticated by the Vice-Chancellor on 30 September 1918.

As a result of the poll in the Parliamentary Election, declared on 27 December 1918—a result arrived at by the proportional representation system of vote-counting, the three representatives of the Scottish Universities constituencies were Sir W. Watson Cheyne, Mr. D. M. Cowan and Sir Henry Craik, K.C.B. Of all Scottish graduates only 48 per cent. voted but the proportion of possible Aberdeen voters was 60 per cent. This difference in interest would give some support for what we would like to think is true—that of all Universities, none has more loyal and interested graduates than Aberdeen.

Further proof of hopeful stirrings of academic life might be found in the number of proposals for new degrees that are the subjects of Ordinances in the later months of wartime. Combination degrees English-Philosophy, French-English, History-English—as well as an entirely new kind of degree, Bachelor of Commerce, came up for consideration. This expansion gathered momentum throughout the nineteen-twenties and the early thirties, when Ordinance followed Ordinance, instituting new degrees, particularly in Science, and endowing new Chairs, such as in Engineering, in French, in Geology, and in Political Economy, the Foundation of the last-named due to the munificence of Sir Thomas Jaffrey. Each Ordinance in turn was scrutinized by the Business Committee and occasionally it was recorded " with satisfaction " that an Ordinance had been adjusted according to the recommendations of the General Council.

Within the Council itself the resurgence of hope was expressed in the setting-up of a number of new forward-looking committees—a Sub-Committee on Education (Scotland) Bill, a Sub-Committee on Systems of Residence and a Sub-Committee on Post-War Development. Under the last-named umbrella-like title six different topics were selected for report by six individual members of Council—Research, Finance, Extension of University Teaching, the Arts curriculum (that perennial!), Relations of the University to Central and Collegiate Institutions within its district and Relations of the University to the Universities of our Allies.

It is interesting to see the question of University residence cropping up again; since first raising the matter in 1870 the General Council had been importunate in urging the need for it. Now under the chairmanship of Mr. Henry Alexander, whose skill in scholarly research on behalf of the University and its General Council was again in 1923 put at their services in a report jointly prepared with Mr. P. J. Anderson on the history of the M.A. Hood, a most interesting report was drawn up and presented to the General Council in April 1918. And if the conclusion again finally reached by the University Court in January 1921, was that the time was not yet opportune for the launching of this project, at least the researches of the Committee provide entertaining and probably historically valuable reading.

From the foundation of King's College up until near the end of the eighteenth century, residence would appear to have been imperative on students. Even in the nineteenth century up until the session of 1824-25 some students were in residence and it was only after the fusion of King's with Marischal College, that the vacant dormitories at King's were taken down. At Marischal College the dormitories had been converted into classrooms or residences for Professors.

The arrangements for boarding the students were in the care of the Economist who had to submit a bill of fare for approval by the Faculty. Alexander Leslie, " vintner in Edinburgh ", was appointed Economist at King's College in 1753 and the bill of fare drawn up by him has happily been preserved. Students eating at the First Table paid 50 merks Scots (£2 15s. 6d.) per quarter and students eating at the Second Table £2 per quarter.

Supper and breakfast dishes for the First Table included " dropped eggs, parsnips, cold meat, milk and rice, finnan haddies and butter, ale saps: any of the above as called for " while the humbler Second Table supplied for supper " porridge and milk or ale, milk and bread, and sometimes a fricasée " and for breakfast " porridge and ale or milk, bread and drink ". Contrasting standards are to be seen too in the provision for dinner, presumably served at midday. Tuesday's dinner, for instance, provided " pease soup or white broth, saddle of roast mutton followed by apple pie or veal pie " for the First Table, but for the Second, " fish and potatoes, cold meat ". On Thursday, while the poorer sort—or the thriftier—ate pease soup and tripe, the gourmets fed on " green soup, roast ducks or pullets, pigeon pie ". Not only on the life of the student of the period but probably on the eating habits of the people as a whole does this report throw an interesting light.

Of the other Scottish Universities, St. Andrews, in 1918, had a residence for fifty women and none for men; Glasgow had a residence for women, one for nineteen Divinity students of the Church of Scotland, and two hostels for Medical students. Edinburgh had five houses accommodating 140 women students, these hostels having been built by a joint arrangement between the University and the Provincial Committee for the Training of Teachers. The Aberdeen Provincial Committee had before the war prepared a scheme of residences for its women students. It acquired 20 acres at Hilton and invited the Aberdeen University Court to combine with it and make the project a joint one as in Edinburgh but the Court did not see its way to do so and the Provincial Committee went on after the war to carry out its own scheme.

Mr. Alexander and his Committee considered with great thoroughness residential schemes in Oxford and Cambridge and other English Universities as well as schemes in Canada and the United States. Their report was submitted to Court and Senatus and to the Carnegie Trust and it was recommended that the Business Committee continue consideration of the subject with a view to " more definite proposals at the first suitable moment ". The Committee, continued in being as a Joint Committee working with the Senatus, proposed in 1920 the erection and equipment of a Hall of Residence to hold fifty students, the whole to cost £40,000, and considered other expedients to cope with the greatly increased number of medical students. For lack of money the whole scheme was postponed. On the recommendation of the University Court, the Joint Committee of the General Council and the Senatus on Halls of Residence was continued and a comment on its activities appears in the Minutes of the Council Meeting of October 1924.

One interesting feature of the century of life of the General Council has been the way in which it has provided a forum for the expression of some aspect of University opinion not always sympathetically listened to in Senatus or Court. The warring Professors in the matter of the Extended Session in the years 1907-8 had used the General Council as a sounding-board and now members of the University staff under professorial rank sought an outlet for their grievances through the Council. One natural result of University growth in the first decade of the century had been increase of staff. Not only were additional members working under the Professor added to existing Departments but new and independent Lectureships were founded. No one under the rank of a holder of a Chair, however, had any voice in the affairs of the University as dealt with in Senatus or Court.

Before the war, in 1913, the Association of Lecturers and Assistants had approached the University Court and the Senatus about the situation but, although both bodies considered the Association's resolutions, neither took any action and now the Association found itself compelled to consider " different methods ". A Sub-Committee of the Council's Business Committee under the Chairmanship of Dr. Rennie and working in conjunction with the Status Committee of the Lecturers' Association drew up a long and detailed report which was sympathetically received by the General Council in October 1917. In September of the following year a Conference of representatives of the four Scottish Universities, presided over by Mr. D. Milligan of Aberdeen, was held at Perth. The recommendations of this Conference were approved by the Aberdeen General Council in October 1918, and the clauses of a necessary Act of Parliament drawn up by the Committee. In April 1919, the General Council resolved to transmit to the University Court the approved Report of the Business Committee. But it took years of further skirmishing with the University Court, further Conferences, more Committee reports, before in 1922, the Universities' (Scotland) Bill, embodying some of the Council's proposals found its way on to the Statute Book. By the Act, Lecturers or Readers could be admitted as members of the Senatus; and a Lecturer or Reader after one year in service became *ex officio* a member of the

General Council of any of the Universities. On payment of a registration fee, a Lecturer, so entitled, had his name put and continued on the Council's Register during his life. As a result of this latter provision the names of twenty-three members of University staff not graduates of Aberdeen were enrolled in the General Council in 1923. In the near-forty years since these first concessions to the underprivileged members of the University staff, the Association of University Teachers—the Aberdeen Branch, as a limb of the the Scottish Association was formed in 1923—has appealed more than once to the General Council when they have found the University Court a stiff-necked people.

Much more harmony and much less delay accompanied the poignant task of the War Memorial, a first consideration after the Armistice of November 1918. In January 1919, the Principal proposed to the Senatus that the question of a Memorial should be brought before the Court, the General Council and the Students' Representative Council, and a joint-Committee of these Four Estates was formed. The General Council was represented on this joint-Committee by the Convener and the Clerk and three other members of the Business Committee. Mr. David M. M. Milligan, Convener of the Business Committee, acted as Honorary Treasurer of the War Memorial Fund, the major part of which was devoted to the cost of " a stained glass window in the antechapel by Mr. Douglas Strachan, with oak panels of about 10 feet in height, placed round three sides of the antechapel and bearing the names of the fallen carved in raised letters and gilded, the fourth side being filled by the screen ", the whole design being carried through under the direction of Dr. Wm. Kelly. Miss Mabel D. Allardyce with the help of voluntary assistants, compiled the Memorial Volume, comprising the Roll of Service with about 3,000 names of graduates, alumni, students and appendices containing the names of civilian prisoners of war and officials of the University who rendered war service, and an In Memoriam section with over 300 names accompanied where possible by photographs and brief biographies. No one could have foreseen when the work was completed in 1921 that less than a generation later another Memorial Volume would be needed and more names " in raised letters and gilded " would be added to those beautiful oak panels in the ante-chapel at King's.

A link with the early years of the General Council was broken when in October 1920, Dr. Robert Walker died, leaving a host of legends behind him. In these days of specialization and yet more specialization his list of offices has an almost Gilbertian ring. Assistant Professor of Mathematics, appointed in 1866, Examiner, Librarian, Registrar, Secretary of the University Court, Clerk to the General Council—he had been all of these, and his early nickname of " Function " earned in the mathematics classroom later became appropriately " Functions ". The Minutes of the Business Committee are engrossed in his handwriting from 1 October 1877, to 27 November 1906, and the Register of the General Council was compiled by him down to the issue for 1915, fitting memorials to the " meticulous conscientiousness " with which he served the General Council as well as the whole University. A member of the Business Committee till his death, Dr. Walker had resigned as Registrar in 1918, but he was retained on the list of the University staff with the title of Registrar Emeritus, and continued to rank as the Senior Official of the University. From the date of his resignation as Registrar in 1918 the care of the Register of the General Council, according to the recommendation made by the General Council on 11 October 1905, was entrusted to his successor as Clerk, Mr. P. J. Anderson.

It is time now to take up again the tale of the Elphinstone Tomb, the last report of the matter of its reconstruction having been submitted to the Council in April 1915. It was in keeping with the renewed hope of the twenties, with the verve and vigour of the returned soldiers filling to overflowing the classrooms come to life again after the sad depletion of the war years and infecting their seniors and juniors with optimism, that as well as new causes, near-lost old causes should find champions. The correspondence with the sculptor, Mr. Henry Wilson of Borough Green, Kent, was renewed in December 1918, and a year later a promise was extracted from him that he would travel to Italy in March 1920, to supervise the casting in bronze of the figures; he anticipated that the Tomb would be ready and in position in August 1920. So far as the General Council Minutes are concerned, the rest is silence until April 1927, when Mr. P. J. Anderson, the Secretary of the Reconstruction Committee, " informed the Council that the bronzes had at last arrived from Venice and were at present temporarily assembled round the tomb in King's College Chapel ". It only remained for them to be put in place. But a year later " the excessive dimensions of the bronzes as delivered by the artist " were still creating an almost insuperable difficulty. As offered by the sculptor, the total monument was about 16 feet long, 10½ feet broad, and over 6 feet high instead of the specified 9 feet 9 inches of length, 6½ feet of breadth and 4 feet 4 inches of height. Two expedients were considered and each in turn tried; " first on the original site according to a scheme which secures a reduction in height by sacrificing the tomb chest and the sculptures on the sides; and secondly according to the full design as submitted by the artist but erected in the ante-chapel ". In the Spring Term of 1928 the bronzes and model base were erected on the original site within the chapel and in the Winter Term of the same year they were set up in the ante-chapel according to the artist's full design. At the General Council Meeting of October 1928, all members were urged to form an opinion on the position of the monument, as a report by the 1909 Committee would be made at the meeting in April 1929. The recommendation then made by this Committee and accepted by the General Council was that " the only satisfactory solution " was to erect the monument in the ante-chapel and in this decision Court and Senatus agreed. By this time a further sum of £1,500 was needed to complete the work and discharge the Committee's obligations.

It is understandable that the Committee viewed with " grave mis-giving " the prospect of having to make another appeal to graduates and friends of the University and that it was with " acclamation " expressing " the liveliest satisfaction " that the General Council at their meeting in October 1929, heard the good news that two very generous offers eased the financial situation. The University Court had lent the Committee a sum of £675 which they now decided to give the Reconstruction Committee along with any interest thereon; and Sir Thomas Jaffrey, on the understanding that the Court would cancel its loan, " offered to meet the cost of erecting the monument in the Ante-Chapel and of suitably treating the original Tomb in the Chapel, up to the sum of £1,000 ". The estimated cost of the whole work came well within this sum. Started in the summer vacation of 1930, the work was finished by the end of the year and its completion fitted in well with the University celebrations of the five-hundredth anniversary of the Founder's birth held in April 1931. The dedication of the Memorial to Bishop Elphinstone in the ante-chapel at 2.30 p.m. on 4 April 1931, provided the opening ceremony of these celebrations. The final report of the 1909 Committee was presented to the General Council at their meeting in October 1931, and one can well imagine the relief with which the Committee's discharge was both sought and given.

It is natural that in the course of an undertaking completed only after the lapse of twenty-two years, the Committee should suffer consider-able loss by death and otherwise among its members. Mr. P. J. Anderson's death on 12 May 1926 bereft the Committee of its Secretary and of one who " gave his services to the movement with a rare devotion and enthusiasm ". Dr. W. Douglas Simpson, Mr. Anderson's successor as Librarian and Clerk to the General Council, took over the Secretaryship of the Committee. In 1929 Professor Harrower, who as Convener of the Committee since 1909, had shown unwearying interest and patience through many difficult years, resigned. His place was taken by Dr. Gordon J. Murray who guided the Committee from a state of deadlock to at least a dignified, if not entirely successful, conclusion. For it was not long before the great bulk of the memorial in the ante-chapel brought protest and objection and a tailpiece had to be added to the story.

In the immediate post-war years the machinery of the General Council slipped into gear again. The elections for Assessors on the University Court, halted during the war years, resumed their biennial course, a poll being demanded after the election of October 1921, when three candidates were nominated for two seats. The poll upheld the election made at the meeting of the General Council when Mr. Milligan was returned and Mr. George Duncan was elected. This was the last postal vote until the historic Extraordinary General Council Meeting of November 1937. In the intervening years the elections were more or less automatic, the retiring members being re-nominated and elected without challenge. The Rev. Gordon J. Murray, M.A., D.D., succeeded to the vacancy caused by the death, before his term was completed, of Mr. D. M. M. Milligan, whom he also succeeded as Convener of the Business Committee. Sir Ashley Mackintosh succeeded in April 1930, to the vacancy caused by the death of Dr. J. Scott Riddell and, when Dr. George Smith did not seek re-election in 1931, his place was taken by Mr. Wm. Riddoch. When Mr. Riddoch resigned in April 1937, his place was taken for the remainder of his period in office until 1939 by Colonel James Dawson. The death of Sir Ashley Mackintosh in October 1937, created a vacancy which was to be filled at an Extraordinary Meeting of the General Council on 6 November 1937. For the first time a woman candidate, Dr. Mary Esslemont, was nominated and at a largely attended meeting defeated the other nominee for the seat, Dr. A. Greig Anderson. Dr. Anderson's proposer demanded a poll which overturned the decision of the meeting, Dr Anderson securing the seat by a majority of 134 votes out of the 4,556 valid votes received at this last election of Assessors before the outbreak of the Second World War.

In spite of a growing murmuring against the privilege, the Universities continued to hold Parliamentary seats throughout the inter-war years. In the Parliamentary Election of 1922, Sir George Andreas Berry, LL.D., of Edinburgh, was nominated in place of Sir W. Watson Cheyne and along with the other two nominees, the retiring members Mr. D. M. Cowan and Sir Henry Craik, was duly elected, as again in 1923, there being no other nominations, to represent the Scottish Universities. These three were re-elected in 1924 but this time the seats were contested by a fourth nominee. Sir Henry Craik, who had faithfully represented the University of Aberdeen in Parliament for over twenty years, died in March 1927, after a life of " devotion to education, literature and service to the State ". In June 1928, four candidates again stood for the Parliamentary seats, the three elected being Sir George A. Berry, Mr. John Buchan, LL.D., and Mr. D. M. Cowan. In the Representation of the People Bill of 1931 came the first proposal to abolish the University seats, a proposal strongly opposed by all four Scottish General Councils. In the election of this year, Sir George A. Berry did not offer himself as a candidate and his place was taken by Mr. Archibald Noel Skelton who along with Dr. Buchan and Dr. D. M. Cowan were returned unopposed. Dr. D. M. Cowan died in December 1933, and a by-election was necessary to fill the vacancy. Two candidates were nominated and of these Dr. G. A. Morrison, retired headmaster of Gordon's College, was elected by an overwhelming majority. The Aberdeen General Council took especial pleasure in the success of one of its own graduates and a member of its Business Committee. Another by-election was necessary in June 1935, owing to the vacancy created by the elevation of Mr. John Buchan, by this time Lord Tweedsmuir, to the Governor-Generalship of Canada. The seat was overwhelmingly won by Professor John Graham Kerr of Glasgow after a contest against Mrs. Naomi M. M. Mitchison, and in the election in November of the same year, the three sitting members,

8

Professor Graham Kerr, Dr. G. A. Morrison and Mr. A. Noel Skelton, were voted in against a fourth nominee. An unprecedented situation was created by the death of Mr. Noel Skelton on 22 November while the election was in progress. In the by-election which had to follow in January 1936, the Rt. Hon. James Ramsay Macdonald, P.C. LL.D., Lord President of the Council, was elected out of three candidates but his period in office was destined to be short. He died in November 1937. In the by-election which followed, the last election before the years of the Second World War, the Rt. Hon. Sir John Anderson was elected out of four candidates. The matter of the abolition of the University seats was being pressed throughout the thirties and in February 1936, a debate on University Franchise, arising out of a private member's motion, took place. The motion was defeated by a large majority; the time was not yet ripe.

The third piece of elective machinery of the General Council arose out of the annual retiral of seven members of the Business Committee. In the early days of the General Council the Business Committee began as a group of twenty-one interested members appointed at one meeting by authority of the University Commission to prepare the business for the next meeting. The 1889 Act gave fuller recognition to the Business Committee for by this Act the Council was permitted to appoint committees to investigate work and report upon any matter remitted to them or to carry out instructions given to them by the Council. As the numbers in the General Council grew and the items of business multiplied it was necessary for the Business Committee with its specially appointed Sub-Committees to take over more and more of the affairs of the General Council. In 1918 the General Council granted to its Business Committee the authority to deal with Draft Ordinances or Alterations in Ordinances without summoning an adjourned or special meeting of the General Council. In April 1924, regulations for the nomination and election of the members of the Business Committee were drawn up. Apart from the *ex officio* members, that is, the Principal, the four Assessors on the University Court and the Clerk of Council, twenty-one were to be elected, seven of whom were to retire annually in order of seniority as members of Committee. The retiring members could be re-elected and might be nominated by the Business Committee, such nominations to be intimated in the Notice of Meeting sent out by the Clerk seven days before the meeting of Council. To these nominations might be added others made by any two members of Council of which notice in writing had to be given to the Clerk not less than fourteen days before the meeting. If nominations exceeded vacancies in numbers, voting was to be by a show of hands at the meeting of Council. An amendment of April 1926, to Standing Orders allowed for the filling of any casual vacancy in the Business Committee by the Business Committee itself. So far as one can gather from the Minutes of the inter-war years, re-nomination and re-election of retiring members by the Business Committee itself was automatic and there is no evidence of competition among the members of the Council for a place on the Committee. How very different this has been in the revolutionary years since the Second World War! These years have seen the abolition of Parliamentary seats for the Universities but an unprecedented interest in the composition of the Business Committee, which more and more has become the tail that wags the dog, and in the Assessorships on the University Court. Lively-minded vigour linked with balanced judgment rather than venerable seniority has become the desirable criterion.

As might be expected at such a time of re-appraisal as followed the First World War, the whole question of University Entrance came up for renewed consideration, as did the composition of the Ordinary Arts degree. For the first time medical students by General Medical Council Regulations, which dealt with many aspects of medical training, had from 1 January 1923, to qualify for University Entrance on the same standard as entrants to Arts and Science. But apart from the fact that a Group Leaving Certificate of the Scottish Education Department or its equivalent was acceptable for matriculation, what exactly the passes endorsed on that certificate should be for any University entrant was a matter of several years of long dispute between the Scottish Universities Entrance Board, born in 1918, and the twelve groups—Court, Senatus and Council in each of the four universities—besides the other bodies it had to satisfy.

In February 1921, the Entrance Board drew up Regulations which, with the idea of unifying minimum requirements for entrance to the different Faculties, recognized for matriculation a Scottish Leaving Certificate which carried four passes, three on a Higher and one on a Lower standard, these passes so arranged as to guarantee a certain " hard core " of intellectual attainment on the part of the candidate. These Regulations met with the approval of the Aberdeen General Council but all four Courts dissented. In June 1921, the Entrance Board issued a second set of Regulations which by specifying certain requirements for Arts, others for Law and others for Science, destroyed the idea of a common minimum basis for all University study. Of these, as of a third set of Regulations issued in 1922 and a fourth set in 1923, the Council resolutely disapproved, re-affirming approval of the original Regulations. When in 1924 the 1923 set of Regulations was disallowed by His Majesty in Council, the Entrance Board had to begin again and in 1925 the Aberdeen General Council had the great satisfaction of finding that the Regulations as finally accepted were substantially the same as the original Regulations of which they had approved. In 1928 an amendment giving the Natural Sciences a place in the possible acceptable Leaving Certificate passes was in keeping with the new educational emphasis of the times. This was followed belatedly in 1930 by a similar adjustment in the Regulations of the Universities' Preliminary Examination. Apart from minor alterations these Regulations remained in force until after the Second World War.

The same desire to safeguard standards and yet to fit in with the changing educational pattern has meant periodic review of the Regulations for the M.A. degree. The eminently readable report of Dr. George Smith, the member of Council to whom the task of investigating the Arts curriculum was entrusted as one of the themes for consideration under the general heading of Post-War Development, was presented to the General Council at the meeting of October 1918. Dr. Smith recalled that the rigid, traditional Arts curriculum fixed by the Ordinances of 1856 and 1861 had been swept away in 1892 when new Regulations of great length and complexity were introduced. It was then obligatory on every candidate to include among his seven basic courses Latin or Greek, Mathematics or Natural Philosophy, Logic or Moral Philosophy, English or a Modern Language or History. The Ordinance of 1908 had removed all these restrictions and the Senatus was entrusted to make from time to time groupings of subjects. In the too-elastic curriculum permissible thereafter no fewer than 617 alternative courses in Arts were open to the Aberdeen student. Dr. Smith suggested that the first half of the curriculum ought to be obligatory on all entrants. English should be compulsory and a fair field should be given to Modern Languages in competition with Latin and Greek. In the second half of the course the student would have to take at least one subject from the Moral Philosophy Department but would otherwise be free to make his own selection of subjects to finish his course.

It was April 1924, before the matter was raised again when a sub-Committee of the Business Committee under the Convenership of Dr. Smith once more reported, re-iterating the opinion that each candidate should study a certain nucleus of basic subjects before entering on the period of options and that every curriculum should begin with school subjects at a University level. Two sketch curricula along these lines were worked out. The General Council made representations accordingly to the University Court. New M.A. Regulations, issued under Court Ordinance by the end of 1925 and to come into force on 1 October 1928, embodied as " the core " Mathematics and Natural Philosophy, Logic or Moral Philosophy, Latin or Greek, English or another Modern Language, and put some restriction on other subjects recognized for the minimum curriculum, it being a cause of " gratification to the General Council " that the new curriculum was " substantially identical with that recommended by the Council ". These Regulations were in force until just before the outbreak of the Second World War in September 1939, a new set of Regulations for the Ordinary M.A. degree made the Course in Mathematics and Natural Philosophy no longer compulsory.

Perhaps the biggest change of all in University development followed the setting up in July 1919, as a Standing Committee of the University Grants Committee, appointed by the Chancellor of the Exchequer " to enquire into the financial needs of University Education in the United Kingdom and to advise the Government as to the application of any

Grants that may be made by Parliament towards meeting them ". This august body, in whose power it has been to grant huge annual sums of money to the Universities, moves on a very different plane from the General Councils, but its reports are communicated to the General Council and extracts from the second Report, received in February 1921, are quoted in the Council's Minutes of that year's April Meeting in so far as they had a bearing on subjects dealt with in Reports by the Business Committee. For example, on the Tenure and Status of University appointments other than those of Professors the Report states the necessity for Lecturers, " no longer to be regarded as merely assistants ", to be given " an effective voice in internal administration and in the regulation of courses of study and of discipline ", and special emphasis is laid on " the importance of adequate status for women teachers ". The need for sufficient salaries and for suitable provision for superannuation is stressed as is the importance of the University's " central organ "—the Library—as well as the important status of the Librarian. Under " Social Needs " the desirability is stressed of properly-equipped Halls of Residence, each to hold about seventy-five students, each of whom would pay from 50 to 60 guineas for an academic year of thirty-two weeks.

At the General Council Meeting of October 1921, the Business Committee submitted to the Council some interesting statistics culled from the 305-page Parliamentary Paper entitled, " Returns from Universities and University Colleges in receipt of Treasury Grant, 1919-1920 ". For instance, the number of students in attendance during 1919-20 was 1,638 compared with 1,069 in 1913-14. Of these about 600 were in Arts, 700 in Medicine and only 100 in Pure Science. More than half of the students lived in lodgings, the cost of which—none lower in the University towns of the British Isles—was from 30s. to 35s. per week. These figures of the post-First World War bulge, impressive at the time, become insignificant when set beside those of more recent years.

Perhaps as good a pointer as any to the changed cost of living in the twenties is the price at which Volume IV of the printed Minutes of the General Council was to be sold. This fourth volume, begun with the meeting of October 1915, is concluded with the meeting of 12 April 1924, thus covering the momentous period of the last three years of the First World War and the early years of adaptation to post-war conditions. In the first Minute of Volume V it is stated that a copy of the completed volume " will be sent to each member of the Business Committee and as far as possible to any member of the General Council that pays five shillings to the Clerk "—twice the cost of the earlier volumes!

VIII. THE LATER TWENTIES AND THE THIRTIES

It was in September 1925, that, following his letter on the same subject published in the *Aberdeen Press and Journal* in the summer of 1925, Dr. J. M. Bulloch wrote from London to the Clerk of the General Council, Mr.

P. J. Anderson, suggesting that " Colonel Johnston's wonderfully well-done ' Roll of Graduates, 1860-1900 ' " should be brought up to date. The Business Committee in October 1925, recommended that the General Council should represent to the University Court the desirability of having such a Supplementary Roll prepared and printed. A few weeks later the Court authorized the preparation and printing of a supplement covering the years 1901 to 1925 and appointed Mr. Alexander Macdonald, retired headmaster of Durris Crossroads School, to be Editor. Very soon thereafter failing health forced Mr. Macdonald to give up the task and Mr. Theodore Watt was appointed Honorary Editor. Mr. Watt accepted the post with the stipulation that in addition to compiling the Roll for 1901-25, he should be authorized to revise the Roll for 1860-1900 and bring it up to date. The Court very gladly agreed to this condition and it was accordingly decided that the new Roll should consist of two main parts—the first and larger part complementary to Colonel Johnston's Roll, containing a brief record of all who graduated between 1 January 1901, and 31 December 1925; and the other part, supplementary to Colonel Johnston's Roll, containing the names, with additional annotations, of all Graduates mentioned in that Roll and not recorded in it as having died before the date of its publication in 1906.

When Mr. Watt started work in January 1927, on the Roll, he had behind him the experience of similar work, having edited the *Aberdeen Grammar School Roll of Pupils, 1795-1919* published in 1923. He began work on the Roll in January 1927, and for nearly nine years devoted to it all available time apart from his full business life. Completed in 1935, the Roll recorded 3,280 of the 4,360 names for the period 1860 to 1900, and 4,539 entries, nearly all annotated, for the new period, 1901 to 1925, 7,819 names in all. Marriages were recorded, references made to records of war service in the University Roll of Service as well as to obituary notices in the *Aberdeen University Review*. Appendices added other information of interest, such as an analysis of professions or occupations of graduates, an analysis of degrees conferred between 1901 and 1925, a record of Honours, including war honours, a record of money gifts by graduates to the University and the names of Honorary graduates from 1901 to 1925.

The generosity of the University Court in helping to defray expenses made it possible for the volume to be sold to subscribers for 10s. and to non-subscribers for 12s. 6d. Much appreciated at the time of its publication, this " monumental work "—to quote the Business Committee's report to the General Council in April 1936—has enjoyed great popularity in the generation since its publication and continues to be a work of constant reference among Aberdeen graduates and others.

In November 1924, two men who had given long and distinguished service to the General Council died. The Rev. James Smith had been a member of the Business Committee since 1891 and had served for six years, from 1915 till 1921, as an Assessor on the University Court.

Mr. D. M. M. Milligan, appointed to the Business Committee in 1892, was its Convener from 1909 and had served as Assessor on the University Court from 1921.

The Business Committee suffered further loss with the death in December 1929, of Dr. John Scott Riddell, who as well as being distinguished surgeon, Territorial soldier, athlete and scholar, gave of his services to the General Council, as a member of its Business Committee and as an Assessor on the University Court from 1916.

The death of Mr. P. J. Anderson, M.A., LL.B., Clerk of the General Council, in May 1926, was sincerely mourned at all levels of University life, for, to quote Professor Rait, Mr. Anderson " was the University ". A member of the General Council since his graduation in 1872, he joined the Business Committee in April 1886, and was its senior member at the time of his death. He succeeded Dr. Robert Walker in three capacities— as Librarian in 1894, as Clerk to the General Council in 1907—he had acted as interim Clerk as far back as 1892—as Registrar to the University in 1918. During the forty years of his association with the General Council he took an important part in most of the special projects of the Council— the various movements that led up to and followed upon the Universities (Scotland) Act, 1889, being the authority on the Ordinances arising therefrom; the promotion of the degree in Education, the campaign for the improved status of Lecturers. He prepared in 1908 the valuable and interesting Note on the Evolution of the Arts Curriculum and was joint-author with Mr. Henry Alexander of the 1923 Report on the M.A. Hood with its interesting information on the evolution of academic dress. He further made history in the University in July 1892, when he sat on the University Court as Rector's Assessor, by carrying a motion which allowed women to graduate in all Faculties of the University of Aberdeen. As Convener of the Publications Committee at the time of the Quatercentenary Celebrations in 1906, he edited *Studies in the History and Development of the University of Aberdeen* and other kindred works. For many years he was a most vital member of the Committee of the General Council's *Aberdeen University Review*. For some who never knew P. J. Anderson except as an honoured name, he is immortalized as the Bajan of the Scarlet Gown, and a print of Sir George Reid's water colour hangs in many a study the world over.

When Mr. Anderson was appointed Clerk on 10 April 1907, the Minute of the General Council stated as one of his duties " To draw the attention of the Business Committee to all questions coming to his knowledge affecting the well-being and prosperity of the University ". During his nineteen years as Clerk, ever watchful and most keenly and lovingly interested, he inspired much of the achievement of the General Council.

He was succeeded in all three offices—Librarian, Registrar and Clerk to the General Council—by Wm. Douglas Simpson, M.A., D.LITT.

A sub-committee of the Business Committee, set up to consider a memorial to Mr. P. J. Anderson proposed a two-fold scheme—a commemorative tablet in the Library and a Memorial Lectureship. The response to the appeal made both suggestions practicable. An oak tablet designed by Dr. Wm. Kelly, the Latin inscription thereon composed by Professor Souter, was set up in the Library and on 12 February 1932, it was unveiled by Dr. J. M. Bulloch " in the presence of a large and distinguished company ". Colonel E. W. Watt, Convener of the Memorial Committee, presided and others who spoke were the Principal, the Convener of the Business Committee (the Rev. Gordon J. Murray) and Principal Rait of Glasgow University. In addition, a sum of more than £346 was handed over to the University Court for the endowment of a P. J. Anderson Memorial Lectureship. A lecture under the Fund was to be delivered every three years, the proposed field being the whole subject of University Education both past and present, with special emphasis upon the history of our own University, a theme of life-long interest for Mr. Anderson. The University Court generously decided to contribute the fee of the first Lecturer so that the whole sum available in the Memorial Fund might be invested. The first lecture was delivered in the autumn of 1932 by Principal R. S. Rait, of Glasgow University— an early disciple of Mr. Anderson—his subject being " The Place of Aberdeen in Scottish Academic History ". The most recent lecture of the series was delivered in the autumn of 1960 by Dr. Leslie J. Macfarlane, on the theme of Bishop Elphinstone.

Since April 1907, no meeting had been held of the University Endowment Association founded by the General Council in 1896. Indeed, since its contribution of £1,000 to the Foundation of the Burnett-Fletcher Chair of History and Archaeology, its activities had fallen into abeyance, the purposes for which the Association had been founded having been largely taken over by the Carnegie Trust. By 1926 the funds of the Association had accumulated to the amount of £1067 and the surviving representatives were asked by the University Court to hand over this sum towards the endowment of the Forestry Chair. At a meeting of the Association held immediately before the General Council Meeting of 17 April 1926, it was resolved to hand over to the University Court the sum of £300 towards the Endowment of the Chair of Forestry. In addition the sum of £450, bequeathed by the late Dr. David Mackie in 1911, along with interest accrued, was also handed over to the Court with the request that the Court would carry out the conditions attaching to the legacy—" for the purpose of founding a Bursary in the Faculty of Science ".

Evidently the terms of the foundation of the Endowment Association made it impossible for the whole of its assets to be handed over for the endowment of a Chair. Nothing further is recorded of the Association in the Council's Minutes until December 1939, when the Secretary, Mr. Patrick Cooper, who along with the Lord Provost, a Vice-President ex officio, was the sole survivor of the Board of Management, wrote to the

Clerk of the Council, suggesting that as the Association had ceased to function, its funds, now standing at £129 10s. 5d., should be handed over to the recently-formed Aberdeen University Alumnus Association, as such would fall under the objects of the Endowment Association. The General Council agreed that the affairs of the Endowment Association should be so concluded, and Mr. Patrick Cooper who had been Secretary of the Association since its inception was cordially thanked for his services.

The 1929 Union of the Churches—the Parish Kirk and the United Free Kirk in Scotland—healing in the main the rupture of 1843, and the discussions throughout the preceding years impinged upon the business of the General Council. The systems of the two Churches as regards the Training for the Ministry had certain well-marked distinctions. Broadly speaking, the Divinity Professors of the Church of Scotland, while subject to the discipline of the Church and partly paid by the Church, were Professors in the University, accepting the responsibilities and enjoying the status and the rights of all other University Professors, while in the United Free Church the Professors were appointed and controlled and their stipends paid wholly by the Church. It was obvious that much delicate adjustment would be necessary.

Realizing the importance of the working out of a nice balance between authority of University and Church, the Business Committee in October 1927, asked successfully from the General Council a remit to consider the whole question which at that time was being discussed in all four University Courts. It has happened quite often in the century of life of the General Council, that interested experts on its Business Committee have been able to throw fresh light on some intricate matter. Until 1931 the Business Committee kept, as it were, a watching brief and when in January of that year a copy of the proposed Churches' Bill—Universities (Scotland) Act, 1930—was sent by the University Court to the General Council for comment, the text was meticulously considered and recommendations made for insertions and omissions. The University Court approved substantially of these recommendations and it was a source of gratification to the Business Committee that the Bill before Parliament in the spring of 1932 embodied the recommendations proposed by the Committee and approved by the Council the year before. When in the autumn of 1933 the University Courts of St. Andrews and Glasgow protested against certain aspects of the Aberdeen Ordinance governing the new Theological Chairs arising out of the Union, the Business Committee, maintaining its watchful interest, intimated its entire approval of the stand taken by the Aberdeen Court, and in the following year its gratification when " an agreement satisfactory to all parties " had been reached. This welcome harmony in the relations between Court and Council over the Universities (Scotland) Act, 1932 and its aftermath was very different from the state of tension and disagreement over the previous Universities (Scotland) Act of 1922.

On 18 January 1928, the Chancellor of the University, His Grace the Duke of Richmond and Gordon, LL.D. died at his home at Goodwood in his eighty-third year.

Following the precedent set by the General Council in October 1903, April 1914, and April 1917, the Business Committee co-opted for arranging the nomination of a new Chancellor any members of the General Council on the University Court in addition to the Rector, the Lord Provost, the Rector's Assessor and the Town Council's Assessor and from the Senatus Academicus the Deans of the Faculties of Arts, Science, Divinity, Law and Medicine. This augmented Committee of thirty-nine nominated as Chancellor one of our own graduates, the Rt. Hon. Baron Meston of Agra and Dunnottar, K.C.S.I., V.D., LL.D., whose election was upheld at the General Council Meeting of 21 April 1928. The installation of the new Chancellor took place at an adjourned meeting of the General Council in the Mitchell Hall on 3 July 1928, and was followed as was customary by the graduation ceremony.

It is always a sign of a certain harmony of mood and expansiveness of spirit when, in the life of a corporate body as in the life of an individual, opportunity can be taken for celebration. This would appear to be true of the University when, a measure of rhythm re-established after the adjustments immediately following the war, plans were made in 1930 to celebrate the Quincentenary of the birth in 1431 of its Founder, Bishop Elphinstone. The suggestion of the appropriateness of such celebration was made to the University Court by the Business Committee of the General Council, and a Joint Committee of the Court, the Ceremonials Committee, and the General Council made the detailed arrangements. The Business Committee suggested that the Summer Term might be more appropriate than earlier in the year and accordingly the dates agreed on were 4 and 5 June 1931. The celebration opened appropriately on the Thursday with the dedication of the memorial to Bishop Elphinstone in the Ante-Chapel. Then followed the opening by Lord Meston, the Chancellor, of the New Elphinstone Hall—a notable contribution in University building to post-First World War expansion.

On the Friday the laureation of Honorary Graduands in the forenoon was followed in the afternoon by a Garden Party at King's College to which members of the University, including students, were invited. A dinner attended by 350 men was held in the Elphinstone Hall in the evening. Not officially arranged in advance, a dinner for women graduates of whom 170 were present was held co-incidentally with the men's dinner. The Minutes of the General Council record that " complete success marked all the proceedings ".

On 16 October 1936, the Quatercentenary of the death of the first Principal of the University, Hector Boece, was also marked. Hector Boece, a native of Dundee, completed his education in Paris from where he was called by Bishop Elphinstone to be the first Principal of his new foundation, the College of St. Mary in the Nativity within the University of Aberdeen, otherwise known as King's College.   The celebration on this occasion was on a smaller scale, being confined to one day.   In the morning a lecture was given by the University Librarian, Dr. W. Douglas Simpson;   thereafter a short commemorative service in the Chapel was followed by a lunch to which representative persons were invited.   In the afternoon an exhibition of books written by or belonging to Hector Boece or associated with him and his colleagues was on show in the Library.   After tea, Professor Black of the Chair of History gave a lecture on Boece's position as a writer of history.

Apart from a reference to a restoration made in 1936 by the Chancellor of the Exchequer to the University Grants Committee of the sum of £150,000 " set aside out of the 1930-31 grant allocation which was surrendered to the Exchequer ", the records of the General Council bear little direct evidence of the financial crisis of the year 1931 but some re-adjustment of various aspects of money matters may indicate the national concern with ways and means throughout the early years of the thirties. For instance, while the fees of necessitous students were paid in full, demands on the Carnegie Trust for grants towards students' fees had to be restricted by the insistence that grantees should enter the University with more than the minimum qualification for matriculation.   From October 1932, three passes on the Higher level at Leaving Certificate or Preliminary Examination were required.   In 1932, a new Ordinance was framed, giving the Senatus " discretion from time to time to amalgamate bursaries of small value "—a necessary result of the changing value of money and accepted as such by the General Council.   But the crude and " spoliatory proposals ", and the intended " wholesale plunder ", of the Educational Endowments (Scotland) Commissioners brought spirited protest from the General Council and an assurance to the University Court of " its utmost support in the resistance which it is making to the schemes of the Com-missioners ".   It was fitting that the motion of protest fervently made and strongly supported at the General Council Meeting of April 1934, and forwarded thereafter to the University representatives in Parliament should have been made by Dr. C. S. MacPherson, Rector of Banff Academy, for the well-endowed County of Banff was threatened with serious loss because of the unimaginative policy of the Commissioners. Indeed, the result of the schemes of the Commissioners would have, by diverting the money to public funds which might be used for " such grotesque items as free seats at entertainments and free trips to zoos ", deprived the students of Aberdeen University alone " of the certainty of receiving the sum of no less than £1,574 " annually.   At the end of 1934, such had been the storm of protest throughout the whole country, the powers of the Commissioners were somewhat restricted and the battle against their depredations was largely won by the end of 1935.   As late as the autumn of 1936, however, the Scottish Education Department rescued for the University another substantial bursary from being merged in the general fund to be handed over to the Aberdeen County Council.

In 1934 the Business Committee were " much gratified to report " that under the title of *The Four Nations of Aberdeen University and their European Background*, an interesting and scholarly work about a subject of which no adequate account had appeared in English, and written by Mr. W. M. Alexander, was published as a University Study. The idea for such a piece of work had arisen out of a motion put to the General Council Meeting of April 1932. Like his brother, later Sir Henry Alexander who became Provost of Aberdeen in 1933, whom Mr. Wm. Alexander succeeded as a member of the Business Committee, he most willingly put his aptitude for historical research at the services of the General Council and as recently as 1957 prepared at the suggestion of the Convener (Mr. John N. Milne) of the Business Committee an interesting memorandum on the Order of Precedence of the Faculties, submitted to the Statutory Meeting of Council on 28 December of that year.

Perhaps the most notable event of the nineteen-thirties in the history of the University was the change of Principal. At the end of October 1935, Sir George Adam Smith retired after twenty-six years of outstanding service. The Business Committee, reporting to the General Council at the meeting of that month and conveying to Sir George and Lady Adam Smith the good wishes of the General Council, commented: " For the General Council, consisting as it does of the whole body of graduates of the University, the predominant feeling, on the present occasion, will be one of profound thankfulness that our Alma Mater has been so greatly favoured of fortune as to enjoy the guidance, through so long and in many respects so critical a period, of a man gifted with such rich and out-standing qualities of heart and mind and soul as Sir George Adam Smith."

By a happy chance the news of the appointment as successor to Sir George Adam Smith of Dr. William Hamilton Fyfe, Principal and Vice-Chancellor of Queen's University, Kingston, Ontario since 1930, was announced on the morning of the General Council's Statutory Meeting of October 1935, and it was agreed to send a cablegram conveying to Dr. and Mrs. Hamilton Fyfe loyal greetings and the assurance of a hearty welcome from the General Council. At the meeting of 18 April 1936, at which Dr. Fyfe was present, he was bid welcome in person and again promised the loyal co-operation of the General Council.

Perhaps one penalty of the growth in importance and power of the Business Committee and its almost closed-shop method of elections had been a lessening of interest among the rank and file of the General Council. Whatever the reason—and it may have been merely the mood of the times—the thirties brought among some graduates stirrings of dissatisfaction with the opportunities to keep in touch with each other and with the University. As not all graduates are punctilious in keeping the University informed of changes of address, it has always been difficult to keep the Register of the General Council up to date, and with the cessation of Parliamentary elections, which always brought in hundreds of corrections, the difficulty has become much more acute. Yet even before this, by 1931 the Register was badly in need of revision and the Business Committee itself had prickings of conscience about this. Among the seven to eight thousand names on the Roll, several hundreds had faulty addresses and many deaths had not been noted. The unsatisfactory state of the records caused the Business Committee to appoint a sub-committee for the purpose of overhauling the Register. During the First World War notices of General Council Meetings had been sent only to those resident in the Counties of Aberdeen, Banff and Kincardine. In May 1925, the University Court sanctioned the extension of this area to include the whole of the North of Scotland and Orkney and Shetland and five years later, in May 1930, further agreed to the sending of notices of the Half-Yearly Meetings to all graduates resident in the British Isles.

In a letter of March 1933, to the Clerk of the General Council, the Secretary of the University, Mr. H. J. Butchart, writing as a private individual, raised the matter of the dates of the Meetings, asking the Business Committee to consider, with the idea of enabling a larger number of graduates to be present and perhaps arranging class re-unions and " other social and athletic events ", changing the dates of the half-yearly meetings to coincide with the Christmas and summer vacations. Not until October of the following year did the Business Committee report that there was " no sufficient reason meantime " for any alteration of the dates of statutory meetings. In February 1935, Mr. Butchart repeated his suggestion but again the Business Committee did not agree that any alteration of dates would improve attendance. Mr. Butchart's insistence evidently had effect, however, for at the meeting of April 1938, the Business Committee gave notice of motion " that, subject to the approval of the University Court, the two ordinary meetings of the General Council would be held respectively on the Saturday following the last day of the Winter Term, and the Saturday preceding the annual Summer Graduation ". Standing Orders accordingly amended, the first July meeting of the Council was held in 1939.

Over the years of discussion of these changes of dates of meetings, the idea of an Alumnus Association had been canvassed. As early as November 1933, the Yorkshire Aberdeen University Graduates' Society, which over many years has been a very healthy limb of the General Council, forwarded to the University Court a resolution suggesting the formation of an Alumnus Association. And earlier that year, largely owing to the initiative and enthusiasm of Mr. G. B. Esslemont, who wrote to the Clerk of the Council in April 1932, and spoke on the matter at the statutory meeting in October 1932, a Graduates' Athletic Club was created, a project which the Business Committee commended to the " sympathetic attention " of all General Council members.

The final impetus towards the creation of an Alumnus Association would appear to have come from the failing strength of the *University Review*. The statutory meeting of April 1937, considered a letter from

Mr. Theodore Watt, Secretary of the *Review* Committee, in which was suggested, as a means of placing the *Review* on a sound financial basis, the formation of an Alumnus Association, the subscription to which, would cover the cost of sending a copy of the *Review* regularly to each member. A Sub-Committee of the Business Committee, appointed to consider this important proposal, wrote to the Secretaries of all Aberdeen University Clubs in the country; and, encouraged by the nature of the replies received, proceeded to send to all graduates a circular letter, over the Principal's signature, inviting them to become members of the Alumnus Association. By July 1939, about 1,100 graduates had joined the Association which was formally constituted at a meeting held in Marischal College on 6 March 1939, with the Principal as President and Mr. Leslie J. Smith, as Honorary Secretary and Treasurer. The Alumnus Association took over responsibility for the *Aberdeen University Review* whose Committee of Management accordingly lapsed and its assets were handed over to the new Association as later were the assets of the lapsed Endowments Association. A leaflet enclosed with the print sent out for the meeting of July 1939, set forth the main objects of the Alumnus Association—to maintain contact between its members and the University of Aberdeen; to promote educational and social intercourse among its members; to diffuse information regarding the wants of the University; to further the welfare of the University by supporting through any means in its power its further extension and better endowment and by promoting its efficiency as a seat of learning in any way agreed upon by the Association in general meeting; and to further the welfare of the members of the Association. All Aberdeen University Clubs were affiliated to the main body and could be represented on the Management Committee.

The new Association was entertained by the University to a reception in the form of a Garden Party held at King's College on Saturday, 8 July 1939. The outbreak of the Second World War within two months of this happy occasion froze the activities of the Alumnus Association; but since the later forties the Association has been in vigorous life, particularly successful having been the Winter Programme of Lectures for members in or near Aberdeen. These and the *Review* sent regularly to members anywhere anywhere in the world have been excellent value for the modest annual subscription originally of 7s. 6d., raised after the war to 10s. and to 15s. only in 1958.

By the death on 14 October 1937, of Emeritus Professor Sir Ashley W. Mackintosh, the General Council lost a much valued representative on the University Court. After a career of great distinction as medical practitioner in Aberdeen, promoter of the Joint Hospitals Scheme, Professor of Medicine in the University, he joined the Business Committee in 1930 and was in the same year elected as one of the Council's Assessors on the Court. His services in that capacity were especially valuable as he already had the experience of sitting on the Court as a representative of the Senatus up to the time of his retiral.

Three other matters of interest are referred to, two briefly and one at greater length, in the records of the General Council in the years immediately preceding the outbreak of war in September 1939. In April 1937, the Business Committee, while still urging the provision of a Residence for Students, noted " with satisfaction " that the building of the new Union, opposite Marischal College had been taken in hand. In 1938, the Senatus Academicus proposed the extension of the Medical curriculum from fifteen to seventeen terms. And in that same year new regulations for the Entrance Bursary Competition came into force. The main changes in these were that, in addition to candidates from the north of Scotland being able to take the examination in Inverness and the initiation of a four-subject examination, from a choice of fifteen subjects, with an optional higher paper in one of the four selected subjects, the names of successful candidates only were to be published and these without any order of merit; and marks were not to be given to candidates. The allocation of bursaries immediately the results were ascertained superseded the old method of personal attendance of candidates for the allocation of bursaries on the day before the opening of the Winter Term. The Bursary Competition has always been so much bound up with tradition and sentiment in the north-east of Scotland that no change has ever been made without rousing strong protest and on this occasion graduates from as far away as China wrote with feeling on the matter. The New Regulations, however, were generally acceptable as more in keeping with the educational trends of the times and these have been in force without change since 1938. But the fact that the letter of protest has been recorded among the proceedings of the Council is proof that the General Council welcomes and values expression of opinion from its members.

IX.   THE YEARS OF THE SECOND WORLD WAR AND AFTER

The fact that the records of General Council business from December 1939, to June 1946 are contained in a very slim volume consisting of about two dozen pages of typescript speaks for itself. A special meeting of the Council held on 15 June 1940—probably in an atmosphere of sad anxiety at this dark hour in the country's history—agreed that, in compliance with the University Court Emergency Ordinance following upon powers conferred by the Chartered and Other Bodies (Temporary Provisions) Act, 1939, the duties of the General Council of the University of Aberdeen would be discharged by the Business Committee of the General Council. By the smaller body's acting for the larger, which it would have been difficult and expensive to convene, it was possible not to call Statutory meetings of the General Council during the emergency. Further saving of time and money was effected by not printing during the war the General Council list of members in the *University Calendar*. No Statutory meeting of the General Council was called after December 1939 until

December 1943. While the Business Committee had decided that the Statutory half-yearly meetings ought then to be resumed, to save paper, postage and labour, meetings until the emergency was over were called by newspaper advertisement and no print of the business was distributed. The main matter of discussion before this meeting—indeed, probably the reason, along with the fact that war clouds were lifting, for the resumption of the Statutory meetings—was the question of a successor to the Chancellor, Lord Meston, who had died earlier in the year.

The Business Committee had before the Council meeting convened the enlarged Committee composed as on the previous four occasions and this Committee had decided that the election of a Chancellor should be deferred until the following 1 October, a decision approved by the Business Committee. Such a postponement, if agreed to by the General Council, required of the University Court an Emergency Ordinance empowering the office of Chancellor to ke kept vacant. Opinion was divided as to whether the election should be proceeded with or delayed. The decision to delay was made and the Court Ordinance enabled the vacancy to remain during the war. By December 1944, however, the Business Committee's recommendation was to proceed with an election.

At the Statutory meeting of the Council on 23 June 1945, the name of Field Marshal the Rt. Hon. the Viscount Wavell, P.C., G.C.B., G.C.S.I., G.C.I.E., C.M.G., M.C., Viceroy of India, was put forward and his election unanimously agreed upon. Lord Wavell accepted the office and his Installation on Saturday, 25 October 1947, on his return from India was the first notable ceremonial occasion in the University after the end of the Second World War. Mr. John N. Milne who had in June 1946, succeeded Dr. George Duncan as Convener of the Business Committee, Dr. Duncan having held that office for four years after the death of Dr. Gordon Murray in 1942, presented the new Chancellor in an admirable speech happily preserved in the records of the Council. The Vice-Chancellor then tendered to the Chancellor-elect the oath in English, superseding the Latin form hitherto in use, in these terms:

I solemnly declare as Chancellor of the University of Aberdeen, that I will faithfully fulfil the duties of my office, and will at all times do all that is in my power to preserve the rights, the interests and the reputation of this University to which, as my Alma Mater, I hereby declare my fealty and allegiance.

Thereafter the new Chancellor in a charmingly whimsical address based largely on the theme of cricket, set the seal on a memorable occasion. A further memento of the installation is the ballad with its refrain " I left my shaving brush in Aberdeen ", which Lord Wavell sent to the Principal and which was published in the *University Review*.

Lord Wavell's death on 24 May 1950, less than three years after his installation was a matter for deep regret. As the Business Committee reported, in the short space of time that he had been Chancellor " he had won for himself a distinctive place in the esteem and affection of the University, not only by his appearances at Graduations and other public ceremonies, but also by his vigilant action in support of her interests on more than one occasion ".

The limited records of the General Council during the war years and immediately thereafter do not make on the whole very lively reading. One interesting feature of the new stirring of life as the wartime paralysis passes is the interest shown in the elections, both those for Assessorships on the University Court and for places on the Business Committee. At the meeting of 23 December 1939, Colonel Dawson and Dr. A. G. Anderson were returned unopposed as Assessors for a further four years' term of office. But in the next recorded election for Assessors in December 1943, Colonel Dawson did not seek re-election and two heads of schools in Aberdeen stood along with Dr. A. G. Anderson for the two seats. Miss B. M. Rose, headmistress of the High School, who in April 1937, had drawn the attention of the Council to the fact that there was no woman on the governing bodies of the Scottish Universities and who had in November of that year seconded the nomination of Dr. Mary Esslemont, stood, as did Mr. John W. Robertson, head of Aberdeen Central Secondary School. Evidently the time was not yet ripe, however, for the election of a woman Assessor and by the vote taken by a show of hands at the meeting Dr. A. G. Anderson was re-elected and Mr. John Robertson chosen to fill the other vacancy. No request was made for a postal vote.

In December 1945, three candidates again stood for two vacant Assessorships, caused by the expiry of the term of office of Dr. George Duncan and Dr. Theodore Watt, both of whom had been elected by the Business Committee acting under Emergency Order No. 3, on 7 January 1942, for a period of four years. The vote taken by a show of hands returned both Dr. Duncan and Dr. Watt and the seconder of the unsuccessful candidate demanded a postal vote. Withdrawn before the machinery went into operation, this demand, which would have required the exercise of the University Court's wartime emergency powers to lengthen the period of the postal vote because of Christmas and New Year holidays revealed one of the difficulties following upon the altered dates of meetings. Accordingly, with the sanction of the Court, the election of Assessors was changed in June 1946, except when a casual vacancy occurs, to the summer meeting of the Council although the elections for the Business Committee continue to be held at the end of the year.

It was the occurrence of a casual vacancy through the death in July 1946, of Dr. Theodore Watt which led to the election of the first woman to serve on Aberdeen University Court. Dr. Mary Esslemont, defeated in 1937, was one of two who stood for the vacancy in December 1946. She won a resounding victory both in the vote taken at the meeting and in the following postal vote when she rolled a majority of nearly 3,000 votes. In 1960 Dr. Esslemont remains the only woman on the University Court.

In July 1949, Dr. A. G. Anderson and Mr. J. W. Robertson were

9

returned unopposed as Assessors on the University Court and in 1950 Dr. Mary Esslemont and Mr. John N. Milne, who had succeeded without challenge to the casual vacancy caused by the death of Dr. Duncan in September 1949, were also returned without contest.

A great burst of interest was shown in the later war years in the Business Committee elections. At the December 1939 meeting of the Council, as with the Assessorships, there was no contest, seven nominations being made for seven vacancies. It is to be presumed that between 1939 and 1943 the Business Committee remained more or less static, in its composition. At the next Statutory meeting, however, held on 18 December 1943, when four of the seven retiring members did not seek re-election, six nominations were received for the vacancies in addition to the nominations for the other three retiring members. With these numbers voting by a show of hands would have been confusing and Standing Orders were suspended to enable the voting to be done by means of slips of paper, a proceeding necessarily repeated quite often since. Again in the following year nine nominations were lodged for seven seats, a situation repeated in December 1945. Apart from the year 1948, when eight candidates stood for seven seats, there was no contest for ten years, until, in June 1956, two casual vacancies had to be filled and three nominations were made. A further burst of interest came in December 1956, when no fewer than twelve nominations were made for the seven vacant seats. Only in 1958 has the number of nominations exceeded the number of vacancies. In that year Mr. John Mackintosh, Editor of the Roll of Graduates, was elected to fill the vacancy created by the death of Mr. W. M. Alexander.

This healthy post-war interest in the work of the Business Committee which has grown steadily in authority and vitality over the years brought to light a fault in election procedure. The regulations require that fourteen days' notice must be given by any two members of Council desiring to nominate a member; but the members of the Council did not receive intimation that an election was pending until the printed agenda, sent out only seven days before the Statutory meeting, reached them. This printed notice, discontinued during the war years, was sent out again for the 166th Statutory meeting of the General Council held on Saturday, 21 December 1946. The lateness of the information had had the effect of perpetuating the practice whereby the Business Committee elected its own members. Asked at the meeting of December 1945, to consider this position, the Business Committee recommended that one month's clear notice be given by advertisement in *The Scotsman*, the *Glasgow Herald* and the *Aberdeen Press and Journal* of any meeting where an election is to take place; that the advertisement state the names of the retiring members and indicate the rights of members of the Council in regard to nominations. This, the present practice, has had the desired effect of keeping alive interest in the composition and the proceedings of the Business Committee and of encouraging a flow of fresh blood into it.

The procedure for electing a Chancellor and for electing Assessors was also considered as part of the General Council's post-war New Look. A conference of the four General Councils held at Perth on 14 October 1946 agreed that the written consent of the candidate for the office of Chancellor or Assessor should be required; that all such nominations in writing should be intimated to the Clerk three weeks before the date of election and at least four weeks' notice of the nomination date given to graduates by advertisement in the press; that the time allowed for the candidate to withdraw after the election meeting should be extended from three to five days; and that, if a poll is required, the Registrar should be allowed up to three weeks for the simultaneous despatch of voting papers to graduates resident in Great Britain and Northern Ireland. A further recommendation, later invalidated, was that no person over seventy years of age should be elected or re-elected as an Assessor. These changes required a new Ordinance which was not passed until 1949.

The official end of the war in 1945 brought consideration of a fitting War Memorial. When the Edilis Committee invited the opinion of the Business Committee, they suggested that the lower panels of the Memorial to the Fallen of the First World War in the Ante-Chapel should be used for the names of those who fell in the Second World War—about half the number. The " foliaceous enrichment on the stiles " between the upper panels should be continued on the lower stiles and the necessary alterations made in the commemorative inscription over the West Door. A Latin text introducing the second series of names should be added on the horizontal band between the two series of panels. The Book of Remembrance to be displayed in the Shrine should include both sets of names. An appeal to graduates and alumni would provide a fund to enable the work to be done. The recommendations were made on the assumption that the Elphinstone Memorial, too large for the Ante-Chapel, would be removed. The University Court adopted the recommendations of the Business Committee and in June 1946, the Business Committee could report, that the Cenotaph of Bishop Elphinstone had " been removed from the Ante-Chapel, and erected outside the west front of the Chapel ". There with space to give its proportions fitting dignity, the oversize memorial had at last found a suitable setting. The appropriateness of its present position happily gives no indication of the vicissitudes attendant upon its creation and erection.

When the work on the War Memorial was completed the Business Committee reported that it had been " dedicated on Remembrance Sunday, 9 November 1952, in the presence of a great company representing the University and relatives and friends of the fallen." The names of 180 sons of the University who fell in the Second World War have been added on the blank panels below those of the former war and in the niches on either side of the western door have been placed figures of St. Andrew of Scotland and of the Archangel Michael. A finely bound copy of the

Roll of Honour of both wars lies in the Shrine and is available for consultation by all interested. Another copy, similarly bound, is in King's College Library.

" The General Council, as representing the whole body of graduates of the University, has been closely identified from the outset with this matter of the University's Memorial to her gallant fallen. The Business Committee feels that the Council will desire to express its appreciation of the manner in which the University Court has carried out this beautiful and dignified commemoration of the sacrifice of those to whom their Alma Mater and their country owe so much."

In the later forties as in the early twenties, the new life of a post-war generation made itself evident in the changes and adaptations required in the provision of University education. A spate of new Ordinances and alterations to Regulations reflected something of the social revolution of the mid-twentieth century. The extension of University learning and teaching to include a wider section of the community and to meet the needs of the new scientific age as well as to ease the now highly sensitive social conscience had its echoes in the business before the General Council. Provision for teaching in psychology and research in mental health, the deepening and broadening of teaching in Science, the endowment of new Chairs—in Geography, German, Jurisprudence, Social Medicine—the extension of old Departments, the initiation of new Lectureships, changes in direction such as were revealed in the new emphasis on Scottish History and Scottish Literature—all suggest vigorous growth and rapid development, with raised fees as a reminder of new money values. The extension of the medical curriculum to six years roused vigorous objection among the medical members of the Business Committee whose " reasoned statement " was presented to the University Court. The General Council, however, at its Statutory meeting of 3 July 1948, did not adopt this report and the Court was informed accordingly—a proof that the General Council does not always accept the recommendations of its Business Committee.

The shift in educational direction in the schools as well as in the Universities brought new University Entrance Regulations, drafted, revised, changed several times within the ten years from 1944, each new proposal rousing lively comment in which the General Council took a full and influential share. Much of the discussion turned upon the position of History and Geography and also the ever-increasing stress on scientific requirements. The regulations of 1949 were replaced by those of 1955, which, still in force in 1960, laid down as minimum requirement for entrance to the Universities either four passes on a Higher Grade or three Higher passes and two Lower passes, the subjects to be selected on a restricted basis and the passes gained at no more than two sittings of examination. The proposed introduction in 1962 by the Scottish Education Department of a new Ordinary Grade Examination makes necessary further changes in Entrance Regulations. These have already appeared in draft form and were approved by the General Council in July 1959. The Council also gave approval in June 1958 to an Ordinance which reconstituted the Scottish Universities Entrance Board and made the University Preliminary Examination rather than the Leaving Certificate the principal criterion of fitness for admission to a University, a complete reversal of the position in 1916 when the need for the Preliminary Examination was being questioned.

The constantly increasing non-professorial staff in the University— almost trebled in number between 1945 and 1950—became again restive after the war. In 1946, the Business Committee on their behalf asked the University Court to obtain an opinion of Counsel as to whether it was competent for a member of the teaching staff, other than Professors, to act as Assessors of the General Council on the University Court. The affirmative answer led to the proposal in 1948 by the Aberdeen Association of University Teachers that the non-senatorial staff should be represented by two Assessors on the University Court. The Association, seeking the co-operation of the General Council in this matter, were invited to present their case to the Statutory meeting of July 1948. Having heard a statement by Mr. Ralph S. Walker, the Council decided to champion the cause of the Association and accordingly intimated to the University Court their approval of this proposal. The Court replied that the matter of the representation of non-senatorial members of the University staff on the University Court would be raised at the next suitable Inter-University Conference. Two Ordinances of the fifties, one on the Composition of the Faculties, the other on the Admission of Readers and Lecturers as Members of the Senatus Academicus, have been moves in the right direction.

The P. J. Anderson Memorial Lectureship had lapsed during the war years. Indeed, the Advisory Committee provided for in the letter of gift of September 1931 had never been set up. This was remedied in 1947 and the first lecture thereafter under the terms of the foundation was given by Dr. Douglas Simpson in February 1948, the subject being " Gavin Dunbar, Second Founder of the University ".

A special Service for the General Council held in King's College Chapel on the last Sunday of June 1949, was an innovation which has been repeated each year, a special feature being that the preacher on the occasion is a distinguished member of the General Council.

Besides war casualties and the death of two Chancellors, the General Council suffered other losses in the war years and afterwards. Sir Henry Alexander's death in 1940 was mourned by the University, whose service occupied a prominent place in his " singularly full and many-sided life ".

In December of the following year, Dr. Gordon M. Murray, who had succeeded Mr. D. M. M. Milligan as Convener of the Business Committee, died. The Business Committee put on record that with Dr. Murray's death the University " lost a son who served her with a zeal and loyalty in which few have equalled him ".

9*

The same might be said of Dr. Theodore Watt, who in July 1946, died very suddenly. Senior member at the time of his death, Dr. Watt had been on the Business Committee for thirty years and was completing the fourth year of his term of office as an Assessor on the University Court. As the Business Committee reported—" he brought his excellent business gifts, his soundness of judgment, his remarkable power of work and his devotion to the University unstintingly to bear in furthering her interests in every possible direction ".

Dr. George Duncan died on 30 September 1949. A member of the Business Committee since 1921, he was the Convener from 1941 until 1946, and an Assessor on the University Court from 1921 until his death. He also gave fully of his services to the City in whose educational progress he was particularly interested. Again to quote the Minutes, he made " his sound judgment and grasp of business felt in every branch of academic life ".

In the last three years of the decade which ended in 1950, two major events as well as the change of Chancellor occurred in the life of the University—a change of Principal and the abolition of the Parliamentary Franchise. Sir William Hamilton Fyfe who, in 1935, had brought a fresh Transatlantic breeze into the University, retired in 1948 after thirteen years of service which included the momentous war years and the initial stages of the difficult period of reconstruction thereafter.

The appointment of Professor T. M. Taylor as Principal gave the General Council cause for particular pleasure. The letter on behalf of the Council sent by the Convener and the Clerk to Professor Taylor on his appointment said that it was " indeed a source of pride that one of our own men, who has been both student and teacher in the University, should now become her resident head ". The fact that Mrs. Taylor was also a graduate of Aberdeen and accordingly a member of the Council gave added pleasure. Principal Taylor was formally welcomed at the Statutory meeting of December 1948, over which he presided.

Lord Wavell was succeeded as Chancellor by the Rt. Hon. Thomas Johnston, p.c. ll.d., appointed in December 1950 after his nomination by the enlarged Committee created according to the 1903 precedent. Thus Aberdeen University has the privilege today of having as its head the most distinguished of Scotland's elder statesmen. Mr. Johnston was installed with the usual ceremonial on 5 April 1951.

In April 1945, Dr. George A. Morrison resigned his seat as University Parliamentary Representative and in the consequent by-election Sir John Boyd Orr gained the seat. In the July General Election, the three sitting members were returned; but in November Sir John Boyd Orr resigned and was succeeded by Colonel Walter Elliot, who of five candidates for the seat was returned with a very large majority.

The Representation of the People Bill before Parliament in 1948 contained provision for the abolition of the Scottish Universities Constituency and a Special meeting of the General Council was called for

28 February to consider this eventuality. A motion that the meeting was in favour of the retention of the University Vote and authorizing the Business Committee with powers to use all constitutional means to achieve that end was carried by an overwhelming majority, the amendment acquiescing in the abolition securing only three votes. The Convener of the Business Committee wrote to Lord Wavell on the matter and Lord Wavell declared his intention of raising the question in the House of Lords. Nevertheless the University Vote was abolished and with the dissolution of Parliament in 1950, the Scottish Universities Constituency ceased to exist. Of the three members who lost their seats, Colonel Walter Elliot found another constituency but Sir John Anderson and Sir John Graham Kerr did not seek re-election. On behalf of the General Council, a letter of thanks for services rendered, signed by the Principal, the Convener and the Clerk, was sent to the three unseated members, each of whom replied in appreciative terms. And so came the end of another auld sang.

X. THE LAST TEN YEARS

At no period of the General Council's history has it been in healthier condition or more effectively active than over the last decade of its first century. Age certainly has not withered it and its Minutes, ever growing in bulk, testify to the infinite variety of the portion of University life in which it is both its duty and its privilege to share.

Perhaps it is because in one sense the world is shrinking, because the marvels of modern transport make it possible for us to be here today and in America or in Africa tomorrow, or perhaps it is that soon after completing their degrees more than ever of our graduates take off to distant places, but certainly there has never been a time when the " news " of the General Council's activities has reached so far so acceptably and when response to the " news " has come from so many different parts of the world. One very potent factor in linking up graduates here, there and everywhere has been Principal Taylor's Report on the State of the University, delivered to each winter meeting of the General Council since December 1949. These talks—for, lucid and vivid, they are delightfully informal, one graduate talking to his fellow-graduates, as well as having the authenticity of a statement by the Principal of the University—are the highlight of the meetings, as one can tell by the expectant hush that precedes them after the more prosaic routine business has been disposed of. Of necessity only a very small proportion of graduates can be present at the meetings to hear at first hand this Report, but all over the world graduates can read it for it is printed in the notice calling the following meeting of the General Council.

In 1955 it was decreed that the twice-yearly print announcing the General Council meeting should be sent to all graduates with a known address anywhere in the world, instead of merely to those in the United

Kingdom and Northern Ireland. A very delightful sequel in 1957 to this sending far afield of the General Council Notices was a letter from a very old graduate living in Pretoria, perhaps the University's oldest living graduate. The Reverend James Dewar (M.A. 1887) wrote in his ninety-fifth year to say that he had received the Minutes of December 1956, and that he was still interested in his Alma Mater. The Clerk on behalf of the Business Committee and the General Council sent a message of congratulation to Mr. Dewar and since then there has been further news of Mr. Dewar.

Throughout the fifties the speed of growth of the University has been quickened and much of the business of the General Council has been the consideration of new regulations governing the changing shape of University teaching. After a slight decrease in numbers following upon the passing-out of the ex-Service students, a steady increase has begun. At present the number of students in attendance is just under 2000. More and more of the school population aim at University education, and when the post-war " bulge " reaches the University and the overflow from the south have to be accommodated, the expectation of a 4,000-students University may not be widely unrealistic. Small wonder then that the chief burden of the Principal's Reports on the State of the University has been building and yet more building.

One very delightful feature of this expansion of the last decade and of the growth in prospect has been what one might call the return to King's. Without any weakening of the pulse of life of Marischal College—indeed the recent re-building and the nearby presence of the expanding Union give it ever new strength—more and more of the work of the University is done in the Old Town. One man more than any other had the foresight to visualize the " ville universitaire " that gives Old Aberdeen much of its charm and its interest. Colonel H. J. Butchart, as Secretary of the University, encouraged the buying of land in Old Aberdeen, a wise and far-sighted and profitable policy. His resignation as Secretary of the University marked the end of an epoch; but happily he remains an active member of the General Council who, as his vehement opposition to one clause in the Draft Regulations for the new Diploma in Statistics bore witness, speaks out loud and clear when occasion demands and who, as its Law Agent, guides the General Council on controversial matters.

In bidding him farewell in the summer of 1952 on his relinquishing his post after thirty-three years, the General Council saluted " with mingled pride and affection a great servant of the University ". The Council joined in the presentation of Colonel Butchart's portrait and in January 1953, the Business Committee gave him a Complimentary Dinner.

Mr. Butchart's successor, Mr. W. S. Angus, who was welcomed at the December meeting of 1952, gave particular service to the General Council by acting as its Clerk during Dr. Simpson's illness in 1954 and in the early months of 1955.

The beginning of a new half-century turned the thoughts of the Business Committee towards the need for a third Roll of Graduates to cover the period from 1926 to 1950. Bearing in mind the great movement of graduates in the course of the Second World War and thereafter, the Business Committee in 1952 suggested to the University Court that, as a preliminary to a third instalment of the Roll and for the use of the Registrar and the Editor of the *University Review*, a card-index of all graduates and alumni should be set up—a revival of an old practice authorized by the Court in 1914 as a result of a General Council suggestion —and maintained in the Offices of the University. In 1954 the University Court agreed to this and agreed too to provide records on which could be based a Roll of Graduates and Alumni, leaving the biographical work under the control of the Business Committee, at the same time decreeing that, because of the expense involved, immediate production was not practicable.

In the summer of 1957, Mr. John Mackintosh agreed, on his retirement as Head of the History Department of Gordon's College, to undertake the Editorship. After the delay, it was decided that it would be more suitable if the period covered by the Roll was the thirty years between 1926 and 1955 and that the publication could be a feature of the Centenary Celebrations already under discussion. Mr. Mackintosh's huge task, now completed, contains almost twelve thousand entries, for its Supplement brings up to date records of earlier graduates. This third volume now stands along with the two earlier publications as worthy evidence of the zeal, devotion and skill of three distinguished members of our University.

As a result of the collecting of information for the Roll of Graduates, many corrections were made in the General Council Register. The abolition of the University Franchise in 1948 had made unnecessary the Parliamentary Register of the Council. The opportunity was taken to restore to the *University Calendar* the list of members which had been discontinued during the war and to re-cast it in a form suitable for use in a postal vote for the Election of a Chancellor or an Assessor. Separate copies of the Register were also printed. In 1955 the University Court, in order to reduce the bulk of the *Calendar*, decided to discontinue printing the General Council list. Since that time the list has been issued separately, the first issue being published in 1957. With the exception of the year 1958, the list has been issued annually, authenticated as to 1 January of that year. But only the care and courtesy of the members of the Council in intimating changes of address can keep the information in that Register up to date.

This matter of a separate General Council Register raised the question as to whether, when such a list was maintained, it was also necessary to keep a Registration Book. The Law Agent proved that both lists must be maintained, the Register as distinct from the Registration Book having to be authenticated by the Vice-Chancellor on or before 31 December in each year.

Perhaps the matter that has roused most controversy both in the Business Committee and in the Council in the course of the past ten years has been the new Higher Degree in Law. In the winter of 1953, the proposal of the Senatus that the title Doctor of Laws (LL.D.) be given to this suggested degree was disapproved of by the Council, on the grounds that the Scottish LL.D. given *honoris causa* had a distinctive character and tradition which should not be confused with a degree awarded by thesis only. The University Court invited representatives of the Senatus and of the Business Committee to state their respective cases before the Court. This resulted in the rejection of the recommendation. Early in 1955, however, the University Court decided to join the other three Scottish Universities in the promotion of the Ordinance governing the new degree but the Business Committee adhered to its previous decision. Eventually in the summer of 1956, when a revised Draft Ordinance establishing a Higher Degree of Doctor of Laws had been approved by the four Scottish University Courts, the Business Committee decided to recommend approval on the grounds that the new Higher Degree was subject to severe restrictions and could not be given except for work that represented " an original and substantial contribution to the study of law ". The General Council, while agreeing that the use of the title LL.D. for both an honorary and a higher degree was regrettable, concurred in the decision of the Business Committee.

The same meeting which gave grudging approval to the LL.D. degree also accepted the new conditions of the M.A. degree. These turned upon the abolition of compulsory Latin—the end of even a pretence at a classical basis for the Ordinary Arts degree—and the consequent reshaping of the various options open to undergraduates. The Business Committee in spring 1955, had discussed thoroughly the proposed changes and a report with intimation of the points raised was made to the Court, with the recommendation that the proposals be referred back to the Senatus. Eventually the Dean of the Faculty of Arts attended the summer meeting of 1956, and explained the New Regulations to the satisfaction of the General Council.

This attendance of the expert at the meetings of both the Business Committee and the General Council has been a feature of the last ten years or so—an innovation introduced by the present Convener of the Business Committee, Dr. John N. Milne. Such a policy, whereby members of the Senatus have explained desirable changes in curricula and regulations governing the many new courses in the rapidly-expanding range of teaching in the University, has given added interest to the work of the General Council.

Another evidence of the healthy relations between graduates and the University generally has been the spontaneous desire shown by various groups to give a present to their Alma Mater. For instance, 1880-4 Arts Class presented in 1937 a clock to King's College Library, and the Arts Class of 1890-94 gave in 1954 a sum of money for the purchase of a chair for the Chapel and in December 1955, the Principal opened his Report on the State of the University by telling of the attendance that week at the University Court meeting of two members of the Medical Class of 1922-27, Mr. Norman Logie and Dr. James Gill, " who presented to the University a very fine silver candelabrum subscribed for by members of the class now practising in various parts of the world ".

These presents have led to gifts by other classes. And Mr. Logie's desire to encourage such acts of piety which would at the same time furnish the University with silver plate for ceremonial occasions inspired his suggestion to the Business Committee of the Centenary Silver Fund to which graduates have contributed the sum of over £2,100. Dr. Douglas Simpson in his account of the Centenary Celebrations has told at greater length the story of the Fund.

It was after hearing a statement by Dr. Simpson about the important events of the autumn of 1860—the year of the fusion and of the Inauguration of the General Council—that the General Council at its meeting of December 1955, agreed to recommend to the University Court that the Centenary of these events should be celebrated in 1960. The story of the planning and successful carrying out of the Celebrations has been told in a preceding section of this volume.

It is necessary to go back to the year 1952 to complete the story of the Assessorships. In that year, both retiring members, Dr. A. Greig Anderson and Mr. John W. Robertson, were re-elected as were in 1954 and again in 1958 the retiring members, Dr. Mary Esslemont and Mr. John N. Milne. An unusual situation arose in the winter of 1954 when Dr. John W. Robertson, because of his appointment as Lecturer in Methematics in the University, had to resign his Assessorship. He was eligible for re-election, however, and at an adjourned meeting of the Council held in January 1955, he was re-appointed to the Court, although another nominee also stood for the vacancy. In 1956, however, at the end of his term of office, Dr. Robertson, after thirteen years of " very distinguished services ", did not seek re-election. Three nominations were lodged for the two vacancies; the vote at the meeting was confirmed by the poll which followed and Dr. A. Greig Anderson, the other retiring member, was returned along with Mr. Frank Scorgie, retired Director of Education for the City of Aberdeen. The Centenary year, 1960, brought a lively contest in the election for Assessors. When Sir Alexander Greig Anderson, because of the increasing burden of ill-health, intimated after twenty-three years of " arduous and unwearied services " that he did not wish to seek re-election, three nominations were lodged. The vote taken at a crowded meeting gave the seats to the retiring member, Mr. Scorgie, and to Dr. Alexander Lyall. The proposer of the loser demanded a poll and as a result, after a close contest, the sitting member lost his seat and Dr. Lyall and Mr. Maurice Cramb were appointed to the Court.

The frequency of a poll for the Assessorships had revealed new difficulties in the timing of the election, moved from the December meetings to avoid the Christmas holidays. Now the Trades holidays in July make it difficult to have the necessary printing and despatch to an ever-increasing number of graduates done in time. This was considered in 1956 but no change was recommended. In 1960, the difficulty again required that the Clerk be allowed the maximum permissible time to conduct the poll. The hour of the Statutory meeting has also been reconsidered during the past decade. In 1952, Mr. John R. K. Pirie pointed out that business men found it impossible to attend the Saturday forenoon meeting of the Council and he suggested an evening meeting. This, however, would be difficult for country members. The Business Committee considered a compromise, that the summer meetings might be held in the early evening; but, with insufficient evidence to prove that this would be advantageous, the suggestion was not adopted. It seems difficult to find the ideal time of meeting but the Lecture Hall as the place of meeting since 1956 has met with unqualified approval.

It is good to be able to close this account of the General Council with the story of a recent contribution made by the Council to forwarding the work of the University. Out of a discussion in the Business Committee in the summer of 1958 of a Regulation devised to meet the case of candidates desiring to proceed to the degree of B.SC. after taking the degrees of M.B., CH.B., the question of the need for teaching medical physics was raised by Dr. Lyall. A Sub-Committee under the Convenership of Dr. Lyall was formed and with the assistance of Mr. Harry D. Griffith of the Natural Philosophy Department, a memorandum was drawn up. Information was obtained as to what was being done in this direction in Glasgow and Edinburgh as well as in the various Departments of Medicine in Aberdeen. The Sub-Committee reached the conclusion that there was great need for instruction in the fundamentals of the new techniques in radiobiology and in the use of isotopes for clinical purposes. To meet this need a course in Radiobiology was necessary. The Council informed the University Court of their hope that, when circumstances allowed, such a Course would be established in connection with the new degree of B.SC. sequent to M.B., CH.B. In the autumn of 1959 the University Court gave their approval and the first course in Radiobiology was given in the Winter Term of 1960. There is every expectation that a further course will be held in 1961.

The General Council is glad to be of service in this way. As the new century of its life starts under the vigorous, knowledgeable and experienced leadership of Dr. John N. Milne as Convener of the Business Committee and Dr. Douglas Simpson as Clerk and Registrar of the General Council—both men appropriately received laureation at the Centenary Graduation—the prospect is bright.

Very new graduates have little idea of what the payment of one pound sterling to have their name put in the Register means. As well as being, since 1881, a statutory preliminary to graduation, this enrolment, however, makes them one of a great company bound by a common loyalty.

By means of the General Council—to quote from " Reconstruction in the Universities ", a series of articles originally appearing in the public press and issued in 1918 in book form—" every graduate receives a stake in the fortunes of his Alma Mater. In it is capitalized the accumulated interest of thousands of educated men and women scattered all over the world. It focuses and reflects extra-academic opinion and influence." But perhaps the neatest and most attractive description of the General Council is that of Principal Taylor in his 1955 Report when, speaking of the University as " a communion of memories as well as of hopes ", he said the General Council " is at once the repository and the custodian of our traditions ".

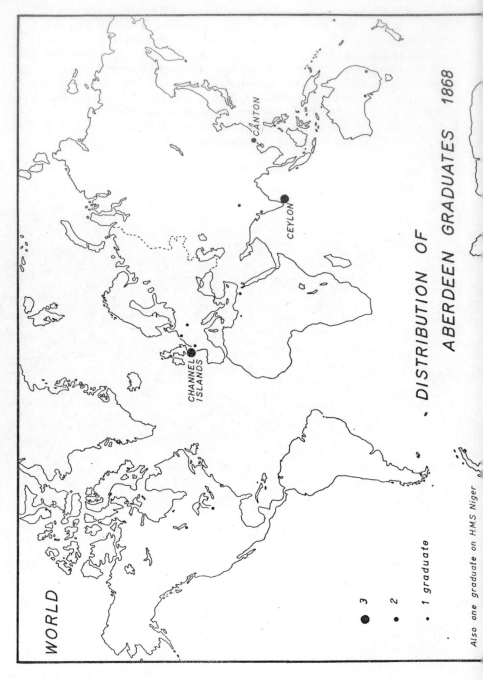

WORLD

DISTRIBUTION OF
ABERDEEN GRADUATES 1868

CANTON

CEYLON

CHANNEL
ISLANDS

3

2

1 graduate

Also one graduate on H.M.S Niger

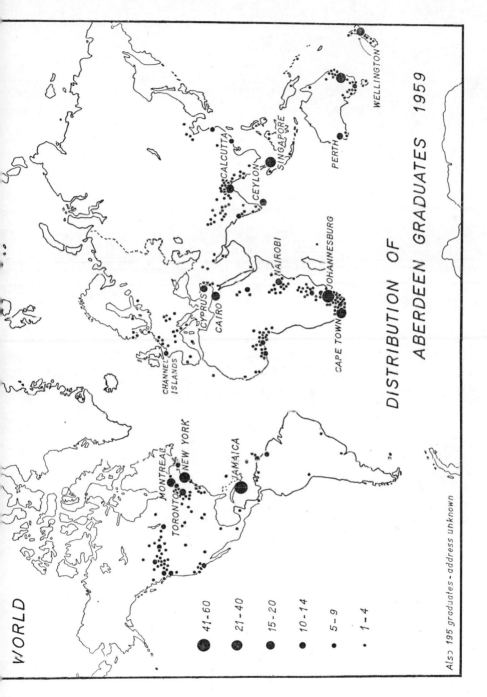

WORLD

DISTRIBUTION OF
ABERDEEN GRADUATES 1959

WELLINGTON

PERTH

SINGAPORE

CALCUTTA

CEYLON

JOHANNESBURG

NAIROBI

CAPE TOWN

CYPRUS

CAIRO

CHANNEL
ISLANDS

MONTREAL

NEW YORK

TORONTO

JAMAICA

41 - 60

21 - 40

15 - 20

10 - 14

5 - 9

1 - 4

Also 195 graduates - address unknown

4

THE UNIVERSITY REVIEW[1]

LEARNED DOCTORS AND MASTERS

" I ask you to look back on your careers at King's and Marischal Colleges.
You have forgotten much of what the professors taught you, but one thing
you have not forgotten—a living factor which is still at work in you—
and that is the personality of these men. . . . I tell you, you cannot have
real teachers unless you give them liberty."

ARTHUR KEITH

*A survey of the staff of Aberdeen University, from the Fusion of King's and
Marischal Colleges in 1860; made in 1960, but treading delicately among the
living. For the long-dead, whom no one still alive could have known, we have
drawn on older publications such as Class Records, early numbers of the* REVIEW
and of Alma Mater, *W. Keith Leask's* Interamna Borealis *and the volume
edited by P. J. Anderson called* Aurora Borealis Academica. *We thank all
our living contributors, and those who sent us tales and reminiscences, even though
not all of these could be used. Quotations from older publications have appended
the initials of these publications (e.g. A.U.R. = Aberdeen University Review).
The insets in small type have come from many contributors and the writers of the
main articles are not responsible for them.*

The illustrations are cartoons from old numbers of Alma Mater.

[1] The fourth part of this volume, being a reprint, *in toto*, of the Centenary issue of
the *Aberdeen University Review*, Vol. XXXVIII, No. 123, September 1960, edited by Miss
Nan Shepherd, M.A.

KING'S ...

> There's an old University town
>   Between the Don and the Dee
> Looking over the grey sand dunes,
>   Looking out on the cold North Sea.
>
> WALTER C. SMITH

> I love this place, all seasons of the year.
>
> Elphinstone, in G. R. HARVEY's play of that name.

> Greatness hung in the air of King's.
>
> JOHN MURRAY

> And the vivid folk are going to King's in Aberdeen.
>
> RACHEL ANNAND TAYLOR

> Young venturers in mind's astringent story.
>
> C. COLLEER ABBOTT

Principal Geddes and King's College were one and indivisible.   He told Mr. Leask that he believed the Crown would be found in his heart as Calais was in Mary's.

" King's College, Sir, is an oasis in the midst of modern so-called progress, from which may the gods preserve us."

Alma Mater, 1919

> To that grey city by the sea
> Ma thochts will turn until I dee:
> The winds sae keen, the nichts sae snell,
> The snaw that drifts o'er muir an' fell.
>
> Ay, Aiberdeen an' twal' mile roun',
> The words come wi' a couthy soun':
> The Tower, the Crown, the Don, the Dee,
> An' aye the sabbin' o' the sea.
>
> W. SOUPER

> What marvellous mad hopes were cherished
>   In Aberdeen!
> Oh, that's a city to be born in.
>   The pure air kindles you, and witty
> Your mind goes dancing.   To learn scorn in
>   Oh, that's a city.
> Under the Crown that dreams of Flodden
>   And Borgia, in scarlet gown
> Youth lightly treads where Youth hath trodden
>   Under the Crown.
>
> RACHEL ANNAND TAYLOR

> Crown of King's! and yonder the infinite thunder of Ocean.
>
> A. W. MAIR

... MARISCHAL

Marischal College was a leaf from a European tree.

G. D. HENDERSON

In our second Founder as in our first, educational enthusiasm was hallowed by religious principle.

H. COWAN

Masson on Marischal: Old Marischal College, as he knew it, had none of the architectural graces of King's, but to that gaunt pile he made his confession of loving allegiance, and would not depart from it even when Simpson's finer lines had usurped the site. For him there was but one Marischal College, the College of Dugald Dalgetty, a house rude and plain of feature, but ever memorable and dear, a thing to lift his imagination to the frosty stars.

J. D. SYMON

Marischal College and Mitchell Tower—I have seen them at all hours of the day and night. In the first half-light of dawn, when the quadrangle is grey, empty and silent. . . . At midnight, when the tower seems to stand aloof, withdrawn among the stars. . . . But I love college and tower most of all when I see them against the placid grey sky, shot with silver, of early evening—the hour and the hue that goes deep into the heart of the Aberdonian who cares for the peculiar beauty of his own city. It is in such an hour that the city and its granite become intimate and revealing.

G. R. HARVEY

Each hoary pinnacle and frosty spire.

R. C. MACFIE

A wedding cake in indigestible grey icing.

A.U.R.

The fourteen hundred golden flaggs
  Stiff in the windless air,
The pinnacles and minarets
  Most excellentlie faire,
The carven stone, the blazoned pane
  All cunningly bedight,
It was the Stout Earl Marischalle
  Made them for our delight.

O all the prayers of Holy Church
  Are Bishop Elphinstone's;
But for the good Earl Marischalle
  God rest his jollie bones.

Alma Mater

PROFESSORS AND STUDENTS

THESE pages are for the most part an Act of gratitude for the variousness, the plenitude and the surprise of human nature. They are our Grace after Meat—though we have not disdained the occasional asperity, the plaint of the man who went hungry because the food was not convenient for him. We have been taught by more than the words from our teachers' mouths, as some of the things said here may testify. We have savoured the quirks and relished the quips, appreciated the courteous, taken as tonic the dry, comment, admired achievement, and now and then recognized greatness.

In 1860 the staff comprised a score of professors between whom and the general run of students a gulf was fixed. This is amusingly illustrated by a writer in *Alma Mater*: " The first thing that strikes one on entering the Greek classroom is the exceedingly comfortable position of the lecturer (' Homer ')—large screens protect him from draughts and the glare of the fire, a softly cushioned and ample *cathedra* ensures that he shall not be troubled with the same affliction as the students who rest on hard deal forms." Several writers attest that for a professor to recognize his " men " on the street (even those whom he knew well in class) was so unusual as to be memorable. " I never heard of a student dining with a professor in my day," says Robertson Nicoll, though this is contradicted by others who say that Honours men were invited to one or two professorial homes. On the other hand, there is abundant evidence of the practical kindness (sometimes surreptitious, as though the donor feared to embarrass the recipient—Professor Fyfe even disguised his handwriting when enclosing largesse) of several of the professors towards students whom they suspected to be in want; and it has to be remembered that the majority of the students were poor, that they lived in bare lodgings, often on very meagre fare (" when the potatoes gave out and only the meal was left, brave hearts sank. In spite of our happiness, and it was very real, I think now that we were too young and too poor ") and that they had no social centre to provide them with warmth and light, to put it no higher, on winter evenings. A large number were too poor to lay down the £1 deposit that was required until as late as 1904 for the privilege of withdrawing books from the University Library. Walter Besant speaks of the " shifts by which the poorer undergraduates of Aberdeen continued to live ".

(Poverty wears a scarlet cloke
In my land)

The wastage in human life among the students and young graduates of the sixties, seventies and eighties was almost certainly the result of serious under-nourishment. " It was a steady grind for most of us. Men

(Poverty has the Gaelic and the Greek
In my land)

worked insanely. Lives were sacrificed and others injured beyond recovery. Bain predicted that of his three most distinguished pupils none would see fifty "—a prediction that came true with the deaths of Robertson Smith, Minto and Hunter.

SHON CAMPBELL

Shon Campbell went to College
  Because he wanted to,
He left the croft in Gairloch
  To dive in Bain and Drew;
Shon Campbell died at College
  When the sky of spring was blue.

Shon Campbell went to College,
  The pulpit was his aim;
By day and night he ground, for he
  Was Hielan, dour and game;
The session was a hard one,
  Shon flickered like a flame.

Shon Campbell went to College,
  And gave the ghost up there,
Attempting six men's cramming
  On a mean and scanty fare;
Three days the Tertians mourned him—
  'Twas all that they could spare.

Shon Campbell lies in Gairloch,
  Unhooded and ungowned,
The green quadrangle of the hills
  To watch his sleep profound,
And the Gaudeamus of the burns
  Making a homely sound.

And when the last great roll is called
  And Adsums thunder loud,
And when the Quad is cumbered
  With an eager jostling crowd,
The Principal who rules us all
  Will say, " Shon Campbell, come!
Your Alma Mater hails you
  Magister Artium! "

              W. A. MACKENZIE

In the early part of the time with which we deal many of the professors were of native growth.

In the good old days we love to praise
Our Profs were a home-grown lot,
With homely ways and a Doric phrase,
For each was a sturdy Scot.
  They came from the shafts
    Of the rustic plough
  From diverse crofts
    And a country knowe.

          J. M. BULLOCH

There may have been an air of self-sufficiency about—

> You may talk about Arenas in the South
>   And eulogise the Isis and the Cam;
> You may glorify a Porson and a Routh,
>   And compliment the English college cram,
> And possibly these rivals may amass
>   More knowledge
>   Than the College
>   By the Dee;
> But I'm also very sure they don't surpass
>   Its weather
>   And its heather
>   And its sea.

J. M. BULLOCH

This may be a local patriotism so narrow as to be parochial, yet it catches something essential to the region from which our University draws its life—snell, bracing, with the taste of wildness on it, breeding men with the heather stride and eyes that are used to scanning long horizons, " the threat and promise of the ocean ". The comment on Grierson turning gradually side-on to his audience and declaiming raptly to the window—" delivering his lecture to the North Sea fishermen "—is a portent: for the North-East has never been purely bucolic, as Rachel Annand Taylor knew:—

> My roots were set in that north-east
>   Where ironies prevail—

and soon Aberdeen men were hastening to the " Arenas in the South " (so often on the lips of " Homer ") and returning not only to bring to Aberdeen something of the new knowledge that was transforming the world, but to create it there: nor did they always require to go south first.

For as the century went on, one thing that no thinking mind could escape was the stupendous growth in knowledge. The very substance of the earth around us became new; our bodies and our brains were altered; time was not what it was; distance had new dimensions; and as the tree of knowledge proliferated in every direction, so the staff grew, not only to teach the new knowledge but to discover it. Research became an integral part of the University's life. A new Faculty (Science) was created, new Departments, new branches within the Departments, readers, lecturers, assistants and research fellows, with clerical staff, technicians, photographers—a complex whole bewildering to those accustomed to the simpler airs of a world that did not know too much. The classic comment came from " Boothie ", so long the sole attendant in Medicine, Surgery and Midwifery. Asked how things were going under Sir Ashley Mackintosh's successor, he made reply, " Ach, I dinna ken what things are comin' tae. What wi' the Perfesser, and this chielie Mac—, twa stenographers and the dictaphone—michtie me, me and Ashley managed it a' oorsels."

Each of the world wars of our century, being a forcing-house of invention and discovery and conjecture, was followed by a period of intense University development, with new Chairs and new lectureships, and this not only in Science and Medicine. A new knowledge was demanded of the life, language and history of other peoples, and thought had to rediscover its own bearings amid the welter of new information. There were still people about in the twenties (and perhaps later) who believed that a professor had nothing to do but repeat the same lectures year after year (" here is a joke "), that a professor's was a leisurely life. It was a professor of mathematics who realized that those who adventure into unknown countries—whether through the Looking Glass or the crystal—have to run as fast as they can even to remain in the same place. The conception of professor and student as fellow-seekers after a truth not yet established was alien and difficult.

The sheer size of the staff in the later part of our hundred-year period makes it fantastic to attempt to portray them all. They have come to us from many lands and many seats of learning. For some we have been no more than a rock in the ocean on which they have alighted for an hour on their further journey; others have stayed and added lustre to our name in achieving it for themselves. Young graduates have told me that there are now-a-days no " characters " among their professors: which is odd. Perhaps there is too much knowledge to amass for us to loiter over oddity; perhaps we are all too busy to dwell lovingly on individual traits, too little serene to let ourselves enjoy a man simply being himself. Perhaps a generation that paints abstract pictures despises the personal. Or it may be that the dehumanisation of knowledge—when the poet's " sound within the growth of trees " becomes measurable by machinery and the mystery of nativity is subjected to pipette and balance—detracts from the value of personality as the medium through which truth is conveyed and apprehended; personal idiosyncracy, far from conveying truth, invites error and must be neutralised. Science grows more dominant and science, as a writer on Einstein has said, is " an escape from the merely personal ". There is the further consideration that thanks to research expeditions, travelling scholarships, exchange visits and other such apparatus, the student of today crosses more frontiers and meets more men, and a wider variety of them, than his predecessor ever did; and gives to none of those he meets the loving concentration the older student afforded to his professor, out of which was partially created the " character " he carried away in his memory. However this may be, the tales that have been sent to us have been mostly of the older race of heroes. We keep our own counsel over this, for we have little doubt that the later races will be suitably enshrined in myth long ere they are dead. And the tales that will be told may not be so very unlike the tales that have been told.

Of these tales a surprising number are of the quick-witted professor scoring off the student—not the other way about: as of Professor Arthur

Thomson, pacing in his measured way along the beach and giving instant identification to the flotsam and jetsam presented to him by students —" a sea-urchin, a piece of sea-mat "—when the offering was a scrap of leather sole saying with no change of gait or mien or voice, " A piece of impertinence ", and passing on; or " Charlie " Niven confronting the student who had seven absences to explain and could muster only six excuses, " And the seventh day, Mr. R—, you rested "; though who scored off whom I am not quite sure in the story of the man who followed Professor Grierson to his room to complain that he could not read the comment written on his essay. " Sir," said the Professor, disentangling his own script, " I cannot read your writing." Of Grierson too (he was not yet Sir Herbert, as the Natural History Professor was not yet Sir Arthur Thomson—certainly for the former the Aberdeen student had no name but the plain all-sufficient *Grierson*)—of Grierson the best of the absent-minded tales are told: the one, for instance, of how he telegraphed his wife to say, " I am in Perth station—where ought I to be ? " Perhaps her reply, " Look your ticket, dear," is apocryphal. How endearing too is the tale of Professor Jack coming out of a daze as the tramway inspector made a third request for his ticket and pulling a handful of used tickets from his pocket as he said with a disarming smile, " I think it must be one of these."

The human kindliness of the staff is remembered too—" My home ", writes an English Honours graduate, "was in the Island of Raasay, from which one could not lightly sail away to the British Museum for research. After I had given up my original idea for a thesis, a parcel arrived with Professor Jack's handwriting on it. Inside were two source books invaluable for my purpose with a note: ' I found these in Low's. I paid nothing for them as he didn't know he had them.' I treasure a Capell's Edition of Shakespeare that I was startled to find was not a loan but a gift." And it was a Highlander who walked to his lecturer's rooms to tell him he was called away to his father's funeral and had nearly reached his own digs again when he heard running footsteps and someone puffing and blowing: it was the lecturer, afraid lest the youth had not enough money to take him to his Inverness-shire home.

Many of the vividly remembered instances contain a point of superb teaching—something driven home by a presentation that was never forgotten. " The length? " queries Sir John Struthers. " Half-an-inch, sir." " Have you measured it ? " " No, sir." " Let us measure it— yes, I thought so, three quarters of an inch." " It's much the same, sir." " The same! No, sir—miles of difference, *miles* of difference." Or Professor Fyfe returning to its writer an essay copied word for word from Principal Pirie's *Natural Theology* with the sole sufficient comment written on it: " Verbose rubbish." Or Professor Jack, grieved over a vulgarism in an Honours student's essay, standing hesitant and then plunging, " It's—it's as though you took your soup plate to your mouth ". Or the startling splendour of Professor Lockhart's similes: " The colour in muscles of rapid motion—the honey bee's rosy red layer in the Himalaya hybrid ". Or Professor Arthur Thomson, talking on the division of the ovum after fertilization: " This pattern is followed among certain of the mammals, the primates "—a quiet impressive pause—" man himself." To young women students whose girlhood had been passed under Victoria, that quiet pause was teaching of a very high order.

Then there is the professor or lecturer who could save the situation for a student under examination, as Dr. Richards jingling the pennies in his trouser pocket when an examinee couldn't think of copper; or Professor Gibb replying, when the co-examiner complained that the student didn't know what was on the back (of a stone displayed for ice-markings) because he hadn't turned the specimen over, " To tell the truth, neither did I." There was a point, however, beyond which complaisance would not go. Professor Nicol, the Natural Historian, was said to refuse no man a pass. There came a day when he failed a man who would therefore be unable to graduate and representations were made to the professor: who remained adamant. " He said that the cow had no anal opening, and I cannot pass him."

Froth upon the water? Perhaps. But froth is thrown upon a river that is running strongly; and from these stories—passed from lip to lug over half the world, and, like folk-ballads, not always in the same form (I have been given three variations of one tale already quoted here)— from these the myths grow. Where myth is created, there is always a deep inner energy at play, vital to the true functioning of a university.

Of the strong river—the power and achievement of our University— there are glimpses in the pages that follow.

NAN SHEPHERD

THE PRINCIPALS

Seven Principals have presided over the University during the century 1860-1960. The first three held Chairs before their appointment as Principal (Greek: Church History: Greek); the next three came to us from without our borders; the seventh, our present Principal, Sir T. M. Taylor, was again one of our own Senatus (Law) and also one of our own graduates, as were Principals Pirie and Geddes.

PETER COLIN CAMPBELL

Professor of Greek in King's, 1854
Principal of King's, 1855
Principal of the University, 1860-1876

The first Principal of the combined Colleges was an Argyllshire man who, after being ordained in the Church of Scotland, became Professor of Classics in Queen's College, Kingston, Canada, but returned in 1845 to take up a charge in Perthshire. From there he came to Old Aberdeen as Professor of Greek, then as Principal, finally becoming Principal of the University in 1860.

" We saw him ", says the author of *Meminisse Juvat*, " at Graduations, at the Installations of Rectors, and on Sundays in the Chapel, where a window now commemorates his connection with the College."

Another writer says: " Dr. Campbell was a scholarly man, had a great regard for academic tradition and propriety, and hid a kindly nature under a somewhat austere manner. He presided with dignity and firmness over University cere onials, and successfully upheld the reputation of his office."

WILLIAM ROBINSON PIRIE

Professor of Divinity, Marischal, 1843-1860
Professor of Church History, 1860-1877
Principal, 1877-1885

> An outstanding figure of the time, and a man remembered for the vigour of his character and the strength of his intellect. . . . His great theme was Happiness. " Ye can't be happy," he was said to have once declared, " so ye needn't think ye can."
>
> A. SHEWAN

Those who studied church history under Dr. Pirie are not likely ever to forget his outward appearance and manner. His short but compact figure, his erect and vigorous gait, his bold strong features surmounted by a heavy crown of tangled hair, his easy confident manner, and his almost ostentatious carelessness of dress, could not but arrest attention. His broad Aberdeenshire accent, and the metallic tones of his voice served only to heighten the impression produced by his remarkable readiness and fluency of speech, his deft ingenuity in argument, and his somewhat scornful humour. The whole set forth one whose natural confidence in himself had been fully justified by results.

[As Principal] though not possessing an imposing presence, nor caring greatly for academic tradition when it obstructed his path, nor having much love for ceremonial display, Dr. Pirie brought, to the performance of his duties as Principal, a long experience of university work and life, and a well-recognized business capacity. In his time the Senatus was the executive of the University. Its proceedings took place with closed doors, but rumour reported that the discussions were often lively and the debates warm, and that the chairman needed a clear head, a quick judgment and a strong hand to guide their deliberations with success. These qualities were already fully developed in Dr. Pirie before he became Principal, and enabled him to give eight years of valuable and effective service as the ruling head of the University.

STEPHEN REE: *A.B.A.*

No account of Dr. Pirie would be complete which did not take notice of his wonderful power as a debater. His good humour was imperturbable, but his assault on an opponent's position always struck with unerring instinct at the weak point; and I do not think that any man was ever readier of speech, or keener in wit, or more irresistible in his combination of facts and principles in establishing his own case. It was often noticed that he was never taken by surprise, and the reason was that he had pondered the whole subject so thoroughly that he had anticipated every possible argument, and was pleased rather than perplexed when someone suggested an objection—especially if the suggestion was by way of interruption of his speech [in the General Assembly]. Then the spectacles were pushed further back on the broad brow, and the kind eyes twinkled with fun as he ridiculed the luckless interpolator. We shall not see his like again: it seems to be so hard to have humour without personalities, and incisiveness without invective.

REV. PROFESSOR CHARTERIS: *Memoir*

WILLIAM DUGUID GEDDES

Professor of Greek, 1860(55)-1885
Principal, 1885-1900

" Homer."

" The Hierarch himself, standing stately and grave."

Tall with the wonderful grace of the Greek,
Solemn as Consul at Rome. . . .
Bound to the story and life of the Crown,
Bound by unbreakable tie. . . .

J. M. BULLOCH

An etching of the Crown by Sir George Reid hung over the fireplace of
his drawing-room. " It holds, you see, the place of honour, and I sometimes believe it will be found in my heart, as Calais was in Mary's. Well,
I hope it is the last object I shall see. I can remember like yesterday the
feelings with which I first beheld it, as a boy."

W. KEITH LEASK

" I owe Geddes ", said Garden G. Smith, " rather a grudge. For he
once made a remark that let me see that Poetry was concerned with the
Infinite, and it has made me profoundly miserable ever since."

A.U.R.

The artistry of words was practised and inculcated in the Greek classroom.
The luckless wight who dared to give the literal rendering " Twelve little
pigs " was immediately hauled up with the indignant appeal: " Oh,
Mr. ——, can you imagine Homer saying, ' Twelve little pigs '? Would
he not rather have said, ' Piglings ten and twain '? " It is related that
one of our Bajans, when called upon to deposit a copper coin of the realm
as tribute for being late, expostulated and claimed exemption on the ground
that the College clock was two minutes fast by his watch, only to be met
with the withering question: " How dare you, Sir, compare your paltry
chronometer with our academic horologe? "

J. SCOTT RIDDELL

The state of Greek which he found in 1855, and which he left in 1886,
can be appreciated only by those who have examined in detail the papers
and traced the raising of the standard. It had to be fought for both outside and inside the University, and it would serve no good purpose now to
recall the " Boor " bombardment of vulgar personalities that used to
enliven the meetings of the General Council. Many of his colleagues
had no real conception of the function of a university; each was only bent
on advertising, extolling, or unduly popularizing his own subject, while
outside, the late Principal had to create his own public by reinforcements
of graduates trained under his eye to the schools all along the line in the
North.

W. KEITH LEASK: *I.B.*

The chapter from the Bible reverently read, we commence the morning's work and pursue it for a solid hour. A " man " is called up and
scrambles through a few lines of the passage prescribed. The *Orestes*,
Arrian's *Anabasis*, fragments of Theognis and Solon, and of course the
Iliad, were some of the works we read. As the translation proceeds,
Geddes corrects and helps, kindly and sympathetically, and often repro-
duces the text in his own, his very own, English, which he mouths in
his efforts to fit it to the original. If sibilants predominate in a sentence,
the English must also hiss. If alliteration is detected, it must not be lost
in the reproduction. The result is often comical, even to the Professor
himself. Good plain Anglo-Saxon or broad Scotch words are not to be
disdained, but rather to be preferred. A spade is to be called a spade.
The moisture induced by the Homeric hero's toil " along the highways
of the battle " was sweat, not perspiration. Buttocks were buttocks,

naked and unashamed. Even a sprinkling of slang was admissible, τὸ κάρτα was "with a vengeance". Onomatopoeia must *never* be neglected. Heavens! what contortions of the Professor's visage the fights of the *Iliad* produce, as he travails to bring forth something worthy of the original! He matches δούπησεν δὲ πεσών with "he came down with a THUD," and ἄσπις ἄρ' ἀσπιδ' ἔρειδε with "buckler GRIDED on buckler". The πότνια, πότνια νύξ of the *Orestes* beats him utterly, and he gasps for something of adequate solemnity. He sways slowly and heavily the while like a liner lying to; his brows drawn down recall the Olympian Zeus.

A. SHEWAN: *Meminisse Juvat*

Order reigned supreme in the Greek classroom: there the spontaneity or the original sin of the natural bajan never came within distance of giving trouble. . . . His presence, venerable even at a time of life when other men could have no claim to such an epithet, was a power of discipline in itself. He left no room for frivolity. He commanded respect from the first. . . . Sympathy for the student character in general, and special sympathy for individual students, where it was needed, were given in plenty. He won the hearts of Highland students by learning Gaelic. . . . And in the cases of the ordinary students, where some knowledge of home or private circumstances might settle a doubt as to a pass, examiners for degrees in Classics ever found the Greek professor ready with the quietly-given information which determined the case in favour of many. . . . It cannot be forgotten that during many years Sir William Geddes had not only to do his work, but to fight for the doing of it, to justify its existence and the part he considered it should bear in the training of Scottish youth. The way in which he did that work, bringing to Aberdeen not only a new knowledge of Greek, but what may fairly be called a new ideal of scholarship and of a scholar's life, constitutes a lasting title to gratitude and fame.

ROBERT A. NEIL: *A.B.A.*

When seventeen years of age he was a schoolmaster [at Gamrie]; two years later he taught in the Grammar School; at twenty-five he succeeded Melvin as rector; and at the early age of twenty-seven he was Professor of Greek in King's College. For thirty years he shed lustre on the professoriate and established for his University a widespread reputation as a seat of Greek learning. As Principal, his activities were directed into wider channels and in many ways he fostered the interests of the University. The Restoration of the Chapel was mainly due to his efforts, and the Extension Scheme was the great work of his later years. As scholar, as author, and as head of the University he served his day and generation with high distinction.

Alma Mater, 1900

JOHN MARSHALL LANG

Principal, 1900-1909

> Great master of the happy phrase, he knew
> To shape the common thought in winged speech.
>
> A. MACKIE

Lord Balfour, Secretary for Scotland in 1900, knew his man when he selected the successor of Sir William Geddes in the Principalship of the University of Aberdeen. To many it appeared a daring experiment to appoint one who was already well advanced in years and whose sphere of work had lain wholly, and for nearly half a century, within the Church. Dr. Lang was well known as one of the most eloquent preachers of his time, as a trusted leader in the councils of the Church and as a man of considerable administrative experience; but he entered his high office without the preliminary experience of a professorship, or of any appointment which might have familiarized him with the intricate workings of a university. It was therefore a signal achievement that so handicapped by age and lack of special knowledge he should now be regarded, after a few years of office, as worthy to rank with the most successful of the long line of distinguished men who have occupied the Principal's seat. His success was due partly to his own qualities and partly to his opportunities.

He came to the University at a time when the Court was about to resume its efforts to carry through to a finish the great scheme of extension which had been begun ten years earlier. The large part of this extension had been made before Dr. Lang became Principal, but the plans for the closing of the front of the Marischal College quadrangle were still under consideration, and the very difficult and delicate question of their relation to the old Greyfriars Church required the most careful handling. The Principal's great tactfulness and his popularity with both Presbytery and Town Council were of much help in bringing the negotiations to a satisfactory close.

The final stage of the extension was opened by His Majesty the King in September 1906. During the actual celebrations, as resident head of the University, Dr. Lang was a central figure. No one could have filled the position of chief host with greater dignity and graciousness. To every one his welcome was equally warm, whether the guest was academic or civic, and whether he was a savant of world-wide reputation or a humble alumnus from an obscure Scottish parish. But his outstanding service was the delivery, without a single note, of a magnificent oration of welcome to the assembled delegates in the Strathcona Hall. It was a great effort and worthy of a great occasion.

There never was a more tender or generous heart. He was always generous in his estimate of the work of others, and had a disparaging word for no man. But no part of his academic constituency so excited his sympathies as the students. He seized every opportunity of knowing them personally. He was ever the first in the Councils of the University to defend their rights or plead their cause. For him, escapades that seemed to others to call for strict disciplinary measures were only the results of a little youthful exuberance, a little excess of high spirits, that might well be met by the gentlest of admonitions. The students will not soon find so generous a friend.

Principal Lang was a man of dignified and courtly bearing scarcely inferior to that of his immediate predecessor. Along with his dignity was an obvious desire to conciliate and please, an abundant kindliness and accessibility. His popularity was in part due to his enviable gift and distinction as a speaker. His unbroken flow of language, graced with felicitous phrase and apt idea, and not lacking in the sparkle of quiet humour, was almost marvellous. He was peculiarly happy in his short eulogistic speeches, such as he had frequently to make as acting President of the University Court. It would have been impossible to improve them in either substance or manner.

MATTHEW HAY: *Alma Mater*, 1909

GEORGE ADAM SMITH

Principal, 1910-1936

William Robertson Smith, probably the greatest Semitic scholar that the Scottish Church has produced, had been " suspended " from his Chair for heresy. . . . His church now appointed this youth of promise [George Adam Smith] as interim lecturer. When he arrived in Aberdeen he went to call on the suspended Professor, whom he found in combative mood. " What would you do ", said the older man to the younger, " if I should refuse to obtemper the decision of the Assembly and insist upon taking the class myself? "   " Then," said the younger, " I should be proud to go to it among your students."

To come to know George Adam Smith was an event in one's life.

H. J. C. GRIERSON

Professor Drummond proposed that a plaque should be placed on Barbour's house at Bonskeid [where George Adam Smith used to go for quiet to write]: " Here was Isaiah hewed in pieces for the second time."

When " Ian Maclaren's " books appeared, George Adam Smith guessed the author from internal evidence and told him so. Back came a postcard: " Well done, Higher Criticism."

G. A. Williamson, o.c. o.t.c., speaks of " the honour paid to the contingent by the Principal going specially from Aberdeen to Fleetwood to be with officers and cadets for a few days. [1922]

" The Unit owes its existence to the Principal and his interest in it has never weakened. . . . It is only right that students in general should know we were the envy of all the other contingents as being the only Unit visited by the head of its University . . . other contingents requested that they might be allowed to attend the open-air service on the last Sunday in camp, for ' they would never venture to go back and have it said that they got the chance of hearing George Adam Smith and did not take advantage of it '."

I first experienced the impact of George Adam Smith's personality long before I went to Aberdeen to become an Aberdonian. It was in

Edinburgh—probably round about 1901—when the fickle Edinburgh undergraduates were transferring their devotion from Alexander Whyte of St. George's to John Kelman of the New North. And so there came an evening when the pulpit of the New North was occupied by the rising and distinguished Professor from Glasgow. I cannot now recall his heads, if he had any; but I can truthfully record that my initial annoyance that John Kelman was taking a night off (or was he?) had evaporated before the end of the evening. And I can also report that the text was taken from Psalms xix. 9: "The fear of the Lord is clean, enduring for ever." And of how many sermons can one remember so much after close on sixty years?

To my next confrontation with Sir George Adam Smith, I can assign a precise date. It was on 5 August 1921, when I was interviewed by the University Court of Aberdeen in connection with the newly founded Jaffrey Chair of Political Economy. It must have been a somewhat ludicrous interview! I had no desire to be a Professor of Political Economy—even in Aberdeen! I had sent in a hastily drafted application at the last moment, in order that I might collect testimonials from my superiors in Whitehall, in the hope that they might infer from this that I was quite prepared to flee from their bondage, unless . . .! It is the kind of thing that young men do! And I imagined that this was quite a safe game to play, in the confident belief that my application would be the first to go into the waste-paper basket. But I was scared beyond measure when I realized that my application was being taken seriously —so scared indeed that post-haste and by telegram I at once withdrew my application, and I again breathed freely for two nights. But I was not allowed to return to my wallowing in the mire of Whitehall. A characteristically gracious letter from the Principal persuaded me that I ought to go north for a general talk with the Court about things at large. And so on 5 August I was interviewed—I suppose it was an interview—by the Court. I spent my time enumerating and underlining my many deficiencies, and urging them to appoint someone better qualified for the post and not wholly inexperienced. I have given so much of my allotted space to my introduction to Aberdeen, because it impressed me, above all in retrospect, with a strong realization of the Principal's skill in managing the Court, for it was obvious that some of my interviewers were in complete agreement with me in the matter of my inadequate qualifications. And who shall blame them? Even now the only excuse I can find for the extremely rash and risky action of the Court in appointing me is that in the early post-war years the academic fields were deplorably denuded of the young. And also I realized how skilfully the Principal had managed *me*! But a fish that has no desire to be caught should not even look at the bait, especially when the rod is in the hands of so skilful an angler as the Principal.

And so I came to Aberdeen, where I remained for somewhat over thirteen years, and among these were some of the happiest of my life.

In contrast to London which, as I had known it, was a city of strangers, with friendship confined to office-hours, I found myself in an atmosphere of benevolence and—if I may use the word—of love. The older professors, —" Bourtie ", Cowan and Matthew Hay—were almost too good to be true; and I wondered whether thirty years of Aberdeen might transform me into another such miracle of loving-kindness. And over and above the friendly companionship of my colleagues, there was the influence of what it is now customary to call the " Establishment " represented by the Principal and Sir Thomas Jaffrey. For it was largely they, with the Principal at the centre of all things, who made Aberdeen for me.

Is it possible to find the secret of the quite extraordinary place which the Principal had in our academic society? I doubt it, for he manifested his greatness in so many ways that no simple summary is possible. But in seeking to bring together my memories of the Principal during that period which ended twenty-five years ago, I should begin first of all with the man himself. And here the outstanding feature of the Principal's make-up was his unaffected humility. He was essentially a simple companionable man who could freely meet and speak to all his fellows. The little shop-keepers in the Gallowgate felt no restraint in having a passing word with the Principal on his way to Marischal. If, as we are told, a Bishop should be given to hospitality, then George Adam Smith had at least one of the essential non-professional qualifications for a bishopric! Chanonry Lodge was in a very real sense the centre of the University. Inevitably such a transparently honest and sincere man was on the best of terms with the students, who accepted his greatness unquestioningly, but loved and honoured a man who met them as one of themselves.

He was, in short, an easy and helpful man to go to. If I may again refer to my own personal relations to him, there are two occasions which remain in my memory. In my earlier years some attempts were made to lure me from Aberdeen. Two in particular caused me much heart-searching: one was an invitation to return to government service, the other was to accept a distinguished academic post overseas. Of course I consulted the Principal; he was that kind of man! Without endeavouring to influence me one way or another, he was on both occasions a most helpful counsellor. And I have ventured to recall this because it brings back one of the happiest of my memories of the Principal. I shall never forget the extremely friendly and gracious manner in which he shook hands and thanked me when I finally told him that I had rejected the allurements of the south.

Of course none of us outside the Faculty of Divinity (and probably none of them!) was qualified to appreciate the Principal's profound scholarship, but we knew that in his own field he was supreme, and we also knew that while still a young man, with a Kirk to look after, he had been known among the elect as " Isaiah Smith ". One of the little vanities of this so modest man was that, although a clergyman, he was by no means a child in worldly affairs, despite current libels which would regard such a

11

prodigy as a contradiction in terms. In fact he was an admirable Chairman of the Senatus, pre-eminently so in the earlier years of my sojourn in Aberdeen. He always came master of the business before the meeting, having conscientiously done all his homework; and he knew his way through all the complicated questions of finance and all the other devilries which plague the administration of a modern university. Another matter in which the Principal was not ashamed to show a very legitimate pride was his authorship of *The Historical Geography of the Holy Land*. I remember his reaction on one occasion when the suggestion had been made that the authorities were unsympathetic to the newer subjects, and in particular towards Geography. How could they say that? queried the Principal, when he himself was a geographer, and a geographer whose geographic studies had been of the highest possible practical value! Lord Allenby's testimony to his reliance on the *Geography* during the campaign in Palestine naturally gave the Principal much pleasure which he was in no way concerned to conceal.

But great as he was in whatever he undertook, there was one field in which he was pre-eminent. George Adam Smith was a great preacher; one is tempted to say (doubtless on insufficient experience!) that he was the greatest preacher of his generation. Always he spoke with a deep and moving sincerity; although his utterances were the fruit of profound scholarship and thought, the final result was always a message within the grasp of ordinary men and women—and ordinary students. And above all, what made the Principal so persuasive, what compelled the congregation to listen, and to continue listening, was the marvellous quality of his voice, rich, musical and vibrant. His voice was in itself a benediction.

And something of this quality coloured all the Principal's utterances on the great occasions. I have an idea that he rather enjoyed lofty ceremonial. Anyone who remembers the laureation of Queen Mary or the Elphinstone celebrations will recall how his old-fashioned courtliness (and the music of his voice) added to the dignity of these memorable days.

As the years went on our Principal, eminent in many ways which have not been touched upon here, became more and more the embodiment of the spirit of Aberdeen. Perhaps surprisingly so, for his roots were in Edinburgh, and much of his later " adult " education came from these years of intense and fruitful activity in Glasgow. But he became as proud of Aberdeen as any Aberdonian (can one say more?), and proud of the great traditions of the University of which he was the distinguished head. And the Aberdonians realized that he was one of themselves, and this was gracefully acknowledged when he was made a Freeman of the City. Nor until the end was there any decline in his great mental powers, although he may have become somewhat less instinctively sensitive to the atmosphere of thought of those around him. But it is significant of the vigour of his intellectual powers in his venerable old age that one of the highlights in his career as a preacher was reached in the sermon which he delivered on the occasion of the visit of the British Association to Aberdeen in the late summer of 1934.

In trying to present to others what those of my generation most clearly remember of our Principal after twenty-five years, I suppose we naturally place in the forefront his profound scholarship, his great services to the University, his eloquence in his country's cause in a war in which he and his wife suffered so cruelly. But as so often happens, all that is but a framework, and the man himself is more memorable than anything he did. The most enduring memory is of his gracious and kindly personality, his courage, the example he gave to us all in the art of living. These things cannot easily be summarized, or conveyed to those who did not know him. Perhaps in the end we get as near as possible to the core of things if we fall back on the simple, and yet majestic, language of one of his own prophets, and say of him that he was a man who walked humbly with his God. For therein lies the essence of all that George Adam Smith was and did.

ALEXANDER GRAY

WILLIAM HAMILTON FYFE

Principal, 1936-1948

> Invited to attend the Evans pre-rectorial speech the Principal refused, as it was a student affair. The promoters, fearing for the Mitchell Hall, pressed their invitation: whereupon he attended in a grey lounge suit and remarked that the meeting would see from his " state of academic nudity " that he was not officially present.

> The Principal passed on to the REVIEW the Ballade *I left my shaving-brush at Aberdeen*, composed by our Chancellor, Lord Wavell, with help from his host, Colonel Bernard Fergusson, when, the morning after a Graduation ceremony in Aberdeen, he announced at a breakfast table in Germany the oversight of his shaving tackle. The Principal's comment: " Lord Wavell imputes paternity to Colonel Fergusson, who claims, however that the Chancellor is responsible for five-twelfths of the lines. Whether they are seeking to claim credit or to shift blame is not clear. But it is nice to know what the Higher Command do at breakfast."

The position of Principal in a Scottish University is an important and exacting one, and it has been filled by men of diverse gifts and interests. Few, if any, however, have been so intimately connected with so many aspects of education as Sir William Hamilton Fyfe.

After being educated at Fettes and at Merton College, Oxford, he was for a short time an assistant master at Radley. He then returned to Merton as a Fellow, and later occupied the post with the somewhat misleading designation of " Principal Postmaster ". He then became headmaster of a famous school, Christ's Hospital. The writer knows one of his former head boys, now a distinguished classical scholar, who spoke with affection and respect for his former headmaster. The next step in his career took him across the Atlantic to become Principal of Queen's University, Kingston, Ontario, one of the smaller but more attractive universities in North America. Sir William and Lady Fyfe have given hostages to Canada; their elder son is a successful lawyer in Ottawa, and some of their grandchildren are Canadians.

In 1936, he crossed the Atlantic once again to become Principal of our University. The period of twelve years during which he held this office was broken by the Second World War. Indeed he had scarcely settled down before the work of the University was disrupted and improvisations of all kinds became necessary. It is a tribute to the resilience of the human spirit that even in the darkest days of war one looks forward and plans for the future. The University did so and formulated post-war development plans under the leadership of the Principal, assisted, in particular, by the then Convener of the Edilis Committee, Dr. John Ross, and the Secretary, Col. H. J. Butchart. Sir William paid tribute to their help in this and in other spheres of University activity, when the Court and the Senatus entertained him to lunch on the occasion of his retiral. These three men were entirely different, but each made his own distinctive contribution to the development of the University in his time. When the War ended there was a surge of students to the universities, and the number of matriculated students at Aberdeen reached the highest level in its history so far. This created problems for all and not least for the Principal.

Although the sphere of Sir William's interest in education was already so wide, new fields were opening up which called for his gifts and experience. He was appointed Chairman of the Scottish Advisory Committee on Education in 1942, and he guided and helped to formulate the valuable reports which it published on the future of education in Scottish schools. It gave him pleasure also to be a member of the Advisory Committee on Colonial Colleges, and he visited West Africa on several occasions in connection with the setting up of University Colleges there. His wide experience and liberal-minded views enabled him to make a distinctive contribution to this important and timely work. It must have given Sir William great pleasure when earlier this year Kenneth Diké became the first African Principal of Ibadan University College. He was one of the first Africans to graduate at Aberdeen, and he showed, as so many have since, that Africans could have high qualities of mind. Sir William took a keen interest in him from the time of his sojourn in Aberdeen.

Sir William had a keen and genuine interest in the young and their problems. No Principal could have been more accessible to students, and they made full use of his help and informal friendliness. This was particularly valuable to the life of the University in the immediate post-war years when so many students had special difficulties. Moreover that accessibility did not stop at student level; many members of staff valued his advice and he was particularly concerned and helpful about their housing problems.

He had outstanding gifts, not as an orator, but as an elegant and witty speaker. He was the master of the well-turned phrase, always apt and sometimes scintillating, and occasionally even indiscreet! His hearers listened with expectation for the flash of wit, and perhaps also for the possibility of an indiscretion, just as radio audiences—not interested in art—still tune in to speeches at Royal Academy banquets.

Although a Scot, Sir William spent most of his life furth of Scotland, and he was more Anglo than Scot. If our community tends towards parochialism, as some think, he helped to correct such a fault.

H. M. STEVEN

THOMAS MURRAY TAYLOR *has been Principal since 1948.*

11*

ARTS

GREEK

Our Greeks are immortals: or at least have the secret of long life. From 1860 to 1960 only three men have held the Chair; and indeed, Sir William Geddes had already for five years been Professor of Greek at King's College before the Fusion, and the present holder, Professor ARCHIBALD CAMERON, *installed in 1931, will, we trust, hold it for many years yet. To look even further back, while our first post-Fusion Principal, Colin Campbell, held the Greek Chair for one year (1854-55), his predecessor Hugh Macpherson sat from 1797 till 1854, thus making the astounding total of 162 years incumbency for four individuals. Whether it was for the good of Greek that the last-named gentleman remained so long in office (he was " believed by the students to be kept embalmed while an assistant did his work ") the story of Sir William Geddes may reveal; and as that has already been told, we pass to his successor.*

JOHN HARROWER

Professor of Greek, 1886-1931

My spirit contracts yet as I recall that dark frown. . . . His stern discipline, his relentless perseverance with class work, fitted in with my scheme of life, and I respected where I did not revere.

G. WATT SMITH

He could be polite and pungent in the same breath. Introducing myself after twenty years, I said I had been in his Greek class. " Yes, but," he said apologetically, " I've had so many. Your name is? " " Mac-Echern," I said proudly, " Ah yes, of course, I remember you—as a footballer."

Johnnie Harrower is usually ranked as a superlatively good teacher, but I personally did not find him so. He left me entirely blank as to what the Greeks as human beings stood for.

A MATHEMATICIAN

There he stands looking down at us from the canvas of Douglas Strachan's magnificent portrait. As we gaze at him the years roll back and we are Bajans again, armed with new lecture books just bought at Bisset's, walking over the Spital, catching glimpses of the gray sea as we go, making for King's and the Greek Class at 10 o'clock. Arrived there we see Dan's martial figure in the corner of the Quad. When the bell rings, he opens the door and says," Come away you gentlemen, please," and in we go. Taking our seats, we look around. There are some plaster busts, a relief model of the Piraeus, a glass case with a silver pen, and a brass plate bearing the legend: " Nomina eorum qui praemium Simpsonianum reportaverunt." So this is the Varsity at last.

The ante-room door opens and in comes the Professor, tall and portly with an air of mingled arrogance and benignity. From Semis and Tertians we have heard the fame of him with our ears and now here he is in the flesh, " Hawa ", the greatest teacher of Greek in the country.   There is about him a certain sartorial amplitude which invites the comment of the Aulton youth.   But here in his own domain he allows no liberties to be taken.   He is an old Tory hating innovations, openly contemptuous of those who spend their time " playing with bottles ", of " soft options " (which means everything but Classics and Mathematics), and of many of his colleagues, including the Professor of Humanity.

The study of Greek, its promotion and defence, is the grand loyalty of his life.   For this no pains are too great.   He will defend the cause in speeches, newspaper articles or correspondence.   He will travel far to encourage a classical master in some remote country school.   If a student is one of his men, he will go out of his way to help him in distress or to prevent him from giving up his course in some mood of despondency. He is no scholar in the technical sense and no book is called after his name.   But his lectures, the fruit of the years, in bound volumes which now repose in King's Library, are scrupulously prepared and the

The Eighth Wise Man of Greece.

same kind of care is expected from his students.   Let any Bajan think that accents don't matter, he will be told that " correct accentuation is the mark of a scholarly mind ".   Mistakes in prose or verse are chidden in the tone grown-ups use to little children: " Oh dear, dear, we're not clever today.   Quite a superfluous piece of naughtiness, Mr. Taylor ".

One of his foibles is to feign dismay when a class confesses ignorance of simple common things like the felloe of a wheel.   With what relish he expounds that mystery!   He has many pet aversions, especially radicals of all kinds.   " Euripides—lovely lyrics, gentlemen, but the man could no more write dramas than my cat."   And, of course, Gilbert Murray, perhaps as a " translator " of Euripides, perhaps in his own right.   Cold print cannot convey his contempt for modern translators of the Bible. " Those cows, for they are nothing else, trampling with their bovine hoofs over the green pastures of the Authorised Version, have produced this abortion."   The modern taste in literature fares no better.   " There once was a man named Sir Walter Scott.   Of course nobody reads him nowadays.   But we all know our Russian novel."   Our Russian novel! It is the quintessential Hawa.

His Honours men are his principal care and on them he lavishes the reading and observation of the years.   Now he lectures on the unimagined subtleties of prose rhythm illustrated from many a source.   Listen to him declaiming the great imprecation of Meg Merrilees—" Ride your ways

Ellangowan. . . . " Now the theme is Thucydides, recalling at one time the immortal words in which Pericles set before his people the splendours of the City Violet-crowned, at another the language of incitement in which lesser men drove the same people to deeds of shame with the taunt that a democracy is incapable of bearing imperial sway. Now it is Plato, and his friends are recalling Theaetetus fallen in the wars and how his voice, when he spoke, was like a river of oil noiselessly flowing. Now it is Homer, and there is the helmsman sitting at the tiller all night long while the great constellations wheel overhead. Now it is the Agamemnon, greatest of man's imaginative works, and the lecturer wrestles with untranslatable loveliness so poignant that his voice breaks and there is a silence. . . . No scholar, maybe, but at the end of the day we are aware that through him we are in touch with the language of Hellas, the loveliest and subtlest, the most flexible and accurate medium for the expression of human thought which the mind of man has ever known. This is Hawa's great gift to his students and it is their possession for ever.

For those who, not knowing the language, have to wait outside in the court of the Gentiles, he does his best by providing public courses on art and architecture which he calls " Greek without tears ". " Very jolly," he will say as he shows the Aeginetan smile on the antique statues. But not so jolly when he refers to the Aberdeen architect who, copying Lysicrates, puts a choregic monument on top of a kirk in King Street. Another missionary effort is the production of the Antigone in the Music Hall. After that, after hearing George Rowntree Harvey as the messenger bursting in with the tragic news, who will dare to say that Sophocles is cold?

This production recalls the part that his wife plays in all that he does. She is the only child of Principal Geddes, " old Homer ", who came up the hard way from Glass—first the toil at the oar and then the fair breeze, as his memorial bears. She is a formidable figure, a scholar in her own right, who, when she lectures on Dante to a university society, appears in evening dress, as her husband also does on similar occasions. She is very much the grande dame in the Greek manse, where a dinner party is an affair of style, with a full muster of resident maids and the beadle from the West Kirk enlisted as butler. For a special occasion, like the triumph of the Antigone and a double in the Ferguson, the menu will be in azure and or, printed throughout in Greek. His successors, breathing a less ample air, will never know what it once meant to be a professor at King's.

All this is a memory of half a century ago. This year, in terms of his own bequest, the University will found the Harrower Chair in Greek Art and Archaeology. This is the memorial which he himself desired to have. But none knew better than he that there is also another memorial written into the lives of those who were known to him always as his own men.

T. M. TAYLOR

HUMANITY

ROBERT MACLURE

Professor of Humanity, 1860(52)-1868

> His scholarship we admitted to be not without elegance, but his teaching was of a very easy-going Capuan description. His class-room was a Lotus-land, where it " seemed always afternoon ". . . . When the hour was up, we shut our books with a bang at the first stroke of the bell, even if Maclure or his victim were in the middle of a sentence, and were out in the quadrangle in a twinkling.
>
> A. SHEWAN

> " It was Maclure ", cried Geddes angrily, " that let down Latin and began to sap the North."

Perhaps the truest definition of him would be to say that he was a good schoolmaster. He was a handsome, somewhat corpulent and stately old man, who walked very erectly and demeaned himself as according to the ideas of those times a professor should.

For Dr. Maclure there was but one name. He was universally and invariably spoken of as " Cocky ". Sometimes he would be called Cocky Maclure, but this was rare. His whole aspect suggested his nickname, and as he grew older, he advanced in a certain haughty and imperturbable style. I do not suppose that the feelings of his students would have ever given him a moment's concern. They were remote indeed from his exaltation. But he was not by any means an inefficient professor, and he was rather a favourite than otherwise. He had the gift of governing his classes, for no rebel could stand out long against that stony stare. He also communicated a good deal of information, and had a real perception of literary beauty. Sometimes his illustrations of the Latin writers from modern literature came like a cool wind. I am not at all surprised to find that in early days he lived among literary men.

W. ROBERTSON NICOLL: A.D.A.

JOHN BLACK

Professor of Humanity, 1868-1881

> " Black—large and cumbrous, with a kindly heart and much humanity in his unwieldy frame; a contrast to his co-Professor in the Classics in his freedom of style, his humaneness, his readiness to enjoy a joke."
>
> G. HENDERSON

Black succeeded to the Latin Chair in 1868. Before that he had been engaged as a school inspector of the old *regime*. That kind of work is not favourable to the retention or to the development of scholarship, and the results were obvious in the Chair. Yet he had the virtues of his very defects; he was unquestionably the best formal teacher in the University. Indeed, he was a born teacher in so far as the attitude and the manner are concerned, and any lack of touch came rather from indolence than want of ability.   He was himself at his ease and at once set others at theirs, and it was to most a feeling of relief to turn from the discipline of other classes to his.   No man ever held the curb easier and yet with greater success; by him all paedagogic tricks and traditions were dismissed, and over the northern counties today his influence on teaching and on teachers has been more marked than that of his colleagues.   He aroused interest in the subject, and his method of maintaining discipline was, like that of Professor Fuller, his always having something to say and knowing that he could say it.

He knew his strength and his defects, and he wisely made no pretence to finished or widen Latin scholarship. . . . He had not more than a popular and vague knowledge of Roman history, and beyond Arnold we do not think that his sober wishes had ever learned to stray.   Greek he had well-nigh forgotten, and philology beyond Peile he did not profess. But what he knew was all living and vitalized knowledge, and with greater industry he could have done justice to his undoubted natural ability.

He did much to promote a genial intercourse between the students and himself, and to thaw the old geological era of barrier reefs and icebergs. He recognized his men on the street, and this he alone did of the professoriate in his day.   An epoch was introduced in 1875 by asking him as the first professorial chairman to a class-supper.   It looked, as was confessed at the time, rather hopeless and against all precedent; as soon might the Pope of Rome or the Emperor of All the Russias have been thought of to open the Debating Society.   He was a little late in arriving, and the " bookies " were jubilant over their free offering of long odds; but a rattle of the cab up to the door soon ruined their bets and restored the general equanimity.   He had had no hesitation about coming, and never was there a better and an easier chairman.   It was the day of small things, and the speeches were of a subdued cast.   The organizer of the supper and the author of the invitation was entrusted, as the wit of the class, with the toast of " The Ladies ".   His rising was the signal for an ovation; but, getting no farther than these two words, he sat down in funereal silence.   Genially then did the chairman congratulate the speaker on his terse and happy style!

W. KEITH LEASK: *A.B.A.*

JAMES DONALDSON

Professor of Humanity, 1881-1886

Professor Black was followed in the Chair by James Donaldson, a popular if not inspiring teacher.   He is said to have broken the tyranny of the Latin version, not so much as a discipline in Aberdeen training as an arbiter in the all-decisive Bursary Competition.

Professor Donaldson's appearance and physiognomy are remarkable enough to call for a few words in passing.   When we look upon his radiant visage, there rise before us visions of those genuine works of art which are still to be seen on the sign boards of quaint old hostelries in English counties, and are labelled the Rising Sun or the Sun in Splendour. A benignant smile constantly overspreads his good humoured face, though, it is true, he does occasionally attempt to frown. . . . He assumes a very free-and-easy sitting posture when lecturing, and stuffs his hands deep into the pockets of his nether garment, as if he expected to find there the key to the Old Etruscan language. . . . He talks to his students like an ordinary mortal and not like one of the heroes or demigods of antiquity. We can approach him like " children to a father ", for he has always shown himself the friend and champion of our cause.

Alma Mater, 1884

WILLIAM MITCHELL RAMSAY

Professor of Humanity, 1886-1911

In 1886 for the first time the Latin chair was filled by a man with a European reputation. His travels in Asia Minor had made (later Sir) William Ramsay an authority on that part of the world, and the heady delights of re-discovering lost civilizations got between him and the plainer of his students. Inscriptions " discovered by myself, gentlemen " did not help them to a " sign-up ", and dissatisfactions between them culminated in a complaint to the S.R.C. over what the students felt to be arbitrary and inconsiderate treatment of examination papers. Reading the exchanges after sixty years one has to admit that the great man could be peevish. It is pleasant to set against this such tributes as those of Professor Rudmose Brown, John Fraser, Agnes Mure Mackenzie and the brilliant Honours man of the nineties who contributes the main part of this conspectus.

That little insignificant figure in his shabby buff overcoat was, with Grierson, the greatest teacher that it has been my fortune to " sit under ".

T. D. RITCHIE

" In season and out of season, I say, gentlemen, remember the ancients."

He is before my eyes again, sitting on one foot, twirling a pencil, the background of his desk suggesting ancient Rome, he himself most carefully groomed, just like a leading draper in my native town.

G. WATT SMITH

Professor Ramsay is startlingly original and is one of the very best authorities on Ancient Research now living, but he is undeniably a failure as a teacher . . . his lectures are uninterestingly dry and pitifully stale.

Alma Mater, 1887

I may not know a great deal of Latin, but when I left his class I understood what *res Romana* meant.

AGNES MURE MACKENZIE, 1910

Ramsay had limitations as a teacher of average undergraduates . . . To more advanced pupils, who had had more experience of other teachers, Ramsay's unique character in the King's College of those days as (to quote the words of a scholar eminently qualified to judge) " a gifted maker of

knowledge " was more evident. He could now pass more freely beyond
the bounds of the syllabus and indulge in University teaching in the full
sense of the term. The result was practical classes in epigraphy and
numismatics, which revealed the mysterious sources of knowledge. We
knew already that historians had written impressive books, and now we
saw one of the greatest of the tribe show, step by step, how the thing was
done.

JOHN FRASER

Ramsay was Professor of Latin but his proper title was Professor of
Humanity, and he was faithful to this title. Just about the time when I
first knew him, in the winter of 1893-94, he stated in *Alma Mater* in an
obituary notice of Professor Minto that he himself had always voted against

the misdirection of classical studies,
debasing them to be fetters instead
of wings for the free modern spirit,
and that the aim and crown of all
literary education is to understand
and appreciate the spirit of our own
age. In a book entitled *Historical
Geography of Asia Minor* which
Ramsay had written some time
previously and which he presented
as a prize at the end of my bajan
year, this sentence occurs: " If we
want to understand the Ancients,
especially the Greeks, we must
breathe the same air as they did
and saturate ourselves with the

same scenery and the same nature that wrought upon them. For this
end correct topography is a necessary though a humble servant."

In class, in a quiet but very persuasive tone of voice, he often impressed
on us the need for wide reading and broad views, but there was another
side to his teaching. Nothing stands out more vividly in the memory than
Ramsay's translation of the word " diligentia ": " minute attention to
details " with emphasis on the word " minute ". Like Mommsen whom
he had known personally, and by whom as by other German scholars he
was much influenced, he combined mastery of detail with the power of
broad generalization, though I cannot think that Ramsay would ever
have gone quite so far as Mommsen in exaltation of Julius Caesar and
depreciation of Cicero.

For evidence that Ramsay's own reading was very wide we have only
to look at the index of ancient authors quoted in the above mentioned
book on Asia Minor. There was apparently no book in Greek or Latin
which he had not read and the range of reading extended far into the
Byzantine period. He had developed a special interest in the early
growth and spread of the Christian Church in the Roman Empire and it
was of course necessary that he should keep in touch with the most recent

writing on the subject, whether English, French or German. He had become particularly interested in St. Paul and his travels in Asia Minor and elsewhere. He himself had spent many of his long vacations in travel, particularly in Asia Minor, often accompanied by his wife, and both had to endure and harden themselves to life in very primitive conditions. It was no wonder that Ramsay used to impress on us the need for physical as well as mental fitness. He admired very much the combination of scholarship and athletics which was then very common in the English public schools and the two older universities but was in those days very uncommon in Scotland, where the two were seldom combined. (A notable exception was A. M. Mackay, later Lord Mackay, who, in my time, combined the highest honours in mental philosophy with the tennis championship of Scotland.)

In the Summer Term after our third Winter Session, Ramsay being then at home used to invite some of us honours men round to his house in the evening. On one of these occasions he asked us to write an essay on the views of Horace concerning family relationships. For this we had to get a general view of the whole of Horace, whether in the original or in a translation, and use our own judgment and Ramsay was well pleased with the result. It was unfortunate that this experiment was not further followed up. Ramsay was in fact so much obsessed with his own special work that he did not in his teaching in class give full effect to his views as to the proper aim and scope of classical education. Even on these summer evenings he sometimes had long periods of silence. He would apologize and explain that he could not take his mind away from the work he was then pursuing. On one of these evenings he revealed the reason for his especial interest in Rome of the imperial period. On a long view Caesar was justified in putting an end to the Republic and establishing a rule more or less despotic. For some centuries there was a Pax Romana in the civilized world as then known. There were good roads and means of communication. Thus the Christian religion, despite the persecutions to which it was subjected, was enabled to spread throughout the empire and eventually to triumph.

Ramsay's assistant Middleton took much of the burden of the class work off his shoulders. He was known as Caesar, for there was a re-markable resemblance between his features and the small bust of Julius Caesar suspended on the wall above the professorial chair. Middleton was an exact scholar, an advocate of pure classics, of an accurate grounding in knowledge of a few books. In this Ramsay gave him full scope; with his own appreciation of the value of detail he probably thought that Middleton's methods provided a sound foundation for the wider studies to follow later.

In class Ramsay made a new departure by reading with us Tertullian's apology and Minucius Felix, another late Christian writer. I cannot remember that any work of Cicero was read except a few of his letters. On one occasion in class, in some connection which I cannot recall, he told us in his ordinary quiet and persuasive voice that no statesman ever so much misunderstood as Demosthenes the character and needs of his age. Evidently those eloquent periods in which Harrower revelled did not satisfy Ramsay. But the prose of Demosthenes was an excellent model for Greek versions, and Cicero was a much better model for Latin versions than Tertullian. It was no wonder that at Balliol when I tried later for a scholarship or exhibition my Greek prose version was thought superior to my Latin version.

When reading in class the *Miles Gloriosus* of Plautus he told us in naive fashion that no brand of ancient literature appealed to him so little as Roman comedy. Evidently like Mommsen he judged it too moralistically. On the other hand Ramsay was at his very best when reading with us the first book of Seneca's letters to Lucilius. The remarkable sympathy of moral feeling between Seneca and St. Paul would of course appeal to him. Many years afterwards, when feeling one Sunday a need of moral uplift after some previous depression or delinquency, I read at one sitting the bare Latin text of the twenty books of the letters to Lucilius, finishing in the evening to realize that since breakfast I had had neither lunch nor tea.

On one occasion Lord Bryce, then a member of a Liberal Government, having delivered a speech in Aberdeen saw Ramsay in the audience and called upon him to come forward and speak. Ramsay complied and spoke in his usual quiet and persuasive voice, more impressive than any oratory. I was present but all I can remember was his mention of the calamity suffered by Parliament when the Westminster electors in 1868 ejected John Stuart Mill, a philosopher above party who valued only the really vital interests of the body politic. So here was Ramsay on a liberal platform, Ramsay who condemned Demosthenes' fight for the freedom of Athens as an independent City State and defended the policy of Caesar and imperial Rome. But truth has many sides and Ramsay had a multiple mind. Ramsay, the " subtle " Ramsay as Rachel Annand Taylor used to call him, would have been well able to defend his position.

W. A. ROSS

ALEXANDER SOUTER

Professor of Humanity, 1911-1937

> Lively lady, to her monosyllabic young dinner partner: " Is there any-
> thing you are interested in, Mr. Souter? "
> " I have a passion for the Classics."

The painter of a portrait makes several sketches each showing a characteristic pose of his subject; in this short word-portrait I shall attempt to follow the same plan. The first glimpse I had of Souter, an experience that was repeated once a week over several years before ever I became one of his students, was of his progress every Sunday morning *en famille* from Humanity Manse in College Bounds along the Spital to church. This is in many ways the most characteristic aspect of Souter, for, above all, he was a devout Christian and a staunch Congregationalist and his religion was the basis on which his whole life rested.   Even in the world of learning it will be the Patristic scholar [1] rather than the Latinist who will be remembered; his *monumentum aere perennius* is his three volumes of *Pelagius' Expositions of Thirteen Epistles of St. Paul*.   Often, too, he could be seen abstracted in thought waiting for the 'bus at the Mounthooly stop with the end of a cigarette hanging forgotten from his lips; later he solemnly renounced smoking.   No one who saw the handsome and distinguished figure, with fresh complexion and silver-grey hair, could ever forget him.   Almost invariably he carried (incongruous as it may seem) a racegoer's umbrella, complete with golden pencil in the handle; I remember a humorous demonstration he once gave me of the use to which this pencil could be put on the racecourse, not that he had any first-hand acquaintance with the turf.

The first time I met him was when I called for advice at Humanity Manse and found him seated at the piano in his shirt-sleeves; music was one of his constant recreations.   The informality and friendliness of his welcome and the trouble he took to advise a *tiro* was characteristic of the man.   Walking was another favourite recreation and his companion was regaled with a fund of anecdotes and reminiscences and many a pun, for he was partial to word-play (some would perhaps have thought his humour pedantic); on one occasion, when we travelled by 'bus together he insisted on paying my fare, saying with great delight, " Ça, c'est mon affaire ".   When the weather prevented his usual afternoon walk, he would find relaxation in the cinema of which he was an ardent fan.   He was a great traveller and spoke Spanish, French and German fluently and often more correctly than the natives; he related to me how once in Switzerland he was taken for a Pfarrer on his pastoral rounds.

Souter was a great lover of words, which he collected with the zest of a schoolboy, but he sometimes betrayed a curious insensitivity to style; he would read dictionaries in preference to other books.   His posthumous *Glossary of Late Latin* was the fruit of a lifelong pursuit of lexicography. In class he would inveigh against the iniquities and shortcomings of Lewis and Short, and, tugging vigorously at the lower points of his waistcoat, would announce: " Lewis and Short are wrong; this word occurs six times in Jerome and seventeen times in Ambrosiaster."   His enunciation of Latin in lectures was correct almost to the point of pedantry; he invariably spoke of " cone-suls " and " Aissha Minor ".

Class teaching was not Souter's *métier*; he could not plumb the abysmal ignorance of the Ordinary Latin Class.   He tended to assume

[1] An agreeable proof of this fact is to be found in *The Oxford Dictionary of the Christian Church* (1957) which has accorded Souter an entry (p. 1274) on his own as a " New Testament and Patristic Scholar "—the entry is, incidentally, an admirable short appreciation of Souter himself and of his life as a scholar.

The Humanity god SOU-TER conferring the benefits of Roman History upon mortals.   The cherub is "Johnny" Fraser.

that everyone had read the normal run of the Classical authors, and so the prescribed books included such near-esoterica as Statius's *Silvae* (on which he had done his own first research in Madrid) and Seneca's *Benefits* for the first year, with Augustine's *De catechizandis Rudibus* or Tertullian's *Apology* or Apuleius for the advanced class.   As a scholar his industry was prodigious; indeed everything he did was done with an almost Teutonic thoroughness.   Every evening he would conscientiously withdraw to his professional books, like Browning's grammarian, to " settle *Hoti's* business ", believing like the Elder Pliny, whom he closely resembled in his attitude here " that all time was lost that was not given to study " (*perire omne tempus arbitrabatur, quod studio non impertiretur*). But, if he was not a great teacher, and if he did not succeed in imparting to his students his own love of Latin, he was in himself the living embodiment of the Platonic " idea " of scholarship, and his Aberdeen classes may not always have realized that they were in the presence of a scholar with a world reputation in his chosen line.   His unflinching devotion to *Wissenschaft* gave me a vision of scholarship that I gained from very few of my teachers.

J. M. R. CORMACK

Professor Souter was followed by one of his own most brilliant students. PETER SCOTT NOBLE, *1937-51, who left us to become Principal of King's College, London.   A Buchan man, shrewd, balanced, quick-witted, broad of shoulder as of mind, Professor Noble had a Cambridge career of almost unequalled brilliance, having achieved first class in Parts I and II of the Classical Tripos and*

Parts I and II of the Oriental Languages Tripos.   His research in Sanskrit and other Oriental languages led some critics to put his name on a level with those of Robertson Smith and Dr. Giles.

The present holder of the Chair is w. s. watt, *1951.*

MORAL PHILOSOPHY

WILLIAM MARTIN

Professor of Moral Philosophy, 1860(1846)-1876

It is difficult to do justice to Professor Martin.   I have the best evidence that for years he was an efficient and respected professor, and of his unfeigned religious zeal and high character there could be no doubt. . . . But during my time at college it must be admitted that he was something like the butt of his class.   No honest sketch could possibly be written without recognising the facts.

What his claims to be a professor of philosophy were I have not the least idea.   His only publications I can trace are two tiny pamphlets, one of them an address delivered to the Evangelical Alliance in 1822, on *British Infidelity: its Aspects and Prospects.*   The other is a pamphlet called *Creed and Circumstance.*

The professor must have been fairly old in 1870, but it would have been hard to tell his age.   He had a long brown beard, only slightly whitened, and a wig.   His wig was no specious production of art.   Everybody could see what it was.

His lectures were "eloquent" at times, and very old.   The most famous of the number was on " Conscience ", " The Terrors of Remorse ", etc., etc.   It was always known when that lecture was to be delivered, and as the professor rolled off his periods, they were followed by such frantic and prolonged applause, that if I recollect well, he had to carry the thing on for some days.   No doubt as to the genuineness of this applause ever visited him.   He honestly believed the lectures to be the greatest thing in the eloquence of the world.   His class was often, and indeed for the most part, noisy, and his habit was to inflict fines on offending students.   Often, however, he was unable to discover them. One student in my class had an extraordinary gift of whistling in such a manner that nobody could detect the culprit.

Out of the goodness of his heart, Dr. Martin held a Bible Class on Sunday evenings.   It used to be conducted at his lodgings, but the scenes became so violent, that it was transferred to a room in the Music Hall.

w. robertson nicoll: *A.B.A.*

Men who were candidates for Honours in some other Department might scrape through with the barest minimum of ethical knowledge.

12

Others, who could almost say you the lectures by heart, had the Plough driven over them. Attendance at Martin's Sunday Bible Class, so it was whispered, saved many a poor wretch from being " cast as rubbish to the void ". . . . In one case, a candidate for mathematical honours coolly disregarded Martin's embargo, entered the examination room and sat down to the paper. He was promptly ejected by Fuller.

A. SHEWAN: *Meminisse Juvat*

JOHN FYFE

Librarian, 1860(1857)-1876

Professor of Moral Philosophy, 1876-94

> " Here too the Moralist, that lovable man with the broad-brimmed tile, the short breeks and the socks, may have polished his periods about Binnie the Beaver, have drawn up the weird diagrams, and may have interviewed members of our Class—for guide, philosopher and friend, and clandestine benefactor, he was to many."
>
> J. SCOTT RIDDELL

John Fyfe, an Angus man, graduated at King's in 1848 and thereafter, almost continuously till 1894, he served his alma mater *in one capacity or another. In 1854 the Professor of Moral Philosophy, Hercules Scott, fell ill, and till 1859 Mr. Fyfe deputised for him. In 1857 he became also Librarian of the old Library which then occupied part of the Chapel at King's, in 1860 Librarian of the University, in which capacity he performed two great services, the transfer of the books from the Chapel to the new Library building and the compilation of a complete Author-Catalogue of the contents of the Library, " a colossal task described as ' utterly impossible ' by the late Professor Milligan ". On the death of Professor Martin in 1876, Mr. Fyfe became Professor of Moral Philosophy.*

His lectures stick perhaps more in the memory than those of any other professor. They were, it must be admitted, almost devoid of original thought. His strength lay not in philosophy but in teaching philosophy—so lucid was he, so methodic in his arrangement—no abstract dreamer, but clear cut, simple, vigorous, a philosopher of the commonsense school in more senses than one. The feature of his lectures was his system of illustration, which abounded in bright humour, not of the dry, grave old Scotch type, but productive of side-splitting roars, which left no dry eye in the house. Against the Experimentalist Philosophy which has so long prevailed in Aberdeen he launched the thunder of his invective and the keen shafts of his wit. Here is one of his tit-bits:

" If it be argued that we are descended from an arboreal type then we must concede that our ancestors had an excellent training in the higher branches."

He loved all magistrands as peculiarly his own flock. " Remember ", he used to say, " on you the moral tone of the whole body of students largely depends." "Ah," exclaimed the genial old gentleman on the last day of a magistrand session, "You don't know how I shall miss you. When the quadrangle is deserted and all my magistrands leave me, I feel as if I had nothing to live for, and my spirits are very low indeed."

A. T. G. BEVERIDGE: *A.B.A.*

He had no other friends but his Magistrands. He used to sit alone with a set of Arts class groups, and from their faces and memories seek to people his own rather lonely sanctum. One friend of ours on official business did once track him out. "Come away," cried the old Moralist, quite boisterously, "I've some friends of yours with me you'll be glad to see again." To his astonishment "Johnny" produced the Arts group of his year, and went over them all in such a style as quite to justify his own solitary quotation of "though lost to sight, to memory dear".

Long ere Andrew Carnegie had been invented with his millions, "Johnny" with his little had been discovering cases of hardship in the class—so we learned in confidence from a friend of a recipient—and inditing cheery little billets (with enclosure) in some modified dislocation or distortion of writing that doubtless led him to hug the delusion that he had quite succeeded in disguising his impossible penmanship. For years he had been at it, no one had known it, and he died believing it unknown.

W. K. LEASK: *I.B.*

W. R. SORLEY

Professor of Moral Philosophy, 1894-1900

A distinguished and influential member of the Philosophy staff at King's College was Professor W. R. Sorley. Unfortunately his tenure of office at Aberdeen was very short—only six years. He came with an outstanding reputation for scholarship, and impressed his students by the solidity and penetration of his lectures. The cordiality of his welcome to Aberdeen was intensified by his relationship to his brother-in-law, later Sir George Adam Smith, who, although his appointment to the principalship of Aberdeen University was still in the future, had in his earlier days made a name for himself as a preacher, especially attractive to students, in one of the leading congregations in Aberdeen.

By the generality of students Sorley was looked upon as a somewhat distant personality, slightly difficult of approach, but on further acquaintance this supposititious barrier was very rapidly removed, especially for the honours students. The regular discussion gatherings at his house were much appreciated, all the more so when one of the most regular attenders was G. F. Stout, then for a short period a lecturer on Comparative Psychology in Aberdeen University; a man whom C. D. Broad described as "one of the ablest all-round British philosophers of the last fifty years".

Sorley's departure in 1900 to become Knightbridge professor in Cambridge in succession to Sidgwick, was a great loss to Aberdeen, but it was felt that this conspicuous appointment at Cambridge was a fitting recognition of Sorley's philosophical ability, and his cordial welcome at Cambridge to former students from Aberdeen showed that he had by no means forgotten his earlier academic connections. His Gifford lectures on " Moral Values and the Idea of God " and his " History of English Philosophy ", both published midway in his thirty-three years tenure of office at Cambridge, were regarded by the many competent judges who knew his work, as amongst the most valuable of contemporary philosophical publications.

W. S. URQUHART

The Chair of Philosophy was then held for two years by ROBERT LATTA, *1900-2, who had entered the Divinity Hall at Edinburgh with the reputation of being the strongest philosophical thinker of his year. He was widely read in philosophy and poetry and in French literature and had travelled much abroad. But after making a brilliant impression here, he went off to Glasgow to fill the Chair of Logic.*

JAMES BLACK BAILLIE

Professor of Moral Philosophy, 1902-1924

Professor (later Sir James) Baillie made his mark in three fields—as a scholar, as an industrial adjudicator, and as the head of a great and growing English university.

He came to Aberdeen in 1902, at the age of twenty-nine, as Regius Professor of Moral Philosophy after a career of unusual promise at Edinburgh and Cambridge. Shortly afterwards he married the niece and heiress of Lord James of Hereford and settled down to live in considerable style at Norwood, Cults. He must have been one of the few philosophers in Christendom to arrive for his lectures in a chauffeur-driven Rolls Royce; and many a student will recall the panic of being disrobed by the butler in the entrance hall of Norwood. But all this was an essential part of the man. His world was not the world of Aberdeen; and it never became so. Possibly because of this, he never seemed to attain an esteem in Aberdeen comparable with his standing in the outside world. For example, he shared with McTaggart of Cambridge the distinction of being the leading interpreter of Hegel at that time. His *Hegel's Logic* (1901), his *Hegel's Phenomenology of Mind* (1910) and *The Idealistic Construction of Experience* (1906) were major works of scholarship and—although the climate of philosophical inquiry has radically changed—are still landmarks in Hegelian studies. But it may be doubted if they were much read in Aberdeen.

There was, however, no dubiety about his success in the lecture-room. Many students took his class, as they took J. Arthur Thomson's, because of the lecturer. The fine presence, the beautifully modulated voice, and the clarity and sensitiveness of his diction made listening natural. He possessed the power of reducing complicated problems to their simple basic elements, and he drew upon the rich variety of human experience to illuminate his points. To succeeding generations of students—and not only to the philosophically minded amongst them—he must have opened up insights and releases which they would not otherwise have found. Many will say that they owe to him their first steps in intellectual maturity. But even here he received less than his due. His supposed attitude to religious faith was the ground of offence. The tragedy of this was that religion was the abiding interest of his own personal life, as his posthumous *Reflections on Life and Religion* (1952) amply shows. But the aim of philosophy is to prove all things and, in this particular context, to substitute convictions based upon reflection for beliefs held merely by virtue of custom and reiteration. And Baillie, secure himself and acutely analytical, made insufficient effort to temper his dialectics to the less mature. It was commonly said, and he himself believed, that his failure to succeed Pringle Pattison in Edinburgh in 1919 was due to the intervention of ecclesiastical interests who represented him as a corrupter of youth. It did not console him that Socrates was once disqualified on the same ground.

But he was by that time moving away from pure philosophy and developing an alternative talent for practical affairs which he had discovered through working in Whitehall during the first war. His last work of scholarship—*Studies in Human Nature*—was published in 1921; and in 1924 he was appointed Vice-Chancellor of Leeds University, where he made an outstanding contribution to its expansion and development, while at the same time giving repeated service as chairman of Government committees, tribunals and inquiries.

W. TAYLOR

JOHN LAIRD

Professor of Moral Philosophy, 1924-1946

This is a tribute, after thirty-six years, to a man whom in my youth and subsequently, I admired immensely, and who impressed himself on the minds of many of my fellow undergraduates and myself as someone very great indeed. This impression on callow minds was confirmed in the years that followed, for when John Laird died in 1946 at the age of fifty-nine his philosophical abilities had been acclaimed in Europe, in America, and all over the English-speaking world, and he was rightly regarded (with Samuel Alexander whom he himself so much admired) as a leading exponent of the doctrines of the school of philosophy to which he belonged. These doctrines ultimately derived from the work of Thomas Reid, the glory of Scottish philosophy: the point is important, for though John Laird eschewed all antiquarian derivativeness and merely historical alignment, the sentiment of natural piety was strong in him. To be sure, as he would have said himself, the speculations of Arnauld played their part, but Reid was the man for John Laird. " I was born in Kincardineshire, in the parish next to Reid's birthplace ", he said, " and I noted the fact in my dreams." So in 1924 he became what we are told he always wished to be, a professor of philosophy in Scotland, and that in Reid's own University. For twenty-two years he performed the duties of his Chair with the most meticulous devotion, superb skill and that saving grace of humour which was such a pronounced feature in his character.

Dr. W. S. Urquhart has given an excellent account of John Laird's contribution to philosophy in the Proceedings of the British Academy, of which he was a Fellow: my task here is to set down in brief what he meant and did for us in the brave days of our youth. In the first place we liked the look of him: he was a bigly-made man; his face had an engaging comeliness; and his whole appearance suggested the open air. This last describes literally the effect his lectures had on us; our minds were cleared of prejudice and cant; we were shown how to think and to face up resolutely to those philosophic problems that were set, in the master's own phrase, by the brute intractability of nature. But the word that best describes the effect his prelections produced is exhilaration: we were transported by the vigour of that intellectual performance, the power of keen logical analysis which allowed nothing to pass without scrutiny, the wide-ranging scholarship so unobtrusively carried, the command of memorable phrase, the quips and quiddities with which he illustrated and enriched his philosophic themes. Thus, in discoursing on the manner in which diverse men interpret the same event diversely according to their several natures: " When anything untoward happens," he said, " one man says, ' Great is Allah ' and another, ' Cherchez la femme '," Many of these illustrations were of such a kind as to come home directly, to use a phrase from Bacon, to our business and bosoms, as when he would cite some witticism of the late Mr. Harry Gordon (of whose unique powers of humour he, as we also, had a lively appreciation) by way of adjunct to some philosophic theme he was developing. We laughed heartily with him and remembered the point he was enforcing.

What I am trying to say about John Laird's effect on us was said years before I was born by a man who never saw him. " Great teachers ", wrote Sir James Cantlie about William Pirrie, Professor of Surgery first at Marischal and then in the University 1839-82, " leave with their pupils an impression, a picturesque presence, well-nigh impossible to convey in writing. . . . A real teacher implants in his pupils' memories, words, sentences, principles, modes of action, groundwork of beliefs and beliefs themselves which are carried into the daily life of the individual and, maybe, handed down to posterity." Such was the influence exercised over us by John Laird.

Of course, we didn't realize at the time that this was what was taking place. What did happen was that we came out of his classroom and carried into the little societies we formed (for the purpose, save the mark, of exploring social and philosophical problems, one of them being called, such is youth, the Iconoclast Society) the logical habits and terminology of our teacher. " This is a question ", we would cry, echoing the Master, "which cannot be settled *ad hoc* ", or : " The whole matter is debatable " : or : " This argument leaves my withers quite unwrung." And with what indescribable glee some of us marshalled our arguments, as he did, under *Imprimis, Amplius, Praeterea,* and *Adhuc,* throwing in a *per contra* occasionally by way of good measure. But none of us could emulate that deprecatory shrug of the shoulder which invariably accompanied his logical sallies or the charming smile which always went with them.

John Laird had on his desk in his study a photograph of McTaggart, the celebrated Cambridge philosopher, for whom he had much esteem. I remember speaking to him in terms of admiration of Broad's biographical account of McTaggart. " Yes," said he, " Broad has written of McTaggart about as well as one human being can write of another." The remark was characteristic. Though much of our knowledge of human personality and human relationships is at best fragmentary, and our moral intuitions often confused and obscure, yet on occasion we can, and do, overcome the difficulties set by our material, and the limitations imposed by our mental and moral equipment. And that it is our plain duty to make these occasions as frequent as possible was not the least important of the lessons impressed by John Laird on those who were fortunate enough to come under his care.

WALTER R. HUMPHRIES

From 1947 the Chair was held by DONALD M. MACKINNON, *who leaves us this year (1960) for a Chair in Cambridge.*

LOGIC AND RHETORIC

ALEXANDER BAIN

Professor of Logic and Rhetoric, 1860-1880

Grierson has written of the " rigid rhetorical training associated with Bain ", but in conversation speaks of his kindliness, even after he had given up lecturing, to young men of promise. A young American, when Bain was in his seventieth year, spent an evening in his company : " I want to give him a chapter in my book when I go back, but he seems too complex a personality for anything less than a volume."

He is in his seventieth year but his eye is not dimmed—he is ready to appreciate and discuss what is new in literature or science or politics or social affairs or philosophy.

Alma Mater

His strength lay in science rather than in philosophy . . . he never divined the existence of such a thing as style or melody of words . . . but for clear flowing *arrowy* exposition, we have never seen, and we never shall see his like again.

W. KEITH LEASK

Poetry—To Bain it was a mystery. "There was the door to which he found no key." What to many rendered his English class repellent was his possession by one idea: "Grammar is a science or it is nothing." Bain did but reflect the characteristics of a country which was "a layer of peat-moss spread on a bannock of granite".

G. WATT SMITH

Professor Alexander Bain, the first Professor of Logic and Rhetoric and twice Rector of the united University, was the most distinguished psychologist of the mid-nineteenth century. He also made notable contributions to philosophy, to education, and to English. But it was in psychology, which he did much to free from metaphysical speculation and to establish as a positive observational science, that he achieved his international reputation. Bain laid the foundations of physiological psychology; he stressed the role of habit and learning in behaviour and first formulated what is now known as the "law of effect"; and with his "usual severe analytic dissection" (his own phrase) he applied to psychology the method of classification that was then so prominent in botany and zoology. Although he avoided the cruder over-simplifications of James Mill, he was a thoroughgoing associationist, and at the end of last century this aspect of his work repelled such influential people as James, Ward and Stout. But now there is a revival of interest in Bain, even in his associationism, and it is noteworthy that the leading current authority on Bain is himself an Aberdeen graduate—Associate-Professor James Cardno of the Department of Psychology in the University of Hobart.

A. REX KNIGHT

Though we knew his *Grammar* from our youth, Bain himself we had not seen till that vivid day when, after wandering aimlessly in a drizzle of rain and in quagmires of mud, among the Irish stirks of St. Luke's Fair, we were confronted with his notable personality, and were plunged without preamble of any sort into the first lecture of his English course. That this thin, sharp, almost hatchet face surveying the well-filled tiers of benches belonged to no ordinary man even we, schoolboys as most of us were, could divine. The impression rested on a tripod of countenance, manner and voice—each supporting the others. The prominent and finely formed nose, the small sparkling hazel eyes, the mobile and expressive mouth, made a picture stamped with alertness. The hair brushed athwart the baldness and ending in a tip-tilted point at each ear accentuated the piquant archness of the face, and suggested the fox-terrier as the only just comparison. His movements were like his mind, active and nimble, but noiseless and devoid of fuss. . . . His clear polished elocution, that modulated itself so perfectly to fit all shades of emphasis, completed the charm, and the general effect was magic and immediate.

It was the Logic and Psychology class that invoked the professor's most potent spells. This was his sphere; here he had done his most original work, by which he was known outside his own country—a virtue of great merit in students' eyes. The analytic character of his mind, noticeable in the English class, and sometimes doing him injustice there, was in place when expounding discrimination and the great law of relativity as the basis of all intellectual exercise; and as he, day by day, built up in rigidly logical sequence the fabric of his system, we began to understand the power of the instrument he was placing in our hands.

The one term that describes him best is practicality. Anything dreamy or visionary was alien to his nature. Intellectual sanity and clearness of vision, coupled with a tenacious will that no emotional wave could shake, these were the constituents of his mind.

ALEXANDER MACKIE: *A.B.A.*

His method was simple and thorough-going. He lectured on English Composition three times a week: on Mondays he cross-examined—and he *was* a cross-examiner—on the work of the preceding Friday: then he lectured for half-an-hour. . . . And such lecturing! Everything was in perfect proportion; every sentence and every word were destined to a particular effect and never missed it. There was no proposition in Rhetoric that had not its most telling remark or example, and no example that had not its most telling rendering in speech and gesture. I have been with twenty professors since then but I have never again known perfection in the art of lecturing.

Alma Mater

I never heard of Bain indulging in physical recreation other than walking. I did once hear him tell how he had enjoyed a visit to the St. Andrews golf course. But not to play. The charm to him was in the " beautiful parabolas " described by the balls driven from the tee. It took a fast walker to keep up with Bain. The " expression " of his legs, if I may use the term, was peculiar. No one who had seen him hurrying along could mistake him in the distance on a second view. It is said that he was so weak in his youth that he had to use sticks. But walking exercise, persevered in, cured him, and he kept it up. To a cabman who hailed him as he rushed past with " Cab, sir? " he only shouted, " Haven't time."

A. SHEWAN: *Meminisse Juvat*

Retired, in his house at Ferryhill, he was isolated by mutual distrust from the ordinary professional circles, but in active co-operation with international thought. The old gentleman, slight and gray, with a keen pale face and vivid eyes, sat at the top of his table pouring out endless cups of tea for his guests.   In such a fashion one might imagine Voltaire to have held a reception.

When I told him that my father's name was Alexander Mitchell, Bain remarked, " That would be the red-headed bookseller from opposite Marischal College.   And so he became a minister.   The religious people might be more grateful to me.   I did not pervert their men, but the religious disposition is a queer stubborn thing."

CHALMERS MITCHELL

WILLIAM MINTO

Professor of Logic and English Literature, 1880-1893

> The beaming radiant face of Minto—a face reflecting a kind heart and a great soul, infectious to all who sat under him.   No one who merely knows the books he wrote could guess the power which Minto exercised over a generation of Aberdeen students.
>
> ARTHUR KEITH

> Will there be an Elysium at all without him?   He was altogether human and his subject of English Literature was nectar.
>
> G. WATT SMITH

> If there was ever a man who touched the heart of studentdom, that man was William Minto.   To the outside world he was known for the fame of his mental powers, to us rather for his unfailing courtesy of manner, his rare loveliness of spirit.
>
> *Alma Mater*, 1893

> The Tertians on one occasion captured a Bajan and retained him by force in the professorial chair.   Professor Minto regretted that his teaching had been of so little effect.   " You should have used logic, gentlemen, and persuaded him."

William Minto, born in Alford at nearly the same time as Robertson Smith was born in the nearby Keig, and like him one of Bain's most brilliant pupils, graduated with triple Honours, in Classics, Mathematics and Mental Philosophy.   He began academic life as assistant to Professor Thomson in Natural Philosophy, but turned aside to journalism, and was Editor of the *Examiner* and leader-writer on the *Daily News* and *Pall Mall Gazette*.   When he returned to Aberdeen to succeed Bain in 1880, he brought with him the heady aroma of Fleet Street and personal contact with notable writers of the day.   W. Keith Leask considered that for the sake of his scholarship he " stayed too long in Fleet Street.   Yet for him it had some advantages.   Ulysses-like he had seen many men and known their mind.   He alone of his colleagues impressed his students with the feeling of the old mediæval wandering scholar who had realized and concreted in his own experience the *Universitas*. . . . He thus brought the outside world to the gates and gave the look beyond, which it is the peculiar and indispensable function of a university to provide."

All through his tenure of the Chair, Logic and English Literature remained wedded.   "The commission", says Keith Leask, "that conjoined the subjects of English and Logic in a single chair either had a cheerful belief in the ability of man, or was more likely perplexed by the lack of endowments. There is no natural affinity between the two subjects."

That Minto's teaching of Literature was a new experience to Aberdeen students is borne out by the testimony of many, and when the Commission of 1892 resolved to separate the two subjects, it was well known that Minto's choice was to retain English. But he was not to be allowed to build up the school of English studies he was so well equipped to do. Struck down by illness, the " tenement of clay " proved too frail and he died on a bitter day in early 1893, not yet fifty years of age. Men have told of the desolation that fell on his class when the news was brought to them in the middle of a lecture. He was much loved.

" It was ", wrote Sir William Ramsay, " our common study of modern literature that first brought us together as lovers of the ' romantic ' side in that literature, as believers that the aim and crown of all literary education is to understand and appreciate the spirit of our age.

" There is one quality which beyond all others roused my admiration and that quality Minto had in a remarkable degree—courage. The splendid moral courage he showed seems to me almost the greatest quality in human nature. He never flinched a hair's-breadth from an opinion he believed in, however unpopular or even dangerous it might be."

The Chair was held from 1893 to 1895 by ROBERT ADAMSON.

WILLIAM LESLIE DAVIDSON

Professor of Logic, 1895-1926

> Kindest of men, he never lets his learning over-reach his better feelings. I have heard him " make the worse appear the better reason " for fun—and at croquet! You all remember his jokes in class . . . they are all worth repetition—every year. Many a man might have had his future career wrecked by ignorant professors if it had not been for his intervention. If you are the greatest " waster " in the place he will " understand " your action, and is not that the sum of philosophy?
>
> *Alma Mater*

On the borders of the Garioch district of Aberdeenshire there is a conspicuous hill, formerly covered by a wood on its upper slopes and crowned on its rocky summit by the still easily traced ramparts of a prehistoric fort. There are other links between the present and the past associated with that hill. One is that on its north-western side King Robert the Bruce fought a significant battle with his enemy the Red Comyn, and won it, although the monarch was handicapped by a serious illness and had to be carried on a litter to the battle field. So the inhabitants of the district felt that they had associations with the past of which they could be proud. The wood disappeared but the fortifications remained, stretching the memories of the people into the far distant days.

But with the passing of the years associations change their character and direction, and in the closing decades of the nineteenth century another interest captured the imaginations of the little community in this same locality. To the kirk of Bourtie on the southern side of the hill there came a minister who served his people loyally for a score of years, won their affections and established a reputation in which they shared though not perhaps understanding fully the reason for its steady widening far beyond the bounds of the parish. They recognized that they had amongst them in Dr. Davidson, a minister of a very special character, who could give them good reason for being proud of their connection with him, just as their ancestors had been proud of their outstanding men in days long past of which the memory still remained. Their minister had substituted for the clash of weapons in Bruce's day the study of the harmonies of the " perennial philosophy ", reflecting on it as, almost daily, in his methodical way, he wandered through the woods which covered the ascent to the old hill-fort. The memories of its builders, of Bruce and his followers had grown dim. In the time of my boyhood local interest had concentrated on the spare tall figure of the man whom they so often saw and whose friendly greeting always cheered them. After laying the foundation of an academic reputation, under the non-idealistic training of his beloved teacher, Alexander Bain, he had come to them at Bourtie, where in a quiet environment he softened and broadened his interests. Seeing that he had identified himself so closely with his little parish, it is but fitting that the name of it should refuse to be separated from him, and should take the form of a nickname which through many years indicated the affection in which he was held by the succession of students who attended his classes in the University of Aberdeen.

In the year 1895 he was appointed to the Chair of Logic in the University of Aberdeen. Thus began an association with regular students which was to last for thirty-one years, during which, session after session, the numbers of those increased who at the close of their academic life did not straightway forget what they owed to him and his teaching. He regarded himself as called upon to lay the foundations of a knowledge of philosophical topics, and he did this well and truly. His students do not remember him for brilliant flashes of oratory or for impressive flights of philosophical imagination so much as for the steady enlightenment of their minds on the subjects which he taught, and his preparation of them for work on their own account in the spheres in which they found themselves. Year after year ex-students came back to their *Alma Mater* chiefly with the purpose of greeting their teacher of Logic, renewing their friendship with him and expressing their gratitude; and they never failed to receive a cordial and inspiring welcome and an unfeigned assurance of his interest in their particular concerns.

He could claim the authorship of many books both before and during his long professorial career. One of the earliest and most outstanding was his Burnett lectures on *Theism as Grounded in Human Nature*, a book which has hardly received the attention which it merits.   It is not particularly original and its line of thought is perhaps overmuch influenced by his teacher, the well known Alexander Bain.   But it has seemed to me a most useful book for renewing one's grasp of the outlines of theological and philosophical theories which amongst the multitude of more recent publications have become somewhat dim and confused.   His summarizing is a safeguard for those students who are given to wandering thought. His treatment of those with whom he disagrees may be almost too genial, but occasionally it contains a warning which remains in the memory, as, e.g. when he criticizes the indifferentism of agnosticism by reminding those suffering from this tendency that while a soporific may remove pain it is bought too dearly if it leads to permanent anaesthesia.   Again, his analysis of conscience may be slightly prosaic, but it is a preventive of moral lethargy.   Another important book was the *The Stoic Creed*, which has been highly valued by those who were most capable of assessing the significance of its contents.   A general unity was given to his literary work by his desire to continue a tradition, roughly describable as the Scottish Philosophy, and also by his devotion to his teacher, Alexander Bain, although this latter devotion may have slightly hampered his own undoubted independence of thought and narrowed the range of his interests.

When in our memories we go backwards, we pass easily beyond his published works to the joyous and free personality of the man himself. He came of a sturdy country stock.   His father was a doctor who spent the most of his life in a country practice about ten miles distant from Bourtie, and had become almost a legend in the countryside for his brusqueness of address, which did not, however, by any means diminish an underlying kindness of disposition.   His son inherited the kindliness but very little of the brusqueness, and they were both alike capable of an immense variety of friendships.   It might be said with the utmost truth that Professor Davidson had a unique capacity for friendship—with young and old, rich and poor, with those educated in a formal manner and those who relied mainly on their mother wit.   His friendship extended largely, especially round about the time of his appointment to the Aberdeen chair, with those who had already established their reputation in the world of scholarship, such men as Alexander Bain, Minto and Croom Robertson and especially Professor Campbell Fraser of Edinburgh.   But as already pointed out, after his appointment as professor it extended to the ever growing company of his own students, who increasingly realized how much they owed to him.   The present writer knew him at first at a very considerable distance, and still remembers the day, when, as a small schoolboy he got hold of the morning paper and rushed to his father to communicate the news that " the man over the hill has got an LL.D." But hills of separation, literal and symbolic, gradually disappeared.   I happened to be a member of the newly appointed professor's very first class at King's College and, as he persuaded me to abandon a half-hearted aspiration after classical honours and concentrate on philosophy—a service for which I never ceased to be grateful to him—opportunities for contact and ever growing friendship multiplied rapidly, and laid the foundations of an intimacy which widened and deepened throughout the rest of his life. It was at the beginning of his professorial career that I met him most frequently, and as my destiny led me to a far distant land my opportunities of meeting him became less frequent. But it was one of the joys of furlough from India to visit him in his hospitable home in Aberdeen, where the welcome was always of the most cordial character. I felt that the world had grown sadly emptier when I heard the news of his death.

We did not always agree, especially as regards the planning of a place of vocation, and I remember the regret I felt at advising another student some ten years my junior, not to be unduly swayed by his advice regarding this very question of location. But nothing could disturb my affection for my old professor and nothing will ever lessen my gratitude towards him. As Sir Robert Rait, one of his closest and most distinguished friends, said in closing his beautiful and understanding obituary tribute, " No man ever lived who had less of self-seeking in his nature and in his conduct. . . . It is no light thing to have known wise and good men, and this man was both wise and good."

W. S. URQUHART

ALEXANDER STEWART FERGUSON

Professor of Logic, 1926-1953

After a period in journalism and social work, Professor Ferguson spent two years in the Chair of Philosophy at Newcastle-on-Tyne. There he was associated with the Tyneside and Northumberland Council of Social Service in its early days when it was largely concerned with the survey of the social services, statutory and voluntary, available on Tyneside.   One who served with him on this Council bears eloquent witness to the contribution made by his singularly penetrating and honest mind to a mixed group of churchmen, industrialists, and social workers.

In 1926 Ferguson came to Aberdeen, where in the following years he proved himself very much more than a professor of logic, or even a Platonic scholar.   Certainly his contributions to Platonic scholarship, difficult and scattered in time though they are, constitute a landmark in the study of Platonic metaphysics, especially the doctrines of the *Republic*. No student can dispense with their study, and even if his intensely self-critical methods of working make impossible the publication of the Terry Lectures which he gave in Yale in 1947 on the *Platonic Revolution*, there is no doubt that students for generations to come will be referred to the files of the *Classical Quarterly* to consult Ferguson on " Sun, Line, and Cave ".   But where the University of Aberdeen was concerned, and its Faculty of Arts in particular, there was scarcely an aspect of its work on which he failed to leave his mark.

Ferguson was a quite unself-consciously cultured man, the range of whose interest and curiosity knew no obvious bounds. His conversation was at once a severe test and an unending delight; he seemed quite incapable of counting the most minute details of the human scene too slight for his concern. European literature, the history of art, the world of politics, national and international alike, the detailed history of Old Aberdeen—in all these fields he was at home, and in talk as in the lecture room itself, his utterance would slide half noticed from one to the other.

It was certainly inevitable that such a professor should act as curator of the library, and equally inevitable, that with the support of such good friends of the university as the late Dr. James Crombie of Parkhill, his curatorship should mark a milestone in the history of the library.

In Faculty and Senatus Ferguson was a formidable figure. He cared passionately for what he believed to be the true interests and purposes of a university. In private conversation he would make it his boast that he cared for principles, not for individuals; and few who served with him either on Faculty or Senatus will forget the relentlessness with which he would challenge those whom he perhaps sometimes too easily classed as " barbarians ", and those others whom he thought false sentiment to have made too ready to listen to their claims. Perhaps he loved controversy too much, and sometimes failed in his advocacy by allowing personalities too easily to intrude themselves in what he said. Yet one who knew him very well spoke, after his death, of his underlying benevolence, and among his junior colleagues there were not a few who had experienced his tenderness and who found themselves moved to quite spontaneous grief by the knowledge of his passing. Where his service of the university in matters of high policy is concerned, it must be said that all universities everywhere stand in need continually of such service as Ferguson equipped himself to give. He was the advocate of cultural education, always and without compromise; but his knowledge of the history of science made it certain that the culture which he so powerfully championed, never appeared for a moment archaistic but rather a living tradition, continuous, yet ever requiring and receiving renewal from those capable of making any part of its fullness their own.

Ferguson was not always an easy colleague, and few who served with him, did not find themselves on occasion moved to strong disagreement with his policies and with his methods. But none of them who knew him well, or even began to know him well, could fail in the end to respect him or to acknowledge that their own experience of university life had been enlarged profoundly by their fellowship with him.

D. M. MACKINNON: A.U.R. 1958

Since 1953 ROBERT C. CROSS *has held the Chair.*

ENGLISH

HERBERT JOHN CLIFFORD GRIERSON

Professor of English, 1894-1915

> " Herbert Grierson wore his hair long and never could keep it tidy. He wrote poems early. His first is in *Alma Mater*, vol. I . . . I remember every line of it, for I was present at its birth. I see him, like a storm-wraith lashing his own breast, in the anguish of its delivery. Not so long ago I met him casually, one hot summer afternoon, and we lay on the grass in St. James's Park, he on his back, gazing at the heavens, declaiming volubly. A park ranger eyed us with suspicious eye."
>
> P. J. BLAIR

Of all the subjects for the Bursary Competition in 1895 the dreariest was English. Grammar was but a faint imitation of Latin; for composition the themes set were unreal and abstract and there was a wicked exercise known as paraphrasing, while literature consisted in getting up information about books and authors that we never read.

To pass from this dull and meaningless grind into the English class of the young Professor Grierson was like rising above the clouds into a clear blue sky. Here was a man who revelled in the beauty of the English language, whether using it himself or quoting it, as used by the greatest masters of poetry and prose. His enthusiasm was infectious. We were caught up in a gale of eloquence in which the taking of notes was as futile as it was irrelevant. Now for the first time we could recognize and cultivate the art of expression in good English whether in writing or in speech. At the same time we began to feel drawn to the great works in English literature and to distinguish them from the cheap and the ephemeral—another influence that has lasted throughout life.

An odd intrusion was a short course in Anglo-Saxon of which I have little recollection, except that even in Grierson's hands it was a complete flop: but after sixty-five years I still recall the large glasses and the earnest eyes behind them, with the wrinkled brow and the symbolic washing of hands, while a voice in tune with the winds of Shetland held the class spellbound with

> Fresh as the first beam glittering on a sail
> That brings our friends up from the underworld . . .
> So sad, so fresh, the days that are no more.
>
> JAMES STRACHAN

There are some things that one can never forget about Sir Herbert. One is his voice. I heard it first (he was reading the Ode to Autumn) with a shock of wonder and delight in the old English classroom at King's sixty years ago. Years afterwards I heard him address a crowded London audience. At his first words I saw the same wave of surprise and delight pass over the whole audience like a physical impact. The voice (whose " sound was like the sea ") has been known also to arise from an invisible professor groping on the floor behind a lecture desk for a dropped paper-knife. There was no break in the lecture.

Then there was his stride, swift, rhythmic and a little one-sided. Swift above all. I have a very vivid memory of a marathon from King's Gate to King's College, using what breath was left to me to help in the composition (for immediate use) of a paper on the lesser Elizabethan dramatists—" because I had forgotten all about it till an hour ago."

And his handwriting—like no other on earth. One could learn to read it, but after long study.

But these are only the surface of things. Sir Herbert is one of the immortals.

AUGUSTA RUDMOSE-BROWN

All Grierson's students of my generation—his last in Aberdeen—inherited the tradition that he was the absent-minded professor of legend, to whom many apocryphal stories were attached. There was indeed much truth in the legend. It fell to me, as President, to make the arrangements for his lecture on " Don Quixote " to the Literary Society, the first official occasion on which he visited Aberdeen after leaving it. I well remember the agonized moments of waiting in vain for final confirmation of his plans, and then receiving, after he had been and gone, the letter he had carefully addressed to me at his own Edinburgh house. But those of us—and we were many—who learned to know the man became increasingly conscious of a quality in him which the legend might seem to belie. This was his warm and lively interest in people, their interests and doings, their experience and their minds. He never forgot a student who had once been admitted to his intimacy, in whatever degree and for whatever cause, and as the years passed whenever one met him one began where one left off, in a relationship that was singularly natural and of unaffected warmth. His courtesy was instinctive and often beautiful, sometimes moving to those much younger than himself who recognized the generosity of spirit from which it sprang.

He delighted to listen as well as talk, but being the man he was he did not suffer fools gladly, or those whose mind struck no answering spark from his. He once described the acute boredom he had suffered during a long official dinner where his neighbour was a celebrated classical scholar who " seemed to know nothing but fa-acts ". But on the other hand, when Oxford gave him its Doctorate on the same day as P. G. Wodehouse he was genuinely and modestly entertained by " a very pleasant young man ". He relished every evidence of human idiosyncrasy, and none who knew him will ever forget the gusto and the humour, the enjoyment and the whole-hearted laughter with which he could describe it.

Grierson as his students knew him was a man of deep convictions and strong loyalties which emerged in all that he thought and said; and he respected conviction in others. He did not aggressively profess his views, but it was easy for any intelligent student to see where his sympathies lay. He understood Milton's absolute and individualist Protestantism, though he could not like it; one student, nurtured in the Kirk of the Disruption, has never forgotten the look that came over that mobile face and the sudden deepening of his tone as he quoted Paul Pleydell's words: " I am a member of the suffering and Episcopal Church of Scotland." Of his three universities he had a peculiar tenderness for Aberdeen where he had been young and in his prime, where he had fully discovered himself and his powers. To one of his old Aberdeen students that abiding affection was made vividly manifest one evening many years later in Oxford. He had that day given a notable public lecture, brilliant, packed, delivered with the familiar verve and gathering speed which left all his audience breathless except the two or three to whom this was the well-remembered pace of their youth. In the middle of the friendly dinner that followed he was called to the telephone to learn that he had been elected Rector of Edinburgh University, and for the rest of the evening, amused as he was at the idea of his holding this particular form of academic honour, he was visibly moved, not least because two of the last generation of his Aberdeen students were there to share his feeling.

A passionate intellectual conviction inspired the whole conception of his subject that made him a superlatively great exponent of it. A Greats man with a wide knowledge of Greek and Latin literature and a very Scottish bent towards metaphysics, he had come to regard the study of English literature as wholly satisfying in itself and as an academic discipline of immense potential value in the modern world. It did not embrace all knowledge: to the English-speaking student it did something more real, for it was the living expression of that vast creation of art and thought which we mean by Renaissance civilization—to Grierson Europe's finest achievement. As early as the 1914 war he sadly realized that this civilization, like others before it, was in Paul Valéry's word " mortal ", and that he might be living in its decay. But it was the civilization that conditioned his mind, the faith and experience by which he lived and taught. The famous " digressions " were the natural overflow of a mind so nurtured, a mind of insatiable curiosity, of warm and deep perceptions, of knowledge richly stored. Of them two things may be said. Students intent on taking notes for examinations became impatient, but they were in fact, as many of us saw, never irrelevant to his comprehensive vision of the matter in hand. And in themselves they were a liberal education for us in Aberdeen, immature as we usually were, inevitably limited by very reason of our distance from the centres of culture. Just what Grierson achieved by these digressions is perhaps best known to those of us whose later lot, as university teachers of English ourselves, was to plumb the depths of student ignorance and doing so to recall our own.

His students, then, learned from him what English literature was about and, more important, that it was about *something*. But all the ranging and discursive exposition would have been of little avail had it not been informed and inspired by a passionate love of literature, in a favourite phrase, of the " winged words " themselves. His judgments were often unorthodox, always personal. But it is no mere trick of memory that rather recalls the flow of quotation that poured from his lips in an urgent, often a torrential stream. His voice carried his understanding of the things he loved, and all his feeling for them: the voice unlovely in itself, an organ of vibrant consonants and penetrating vowels, of urgent rhythms, stress and speed, of variations in tone and pitch, like the familiar two-point upward curve on the last syllable of each line. " Just when we're safest there's a sunset touch "; " Tears, idle tears "; " Wilt thou forgive that sin which I have done "; the grave and measured stanzas of the *Lament for the Makaris* with the tremor of voice and feeling in the line that has haunted men's minds for centuries: *Timor mortis conturbat me*—as long as we live some of us will hear these and scores of other passages as we heard them from him long ago. He was hugely amused when he was treated to an affectionate mimicry of them and learned that a friendly contest in renderings was the rule when his old students forgathered. But of course he knew why they were thus remembered: that his reciting was an illumination and a commentary, an immediate contact between his mind and that of his listeners, to whom it brought a breath of that wind of the spirit which he liked to call, with a characteristic chuckle, the " divine afflatus ".

ISABEL BISSON

ADOLPHUS ALFRED JACK

Professor of English, 1915-1938

It is not easy to realize that his well-loved figure will be seen no more— the tallish slight form with the scholar's stoop and the cut-away coat, the bright hair untouched by grey (" a freak of nature ", he called it), the chuckling laugh and the gay conspiratorial glance. No one who watched him bustling to catch a tram, encumbered by a tremendous overcoat (heavily lined), an umbrella and a capacious old black bag filled with books (and clandestinely restored to favour even after his students had given him a handsome leather case) will forget the panting triumph of his arrival. But streets were not his element. He was most himself comfortably seated in the study that was all books, laughing over the vagaries of his colleagues at a Senatus meeting, or if some question of literature was at issue, moving eagerly from shelf to shelf to produce all the evidence. He was a bookman to his finger-tips, instinctive in taste, far-reaching in knowledge. Books overflowed wheresoever he was. Bohally, his other house near Tummel Bridge, gave him the opportunity, gleefully accepted, of making another bookroom. To talk with him about books was an education: to add a grain to his store, a triumph. I shall not forget his reproof when, after buying some bundles at one of the Aberdeen book-sales he delighted in, I was about to discard Hutcheson's *Of the Passions*: " Oh no," he said, " not that: that's a book."

At the dinner-parties he and Mrs. Jack gave before English Association meetings he was a most admirable host. Afterwards, as chairman, with his orator's style, hands behind him, head thrown back and eyes looking far ahead, he would introduce the lecturer with inevitable felicity and afterwards make him think he had contributed something of importance to a Northern outpost, even though—as happened not rarely—what we had been given was thistledown or stone. He was, indeed, so gentle and charmingly diffident on a first approach (and always) that men of the trampling kind often thought he would be easy to devour. But they were in error. On any point of principle he was steel, and would pursue what he thought was right with unfailing courtesy and the utmost tenacity. Not for nothing were the traditions and habits of the Scottish professoriate in his blood.

C. COLLEER ABBOTT: A.U.R. 1946

I was lucky in that the Professor of English Literature at Aberdeen was a rosy man with wondering eyes, a clear high voice, three waistcoats in winter, and a heart in love with Wordsworth and Shakespeare's panegyric tongue. He had the innocence, the capacity for pure amazement, that is the key to Wordsworth; and a learned delight in the compact imagination of Shakespeare. He could impart both knowledge and delight.

He was a bookish man who would have wrinkled with deep laughter to be told there was any belittlement in such a title. His touch was delicate, but his mind robust. In his own house, where every wall was clad with books, his conversation was incurably peripatetic. He would go from room to room, reaching with eager hands to upward shelves— his tail-coat lifting oddly as he stretched—for book after book that would fortify or confirm an observation; till his visitor at last went home with Elzevirs and octavos in all his pockets, three quartos in roughened calf under one arm, and a folio of steel engravings below the other. His regular visitors never arrived without a knapsack or small suitcase.

ERIC LINKLATER: The Man on my Back

The Professor, I think, sometimes doubted his success as a teacher, and never realized, perhaps, its full measure. It was not a ponderable learning he gave, that could be returned, exhibited, and weighed; but incalculable apprehensions, an addition of awareness and sensibility. He never tied scholarship in a neat parcel to hand across the counter, but leaning over to the dark side he opened unsuspected windows, and with a luminous discrimination remarked upon the view.

Teaching, he told me once, grew no easier with time. The lectures he had delivered the year before would never wholly serve again, but must always be reconsidered and refurbished. He spoke seriously of this perennial insufficiency, and then with that sudden change of expression—from grave intensity and solemn eyes, in a moment, to the beaming glance and folded chuckle—" But whether they're improved in the process is a different matter. You don't know till the next year! You see what was certainly a deficiency in your judgment of the year before, and try to amend it. But perhaps you don't amend it. Perhaps you botch it again! "

His dignity was never in question, but its full assurance, perhaps, could only be guessed when one considered how often he trifled with it: in his admirable lectures on the Ballads, for instance, he would mime like a puppet-play; with his own shoulders he would sculpture the still sadness of Wordsworth's old leech-gatherer—and though the spectacle of a Professor drooping over an imagined pool, with hung head and long inanimate arms, should be ridiculous, it was at great hazard impressive and effective. He inspired affection early; respect grew more slowly, but grew the more the more one knew him. His charm was quickly apparent and soon felt; but from what deep wells it came, at first was unsuspected. Now, when we perceive how vivid is our memory of him, how clearly in the mind sound the echoes of his voice's most singular melody, and how bright in recollection are those wondering eyes—now from a distance, when we see him a little larger than life, perhaps we see him more truly. For the spell would not have lasted, nor the impress be so deep, if his stature had been no taller than life's ordinary measure.

ERIC LINKLATER: *A.U.R.* 1947

Thirty-six years ago, when I went up to Cambridge from Aberdeen, the Board of Research Studies appointed Q as my supervisor. Professor Jack was gratified, and my own expectations ran high, but it was as if I had left the warmth and inspiration of a good fire to dance attendance on the aurora borealis. It was characteristic of Jack when I went to report progress some months later, to find his own copy of *Noughts and Crosses* and give it to me, praising Q's gifts in the highest terms. But in literary criticism nothing that Q produced is in the same class at all as that judicious and alive book *Young Hamlet*, absurdly little known.

After the first war, the English assistant at Aberdeen was Peter Monro Jack, no relation of the professor's, but one of his most brilliant pupils, who for many years (until his premature death) held a distinguished place as a critic on the other side of the Atlantic. We met in New York in 1941 to talk much of the Jacks and deplore the ignorance of youth— the green and bland assumption that the experience of such friendship would be repeated in other places at other times. It was on the

enchantment of evenings at 22 Queen's Road that Peter dwelt, with conversation such as one could wish to pursue to the end of time, and Mrs.
Jack going so naturally to the piano.   " I thought I was sure to meet other
women like her.   But they don't exist."

He was right about Lucy, and about those evenings, and yet I find
myself remembering the Honours Classroom at New King's as the place
where the professor was even more at home than in his own study, and in a
particular way in his element.   The illumination of his comments one
might have expected from such a scholar and thinker; it was the team-
work of mind and body that took everyone by surprise—the use of voice
and eye, the turn and tilt of the monumental head with its careless plume,
the teeth now on a thumb-nail and now immobilizing the too expressive
lip.   We know, having since watched the famous actors of our time, that
it was a performance of great virtuosity, entirely honest, entirely free of
histrionics.

We all have favourite memories.   " In the questions on Blake, full
marks will undoubtedly be given to any student quoting Professor Elton
without the usual indication and acknowledgment."   Such a Jackism
would ricochet across the room, and the professor acknowledged the
spurts of appreciation with that smile of friendly relish—a little shy—which
was always so well-timed, never too prompt.   But nothing sank as deep
as those episodes when the major works of literature led him to talk of the
major events of life.   The development of Shakespeare as a dramatist
had to be seen as a normal thing.   As youth passed, life grew dark and
painful; the comic spirit flagged, and the tragic coming to strength, trod
it down.   Jack knew well how unacceptable this was, and how much
would depend upon its becoming in some degree acceptable.   He paused
in his discourse.   The grip of his hands on the side of the desk grew tight
and a look of far more than ordinary gravity came into the large eyes
bent upon the class. " *People die.*"   So blunt, like that, it was improper,
as he meant it to be.   There was no other way to put us on our guard.

LYN IRVINE

GEOFFREY LANGDALE BICKERSTETH

Professor of English, 1938-1954

I have heard it said that he was not easy to approach.   That was not my
experience, and it was my privilege to know him both as student and
later as his very junior colleague.   Certainly artful dodgers among the
undergraduates and self-seeking, wire-pulling academic politicians
could be despatched quickly and unceremoniously; but no one ever
genuinely sought his help or advice in vain.   On the face of it there might
seem to be no strong likelihood that this most English of Englishmen
should trouble to go out of his way to encourage a gauche, perfervidly
Scottish ex-serviceman.   But he was very kind, and diffidence learned

to vanish in his humane presence. I had recently been in Italy and had picked up enough of the language to be able to appreciate his enthusiasm for Dante. It might very easily have been an intimidating experience to find oneself in the company of the most distinguished translator of the *Paradiso*, the editor of Corducci and Leopardi; but it was not so; for Geoffrey Bickersteth was a scholar who knew how to stimulate and encourage others. It was a great joy for me to hear him reading his translation, then in progress, of *The Divine Comedy* (later published by the Aberdeen University Press, 1955). I remember sitting quite often in his study at 51 Queen's Road, fascinated by the beauty and power of his verse-renderings. The scholar in English and Italian, the lover of Dante, and the artist all combined to produce this outstanding achievement.

The dedication of this great work to the memory of his sons, Tony and Julian, inevitably calls to mind the tragic loss which the Professor suffered. The dignity, fortitude and reticence with which he endured it made one proud of human kind; and the well-known words which follow that dedication—*In La Sua Volontade è nostra Pace*—speak more eloquently of the faith that sustained him than any comment we can make. I have always felt, too, that his British Academy Lecture on " The Golden World of King Lear "—justly praised at the time by Charles Morgan—is a kind of confessio fidei. There are passages in it which were born out of deep personal experience.

On another level, that lecture is a lasting witness to Professor Bickersteth's powers of close and sustained reasoning. Certain authors brought out the best in him as lecturer and tutor. Shakespeare was unquestionably one. No one who has ever heard him lecture on the opening scenes of *Hamlet*, say, or the meaning of *The Tempest*, is likely to forget the experience. These things had sunk so deep into his consciousness that he had no need to refer to notes. His love and detailed knowledge of Sir Walter came as a delightful surprise to me, and I vividly recall one afternoon when he gave me an animated and word-perfect recital of Meg Merrilees' speech of denunciation to Ellangowan. It was, by the way, during his tenure of office that Scottish Literature began to assume a more prominent position in the curriculum. And if ever a history of English studies at this university is written, it will stand to the great credit of Professor Bickersteth that he introduced the tutorial system for Honours students at Aberdeen. But some of us will recall him chiefly for more personal reasons. To us he seemed a much greater man than most of those who presumed to be his critics; and we shall always remember him, and his kindly, cultured wife, with gratitude and affection.

JAMES A. MICHIE

The English Chair is now held by GEORGE I. DUTHIE, *1955. Among the many notable teachers of English under professorial rank, W. D. Taylor singles himself out.*

W. D. TAYLOR

Lecturer in English, 1920-1949

When I was an English Honours student at Aberdeen, about thirty years ago, the Department was, of course, very much smaller than it has since become. Its sun and moon were A. A. Jack and W. D. Taylor. Lesser luminaries might come and go, but those two seemed to be set enduringly in the firmament and to constitute between them all that really mattered in the Department of English. In most of our undergraduate eyes, Jack easily outshone Taylor, for he was a rhetorician and something of an actor and his dilettantism made a ready appeal. On our impressionable minds his imaginative aestheticism, his delight in the craftsmanship of literature and his very special gift for communicating subtle and indefinable sensations made their quick, strong and lasting impact. W. D. Taylor was far less obviously appealing—a solid, ponderous, patient, unobtrusive man, with an impediment in his speech—and those most captivated by Jack were apt to be least impressed, at the time, by Taylor, who lacked all the outward graces and had none of Jack's gifts of showmanship.

Looking back over the years, I think one sees more clearly how important Taylor was to us as a counterpoise to Jack's brilliance, whatever we thought of him then. A vastly learned man, he was the incarnation of patient scholarship and the devoted pursuit of knowledge for its own sake. But he was much more than what Jack used to call " a dungeon of learning ". He had, I think, a more catholic taste and understanding than Jack, and perhaps a deeper appreciation of the human qualities that determine literary values. I should not like to seem to depreciate Jack's wonderful gifts as a teacher, but as time passes and his glamour fades a little, like the blue Morris wallpaper with which he insisted on covering the walls of all the English classrooms, Taylor seems to me to stand out more clearly as having been a beneficent and corrective influence on those who passed through their joint hands.

The son of a Falkirk pattern-maker, he had been the most brilliant Honours student of his year at Glasgow and had gone on, after a period of travel and study on the continent, to Balliol. He had spent the early part of his teaching career at Queen's University, Kingston, and had been invited by Jack to come over to Aberdeen primarily to teach language. But he preferred the literary to the linguistic branch of English studies and as the years went on willingly relinquished the language classes to others. At first, too, he had had to lecture not only to advanced students but to the large (and in those days often inattentive and unruly) Ordinary class— an ordeal from which he was thankful at last to be set free. In his final years he was happily confined to the teaching of literature to the Advanced class, and of eighteenth-century literature and Shakespeare Text to Honours students.

Among those of his students who were not unresponsive to his shy interest in them as individuals there was no lack of affection for him. He knew all about us and was obviously happy if he could talk at length to us about ourselves, our recent reading, our tastes and hopes and plans, and he would make such pretexts as the holding of a play-reading or a debate on some literary topic to get us into his house and introduce us to his wife. He and Jack were both warm-hearted men and there was something couthy and intimate about the English Honours school in their day. For all their differences as teachers, they were very much alike in their humane and liberal attitudes to life and they were deeply attached to each other. Wherever they are now, I am sure their students can think of them only as being together, spending a wonderfully contented eternity in each other's company, and completely surrounded, knee-deep and arm-high, by an infinity of books.

RALPH S. WALKER

HISTORY

C. SANFORD TERRY

Lecturer in History, 1898-1903
Professor, 1903-1930

> " He is a musical gourmand, and he is ready to share the delicacies of his taste with the whole community: he has educated not only the student body but the public generally to a high degree of musical culture."
>
> *Alma Mater*

> " He had one of the earliest motor cars in the University, and stuck to it, square and high, long after other models had come in; and in his fatherly way he would give his favourite women students (' fillies ', he called them) lifts that were so conspicuous as to be beyond any emotion but a laughing gratitude."

Recollections of one's professors are generally associated with the class-room. One remembers them as lecturers, with their distinctive manner-isms and eccentricities; Grierson gazing raptly through the English classroom window and endlessly washing his hands with invisible soap, as in unforgettable cadences he intoned " Timor mortis conturbat me "; or Baillie elegantly running his fingers through his hair (I always thought it a rather conscious affectation); or Souter, dearest of men but dreariest of lecturers, monotonously dictating those meticulous notes on Statius, whom one ever afterwards regarded as surely the least inspiring of Latin poets.

Doubtless many of Sanford Terry's former students will remember him affectionately as the Professor of History. He certainly was not a dreary lecturer. He had a warm and attractive personality, and was vivacious, almost effervescent in his manner. The field of European history was much too extensive to cover in one year; so Terry divided the course in two, somewhere, if I remember aright, about the period of the Renaissance, and one achieved an ordinary degree in history on demonstrating

an adequate knowledge of events pre-Renaissance, or post-Renaissance, depending on the year one happened to attend the class.

I attended his class when he gave the former course, an unfortunate circumstance perhaps, for Terry was an authority on the seventeenth century, particularly seventeenth-century Scotland and its relations with the continent. It was to this century that the best of his published work related. But no-one could have attended either course of lectures without being impressed by what Miss Mure Mackenzie described as his power of marshalling intricate masses of detail into lucid and balanced narrative.[1]

But if many will gratefully remember him as the Professor of History, far more will remember him as the Conductor of the University Choral and Orchestral Society, which he not only created, but succeeded in making one of the most popular of the student societies. It required no great musical talent to become a member of the Choral. There were no voice tests or sight-reading tests to pass. If you enjoyed singing, and could pay the shilling membership fee, you were in, and took your place amongst sopranos, altos, tenors, or basses, according as you imagined what sort of voice you possessed.

With such a heterogeneous body of singers, good, bad, and indifferent, with widely varying degrees of musical education and most of them with little or none, it was obviously impossible to attempt choral music of any substantial measure of technical difficulty. Terry contented himself with simple arrangements of part-songs that had a recognizable tune, the most ambitious of which might have been designated M.D. in any musical catalogue, and in which the tenor part fell within the compass of light baritone voices, and the alto part within the range of mezzo-sopranos, authentic tenors and altos being something of *rarae aves* in the student body. He wrote for us an excellent orchestrated arrangement of " Gaudeamus "; composed a first-rate tune for Duff's " Salve Boreale Lumen " which he scored most effectively for four voices, organ and orchestra, thus giving Aberdeen a song unsurpassed by that of any university or college; and a fine setting to " Follow Me 'Ome ", to which we invariably gave a thrilling performance.

Nobody enjoyed these choral nights more than Terry himself. His enthusiasm was unbounded, his patience infinite, his appreciation of our

---

[1] See C. Sanford Terry in *Dictionary of National Biography*.

efforts the apogee of indulgent charity. But the really great nights were the concert nights, when, in the Music Hall, with G. T. Wright perched up in the organ seat, and little Riach of H.M. Theatre leading the orchestra, we showed our paces to an audience that packed the building, and that was prepared to cheer with generous indiscrimination everything we did. I would not say the concert was one of the brilliant musical events of the season, but it was certainly *the* social event. And Terry was never more in his element than when, immaculate in flawlessly tailored evening clothes, he stepped on the rostrum and picked up his baton.

He was a good-looking man, with the most charming manners, but he simply blossomed on that rostrum. He might have been conducting the choir of the Sistine Chapel and the Vienna Symphony Orchestra. Years before I came up to the University, I used to sit in the gallery at these concerts, thrilled to ecstatic rapture as Terry whipped up choristers and instrumentalists to frenzied fortissimos, and expecting him every moment to burst a blood vessel. Dr. Coward used to tell his choirs that three thrills made a concert. We far exceeded that modest number. There was a thrill in everything we sang, even in Archie Irvine dramatically proclaiming that the sailor was home from sea, and the hunter home from the hill.

What very few, if any, of us realised was that we were singing or playing under the baton of a man who was to achieve a far greater reputation in the world of music than he ever did in the field of history. What today impresses me most in my recollections of Terry, is just that he ever condescended to bother with us and our trivial little part-songs at all. For the man was steeped in the music of J. S. Bach, and was to become recognized, in the words of Percy Scholes, as " the world's leading authority on Bach ".[1]

We were ignorant of the fact that he was preparing a " Life of John Sebastian Bach " that was to be hailed with enthusiasm in Germany, and described by Grove as " the most authoritative work on the subject published in any language, and not yet superseded; " [2] that he was busy on the translations of Bach's Cantatas that were to form the basis of the magnificent edition produced by the Oxford University Press; that his three volumes on Bach's chorales, and his monographs on Bach's original hymn tunes, the cantatas, the oratorios, and the great B minor Mass, were to place every serious student of Bach eternally in his debt.

These published works followed each other in rapid succession, and universities were not slow to recognize the vast scholarship and exhaustive historical research that had gone to the making of them. Oxford, Edinburgh, and Leipzig conferred on him the honorary degree of Mus. Doc., and one cannot think of a modern work on Bach that does not refer to him as to an unassailable authority. It was my happy privilege to review for the old *Aberdeen Free Press* his works on the chorales, the hymn

---

[1] See C. Sanford Terry, *The Oxford Companion to Music* (O.U.P.)
[2] See *Dictionary of Music*, Grove.

tunes, and the B Minor Mass, and I can still recall the feelings of embarrassment I experienced then, that, while all of us in the society had held him in the warmest affection, we had so ignorantly underestimated his musical stature. Happy and proud should those be who are still alive to boast: " I sang under Terry's baton."

ALEX SMART

JOHN BENNETT BLACK

Professor of History, 1930-1953

Like not a few other members of our Senatus, John Bennett Black belongs to the band of distinguished scholars trained in the slightly more venerable University of Glasgow. Glaswegian born and bred, he went to Gilmorehill in 1902 as a student ready for any intellectual adventure. Having flirted decorously with Philosophy, Science, and Literature, he fell seriously in love with History and English, but putting History aside for a time, he chose English. The due reward of his devoted attentions to this charmer was forthcoming in the shape of first class honours, with the handsome bonus of a Luke Fellowship. Combined with his natural gifts, his study of English literature flowered in a stylistic elegance not always found in the work of other learned historians.

In 1908 he went up to Balliol to read for the Modern History Schools. He obtained a brilliant " First " and won the Beit Prize for a thesis on " The Relations of European and Maori in New Zealand ". Three years later we find him in Paris. The rich fruits of his labours were served up in a lordly dish and did not pass unnoticed; the volume entitled *Queen Elizabeth and Henri Quatre* won him the Arnold Prize awarded in 1914 by the University of Oxford.

As a prisoner of war in the 1914-18 combat, he assisted in the organization of an improvised " Prisoners' University " and by lecturing on History helped his fellow captives to while away profitably the weary months of waiting. In 1919 he was called to the Chair of Modern History at Queen's University, Kingston, and in 1920 to a similar chair in Sheffield. While there he produced *The Art of History, Elizabethan Seabeggars and the capture of Brill*, and contributed to a survey of *Great French Thinkers of the Age of Reason* a brilliant account of Voltaire's political ideas. This essay interested French literature specialists as well as students of political theory and charmed everybody, notably the then *doyen* of French historians, Professor Henri Sée of Rennes, who characterized it as " cette excellente et fine étude sur Voltaire ". Academic France sets a high value on learning presented in true literary form and soon Professor Black was invited to become an honorary member of the Institut Historique et Héraldique de France.

When Professor Sanford Terry retired from the Burnett-Fletcher Chair he was succeeded by Professor Black—an interesting innovation, for never till then had a native-born Scot occupied a Chair of general history in Scotland. The new Professor, continuing with undiminished zeal his Elizabethan studies, was invited by the Oxford University Press to undertake Volume VIII in the New Oxford History of England—the volume on *The Reign of Elizabeth*. It would be hard to say which must have given him the more pleasure, the prospect of teaching the Sassenachs their own history or the honour of writing what was to become a standard work on its most glorious period.

Here, as in Sheffield, Professor Black freely expended his energy on his academic work, developing a remarkably efficient and scholarly History Department and so expanding it that it now comprises not only British and European History but sections for Scottish, Medieval, British Imperial, Colonial and Dominion History, with satellite departments dealing with International Relations and Political Theory.

To his colleagues he endeared himself by his unfailing kindness and friendly tolerance, for never would he let differences of opinion cloud good fellowship nor his wit demolish an opponent; in discussion he generated light, not heat. He represents no narrow specialization but broad culture, and while preferring the spaciousness of Elizabethan times, he likes to wander off now and again into some new field and light up its darker patches. He also likes to wander off now and again to Balgownie, for he is one of the fortunate beings "born with a silver mashie in their hand"; a distinguished son has inherited the same gift. In the deft stroke with driver or niblick, golfers recognize the impeccable style that historians admire in the writings. Evidently great golfers, like great historians, are artists.

F. C. ROE: *A.U.R.* 1954

The Chair of History is now held by GEORGE O. SAYLES, *1953.*

MATHEMATICS

FREDERICK FULLER

Professor of Mathematics, 1860(51)-1878

"He almost, as King Agrippa said, persuaded men to be mathematicians".

Professor Fuller graduated at Cambridge as Fourth Wrangler in 1842 and after teaching there (Lord Kelvin was one of his students) came to King's College, Aberdeen, in 1851, bringing "the energy of youth and mathematical ability of a high grade" to a university where the teaching of mathematics had been on an elementary standard. In 1860, as Professor of Mathematics in the reorganized University, he carried out brilliantly the new regulations of the Commissioners in instituting Honours Courses, so that Aberdeen men went to Cambridge and became Wranglers or entered the Indian Civil Service through highly competitive examination.

To enter his classroom was to enter a region of clearness, order and precision. . . . Each morning as " Freddy " entered, beaming genially at the class thro' the spectacles he wore, we got the impression of a man happy in the work into which, after prayers, he plunged. There was great activity but no hurry, there was nothing omitted for want of time, no difficulty which the class could appreciate was passed over. . . . He himself practically rewrote the textbooks on the blackboard. . . . From the instant of entering the classroom when prayers were said almost with the chalk in his hand, until the last moment, there was on his part intense activity, and on the students' part almost incessant note-taking. Weariness sometimes overtook the less ardent, and once when he had filled his three blackboards with a proof of the binomial theorem, catching with a sidelong glance a view of an opened umbrella, he merely remarked without ceasing to write, " Does it rain, Mr. ———? " and the umbrella collapsed. It was currently reported that in going anywhere he refused to use a cab on the ground that he really could not spare the time.

W. L. MOLLISON: A.B.A.

His patience, enthusiasm, interest in the work were limitless. I never saw him exhausted. His opening prayer was inaudible, though there ran a legend that some keen hands in the front seat had taken it in shorthand! It was pushed up to the top of the textbook he was using at the time, his watch lying on the desk beside it. His " Amen " fused completely with his rapid " Yesterday, you will remember, I was dealing with the arear of the parabolar "—so eager was he to be again in the thick of it. He was never happy till he got it, filling three large blackboards, and only ceasing from lack of space. Everyone will remember the beauty of his diagrams and figures. Gathering the sleeve of his gown on the right arm under it with his left hand, he would dash off circles as perfect as if they had been done with the compass, the class enjoying the difference of his and the egg-like monstrosities of the victim by his side. Then he would reluctantly leave the board and finish the rest of the work orally, lucid and orderly to the close.

On Fuller there is only one possible judgment. He was, like one of his own circles, *Teres atque rotundus*—perfect.

W. KEITH LEASK: I.B.

The lack of junior members of staff and tutorial facilities at this period was made up for in the case of Mathematics by the ministrations of a famous mathematical coach, Dr. David Rennet, to whose rooms a long succession of students came for treatment. " Davie " was as well-known as any professor, and many a student would have stood little chance of graduation without his tuition. Of the youthful Grierson he is reputed to have said, after looking over his work, " Man, ye micht as weel be in the street as here "; but added, " Faith, I'm wrang—ye wad get in fowk's way."

DR. DAVID RENNET

Mathematics Coach 1860(56)-19??

There's nae sic men a-makin' noo—
Awyte the sayin's unco true.
Jist think o' een
That foe and freen
Ca' naething else bit " Davie ".
Man, he is a swippert craitur
Fu' o' wit an' human natur,
He's a leevin' Alma Mater:
Faur's a chiel like Davie?

J. M. BULLOCH

" A p'int o' licht ", as Dr. Rennet would have said, " hits A an' syne stots aff to B."

Davie has no double: he is *sui generis*. He has been teaching Mathematics all his life, but in the specialising process he has made himself an all-round educational philosopher and citizen.

When Davie started his great campaign—unostentatiously and un-officially—he was confronted by the solid (and shall I say stolid?) battalions of the classicists. For centuries they had had it all their own way, and some of them believed that this was going to last for ever. But Davie was wiser. He felt that his subject had vast possibilities, that the virtue of versions was not the last word, that mathematics was to become an integral part of the educational system, and not remain the mere trimmings of the trencher. He has lived to see his hope become a reality.

J. M. BULLOCH: *A.B.A.*

Davie never ceased to remind us that our " heids were like boiled neaps ", and when we forgot anything, " Pit it doon on yer thoomb nail or ony wye where ye'll no forget it ", but whose parting words were ever, " Man, min' Aberdeen and twal mile roun "—a benediction as well as a challenge to us to do our best in the future.

F. P. MILLIGAN: *A.U.R.* 1914

Everybody knew him as Davie; and yet nobody ever took a liberty in his presence, for he possessed immense innate dignity. . . . He was just Davie, the diminutive connoting finely the small, almost elfin figure and the entire homeliness of his nature.

J. M. BULLOCH: *A.U.R.* 1914

GEORGE PIRIE

Professor of Mathematics, 1878-1904

> Opening address to students: " There are doubtless many of you who find but little pleasure in the Arts Curriculum until you come to the Mathematical class."

Professor Fuller was followed by the son of Principal Pirie, George Pirie, M.A., LL.D., a Fellow of Queen's College, Cambridge, who, while at Queen's took orders in the Church of England and also first prize for putting the weight. He became Professor of Mathematics in Aberdeen in 1878, and after his death in 1904 a memorial window was gifted by old students and friends to King's College Chapel.

The young student . . . is at once captivated by the masterly manner in which the path is made plain before him. He is charmed and set at his ease by the order, energy and lucidity of the lecturer's style, and by the constant courtesy which meets him when under the fire of oral examination. As a consequence he begins to talk more respectfully of mathematical studies and more hopefully of the possibility of attaining the mathematics degree.

Professor Pirie, while far from neglecting the best men, more especially addresses the average men. In his opinion there is very little demand for specialists and first-class scholars [1890] while the existing University machinery is hopelessly inadequate to produce them. What can be done, however, and ought to be done, is to turn out well-educated men, with a good deal of general culture and knowledge. The fact that Professor Pirie so exclusively addresses the average man has given rise to the unjust suspicion that he himself is but an average man. This accusation is largely due to the vulgar error that obscurity is the mark of deeper knowledge. . . . His popularity consists in the universal respect awarded to a man of perfect courtesy and genuine kindliness, who does his work with conspicuous ability and enthusiasm.

Alma Mater, 1890

HECTOR M. MACDONALD

Professor of Mathematics, 1904-1935

> " I shall now simplify this expression, though I do not believe it will be any simpler."
>
> PROFESSOR MACDONALD

An expert member of the Alpine Club, a lover of the sea (" if there is one thing in this world which I really can do it is sailing a boat "), the Senior Bursar of a Cambridge College with a great knowledge of farms and estates, an expert in vintages and the subtleties of cooking, a member of the Council of the Royal Society and its Royal Medallist, head of the Wages

Section of the Ministry of Munitions during the First World War, a very influential member of our University Court for twenty-eight years—these are just a few facets of the personality of Hector Munro Macdonald, a Scottish " lad o' pairts ". Even to mention the ways in which he served the interests of our University and its neighbourhood would require more space than can be given to this account.

Born in Edinburgh, a pupil at Fearn in Easter Ross, then at the Royal Academy, Tain, and the Old Aberdeen Grammar School, an alumnus of the Universities of Aberdeen and Cambridge, he achieved most of the distinctions which are due to a mathematician whose outstanding ability is accompanied by a dogged determination to make each problem yield its solution.

He was appointed to the Chair of Mathematics here in 1904. Three successive lectures on each morning of the five-day week during the Winter and Spring Terms might be replaced by a somewhat lighter burden during the Summer Term. His lectures at all levels were completely lucid but were not interrupted by questions from the class. In general the hard work which honours students had to expend in order to keep their heads level with the intellectual current yielded rich rewards. Turning quickly through two right angles from his position facing the blackboard and uttering the short emphatic statement, " That is quite enough ", Macdonald could quell any undergraduate rowdiness even in the hardiest Scots.

The content of his lectures showed a careful avoidance of the extremes of slipshod plausibility and over sophisticated rigour.

Occasionally he would give a lecture of historical interest to a mathematical society and show an amusing touch of conservatism—" In the course of a long and not uneventful existence I have seen many epoch-making discoveries pass into the limbo of forgotten things and I have no doubt that many more will go the same way."

The intellectual climate which formed Macdonald's research interests was provided by professors and teachers such as Stokes, Cayley, J. J. Thomson, George Darwin, Routh, Larmor and others, and such works as the great treatises of Clerk Maxwell, Horace Lamb and the third Lord Rayleigh.

His pure mathematical work was often related to mathematical functions which are of importance in physical science. Some time after the title of an Adams Prize essay was announced, concerning the zeros of a certain Bessel Function, Macdonald remarked to a friend that " the fun of it is that there are no such zeros ". In general function theory his name is attached to an interesting theorem.

In Mathematical Physics many problems in elasticity, classical hydro-dynamics, electrostatics, etc., occupied his attention, but his most important work was in the field of electrodynamics. His Adams Prize essay, published in 1902 as *Electric Waves*, is a masterpiece. He immersed himself in the work of Maxwell and discussed fundamental problems relating to the energy distribution and the flow of energy in the electro-magnetic field. His formulation of the latter differed from that of Poyn-ting. These are ideas of considerable profundity. Their validity may be judged, not of course by absolute standards, but by standards of self-consistency and, in the main, by their fruitfulness in further developments. By this last criterion Poynting's formulation and its associated ideas have been more valuable.

Another major problem to which he made a decisive contribution and which involved him in considerable controversy was the diffraction of electromagnetic waves by a sphere. This outstanding work on diffraction which has just been mentioned was an attempt to explain the propagation of radio waves round the earth. Although Macdonald solved the diffrac-tion problem, it turns out not to be the relevant physical problem which, as is well known, is related to layers of ionisation in the upper atmosphere.

His rather conservative outlook is well illustrated by his apparent aloofness from the tremendous mental upheaval caused by the basic ideas of relativity and quantum theory. This, however, is not an unusual reaction from anyone who has seen the beauty of a fully developed theory with a considerable realm of validity and is asked to watch the combination of mental groping and almost poetic inspiration which attends the origin of a new, more general theory.

Macdonald's pronouncement " Physics without Mathematics is a fraud " may be quoted nowadays in Physics Departments by anyone with sufficient courage.

We shall remember Macdonald as a man of profound convictions, who served this University nobly and whose many acts of kindness were done quietly without thought of acknowledgment. Indeed some will look back to the friend of their childhood who took them to the pantomime and who had a store of sweets for them in his study. They will remember, too, the wreath which they laid on his grave a short time after he had quietly packed his bag and left his home for the last time.

CHARLES STRACHAN

The present holder of the Chair is EDWARD MAITLAND WRIGHT, *1936.*

JAMES GOODWILLIE

Assistant in Mathematics, 1901-1905

Lecturer, 1905-1939

On 15 June, 1891, the Professor of Sanskrit in the University of Cambridge wrote to his niece, " We had a tremendous excitement in Corpus on Saturday, we had the Senior Wrangler, a thing which has not happened since 1764 ".* The Senior Wrangler was a very quiet undergraduate,

* PATRICK BURY, *Corpus Christi College, Cambridge. A History, 1822 to 1952*, Cambridge University Press, 1952.

James Goodwillie. He was born in 1866 in Liberton, near Edinburgh, and went to school in that city. He became a Fellow of Corpus in 1892, having got a first class in Part II of the Mathematical Tripos. After a period of teaching in Campbell College, Belfast, he came to our Department of Mathematics which he served for nearly forty years. In Macdonald's absence during the First World War he was in charge of the Department.

He was a most conscientious and helpful teacher. Macdonald's lucid but somewhat inexorable lectures were often rather strong meat for the less tough undergraduates, and Goodwillie with care and patience provided at least part of the food value in a form less likely to cause indigestion. He was an enthusiastic tennis player.

His kindness and courtesy were constant and outstanding.

CHARLES STRACHAN

NATURAL PHILOSOPHY

Prior to 1860, David Thomson at King's, powerful in the negotiations for fusion, Clerk Maxwell at Marischal, destined to give mankind new knowledge and change their ways of thought, taught independently. At the Fusion, Aberdeen could keep only one of her two professors and she kept David Thomson: " a decision ", says Professor R. V. Jones, " which must have been one of the most disastrous to its own interest ever forced upon a University." But situated as Aberdeen University was at the time of the Union, there is perhaps some reason to be found in having retained the man who had laboured so hard to bring about that Union. The University lost a man who was a giant in nearly all realms of mathematical physics: his researches in Electro-magnetism in particular, together with the experimental work of Faraday and Hertz, formed the foundation on which the structure of a mighty edifice has been built; though he died before the age of fifty, his imprint on mathematical physics is such that his name will be remembered and his influence felt throughout the world, wherever the subject is taught. She kept an excellent teacher of what a later member of the Department has called the " pre-Union School of Natural Philosophy ", although his uncompromising forthrightness gave him a sarcastic utterance not always beloved by his students. One imagines, however, a rough affection in the epitaph they devised for him, doubtless, like Burns' epitaph on Tam Samson, written well in the lifetime of its subject.

> Here lies auld Dauvit, that damn'd ass
> Who taught for years the Tertian class.
> When here he cracked full many a joke,
> Doon there he steers mid fire and smoke.
> Abiit, evasit, evolavit,
> Thank God we've seen the last o' Dauvit.

DAVID THOMSON

Professor of Natural Philosophy, 1860(45)-1880

> Student (who had failed): " May I sit again, Sir? "
> Prof.: " Oh certainly."
> Student: " If I fail again may I still be allowed to try, Sir? "
> Prof.: " Certainly, but we don't like people coming up when they are approaching seventy years of age."

> Scene, the Spital: Dauvit encounters a student returning home under the influence.
> Next day: Oral examination: Same student being oralled on the impact of two bodies.
> Student: " If a body meet a body . . . " and stuck.
> Prof.: " Yes, yes, Mr. S——. ' Gin a body meet a body, coming frae the toon '—I think we need say no more about yesterday."

During his professorship of thirty-five years, the services which he rendered to the University, whether as professor in dealing with his subject, or as member of the Senatus in helping to shape its policy, were both great and varied. He began these services in his own particular field of Natural Philosophy, by initiating that upward progress in the standard of attainment which continued to the end of his life. It was no small service to raise the University teaching of this important subject from the level of popular lectures to that of an exact science. By doing this he placed the University, so far as his Department was concerned, abreast of the requirements of the day, requirements which were certain to advance with the rapid advance of applied science.

Nor were the deficiencies in the mathematical standard the only difficulties which he encountered at the outset. In the examination halls " copying " and " cribbing " prevailed to a scandalous extent, and in examinations for a " pass " were regarded as very trifling offences. The effect of this upon the value of degrees, and upon the standard of acquirement, not to speak of the even more important moral standard of the students, could be nothing short of disastrous.

To Professor Thomson all deceptions and shams, degrading and demoralizing in effect, as well as essentially immoral in themselves, were an unspeakable abomination. In the interests alike of students and University, and of truth and honesty, he at once attacked the evil. When at the close of his first session the examination papers showed that wholesale copying had been practised, he demanded another examination under stricter surveillance. The students refused. They found, however, that in the new professor they had met an antagonist of an unwonted kind; for he prevailed upon the Senatus to suspend till October the whole of the bursary payments conditionally due in April. It was a severe lesson, and one which none but a fearless and determined man would have ventured to inflict. How much courage and determination were required may be judged by the fact that it was only by a majority of one that the Senatus consented.

His action left him a legacy of temporary unpopularity, and he was referred to among the students as " The Fiend ". But in time that feeling gave place to one of a very different kind, and he was commonly called by the affectionate title of " Davie ".

From the very first, Professor Thomson took an active part in the work of the Senatus Academicus. . . . To quote the words of Principal Sir William Geddes: " Coming while still young into a body of then elderly professors, he was soon appointed secretary, and the qualifications which he showed in the conduct of business made him for a long time the directing pilot on the somewhat troublous period of transition, when the colleges had to be transformed under the pressure of the demand for University extension and reform."

Professor Thomson performed a service of the highest value when with unflinching firmness and courage he held his ground, and contended that there should be complete fusion, or none at all.

WM. L. LOW: *A.B.A.*

CHARLES NIVEN

Professor of Natural Philosophy, 1880-1922

> Charlie Niven, with the wisdom of silence, never saying what he thought of some of us.
>
> F. P. MILLIGAN

> From the standpoint of the student, we believe the greatest difficulty he has to contend with is knowing his subject too well.
>
> *Alma Mater*

> It is one of the features of Professor Niven's teaching that he never requires a note; by sheer force of concentration he can reproduce the most complicated formula. With this genius is associated (we are informed on the best authority) a faculty for forgetting the multiplication table which renders Charlie only the more popular with the men he teaches.
>
> *Alma Mater*

" Charlie " was a product of the North-East and had all the characteristics of that part of the country. He had not much patience with the slacker, but he was kindly disposed to the plodder, even though the latter was not greatly endowed. This leniency towards the weaker members of his class appears in his remark while issuing Class Certificates at the end of term: " I hope the Recording Angel turns away his face while I issue some of the following certificates." He considered the profession a student was likely to follow in judging whether or not to grant a Class Certificate, but even here he imposed a limit—" Well, you know, we must draw the line somewhere."

> From another source comes the cognate story: An Arts student having been refused a " sign-up " appealed in person to the Professor, who, looking over his record, said he could not on his conscience furnish him with a

certificate and a recommendation that would let him go forth and teach the subject. " But, Sir, I am not going to be a teacher." " And pray, what are you going to be? " " A minister, Sir." The Professor produced his pen and promptly wrote a certificate. " Take it, my boy. You know quite enough Natural Philosophy to preach the everlasting Gospel." That student became one of our most successful ministers.

Coming from Cambridge as a Senior Wrangler, Professor Niven brought to the study of physical problems a more extensive mathematical treatment than his predecessor, especially in the branches of electricity, magnetism and heat. Himself a lover of music (Mozart rather than Wagner) he took infinite pains in preparing his class experiments in acoustics and was never satisfied until he got what he considered the right effect. He delighted also in the old Scottish Songs, loving particularly " Wha'll buy my caller herrin' ", which he was in the habit of having sung at the students' At Homes given by Mrs. Niven and himself to members of his class.

But for all his kind-heartedness, " Charlie " could give a shrewd hit when he judged it desirable.

" Sir, I had to attend my grandmother's funeral and had to miss the examination."

" I am sorry about that, but come tomorrow and I will give you an examination to yourself."

The student spent the interval learning everything but what had been in the paper he missed.

Professor to one of his staff next day: " I am afraid I proved too much for Mr. S—. I gave him a copy of the paper the others had and he made nothing of it ".

Then he went off chuckling to himself.

A. E. M. GEDDES

In striking contrast to his mathematical colleague, Professor George Pirie, who was both talkative and precise, Charles Niven was the absent-minded savant of romance. To his students he was a bit of a mystery. We knew he had been Senior Wrangler and we believed he had made important contributions to science which had led to his election as a Fellow of the Royal Society; but even in the honours classes we never came near to guessing in what field these might have lain. He was a silent little man with a twinkle in his eye that indicated a genial disposition, and he certainly had not an enemy in the world.

An incident in the Natural Philosophy graduation class comes to mind. The Professor was working on the demonstration bench with a sonometer, and the notes it gave forth were acquiring an unexplained echo from the back of the lecture room. Without looking up he slowly remarked, " There's another hollow box sounding ". Loud laughter in which students and professor joined. When he returned to the preparation room at the end of the lecture, he was still beaming, and laughed on for a considerable time. Then he tried to explain the incident, but could not remember what he had said that made everybody laugh so heartily.

JAMES STRACHAN

" Charlie " occupied the Chair for forty-two years. Charles S. McLeod, whose first year was Charlie's last, remembers him as " a little old man, giving the impression of being far away from us in a world of his own "—though an occasional joke, accompanied by a chuckling grunt, showed that he was not so absent-minded as he might seem.

GEORGE PAGET THOMSON

Professor of Natural Philosophy, 1922-1930

His tenure of office in Aberdeen was short, but into this short period was crowded an enormous amount of research work in the world of atomic physics. His greatest contribution to science has been on cathode rays or electrons. Through the theory of Prince Louis de Broglie and E. Schrödinger an entirely new conception of the electron arose. Professor Thomson at once started testing this theory experimentally, and in spite of the enormous experimental difficulties, his success was such that his name has become widely known throughout the world of physics. The patience and the perseverance which he brought to the task, the skill which he showed in surmounting innumerable difficulties, the unerring judgment he displayed in the interpretation of his results, all unite in showing that in research and along this line in particular he is a master. The originality of his work received the hall-mark of science in that it brought him the very high distinction of being elected a Fellow of the Royal Society of London.

Professor Thomson has been successful, however, not only in unravelling the hidden mysteries of science, but also in setting forth these mysteries in language which the ordinary reader can comprehend. His book *The Atom* contains a clear and concise review of our knowledge regarding the atom, and from this account mathematical formulae have been almost entirely excluded. The ability to do this rests with a limited few.

A. E. M. GEDDES: A.U.R.1930

Since leaving Aberdeen, Professor (now Sir George) Thomson has gone steadily on to one achievement after another. He received the Nobel Prize for Physics in 1937, headed the first British Committee on Atomic Energy (1940-41) and since 1952 has been Master of Corpus Christi College, Cambridge. Among his academic rewards are the Hughes Medal (1939), the Royal Medal (1949) and the Faraday Medal (1960). He has also been elected President of the British Association for 1960-61. The Faraday Medal had been awarded to his father, Sir J. J. Thomson, forty-five years previously.

JOHN ANTHONY CARROLL

Professor of Natural Philosophy, 1930-1946

Professor Carroll maintained the study of atomic physics developed by his predecessor, though he was more of a mathematical physicist than Professor G. P. Thomson. In 1936 he led an expedition to Russia for the purpose of observing an eclipse of the sun. He had already taken part in four eclipse expeditions (California, Norway, Malaya, Canada) and in the Norway expedition he was responsible for the design and operation of three instruments, one of which was an original device for detecting motion in the coronal material: this device in improved form was also used in the 1936 expedition to Omsk. In 1942 he was called to become Deputy for Research and Development to the Controller of the Navy and Scientific Adviser to the Board of Admiralty. At the close of hostilities he was prevailed upon to remain as Director of Physical Research at the Admiralty, and in 1953 he received the honour of Knighthood.

The present holder of the Chair is REGINALD VICTOR JONES, *1946, who had been Director of Intelligence in the Second World War, and whose activities since coming to Aberdeen have included the development of instruments of precision and the detection of infra-red radiation; and the intricate and difficult process of crystal-growing.*

An important part of the work of the Natural Philosophy Department was the maintenance of the Observatory at the top of the Cromwell Tower at King's College. Originally astronomical, and owing its inception to the enthusiasm of the young David Gill, who had been fired by Clerk Maxwell, it became later a Meteorological post, supplying from 1868 till it was closed in 1947 photographic records of pressure and temperature and other meteorological information to the M.O., London. For forty of those years the observer was GEORGE A. CLARKE (1903-43), *whose photographs of cloud formations, lightning and other meteorological phenomena were of such delicacy that in modern meteorological publications they occupy a prominent place.* A. E. M. GEDDES, *who was associated nearly fifty years with the Department, having been for a time its acting head, and retired in* 1955 *as a Reader in Natural Philosophy, worked in the Observatory both in research and in teaching.*

EDUCATION

JOHN CLARKE

Lecturer in Education, 1898-1925

John Clarke came to Aberdeen in 1879 as headmaster of a school—the Gymnasium in the Old Town—already doomed to decline: one of his pupils in its last years was Herbert Grierson.   After the " Gym " closed, Mr. Clarke became a master in the Grammar School, and when a lectureship in Education was formed in the University he was appointed to it.

He had always been deeply interested in the general problems of education.   It was from him, indeed, that I first learned that there was such a subject as Pedagogics.   The subject was regarded with considerable suspicion by the older-fashioned among us, and was rather unwillingly admitted into the curriculum.   But there is no use in attempting to belittle a subject to which Plato devoted so full, so arresting, so vital a dialogue as the " Republic ".

As I look back over Clarke's life two things strike me—his consistency and the continual growth of his outlook and his sympathy.   He was consistent even in his foibles, his love of contradiction and argument, and of giving you an occasional snub; he was consistent also in his religious feelings, his absolute uprightness and sincerity, his never-failing active interest in any scheme of betterment.   On the other hand, his mind was always open.   He was ready to consider any fresh proposition put before him.   His sympathies were always widening.   If his religious feelings never wavered, he grew more tolerant and generous, and always wiser. He might and did make mistakes, mistakes that sometimes injured himself and stood in the way of getting the full recognition, especially in the University, of his real claims and merits.   But when he came to advise another, his wisdom was unfailing.   He would warn you against mistakes of the kind that he himself fell into occasionally.   To know him was to feel it impossible to be insincere oneself, or to acquiesce indolently in what one felt might be improved.

H. J. C. GRIERSON: *A.U.R.* 1939

Mr. Clarke was followed in 1925 by D R. NORMAN T. WALKER, *who became a Reader in 1947, and whose quiet and courteous guidance will be withdrawn from the Department this autumn.   Dr. Walker has also been Director of Extra-Mural Education.*

PSYCHOLOGY

Comparative Psychology was first expounded in the University in 1896 by
G. F. STOUT, *who stimulated and excited those students who followed him into
the new and strange ways of thought that he laid open.   After a short time,
however, he made wing to St. Andrews.*

J. LEWIS MCINTYRE

Lecturer in Comparative Psychology, 1899-1929

Small, almost insignificant in appearance, but with a wealth of character
and a quiet humorous appreciation of the world, Dr. McIntyre quickly
made his new and unfamiliar subject of study a notable one among his
students.   He devoted most thorough attention to the psychology of
language, which demands close acquaintance with child and animal
psychology.   His successor (to become in time Professor) Rex Knight
said of him that by his sudden death British psychology was bereft of one
of its most independent thinkers.   He was one of the first to give lectures
on industrial psychology and on infant psychology.   His course in experimental psychology was rich in experiments he had himself devised.   He
was a keen lover of the outdoor world, a gardener and a mountaineer and
has been known to toboggan down the slopes of the Hill of Fare on a tea-
tray.   For thirty years he kept apace with all the branches of his rapidly
expanding subject, while remaining so unassuming and so selfless that to
know him was to love him.

Dr McIntyre was succeeded by ARTHUR REX KNIGHT, *a brilliantly persuasive
lecturer whose subject was elevated to a professorship in 1947.*

FRENCH

*It was not until 1893 that the study of other than ancient tongues was recognized
as of importance on a university level.   In that year a lectureship in combined
French and German was instituted and was given to a man with both French and
German in his make-up, being Swiss, and certainly with something of German in
his pronunciation of French*—WILLIAM SCHOLLE.   *When the two tongues were
separated in 1903 it surprised some of his listeners to know that Dr. Scholle chose to
remain the teacher of French.   This he continued to be until he died in 1921.   Dr.
Scholle was a small man, an eminent pioneer in his own field of Phonetics, a painstaking teacher but not an inspiring lecturer, though his good-heartedness commended
him to his students.   One of them recalls the Christmas gift offered by his class to
the good doctor—a turkey and a bottle of whisky (" In those days—1907—the
total cost was probably under £1.")   The doctor seemed embarrassed and asked:*

*" Is it a joke? " " A Bubbly-Joke ", answered the student, to the delight of the class
and the bewilderment of the lecturer.*

From 1921 to 1926 ENNEMOND CASATI *took charge of the Department and
continued until 1933 to give inspiring lectures on French Literature, while the new
Professor devoted himself to philology and the historical study of the French language.*

FREDERICK SIDNEY SHEARS

Professor of French, 1926-1932

*The first holder of the French Chair was an Englishman who, said Sir George
Adam Smith, " brought not a little of his own to our fellowship in this the most
northern of British Universities ". He was stricken with illness in the sixth
year of his professorship and the forty-first of his age, and died in 1932.*

When Professor Shears came to Aberdeen as the first occupant of the
Carnegie Chair of French, one was at once attracted to him by his frank
and cordial nature. Very few men coming from the south, as he did, have
so quickly won the regard and affection of all he came in contact with.
There was in his genial and open manner something which appealed to
every one, students and colleagues alike. His contributions to the *Modern
Languages Review* showed his deep knowledge of Old French Literature
and Language . . . but his main contribution to learning was his book on
Froissart, which to him was a labour of love. For many years he lived
with his author, and his volume will stand for a long time as the most
complete and best study of Froissart in English.

E. CASATI: A.U.R. 1932

The same character of unpretendingness—no payment claimed—may
have concealed from some, in his book on Froissart, the importance of
what he was doing. . . . However well it was reviewed, one can give it a
first reading without at first fully recognizing the variety of equipment
necessary for the presentation of detailed learning in so agreeable a form.
But the addition to our Island knowledge was very real. . . . Shears
lived longer than Burns or Byron, but we all know he was just beginning
to open his store. " The machine through all these years had just been
perfected for its business."

A. A. JACK: A.U.R. 1932

FREDERICK C. ROE

Professor of French, 1932-1957

*Born in Warwickshire, Professor Roe had from the first a strong feeling for France
which, when he came to his Aberdeen post, may have helped him through the old*

association between France and Scotland to feel so thoroughly at home in Scotland as he undoubtedly became. He fell deeply under the spell of King's College and Old Aberdeen, and did all in his power, both as Professor of French and as Chairman of the Franco-Scottish Aberdeen Centre, to encourage contacts between the two countries. One of his best-known pieces of work was on Rabelais and his Scottish translator Urquhart, who was an alumnus of King's College; and his many years of intimacy with France were summed up in his last book, Modern France: an Introduction to French Civilization.

> " A buoyant, exuberant, much-loved Professor."

> E. WITTE

There must be few men of whom I would care to speak with the same warm and affectionate regard I have long felt for Fred Roe. It may be that out almost simultaneous arrival in King's College, more than twenty years ago, played its part in weaving the ties that bound us together. But I am inclined to think that what really attracted me to him, and eventually captivated me, was his forthright manliness; he was essentially a man's man: he still bore the marks of war on him, and the grim memory of Mount Kemmel still lingered in the background. At the same time, however, it would only be fair to say that he won a favoured place among his colleagues because he possessed a quality we seldom look for in men, but frequently admire in women—the intangible and indescribable thing called *charm*. To say that he drenched us with an amazing flood of bonhomie, wit, and humour, persiflage, and gentle leg-pulling would be merely a crude way of describing his richly effervescent personality, which never seemed to grow weary, or suffer from exhaustion. True, he once told me that he was " high-strung " and " suffered from nerves ": if so, this was happily counterbalanced by a singularly high " flash point "—so high indeed, that he did not appear to have one at all. Slow to take offence, he seemed to express in himself the so-called Rabelaisian " therapeutics of laughter ": he usually saw the humorous side of things—seldom the gloomy or seamy side—and he took a sheer delight in passing it on to others. The journey from Aberdeen to St. Andrews for the spring and autumn meetings of the Entrance Board and the Revision Committees, was invariably a sort of seed-plot of merry jests intermingled with shrewd and well-informed comments on celebrities in the political or social world and countless other topics. His love of France was, of course, paramount, inspiring, and always " on tap "; and I am certain that it was warmly reciprocated from the French side, for his association with the literary élite in Paris and elsewhere was virtually continuous.

Of his scholarship I shall only say that it holds a high place among contemporaries at home and abroad. His widespread activities; numerous assignments; books and articles that flowed from his pen periodically, supply irrefutable proof of it; and honours came to him easily and quickly. I am convinced that I never met a harder worker, or a more assiduous pursuer of *le mot juste*. His keen sense for style held him to pen and paper with a grasp of steel, and rendered him quite oblivious to the expenditure of the midnight oil.

J. B. BLACK: *A.U.R.* 1958

The holder of the Chair since 1958 is ARMEL H. DIVERRES.

GERMAN

The first holder of the Lectureship in German was a Scot, JOHN LEES, M.A., D.LITT., a kindly, lovable and scholarly expert on German Literature, whose early death through ill-health cut short a career of great promise. He was succeeded in 1920 by an Englishman, WALTER H. BRUFORD, M.A., who in 1923 was elevated to a Readership, which he gave up on his appointment to the Chair of German in Edinburgh. He is now the distinguished occupant of the Chair of German in Cambridge, upon whom the University of Aberdeen bestowed an LL.D. in 1958. In 1929 ARTHUR H. J. KNIGHT, M.A., was appointed Reader in German, stayed however for only one year before returning to Cambridge to take up a Lectureship and Fellowship at Trinity College. He was followed by DOUGLAS YATES, M.A., D.PHIL., who was Head of the Department from 1930 until his resignation in 1945; he demanded a high level of scholarship from his students and firmly consolidated a flourishing department of German studies. His death at an early age was a great loss to the University and a personal grief to his old students. The acting Head of the Department during Dr. Yates's ill-health, WILLIAM WITTE, M.A., PH.D., DR.RER.POL., became Head of the Department in 1945, Reader in German in 1947, and finally, from May 1951, the first incumbent of the Chair of German, founded in 1950.

EDITH WITTE

SPANISH

In 1920 Spanish was added to the living languages taught in the University, and the first Lecturer was a man of immense vitality and urgency, constantly bursting out of the academic mould, but succeeding marvellously in persuading his students to talk in a Spanish that was understood by Spaniards—CHARLES DAVIDSON (*1920-39*).

Others might teach a language so that for examination purposes students could produce the appropriate subjunctive to suit the catch question, or trace correctly the modification of an ending from the sixteenth century onwards, but C. D. taught us a living language as spoken by people whom it seemed we might meet and talk to in their own tongue the next summer or the Christmas after that. Senatorial heads might be shaken over C. D.'s seemingly casual approach to learning (with a capital L) or the frankness of some of his reminiscences, but the measure of his success was that when some of us did reach Spain not only could we talk to Spaniards in their own language with a creditable accent and a reasonable vocabulary, but we had somehow acquired an understanding of the Spanish point of view and the Spanish way of life which helped to make our visit not only a commercial success but a pleasurable experience and the means of forming enduring friendships. So to teach a language that it becomes a gateway instead of a barrier is no mean achievement.

W. M. MIRRLEES: *A.U.R.* 1959

In 1939 A. A. PARKER *became Lecturer and in 1949 Reader in Spanish, and in 1953 was succeeded by* PETER N. DUNN *and* TERENCE E. MAY.

ITALIAN

Italian was added to the resources of the University after the Second World War. From 1950 to 1957 the lecturer was STANLEY B. CHANDLER. *The present lecturer is* PETER M. BROWN.

SWEDISH

The Swedish lectureship also dates from 1950, when ERIK FRYKMAN *came from Uppsala to fill it. In 1956 he was succeeded by* N. GUNNAR LJUNGGREN.

CELTIC AND COMPARATIVE PHILOLOGY

In 1916 John Fraser, a classical scholar of notable achievement and an impeccable scholar, became Aberdeen University's first teacher of Celtic; but though he went on to the Chair of Celtic in Oxford he will be remembered most widely by Aberdeen graduates as a lecturer in the Latin Department, sardonic and salutary.

JOHN FRASER

Lecturer in Humanity, 1907-1916

Lecturer in Celtic and Comparative Philology, 1916-1921

> A profound and fastidious scholarship is not incompatible with a very keen sense of humour, which often makes Plautus a good deal funnier than Plautus was ever intended by the said Plautus to be.
>
> *Alma Mater*

" John Fraser: *Collected Satires*, Epigrams on Members of the ordinary Latin Class."

Alma Mater

Student flounders in a translation that was supposed to be prepared. Johnny Fraser: " Have you prepared this passage, Mr. X? " " Yes sir." " Then you had better let us hear it as it would be if you hadn't prepared it."

On my first long leave from Natal, in the autumn of 1919, I travelled with a man who was re-visiting his native part of Scotland, which he named as Glen Urquhart. That set me asking if the name of John Fraser (whom I briefly described) " rang a bell " with him. After some cudgelling of his memory he replied, " Yes, I think he must be the boy who was known as Johnny Professor ". That " tore it ". I had then no doubt that we had our sights on one and the same individual.

Yes, John Fraser was undoubtedly " the man born to be a professor ", and a professor he duly became (of Celtic, at Oxford), after a distinguished classical career at Aberdeen and Cambridge, followed by a period of lecturing at his Aberdeen *alma mater*. His death at the comparatively early age of sixty-two was a severe loss to Celtic studies.

But it was not so much for his scholarship as for some other things that Fraser will be remembered by his contemporaries—the sardonic humour, the rapier wit, the devastating repartee. " It should be obvious to the meanest intelligence ", I said once in the heat of a debate. " Is that ", he retorted, " why you can see it so well? " I have always regretted that I did not set myself to " Boswellise " him to better purpose over our eight years of close association: I should have had today, for myself and others, a stock of good things which might worthily have been placed beside the great Doctor's best. But behind the semi-cynical façade which Fraser presented to the world—and here another Johnson contact — there was another John Fraser, essentially human and kindly at heart. I would have gone to him for help in trouble, sooner than to many others, and would not have been disappointed.

Fraser, in his student days, posed as something of a misogynist and affected to regard with a jaundiced eye such of his weaker brethren as were beginning even then to show (as he would have said) signs of disintegration. But it was only a pose. In due time he himself succumbed, like the rest of us, and no doubt, as he would have acknowledged, to his great advantage.

John was an inveterate smoker. He calculated distance not in yards but in cigarettes, that is to say, the number he counted on consuming between two given points. I have heard him say he hoped his last breath would be through a pipe. I like to picture him, now, over his book in a quiet corner of Elysium, enjoying a pipe of his favourite mixture, or, failing that, anything that smoke can be got out of, and sending an unwelcome interrupter about his business with a shattering Fraserian broadside.

ALEXANDER PETRIE

The second Lecturer in Celtic (soon to become a Reader) was JOHN MACDONALD *(1921-56; Reader 1926)*

His scholarship has had no truck with the narrower sort of specialization. The Classics, Philosophy, a deep interest in literature generally, and wide reading in history have helped to make him a philologist in the older, more humane sense of the word. In Celtic studies his range is similarly wide, as can be gauged from his distinguished editing of *Scottish Gaelic Studies*, a periodical founded by the University in 1926. In addition to this work, he edited *Ewen MacLachlan's Gaelic Verse* for the University Studies series, and collaborated with William M. Alexander in editing Francis Diack's *The Inscriptions of Pictland*.

He is remembered by his students as a fruitful, kindly teacher, and by his colleagues as a man of ripe learning and wide-ranging conversation. His Highland accent still proclaims where his roots are.

DERICK THOMSON

The present Reader is DERICK THOMSON, *himself a poet in the Gaelic tongue.*

MUSIC

That music had fallen from grace in the higher reaches of Scottish education, forfeiting its ancient position among the seven cardinal disciplines, need not concern us here: but the recovery is our concern. When Professor Christie agitated for an organ in the Chapel at King's College and his daughter Elisabeth became the first organist (and the first woman to hold office in the University), more was done for the cause of music than might have been anticipated; for Elisabeth Christie was a woman of genius who trained her choir to an understanding of music and her audiences to a thirst for more. At the same time Professor C. S. Terry through the University Choral Society was having a similar influence. During the First World War Miss Christie arranged some memorable recitals in the Chapel, and the quickening of the appetite for music that the war had brought (the Second World War had the same effect) may have played its part in the decision to include music in the series of lectures on the Fine Arts that was instituted in 1918. Mr. Harry Townend on Painting, Dr. William Kelly and later R. Leslie Rollo on Architecture, Professor Harrower on Greek Art and Sculpture and Mr. Willan Swainson on Music, gave among them a course which was allowed to count for a degree, though each series was open also to members of the public. The Second World War ended this enterprise, but after it a Department of Music was created, with Mr. Swainson as lecturer (Reader, 1949).

In 1925 WILLAN SWAINSON entered the University as a part-time Lecturer in Music. At that time University music as such could scarcely be said to exist, yet, as a result of sheer hard work, enthusiasm, and single-minded devotion to his subject, Mr. Swainson was able to leave behind him a firmly-established, well-equipped, and truly progressive School of Music.

The duties attached to the newly created Lectureship were slight; the lecturer had only to give eight public lectures during the session. The University Musical Evenings which soon came into being, the song-study groups, and the largely attended Music Hours, to which graduates from far and near still make appreciative reference, soon made it clear that the lecturer had charged himself with a great deal more than the fulfilment of the letter of his bond.

But the developments he most desired were retarded because the University had no provision for an integrated academic study of music. An early memorandum dealing with this problem had included comprehensive plans for such study, but its proposals, necessarily of a somewhat ambitious character, seemed at that time to be impracticable.

After an apparently quiescent period there was a decided advance, and the scope of the Lectureship was greatly enlarged. A Department of Music was established, Music became a degree subject, an honours course was instituted, and the facilities for study were extended. At the same time the Choral and Orchestral recitals reached a high standard, and soon became a recognized and valued part of the musical life of the city.

GEO. SWAPP

In 1956 REGINALD BARRETT-AYRES *succeeded to the direction of the Department in which he had already worked for several years, endearing himself to the students by the ordering of the music for their annual shows. The Department continues to give highly acceptable concerts and lunch-hour recitals, to give youthful composers a platform and to take part in musical events outside its own area.*

POLITICAL ECONOMY

In 1902 David H. McGregor was appointed to lecture in this subject, followed by Stanley Turner to whom in 1913 succeeded R. B. Forrester. In 1921 a Chair was founded.

ALEXANDER GRAY

Professor of Political Economy, 1921-1934

The first professor of Political Economy was a lad of so many parts that one hesitates whether to praise more his lucid lecturing, his distinguished Civil service, his wide and easy culture, his readiness to serve the city of his adoption and, one feels, his love (Aberdeen), his nimble wit, the felicity of his utterance, his courtesy, his poet's tongue. Like True Thomas he has slept under the Eildon Tree; and if the Queen of Elfland gave him thereafter " the tongue that can never lee ", that seemed to him too dangerous a gift to be expended on bare-faced economics, and (son of a poet and

15

his county Angus) he strode over the bare lands not twelve miles from Aberdeen and made out of the economics of the north-east countryman's life a poem:

Here in the Uplands
The soil is ungrateful;
The fields, red with sorrel,
Are stony and bare.
A few trees, wind-twisted—
Or are they but bushes?—
Stand stubbornly guarding
A home here and there.

Scooped out like a saucer,
The land lies before me;
The waters, once scattered,
Flow orderedly now
Through fields where the ghosts
Of the marsh and the moorland
Still ride the old marches,
Despising the plough.

The marsh and the moorland
Are not to be banished;
The bracken and heather,
The glory of broom,
Usurp all the balks
And the fields' broken fringes,
And claim from the sower
Their portion of room.

This is my country,
The land that begat me.
These windy spaces
Are surely my own.
And those who here toil
In the sweat of their faces
Are flesh of my flesh,
And bone of my bone.

Hard is the day's task—
Scotland, stern Mother—
Wherewith at all times
Thy sons have been faced:
Labour by day,
And scant rest in the gloaming,
With Want an attendant
Not lightly outpaced.

Yet do thy children
Honour and love thee.
Harsh is thy schooling,
Yet great is the gain:
True hearts and strong limbs,
The beauty of faces,
Kissed by the wind
And caressed by the rain.

Professor Gray left for the Chair of Commercial and Political Economy and Mercantile Law in Edinburgh, and was followed in Aberdeen by LINDLEY MACNAGHTEN FRASER *(1935-45), an interesting lecturer lured from us during the war to become one of the most persuasive broadcasters of news to Germany. " German listeners ", said a writer in 1941, " testify to his flair for getting under the Nazi skin. . . . Despite the death penalty for illicit listening, his audience within the Reich is said to be steadily increasing." In 1945* HENRY HAMILTON, *who had already been on the staff since 1923, succeeded to the Chair.*

GEOGRAPHY

One of the developments to follow the First World War was the teaching at University level of Geography, the first Lecturer (1919-1945—Reader from 1923) being JOHN MCFARLANE.

John McFarlane came to the University of Aberdeen in 1919 to organize a department of Geography such as he had previously established in Manchester, and this he did so successfully that, on completion of his labours, the Senatus Academicus received the intimation of his resignation with " great regret " and minuted their appreciation of " the quiet wisdom and modesty, gentleness and sympathy " by which, through a period of twenty-six years, he had " endeared himself to his colleagues ".

Twenty-six years—just over a quarter of a century—but how much he packed into those years, how many difficulties he faced and what serious obstacles he surmounted only the governing body of the University and his devoted wife fully realized. Alike to the inner circle of his University colleagues and to the outer circle of his fellow townsmen he preserved a quiet mien which only too often hid bitter disappointment, when lack of funds or other severe impediment retarded the fulfilment of his great ambition, to have in Aberdeen University an efficient, smooth-running, well-staffed and well-equipped Geography department. The completion of this great task he eventually ensured, although the last two of his aims were fulfilled only after he demitted office. This establishing of Geography as a University subject was a real achievement, done, as it was, almost single-handed, for, during the whole tenure of his office, John McFarlane had no full-time assistant. Yet, so quietly did he work, that few people outside University circles realized what an uphill corner had been rounded and important milestone in educational progress reached. Geography had come alive!

DOROTHY M. MUNRO: *A.U.R.* 1953

His successor, ANDREW C. O'DELL, *Reader in Geography, 1945, Professor, 1951, became the first occupant of the new Chair, which he still holds with energy, enterprise and a staff and equipment that would have delighted the heart of his predecessor.*

DIVINITY

In 1860 there were four Chairs in Divinity—Church History, Systematic Theology, Oriental Languages, which for practical purposes meant Hebrew, and Biblical Criticism, a new Chair founded in the year of the Fusion. Through the century, many of the tenures of these Chairs have been short, the holders passing on to other posts (frequently to Edinburgh), while others, as Professors Pirie, Milligan, Cowan, Gilroy, G. D. Henderson, have had long and honoured careers with us and have left their impress on both city and University. Meanwhile in the Free (later United Free) Church College great men also were teaching—Robertson Smith, Principal Iverach, Principal Cairns—and after the Union of the U.F. and Established Churches the two Divinity Halls came together and in 1933 new Chairs in Divinity were proposed in Christian Dogmatics, and Christian Ethics and Practical Theology. In 1935 these were filled by David S. Cairns and Adam Fyfe Findlay, both names of repute in Christ's College, as the Alford Place Church College was henceforth called. Christ's College undertook the practical training of the aspirants to the ministry.

CHURCH HISTORY

The first holder of this Chair was the redoubtable William Pirie 1860-1877, later to be Principal and already spoken upon among the Principals.

JOHN CHRISTIE

Professor of Church History, 1877-1889

One of the Kildrummy Christies, Professor Christie was a man of wide culture who had set up a printing press in his Kildrummy manse, and whose influence helped to revolutionise music in the college chapel. The first organist was his daughter, Elisabeth, a pungent personality who gave the Chapel Choir a new conception of what music could be.

One recalls the frontal curve with its significant possibilities, the keen dark eyes that appeared to see as far through a stone wall (or a student's head) as any human organs could; the firm, straight mouth with its note of character and reserve. One frames them in a head of iron-grey hair and the beard of a Nazarite. One puts in the crows' feet at the eyes where humour lurked, and the little upward lines from the shaven lip that registered the smothering of frequent smiles. One throws the gown over his broad shoulders, gives him a coloured handkerchief in the right hand, a silver snuff-box in the other, and plants him erectly in his chair.

Symeon Stylites of the fifth century, who selected for his manse a lofty pillar in the desert, would have been, in the doctor's eye, an ungrateful incumbent of a Donside parish—which we gathered was his ideal of ecclesiastical economy. Luxuriously balancing a pinch of snuff, with what a playful glance at his portly form he seemed to say: " You may have your choice, gentlemen, of the model Christian, but in my opinion the Reverend Symeon Stylites of Antioch comes in as a second, desperately behind! " And it would be rash to say that the doctor was wrong.

Staunchly adhering to the literal interpretation of the Westminster standards; innocent of reservations, mental or expressed; untroubled by mystical leanings or by any apparent religious emotion, he made his students feel the remorseless logic of Calvinism. His theological statements were couched in a bald, uncompromising style, more nearly resembling a road surveyor's report than a prelection upon the ways of God to man. The doctor, good man, had his limitations, like us all!

Professor Christie came to the Chair with a long experience of teaching, none the worse in some respects that it was gained in parochial schools. It had the grip, the definiteness, the practical purpose of the parochial dominie, to whom our Scottish scholars owe so much.

He was the last of the Moderates; the last of that long line that distinguished the University of Aberdeen. They were scholars and men of affairs; dignified and benignant; unemotional, but of granite convictions.

DONALD MACMILLAN: *A.B.A.*

HENRY COWAN

Professor of Church History, 1889-1924

It is forty-five years since I last sat as a student in the Divinity classroom at King's, yet I can see, clear as if it were yesterday, Professor Cowan's courtly bow as he entered on the last stroke of the ten o'clock bell; his quick walk to the lectern; his pause to place and open his lecture case; then his quick look up to us as a sign that he was about to begin his opening prayer. Very short but very beautiful were his opening prayers. He had favourite phrases and indeed whole sentences. In the course of our two years in his class we came to know them well and when to expect them. If, for example, it was a bright sunny morning following a succession of dull and wet days we would look at one another with an expectant smile as we rose for the prayer. We knew that it would begin: " O God, who shinest upon our bodies today with the light of thy natural sun, shine into our souls with the bright beams of Thy Sun of righteousness." Then followed his lecture, delivered fairly fast and closely read, his eyes seldom leaving his manuscript except when he had a point which he wished specially to emphasize. He would then raise his right hand, closed except for one finger, and looking up, he would, with something between a shake of the head and a nod, bring his finger down smartly on the lectern.

When I commenced my Divinity course in 1912 Professor Cowan— already OLD HENRY to all his students—had been in the Chair of Church

15*

History for twenty-three years.   He carried on for twelve more years till his retiral at or over the age of eighty in 1924.   I have often thought what a blessing it was for the Divinity students at King's from 1909 to 1924 that there was in these days no compulsion on University Professors to retire at the age of sixty-five.   It would have meant that we should have been deprived of the privilege of sitting under him and that would have been a deprivation indeed. None of us but must feel that our course in Divinity would have been very much poorer and we should have gone out far less well equipped for our work as ministers if he had had to retire before our day in favour of a younger man: for no younger man, and indeed no other man of any age, could have given us all that he gave or been to us all that he was.

He was a born teacher.   His lectures on Church History, divided, sub-divided, and sub-sub-divided and so on, sometimes to the 5th and 6th and even 7th degree, were masterpieces of orderliness, of compactness, of lucidity.   And even better and more valuable were the talks that he gave us, one day a week during part at least of a term, advising and instructing us on a minister's manifold tasks and duties, in church on Sunday and through the week at marriages and funerals and the visitation of the sick.   They were such talks as could have been given only by one who, like him, had been a beloved minister for twenty years before he became the beloved professor, and who during these twenty years had made and shown himself a master of every ministerial duty.   Above all: which of his students will ever forget the lesson and demonstration in sermon making that he gave us on the days when one of the third year students read or preached a Homily before him and the class?   I should perhaps explain that the exercises or discourses which every divinity student has to prepare and read before a professor and his brother students included in my time not only a Sermon but also a Homily.   The sermon was preached before the Professor of Theology, the Homily before the Professor of Church History.   But what exactly is the difference between a Sermon and a Homily even Professor Cowan couldn't make quite clear to us.   But Homily or Sermon—to listen to Professor Cowan criticizing it after the student had read it: pointing out and praising what was good in it, but also kindly, gently, but none the less unsparingly pointing out its faults and showing how they might be amended: and finally suggesting other lines of thought that the student might have followed: was indeed an education on the craft of sermon making.

Yes, Professor Cowan was certainly a great teacher.   None of his students looking back but must feel that they would be sorry to have missed what he taught them. But there was something else that we got from him and which we should all be even sorrier to have missed: the impact upon us during our three years in the Hall of his lovely personality. His was a lovely personality. He was the gentlest, kindest, most Christ-like man that I have ever known: a true saint with never a trace of sanctimoniousness. One could never feel that any one particular student was a special favourite with him for he made every student feel that he was his special favourite. And he must have found it very difficult to give his best students an outstandingly good testimonial because he couldn't give anything save a glowing testimonial to any student. Which meant of course that Vacancy Committees had to be warned not to be carried away by a testimonial from Professor Cowan in favour of one of the candidates, but to consider carefully how far the glowing things that were said in it were backed up by that candidate's testimonials, if any, from his other professors. As a rule the Interim Moderator would be able to give them that warning. For Professor Cowan was well known throughout the Church. And that he was just too charitable in his judgment and tended in consequence to describe all his geese as swans—most ministers were aware that that was his one fault. And I suppose it was a fault. But it is a good fault and a very rare fault. It is found only in the best and most saintly people.

A man then so saintly that all his geese were swans—his students couldn't come into contact with him every day for at least two of their three years in the Hall without being impelled to try to become the swans that he made us feel ourselves to be. That is why he was, and will always in our minds remain, the professor revered and loved beyond all others. I find it hard to believe that there has ever been since, or that there ever will be, in any of Scotland's Divinity Halls another quite so good.

JOHN S. MUTCH

GEORGE DAVID HENDERSON

Professor of Church History, 1924-1957

> Small in stature, he is large in mind. He is tolerant of all things worth the knowing. As a lecturer he is rapid and illuminating, bringing to the understanding of what might be a dead thing parallels of thought and action from many spheres, whether of matters long dead (though never to be buried) or of the mad-cap present.
>
> *Alma Mater*

All who had the privilege of studying under Professor G. D. Henderson have their own particular memories of " the great little man ", but all are united in acknowledging their debt to one whose influence went far beyond that which was exerted in the Church History classroom.

I suppose that most of us were more than a little frightened of " G. D." when first we met him. His austere manner, his very precise speech, his insistence in getting to the point quickly, his impatience with " woolly " thinking; all these helped to create the impression that he was aloof and unapproachable. It was not long, however, before his students recognized that in " G. D." they had one who was genuinely interested in them, and one whose helpfulness would prove invaluable.

The healthy awe in which he was held explains in part the unusually good attendance at his lectures, but the excellence of the lectures was the main reason. He had the gift of making Church History come alive; of transforming the shadowy figures from past ages into men of flesh and blood. As a lecturer he was never " exciting ", but was always stimulating. Scarcely thirty seconds into the room, he had taken out his spectacles, opened his notes and launched out into his subject. He wasted no time in introductory remarks or in recapitulation; he simply carried on talking where he had left off the moment the bell had gone the day before. I doubt very much whether he used one unnecessary word or one unnecessary gesture in all the lectures he delivered.

His one characteristic gesture was the removal of his spectacles but even this was a precise action indicating that what he was about to say, although not part of the lecture, was something of equal importance. On those occasions the historian gave way to the Churchman. Despite his long sojourn in the academic field, he never forgot that the Parish was the centre of the Church's life, and that the vast majority of his students were training to become parish ministers and not church historians. Few men had a greater understanding of the contemporary Church or a greater respect for the Presbyterian heritage. He was constantly drawing significant parallels between the past and the present and doing so with his dry but incisive wit. He introduced into all his lectures practical, down-to-earth advice that was to prove invaluable when we started work in our first parishes, and many of us have carefully preserved some of the memorable asides delivered on those occasions when " G. D." removed his spectacles.

No article on Professor Henderson would be complete without mention of his attitude towards those who had left the College. He followed with the greatest interest the careers of his former students and was tireless in his efforts on their behalf. He visited manses up and down the country preaching for his students; and he responded eagerly to every appeal for his help or advice. With very few exceptions he knew the present whereabouts of everyone who had gone out from Christ's College and few things pleased him more than hearing from his former students. This was brought home to me very vividly on one occasion when I was able to tell him that I had met a minister of the Presbyterian Church in South Africa who sent his greetings. Seldom had I seen " G. D." so excited. The minister whom I had met was one of the very few with whom he had lost contact.

ALAN O. ROBERTSON

As I write this tribute to an admired colleague, a letter has reached me from Budapest, from the Dean of the Faculty of Reformed Theology, eloquent in its expressions of gratitude for the work of Professor Henderson. In this Academy he had been appointed, in 1946, an Honorary Professor, and he is described in the letter as " the patron of our Hungarian divinity students ". The description arises from one side of Professor Henderson's activity as member, and for some years Convener, of the Church's Continental Committee. On behalf of that committee he maintained a strong association with the Reformed Churches of Europe. In particular, he promoted the attendance at Aberdeen, and other Scottish Colleges, of students for the ministry of these churches. They were thus brought into intimate contact for one year with the life and studies of the Scottish Church, and enabled to complete their mastery of English for future reading. This appealed strongly to G. D. Henderson as a means of fostering the unity and mutual knowledge of the Reformed Churches, all owing their origin to the work of John Calvin, but apt to lose effective contact with each other through the wide differences of language and historical development. Professor Henderson was always eager to ensure the presence in Scotland each year of Swiss, Hungarian, Czech, Italian, French, Spanish, or other foreign students of the reformed tradition. His lively sense of fellowship with the historic Reformed Churches was demonstrated in other ways. He had himself studied in Germany at Berlin and Jena. Early in his career he mastered the Dutch language, and later acquired Italian to give him direct knowledge of the writing in theology of the Dutch and Waldensian Churches. He lectured more than once in the Netherlands, reviewed Dutch publications, contributed to French Protestant theological periodicals, and travelled from time to time to visit leading centres of theological scholarship and Church life. He spoke at the German " Kirchentag ". In 1954 he was honoured in Paris with the degree of Doctor of Theology. About 1949, when he attained his semi-jubilee as an Aberdeen professor, these travels took him beyond the Iron Curtain at a time when such journeys were attended with uncertainty, discomfort, and even danger.

It was of course in his work as a historian that Dr. Henderson served the Church most notably, and added lustre to the fame of the University. His status as an academic historian is attested by his admission to the Fellowship of the Royal Historical Society. The special field of his studies was the Scottish Church of the seventeenth century (*Religious Life in Seventeenth Century Scotland*, 1937).

Something should be said about his wit. His temperament was not hilarious, nor his humour easy. But he was very perceptive about both the strength and weakness of other men, and his keen, playfully malicious comment could be very shrewd. At Christmas party or Final Year Dinner his speeches were always entertaining, and on these occasions the students were often emboldened to attempt some good-natured leg-pulling, often involving reference to the Professor's lack of inches, or his habit of pronouncing the word important with a short "o". These sallies were invariably well received and often neatly answered. More difficult after-dinner speaking, where greater subtlety and more sustained sparkle were demanded, found G. D. Henderson fully equal to the occasion.

JOHN M. GRAHAM: *A.U.R.* 1957

Since the days of Grub, Scotland has produced no finer ecclesiastical historian. He shared with Grub the same qualities of cool moderation; and what Grub did from the Episcopalian standpoint Professor Henderson accomplished on behalf of Presbyterianism.

Like all great scholars Professor Henderson was both humble about his own learning and generous in his appreciation of the efforts of others— though it hardly needs to be added that he could deal most drastically with shallowness and fraud. Above all things he was helpful. If one went to him with a query, be it ever so small, he would take a note of what was wanted, and within a day or two the enquirer would receive a fully documented statement of the information and all possible further sources of enquiry—carefully typewritten or, as often as not, written out in his own fair and legible hand.

W. D. SIMPSON: *A.U.R.* 1957

The Chair is now held by JAMES STEVENSON McEWEN, *1958.*

SYSTEMATIC THEOLOGY

ROBERT MACPHERSON

Professor of Systematic Theology, 1860(52)-1867

The Chair of Systematic Theology was the one chair to which appointment was by examination. In 1852 there were two candidates only, and the Chair fell to Robert Macpherson, his opponent Samuel Trail returning to labour for the next fifteen years in his remote Orkney parish, after which he succeeded to the Chair.

Professor Macpherson was only sixty-one when he died, and during his tenure " his powers were in full vigour and there was no falling off to the end. He was always recasting his old lectures or writing new ones. His lectures on the Resurrection (in refutation of Strauss) were the proof of unwearied diligence to the last, and were the crown of his life-work."

SAMUEL TRAIL

Professor of Systematic Theology, 1867-1887

From his post as minister of Birsay in Orkney, Dr. Trail took part in the theological controversies of the day, writing a pamphlet in criticism of Bishop Colenso's calling in question the historical accuracy and traditional authorship of the Books commonly attributed to Moses. He also helped in the production of a chronological Bible. But when in 1867 his second attempt at the Chair was successful, his original writings ceased. He was already sixty years of age and his theological position was fixed. In the brilliant uneasy stimulating days when a Robertson Smith, " man of science and yet a defender of the Faith ", could be struck from the roll of Aberdeen's leaders of thought, Professor Trail kept staunchly to the older orthodox teachings. " In his reviews of modern opinions there was a want of sympathetic appreciation of what was really valuable therein . . . and he had neither the agility of intellect nor the readiness of speech to excel in expository examination."

ALEXANDER STEWART

Professor of Systematic Theology 1887-1894

Professor Stewart was a graduate of St. Andrews and a man of great erudition, and kept himself and his students well abreast of all the newest scholarship on his subject.

In recent years Theology has made greater strides than almost any science and has attracted much scholarly consideration, especially in Germany. Dr. Stewart was among the first to appreciate the worth and import of German thought and to assimilate it. To him Theology is not a thing of merely professional, but of universal interest. He does not treat his subject as a playground for the puerile squabbles of dogmatics, but views religion as a whole, historically, comparatively and philosophically. This session [1891] he has been delivering a course of lectures on Christian Ethics, the first course of its kind in any of our Universities.

Alma Mater, 1891

W. P. PATERSON

Professor of Systematic Theology, 1894-1903

Professor Paterson's reputation as theologian and religious leader was world-wide. His career as a minister began in Galashiels, whence he went to Crieff. During his comparatively short tenure of his Aberdeen Chair he was a valuable member of staff, but he left in 1903 to become Professor of Divinity in Edinburgh. While there he was successively Baird Lecturer, Gifford Lecturer and Moderator of the General Assembly of the Church of Scotland, and a succession of notable volumes came from his pen on theology and the social problems of the day.

WILLIAM A. CURTIS

Professor of Systematic Theology, 1903-1915

Professor Curtis was a man of brilliant erudition who had travelled in Greece and Italy and became a member of the British School of Archaeology at Athens before undertaking his studies in Divinity. He studied also at Heidelberg, Leipzig and

Oxford. While he held the Aberdeen Chair he published A History of Creeds and Confessions of Faith in Christendom and Beyond, " *a learned work which received high commendation.*" *In 1915 he went to the Chair of Biblical Criticism and Biblical Antiquities in Edinburgh.*

WILLIAM FULTON

Professor of Systematic Theology, 1915-1928

A man in the fullness of manhood, immaculately dressed, robed and hooded, carrying a richly tasselled trencher, distinguished by a moustache and wearing rimless spectacles, behind which eyes sparkled that betokened an inquiring mind and a spirit of quiet humour and human kindness—such was the Reverend William Fulton when, early in 1916, he came to King's College to enter upon his duties as Professor of Systematic Theology.

He had won this professorship in the preceding year in a *contestatio* which embraced all the disciplines of the Divinity Faculty and much besides. Frequently when these *contestationes* were in progress—they were held only when this particular chair fell vacant—a dense fog descended on the North-East and the City of Aberdeen in particular, where in the new town it slowed down tramcars and in the auld toun the sturdy Clydesdales that laboured along the causeyed High Street drawing huge lorry-loads of pulp to the paper-mills beyond. This was commonly taken as nature's confirmation of the belief that theology is abstruse and unprogressive, and this belief was apparently in Professor Fulton's mind when in his inaugural lecture he said that he looked forward to a simplifying of theology and to dogma without dogmatism.

His senior colleagues, Professors Cowan and Nicol, had for him the affection that Paul the aged bore Timothy, while his remaining colleague, Professor Gilroy, rejoiced in the fellowship of one who, after busy years in the parochial ministry, could still point and translate unpointed Hebrew. His relations with his students were equally happy. Towards that a minor mishap made a notable contribution. When he was delivering his first lecture, the sleeve of his gown sent the loose leaves of his notes floating to the floor. Students hurried to their rescue and, picking them up, handed them to him. As he restored them to their order, his confusion ended, and with a smile he conveyed his thanks. This incident drew one and all together at a deep level; and without doing any hurt to the due relationships between teacher and taught, it imparted to them a cordiality that never left them.

Orderliness was an outstanding mark of Professor Fulton's thinking. His words were well chosen, and every added sentence made a further contribution to the clenching of his argument or the exposition of his theme. In the class-room he presented the substance of his lecture in a few dictated paragraphs and devoted the rest of the time to elaboration of them. This left room for digressions, but paragraphs and elaboration

alike bore evidence of having been carefully prepared with special attention to lucidity and sequence. " To clarify the issues " was with him a
favourite expression, and to do that was one of his main aims as a teacher.

Erect in figure and alert in movement, he was not a professor after
the common conception. He did not live in the Ante-Nicene period:
he was never seen in Don Street or the Chanonry lost in a brown study:
he was not guilty of absentmindedness. Nevertheless he was a scholar
among scholars. A new book was a joy to him; and frequently, when he
lighted on one that particularly arrested him, he brought it to his classroom
with many of its pages still uncut that he might share with his students
the treasures he had already found in it. How widely read he was and
how well abreast of modern thought, became known to a much larger
circle through his contributions (many of them reviews) to the *Expository
Times*, his articles in Hastings' *Encyclopaedia of Religion and Ethics*, his work
as an assistant editor of the *Expositor's Year Book* and his Robertson
Lectures, published in 1927 under the title *Nature and God*.

Professor Fulton had the humility which accompanies sound scholarship. His sense of the majesty of truth imparted a quiet sanctity to all
his speaking and writing about the things that matter supremely. Knowing the many-sidedness of truth, he refrained from final statements; and
believing that new light would yet dawn upon the inquiring spirit, he
continued to be a seeker. He counselled his students when they became
preachers of the Gospel to adhere to the principle of accommodation and
not disquiet good Christians of long standing with the deliverances of
recent criticism. He also counselled them not to provide their people
with solutions of all their problems, but to encourage them to do some
thinking on their own. " Make a point ", he said, " of sending them away
with a nut to crack."

In Professor Fulton's time the Theology Manse, a beautiful and happy
home, nestled among trees to the north of the Chapel. He loved it
dearly, as did also his gracious lady and their children. But Glasgow was
his alma mater; and when she called him to her service, he responded
dutifully, for *quid est pietas nisi voluntas grata in parentes*?

GEORGE OGG

GEORGE THOMAS THOMSON

Professor of Systematic Theology, 1928-1936

*Professor Thomson came from Edinburgh and Oxford, having graduated with
special distinction in Philosophy and History. He took his Divinity course at
Edinburgh and pursued special studies in Berlin. In 1915 he went to France with
the Royal Scots and then served in the Intelligence Corps. Between the war and his
appointment to Aberdeen he held various charges. He translated Barth's Dogmatik,
and in 1936 left Aberdeen to take up the Chair of Christian Dogmatics in Edinburgh.*

The present holder of the Chair is JOHN M. GRAHAM (*1937*)

HEBREW AND ORIENTAL LANGUAGES

This Chair might be held by a layman, and the first holder, from 1860 to 1870, was a layman of picaresque habit and " haughty Courage ".

ANDREW SCOTT

Professor of Oriental Languages, 1860(47)-1870

Andrew Scott was a stalwart Borderer, " with the echoes of Chevy Chase and the exploits of ' Kinmont Willie ' sounding in his ears, and with the blue Cheviots separating him from the ' Englishers ', whom Andrew rather despised as a ' glaikit kind o' fowk', across the hills that bounded his horizon ". A strain of nomad-adventure ran through his early life. As a naval instructor he saw service on ships that carried him from Spithead to Barbary and Constantinople, he taught in Dollar and then in Canada, where his former fellow-student, the Rev. P. Colin Campbell, had already gone, and from which both returned, determined, says Sir William Geddes, " to get back to the old Scotch frying-pan out of the American and Canadian furnace ". Both were soon established at Aberdeen, Scott to teach Hebrew, Campbell Greek until he became Principal. In 1860, the Professor of Hebrew at King's became the Professor of Oriental Languages in the reconstituted University.

" In the oldest of our calendars he was careful to insert so as to justify his position as professor of *Oriental* languages and not of Hebrew alone, a paragraph to this effect: ' Should *three* or more students come forward, instruction will be given in the Arabic, Persian, Hindustani or Sanscrit languages *two* days weekly at such hours as may be found convenient.' Then followed a billet of books to be used, a very reasonable *quantum*, and this flag was always kept flying, though it is very doubtful whether the requisite *three* ever turned up."

This doughty champion of the East had gathered on his travels many yarns, which he told with gusto at his friends' tables and (continues Sir William Geddes) in places " less appropriate—from the Professor's desk, and the hour which might, could, would, or should have been devoted to the mysteries of Hithpael and the Hebrew verb, passed gaily away with Oriental stories of Algiers and the East, greatly to the delectation of not over studious divinity students." . . . " And yet when Andrew did set to work he did so with considerable ' go ', and he could teach with spirit and even vehemence for a time, making good scholars in this field."

WILLIAM D. GEDDES: *A.B.A.*

JOHN FORBES

Professor of Hebrew, 1870-1887

Andrew Scott's successor did not profess any language beyond Hebrew, which he taught admirably from the purely linguistic point of view, though he gave no attention to the critical questions arising from Hebrew Literature. Sixty-eight years of age when he came to the Chair, he retained a physical vitality and a mental elasticity that enabled him to enter on his work with vigour and enthusiasm, to continue at it for seventeen years, and then to retire with his love for study unabated, as is witnessed by the production of a new publication issued in the ninety-sixth year of his age. Though he dealt only with the outlines of a wide subject, his expositions were at once instructive and stimulating.

ARCHIBALD R. S. KENNEDY

Professor of Hebrew and Oriental Languages, 1887-1894

Professor Kennedy was an Aberdeen graduate in Arts who attended the Divinity Hall in Glasgow. In addition to the Oriental Languages which he professed, he was a fine scholar in modern European languages and made translations from the German, which were highly praised by those competent to judge, of Hebrew, Syriac and Assyrian Grammars. Although his official subject took him far into the past, his eyes were on the future and he strove to give the future ministers with whom he worked a living interest in the thought of their own time. " I advocate," he said, " the recognition by the Church of a progressive but reverent criticism." He started among the young divines a French and German Club where Established and Free Church students met in amity, and gave private classes in Syriac and Arabic which were attended by students from both Divinity Halls.

He left us for Edinburgh and attained his jubilee as a Professor.

JAMES GILROY

Professor of Hebrew, 1895-1932

Were I asked to name one outstanding characteristic of the Reverend Professor of Hebrew, after having met him once I should say, geniality; and having met him a second time, optimism; but upon still further acquaintance I should say, a high ideal of man's duty and a healthy outlook on life—" a radiating focus of goodwill ". The Professor in his class sparkles with ready wit. There are few who have come and gone on the benches of the Hebrew class-room but have experienced the needle-like refinement of his sarcasm, and have laughed to feel the sting. Large-hearted, broad-minded, lending a sympathetic hearing to every man's opinions and never obtruding his own, Dr. Gilroy has quietly devoted himself to the interests of young men and has won from them that confidence accorded to the man pursuing unswervingly a high purpose inspired by a living faith.

Alma Mater

Of oriental impassiveness, better known as " The Simple Sheva ". . . .
Jimmy was renowned for the dinner parties which he and Mrs. Gilroy threw
annually for his students, complete with cigars, wine and bridge. Very
popular functions they were.

T. B. S. THOMSON

Hebrew may have been the language of the Garden of Eden, but it did
not appeal to us young sinners before the First World War; we ought to
have been driven out of the Garden before the Kaiser tried it! But
indifferent Hebrew scholars though we were, many of my class-fellows
proved first-class soldiers, and some—alas, they were the cream—laid
down their lives in defence of the Garden. And " Jimmy ", our dear old
Professor, knew it and was proud. With what patience and what quiet
trust he drew out and stabilised any virtue that was in us.

His lectures on O.T. criticism were surely masterpieces of their kind.
No unnecessary verbiage, but clear, brief and to the point, and delivered
in such a way that we could take full notes. Why, the greatest blunderer
in the Hebrew exercises could now score full marks.

How gently but effectively he could deal with flowery language and
youthful effervescence! In an essay I had submitted on evil and its
effects occurred this outburst, " Ah, this infernal, unfathomable working,
this hyperborean darkness, this boiling up from the nether-chaotic deep ".
" Very impressive ", said Jimmy, with a twinkle in his eye, " but ",
mouthing it with much solemnity, " what or where is the nether-chaotic
deep? " The class guffawed and I have been more careful with my
purple patches ever since.

Of a shy and reticent manner, he could sometimes drop a quiet word
that you could hear long after it was spoken: as a young man, he started as
assistant in Beauly, and returned there to spend a summer holiday when
I, as it happened, was acting as student missionary; and desirous of
making a good impression before my " Prof ", I was in full blast. Afterwards I remarked, " Many changes since you were here—a pipe organ
now ". " Yes," he said with his quiet smile, " more wind now." I kept
a calm sough next Sunday!

We played golf there also. He usually beat me, but oh dear! when
he lost a ball he would search for it with the same dogged persistency as for
some hidden root in an old Semitic manuscript, till Mrs. Gilroy would
come to our rescue. " Oh, come away, James, it will be dark before we
get home." Eheu fugaces! Almost fifty of the fleeting years have slipped
by since then, but his memory is still fresh and fragrant. Often in the
silences we remember his wise words and gentle manners. " Remember,"
he would say, " your people will judge you more by what you are than
by what you know."

G. A. JOHNSTON

The present holder of the Chair is ARCHIBALD C. KENNEDY (*1932*) *son of
Professor A. R. S. Kennedy. Father and son therefore occupied the same Chair.*

Five times between 1860 and 1960 a father and a son have held Chairs in our University, although the Kennedys are the only two who have held the same Chair. The others are Principal Pirie (Chair of Church History) and his son (Mathematics); Professor Trail (Systematic Theology) and his son (Botany); Professor Ogston (Medical Jurisprudence) and his son (Surgery); Professor Cairns (Christian Dogmatics) and his son who, though only a lecturer in the University, holds a Chair in Christ's College.

BIBLICAL CRITICISM

WILLIAM MILLIGAN

Professor of Biblical Criticism, 1860-1893

" You are from Scotland? Did you know Dr. Milligan? His books on the Resurrection and the Ascension are textbooks for all our students of divinity."

Examining Chaplain from South Africa

Firm in the maintenance of his own principles, bold even to daring in their application, he has so borne himself as to forfeit neither the respect nor the good will of those who most differed from him.

W. ROBERTSON NICOLL

I began my Arts course in the autumn of 1863, and I made his acquaintance at once; for, to my great benefit, I joined a Greek Testament class which he then taught every Sunday morning throughout the winter session. I do not remember that I was ever absent: I enjoyed that class so much. I think he shone in it fully as much as he did as a teacher of divinity students. Young as we were, he made us feel at once that we were fellow-students, searching with him, though of course under his guidance, into the inmost meaning of the Holy Scriptures. Freedom, moreover, and reverence went hand in hand with him.

Very soon we and the whole Church were to learn, and increasingly to know, alike the strength and keenness of the intellect and the purity, warmth, and depth of the convictions which were hidden under that modest diffidence of tone and genial gentleness of manner. Years of diligent study were fast making him a master of his subject; and when in 1870 he joined the company who were engaged in the revision of the English New Testament his scholarship was recognized, and he took his place as the foremost of the distinguished band with whom he was associated. If the work of the Revision Committee entailed much labour, he found it stimulus as well; and the last fifteen years of his life (1878-93) were his years of fruitfulness. The harvest of those years was rich and valuable. It included his brilliant article on The Epistle to the Ephesians in the *Encyclopaedia Britannica,* and the two works by which he is most widely known, *The Resurrection of our Lord,* and *The Ascension and Heavenly Priesthood of our Lord.* These books became popular at once.

His time of literary productiveness and of literary grace was his time also of public activity as an educationalist and as a citizen, and, in the Church of Scotland, as at once a courageous champion of the Faith and an ardent advocate of a practical and spiritual reformation.

JAMES COOPER: *A.B.A.*

After the outstanding tenure of Professor Milligan, the Chair fell for a few years into the hands of an Orcadian, DAVID JOHNSTON, *1893-99, " the most interesting ecclesiastical phenomenon in Orkney ", whose ministrations were so little appreciated by the students that they submitted a petition to the Divinity Faculty, asking its members if they could induce their colleague to " behave reasonably ". He refused to preach in Chapel because there was an organ there (an objective for which Professor Christie had worked wholeheartedly), and his conduct of classes was such that " embryonic divinities engaged in theological discussion by hurling at each others' heads, not isolated texts, but whole volumes of Scripture ". He was followed by a man deeply admired and appreciated.*

THOMAS NICOL

Professor of Biblical Criticism, 1899-1916

> Professor Nicol became Moderator of the General Assembly during my Divinity years, and I still can remember our chairing him shoulder high from the Quad to his Manse.
>
> T. B. S. THOMSON

Professor Nicol was pre-eminently a scholar of the very best type of the Classical Scholars of Aberdeen. His culture covered a large field of literature. It was marked by great accuracy and acumen. He knew all that was best in his own subject and all that was cognate and complemental to it. His sympathies were widely balanced between the past and the present. He was alive to the importance of the critical movement, appreciated its processes, and reverently received all its proved results, while rejecting all unverified theories. As a man, he was the most delightful *socius*, a bright talker, overflowing with vivacity and quick at repartee.

W. S. BRUCE: *A.U.R.* 1916

ANDREW CUMMING BAIRD

Professor of Biblical Criticism, 1919-1938

Professor Baird, a graduate of Glasgow in Arts, Science and Divinity, and a specialist student in Berlin of Assyriology and Oriental Languages, was compelled by ill-health to resign from his Chair at a comparatively early age, and died two years later.

As minister of Anderston Parish, Professor Baird was in charge of one of the poorest districts of Glasgow, and this led him to take an interest in social questions which he never lost; it was indeed a marked feature of his character throughout his whole life.   But his preoccupation with his ministerial duties was never allowed to supplant his scholarly tastes. While in Glasgow he delivered a course of lectures on " The Civilization of Ancient Assyria and Babylonia " which attracted much attention, and at one time or another during this period he temporarily occupied every one of the Divinity Chairs in the University.   Indeed, so wide was his scholarship that it was said of him when he came to Aberdeen that there was not one of the Divinity Chairs which he was not qualified to fill.

In Aberdeen Professor Baird at once took a distinctive place not merely in the University but in the general community outside.   He became an elder in the Parish of Old Machar and took a living interest in the affairs of the Cathedral and its people.   Soon also he was appointed one of the governing body of the Aberdeen Endowments Trust and a Governor of Robert Gordon's Colleges, and in many other ways he took a leading part in the affairs of the city.   In his public work he was always distinguished by marked independence of thought, and he never hesitated on occasion to speak his mind freely, while his unfailing sense of humour prevented any differences of opinion from degenerating into anything approaching ill-feeling.   He had, on the contrary, a genius for friendship which sweetened the life of all with whom he came into contact.

But it was in the University that Professor Baird's influence was most felt, not merely in his own Faculty, of which he was Dean, but among the students generally.   He took a special interest in the foreign students who came to the University in considerable numbers during his period of office.   For them, as indeed for all the many strangers who came to preach in the University Chapel during his long Convenership of the Chapel Committee, he always kept an open house.

GEORGE DUNCAN: *A.U.R.* 1940

JAMES A. ROBERTSON

Professor of Biblical Criticism, 1938-1945

> " We don't want Robertson of Ballater: he has far too acute a mind for a professor."
>> Conversation overheard in a railway carriage between two country ministers while the U.F. Chair was vacant.

Small of stature and of a gentle and unassertive manner, Professor Robertson had nevertheless a mind of penetrating freshness and acumen.   He was a graduate of Aberdeen but studied Divinity in Glasgow and Germany and held several charges before becoming, in 1920, Professor of New Testament Language and Literature in the United Free Church College in Aberdeen.   In 1938 he passed to the University as Professor of Biblical Criticism.

In 1945 the present holder, ARCHIBALD M. HUNTER, *came to the Chair.*

Of the Staff of the former U. F. Church College who passed into the service of the University in 1935 none is worthier of note than the Very Rev. D. S. Cairns, its Principal.

CHRISTIAN DOGMATICS

DAVID S. CAIRNS

Professor of Christian Dogmatics, 1935-1937

> Stone perhaps, rather than canvas, might be chosen to represent David Cairns. No medium less massive could so well convey his nobility, his profundity, his calm.
>
> J. A. ROBERTSON

> A great shaggy man, with a brooding powerful face.
>
> LYN IRVINE

David Cairns was a country boy, brought up in the Borders. In his early years he passed through two profound religious crises in succession, both of them closely connected with his intellectual development. The first was concerned with the stern Calvinism of his background and inheritance, and his reaction against it.

Then in his third year at the University he was visited by that desolating experience of complete and comprehensive doubt about the whole truth of religion which was so common among devout intellectuals of the most Christian tradition in the nineteenth century. . . . " I entered here a long dark tunnel of my life from which I only gradually emerged. I remember how cold the starlight seemed on those winter nights."

In 1895 he was elected minister of the United Presbyterian Church at Ayton in Berwickshire, where his shepherd grandfather had at one time had his home; and there he remained for twelve years, in spite of repeated invitations to leave that rural parish for important city churches as well as for theological chairs in America and the Dominions.

During his years at Ayton he was thinking out his faith. And at the same time he was inevitably developing into a Christian apologist. The task of apologetics is one which has to be performed afresh in each successive age, and everything in Cairns' mental constitution and experience had been preparing him for the vocation of commending Christianity to those who should be troubled with doubts and difficulties in the earlier decades of the twentieth century. All his life long he was deeply interested in the problem of the relation between Christian beliefs and the claims and conclusions of modern science, and particularly in the question how room can be found for the conception of divine purpose and activity in the scientific picture of the universe.

When he left Ayton for Aberdeen, he had already come into contact with the Student Christian Movement which was to mean so much both to him and to whole generations of students. He lectured to undergraduates at Cambridge and troops during the 1914-18 war—*The Reasonableness of the Christian Faith*—and, in 1919, he drew up the Report of the Committee " to consider and interpret what was being revealed under war conditions as to the religious life of the nation, and to bring the result before the Churches ". *The Army and Religion* has been called " a classic of its kind, as a document of religious history ".

It was in 1928 that Cairns published the volume which contains by far his most distinctive contribution to theology and which did most to spread his fame, under the title *The Faith That Rebels*. In Cairns' conception the campaign of the Kingdom of God was a campaign against all the enemies of God and man, not only against moral and spiritual but also against physical evils, not only against sin but against disease and pain and death, and with a victory lying not only beyond history in another world but also within history and in this world. Thus he became more and more convinced that true faith, such as our Lord was always looking for and commending when he found it, was not mere resignation and acceptance, but " the faith that rebels " against all evils and uses God's power to drive them out of human life.

His last book arose out of the Baird Lectures, which he delivered in 1932, though it was 1937 until *The Riddle of the World* appeared. In the same year he gave up his Chair and the Principalship of Christ's College.

Based on the Introduction to his *Autobiography*

The other new professorship of 1935 was that of Christian Ethics and Practical Theology, the holder of which, ADAM FYFE FINDLAY, *became in 1937, when the Very Rev. Dr. Cairns resigned, Master of Christ's College. He retired from both posts in 1947. In the Chair of Christian Ethics and Practical Theology he had had almost a pioneer task, and its success was due to his fine grasp of the wide range of his subject.*

The present holder of the Chair of Christian Dogmatics is JOHN MACLEOD. *The Chair of Christian Ethics and Practical Theology reverted on the retirement of Professor Fyfe Findlay (still happily with us) to the care of Christ's College, and is there filled by* DAVID CAIRNS *the Younger, who also lectures in the University on Systematic Theology.*

16*

LAW

GEORGE GRUB

Professor of Law, 1881(43)-1891

> The Faculty of Law is Dr. Grub, one single individual, without him it is nothing.
>
> He is one of those perfectly balanced minds that never suggest a favourite nor suspect the opposite. From the moment of his entering the class-room, and placing his " tile " on the chair specially appropriated to its use, when he unearths from some vasty deep in the back premises of his sombre surtout a huge bundle of quarto sheets carefully folded and tied with the professional red-tape, to the time when his class leaves him behind fondly readjusting the forementioned " bit paperies and tape ", the lecture proceeds with a judicial calmness and deliberation that would grace the woolsack.
>
> *Alma Mater*

On the fusion of the Colleges in 1860, Mr. Patrick Davidson, who held the time-honoured post of Civilist in University and King's College, received the appointment of Professor of Law in the United University. He, however, never took up the work of the chair but appointed Mr. Grub as his substitute, and from the first the substitute entered on the work with zeal and practically performed all the duties. On Mr. Davidson's death in 1881 Mr. Grub was appointed to the Chair and continued to exercise the professorship until 1891.

Mr. Grub thus occupied the almost unique position of having been practically the sole teacher of law in the city of Aberdeen for a period of not less than forty-eight years, and at the time of his retirement there were only twelve members of the Society of Advocates who had not received their training at his hands.

In 1864 he received the degree of Doctor of Laws and, when he retired, the Society of Advocates presented him with his portrait painted by Sir George Reid. In the artist Dr. Grub found a congenial literary spirit, and it is recorded of him that after one of his sittings he remarked: " Sir George knows Scott as well as I do, and that is saying a good deal." When making the presentation, Mr. Davidson said, " He was eminently an historical lawyer. He knew from whence the stones that went to build up our great edifice of law were to be quarried, and he knew the men, the times and the circumstances by which these were all built together into the edifice in which they now lived. He recorded for them the various stages of the development of our legal system and expounded and elucidated for them the principles of our law."

Outside his strictly professional work he will be remembered chiefly as the author of his *Ecclesiastical History of Scotland*, which remains to this day the standard authority on the subject. Written from the standpoint of a member of the Scottish Episcopal Church, that work has been ever considered as an almost unique example of fair and impartial consideration of the course of Church affairs in Scotland. Indeed Dr. Grub used to say that his view of the duty of a historian was to depict events as they happened and to leave others to draw the conclusions which seemed to them most fair.   But he could express his own views clearly enough; and while he never pretended to admire Presbyterianism, he frankly admitted the wrongs of the later Covenanters.   " I cannot," he would say, " understand the man, who, knowing the facts, justifies the proceedings of the Covenanters under Charles I, or the conduct of the Government of Scotland towards the Covenanters under Charles II."

JAS. DUGUID: *A.B.A.*

JOHN DOVE WILSON

Professor of Law, 1891-1901

When Professor Dove Wilson retired in 1901, it was forty years since he had come to Aberdeen as Sheriff, and his Sheriff Court Practice was recognized as a Classic.   During his tenure of the Chair the B.L. degree was instituted (1894).

He was in the lecture room an artist in the perfect sense.   Methodical, clear, ample, fluent, courteous towards the students, with a courtesy that was but the expression of the man's high earnestness, noble simplicity and unaffected kindliness, the Professor of Scots Law ruled in his classroom by the divine right of fitness.   In the letter intimating his resignation, he mentioned three things that when he entered upon office he had wished to see accomplished—the granting of a degree in Law, the teaching of Roman Law and the making of Scots Law thoroughly practical.   We think all three have been attained.

Alma Mater, 1901

NEIL KENNEDY

Professor of Law, 1901-1907

As Dean of the Faculty of Law he set himself to approximate Elphinstone's ideal of making Aberdeen a fully equipped School of Law, not merely a training-place for local practitioners.   All the time he held office in Aberdeen he kept this end clearly in view, working steadily for it; but it was not till after he had demitted his Chair that he had the satisfaction of seeing his ideal attained and the degree of LL.B. established.   Everyone wanted to attend a function if Professor Kennedy were to speak, for he had the gift of infusing interest and humour into such tasks as eulogizing honorary graduands.   This was most conspicuously shown at the time of the Quatercentenary, when it fell to him to introduce the long procession of Doctors of Laws.

A.U.R. 1918

In 1907 he became a Judge of the High Court in Edinburgh as Lord Kennedy.

JAMES MERCER IRVINE

Professor of Law 1907-1919

Professor Irvine did obeisance to each of the Scottish Universities in turn, having graduated in Arts at St. Andrews, in Science and Law at Edinburgh, and lectured for thirteen years in Glasgow before coming to fill the Law Chair at Aberdeen. He was a highly distinguished scholar, but " a hard-headed practical man as well, alert, enterprising and having the redeeming quality of common-sense ". He wrote extensively, was editor of the Scottish Law Reporter *and on the staff of the Official Series of Law Reports. He was also joint author of* Rights in Security.

During Professor Irvine's tenure of the Chair, new lectureships were instituted: International Law—GEORGE DUNCAN (*1908-1936*): *Constitutional Law and History*—R. M. WILLIAMSON (*1908-1933*). *Dr. George Duncan was a citizen whose influence spread widely through the city's life. He was a member of the Town Council and for a number of years Chairman of Aberdeen Education Authority; a member of the University Court and an Honorary Sheriff Substitute of Aberdeenshire.*

ALEXANDER MACKENZIE STUART

Professor of Law, 1919-1935

He was the man needed by our Faculty of Law for its leading position. The fifth in a remarkable sequence of men of scholarly attainment, he could, by mental endowment and training, expound with authority the philosophic basis of our law. He knew profoundly our common law sources. He had made the principles and precedents of our Scottish system a part of his intellectual self; and he added a power—almost as rare as these gifts—of crisp and concise and clear presentment united to an intense distaste for irrelevance either in himself or in others—sometimes, if the truth must be told, slightly trying to the others. Some, indeed, considered him too apt to measure a man's capacity by the acuteness of his sense of relevancy, a little forgetful, perhaps, of imagination and vision for which there is much room even in the humblest of legal practices. Whether that is true or not, it is difficult to exaggerate the value of his exact scholarship and high standards, first to sixteen successive Scots Law classes, and then, as a corollary, to the prestige of the Faculty, still young in comparison with other Schools of Law.

A. C. MORRISON

In 1927 A. C. MORRISON *was appointed to the new Chair of Conveyancing, which he held until 1940. He was a member of the University Court, Clerk of the Peace for the County of Aberdeen and Honorary Sheriff Substitute of Aberdeenshire.*

After the war the Chair was held for a year by WILLIAM ELDER LEVIE *(1945-1946), and in 1946* FARQUHAR MACRITCHIE *held and still holds it.*

The Law Chair was held from 1935 to 1948 by THOMAS MURRAY TAYLOR, *who relinquished it to become our Principal.   Thereafter the Professorship was of Scots Law, held by* T. B. SMITH *(1949-58) and since 1958 by* RONALD D. IRELAND; *while in 1951 a new Chair, of Roman Law and Jurisprudence, was held by* DAVID DAUBE *until 1956 and thereafter by* PETER GONVILLE STEIN.

THE MEDICAL SCHOOL

The development of medical studies, from their scattered condition of 1860 to the Medical School of today with its Hospitals, Clinics and Research Units, is beyond the scope of this study. We can only indicate something of the quality of the men who have made it what it is now.

ANATOMY

Aberdeen's first great teacher of Anatomy was DR. ANDREW MOIR, *who " carried anatomy to a perfection hitherto unattained in the north of Scotland " but " had nothing during his lifetime to look to but being hated as a resurrectionist " (Aberdeen Doctors). He taught in an anatomical theatre in St. Andrew Street, which had been built by some gentlemen who formed themselves into a company and took shares in it; but popular antipathy led a mob to attack the " burking-house ", destroy the surgical instruments and furnishings and set the place on fire. Dr. Moir " jumped out of a shop-window into the back of the town's churchyard, where he lay concealed among the tombs ".*

The Anatomy Chair was held by A. JARDINE LIZARS *from 1860(41) to 1863.*

JOHN STRUTHERS
Professor of Anatomy, 1863-1889

Here is a name to be cherished in the annals of the Anatomy Department. While it is the purpose of this sketch to reveal the character of the man, it is a good thing first of all to appreciate his background and the intensity of his activities on behalf of the University in general and the Medical Faculty in particular. He arrived in 1863, three years after the union, to find accommodation for Anatomy " depressing to contemplate ", indeed, " hopeless ", but his transformations left it " unequalled by any in the United Kingdom ", and in large measure as it is today, still one of the finest. Before the union, King's College had one medical Professor for " Medicine and Chemistry ", and Marischal had five for Chemistry, Anatomy, Surgery, Practice of Medicine, " Medical Jurisprudence and Medical Logic ", lecturers in each college being in charge of other branches. In 1863 medical students numbered 185 but 450 when Professor Struthers retired in 1889, a figure for a five year curriculum exceeding that for the present six year curriculum. Thirty-six students began medicine in his first year and 109 in his last year. He took care that the Chair of Pathology, the second established in the country and for several years the only one, should be full-time and his last act in the Senatus was the introduction of the Science degree.

He was a born teacher and a born fighter. Some legendary incidents may paint him as an autocrat and stern disciplinarian. A constant companion was his little black book with comments upon his students, and he would consult this in his dissecting room interviews. The writer recalls a luncheon party when Professor William Bulloch at the London Hospital recounted with Professor Low an illustrative episode. Sir John, black book in hand, approaches a student. " You, sir, what is your name? " " Smith, sir ". " J. A. Smith? " " Yes, sir ". " J. A., I presume, stands for jackass? " " No, sir, John Alistair ". " None of your impertinence. I find you grossly inattentive in my class and you are not to be permitted to pass the Professional examination." However, he had the interest of every student at heart—witness his own words: " As among the youths of the outside world, and there in greater proportion, a certain number of students in all the faculties are inclined to what is called pleasure rather than to work, and here comes in a difference between one medical school and another, and between one Professor and another. ' Let us deliver our teaching to them, and if they don't work, reject them at the examination; we are Professors not schoolmasters,' is a doctrine I have heard; a cruel one, to me a repulsive one. The seeing to it that this kind of youth shall work may sometimes be irksome but it is our duty, even were it on no higher ground than the good name of the school. I think it may safely be said that such care, exerted over a series of years, has contributed to give the medical school of Aberdeen, apart from what else may be said of it, a well deserved name as a working school; a name, however, that will not long survive unless such care is continued. . . . But the great body of medical students require no compulsion." He was against written examinations. The student is " to get his knowledge at first hand from nature, in the laboratory, not to trust to the word-knowledge obtained from lectures or books ". Written examinations were the vogue before his arrival, even oral examinations were conducted without specimens and there were no clinical examinations even in Medicine and Surgery. He states " far too much importance is still attached to the written part of the examination. Written examinations began in this country within my recollection. They are not a test of real knowledge, and tend to promote cramming."

The valuable array of comparative osteology, the mounted specimens of hippopotamus, rhinoceros, camel, giraffe, tapir, several whales and the finest elephant skeleton he had seen anywhere, are all obvious testimony that he worked hard himself and expected his staff to do likewise during many years, including evenings and vacations. It is related that at length one of his assistants approached Sir John with the suggestion that it might help him in his future general practice to do some more human anatomy instead of articulating the skeletons of whales. " Ah, well," came the immediate reply, " if you have no love for the great cetacean creature, that is your misfortune ". This collection has been repeatedly found of great value. Anyone who has taken the trouble to prepare and mount such specimens finds it most delightful to note the tribute paid by Sir John Struthers " to my faithful attendant, Mr.

Robert Gibb, who took intelligent interest in the work and never grudged sitting with me at extra hours ". (Graduates who remember the Anatomy attendant, James Moir, will be interested to learn that he was a nephew of Robert Gibb.)

The famous case of Professor Struthers and the crocodile involved Mr. Scott Riddell, President of the Aberdeen Medico-Chirurgical Society, in the longest crocodile hunt in history (for 33 years!) The skeleton of the " croc " was presented to the Society in 1822. In 1866 Professor Struthers suggested that the skeleton, then in a most unsatisfactory condition, should be cleaned and remounted and be of some use for his class, but still remain the property of the Society. The wish was granted but four years later Dr. Jamieson, Medical Superintendent of the Asylum, requested the return of the skeleton; a deputation visited Marischal College and reported the skeleton in excellent condition, but produced a long letter from Professor Struthers describing what he had done, that the bones were now beautifully white but that he still required time to prepare the hands and feet properly. After the lapse of another four years, with Doctor Jamieson's anxiety mounting, a resolution that the " croc " be returned immediately was passed unanimously. After the further lapse of another two years Dr. Jamieson had the same motion again passed unanimously. Professor Struthers then offered to pay ten guineas to the Widows' Fund of the Society for the " croc ", but members said it was worth £50. A petition to Sheriff Brown ordered Dr. Struthers to show reason why the prayer for the return of the crocodile should not be granted. The Professor did not appear in Court. The crocodile returned to its home. Dr. Struthers resigned from the Society. But his tenacity had not one whit abated. Six years later in 1882 he rejoined, became President, and at an extraordinary meeting of the Society a motion to present the skeleton to the Anatomical Museum was carried by seven votes to six, four declining including Dr. Struthers, but Dr. Jamieson threatened to resign, two members protested in support and Dr. Struthers was induced to withdraw his application. In 1922 Scott Riddell recommended that the skeleton should be presented to the Anatomy department. In 1939 the skeleton, hitherto tethered to the roof of the Library annexe, was removed to the attic of the Society's rooms. In May 1956 the crocodile, without tears or protest from any member of the Society, was presented to the department, where it stretches its length upon the wall, a tribute to the persistence of Sir John in the acquisition of material for his collection.

Probably at this day, upon occasion, Professors miscall each other—usually under the breath—but in Struthers' day the giants were not averse to the spoken word. Sir Alexander Greig Anderson likes to tell the story: Professor Struthers, crossing the quadrangle, passed some students communicating with companions at a window in the Surgery Department regarding the oral examination one group was about to receive and the others had just had; he sent a message to Sir Alexander

Ogston who requested his attendant, Mr. Booth (known to many generations of graduates), " Mr. Booth, go down to Sir John Struthers and
present my compliments and tell him to go to Hell, at your leisure,
Booth, at your leisure ".

It is a tribute to the character of Sir John Struthers that his personality
persists through the arches of the years, that so much tangible evidence
of his work remains in the Department he created.

R. D. LOCKHART

ROBERT W. REID

Professor of Anatomy, 1889-1925

Cited by Sir Arthur Keith as a typical example of the Short Stone Cist
people, who lived in the North East up to 4,000 years ago, Robert Reid,
popularly known to generations of students as " Bobby ", was slight in
stature, fresh complexioned with a thin grey moustache and endowed
with tenacity of purpose in all his undertakings.

The last of the founder members of the Anatomical Society of Great
Britain and Ireland, and the first of the anatomists in the London schools
to devote his whole time to the subject, his name is perpetuated in Reid's
Base Line concerned with his early, and indeed, pioneer work in relating
the cerebral convolutions to the surface of the head.

Certain of his gestures were characteristic. At the end of some
deliberation he would end the conversation with " Ah well, Mr. So-and-
So ", then, rubbing the back of his stiffened forefinger across his nose
(a movement students delighted to imitate) both hands would grip the
lapels of his coat as he tilted his head back saying " Ah yes "; often as a
variant he would remove his pince-nez attached by a thin black cord
around his neck and cast them down to swing from side to side. One
morning, however, he forgot the cord but not the habit and broke two
pairs of glasses.

He rejoiced in some quaint expressions: " That man, so-and-so ", in
reference to one of his Senatorial colleagues, " the sound of his voice is the
breath of his nostrils ", an opinion which has certainly been entertained by
many in Senates before and since his day, if rarely expressed with such
vital brevity and relish.

A kindly examiner, he kept a watchful eye upon his students as well as
upon his staff; for many years, each Christmas season he would invite
relays of Colonial students to dinner and dance in his home at 37 Albyn
Place where he was so ably assisted by his tall commanding sister, Miss
Reid, very much " a lady of the old school ".

Very proud of his family, he had an active interest in the Tower
of London's presentation of the experiments conducted by his grand-
uncle, the Rev. Dr. Alexander J. Forsyth, in the production of the per-
cussion lock which could have been sold at once to Napoleon for much

more than was eventually received, after long delay, from our own government. There is a commemorative plaque on the walls of King's College just behind the Chapel.

Two of the Professor's brothers were also graduates of Aberdeen University, Major-General Sir John Forsyth Reid, K.C.B., LL.D., and William Reid, M.D., a former superintendent of Aberdeen Royal Mental Hospital.

His public lectures upon Anatomy resulted in the foundation of the Farquhar Thomson lectures upon the form and function of the human body, and the first lectureships in Embryology and also in Anatomy were made during his Professorship. He instituted the anthropometric record of all medical students, a unique series of measurements now conducted over sixty-four years.

Appropriately, his bust presides in the Anthropological Museum, his inception and elaboration of which was a remarkable undertaking. This remains a valuable heritage, always increasing in extent and possessing many rare and valuable specimens. Even to have wiled the classical vase collection to the Museum out of King's College when he did was testimony to his characteristic persistence and tenacity. The setting forth of the Museum catalogue, with its wealth of detail in measurement and description, and the endless reference that must have been made to authorities in the British and other Museums, is witness to the meticulous care with which he weighed and reweighed and rewrote, and this even applied to an every day letter.

A bachelor, he was associated in his museum work with his colleague, the Rev. Professor Gilroy, Keeper of the Coins, whose wife, a well-loved personality in our University's life, is one of Old Aberdeen's oldest residents. The professors would tease each other about the relative merits of the married and bachelor estates, and the compulsory contribution of the bachelor professors to the Scottish Universities Widows' and Orphans' Fund was a frequent subject of discussion, always terminated by Reid remarking, again rubbing his nose with his stiff forefinger and gripping his lapels, " Ah well, Gilroy, maybe it's worth it! "—this presumably from his own point of view.

He died in 1939, aged eighty-eight years.

R. D. LOCKHART

ALEXANDER LOW

Professor of Anatomy, 1925-1938

Serious grey eyes with a pleasant twinkle, set in handsome and distinguished features; an earnest purpose; a gentle unassuming personality; a word that could be depended upon to stand the test of time; courtesy to all people and a kindness to his pupils in sickness or difficulty that invariably took practical form with visits to hospital and gifts of fruit and sweets left unobtrusively at his departure; these qualities endeared him to generations of students. No wonder he was so affectionately known as " Daddy Low ". No wonder that these students presented him upon his retirement with his portrait etching by Malcolm Osborne and a cheque for some £500 which the professor left for the benefit of medical students.

Although usually reserved and reticent he has been known to indulge in delightful description of the fairy spectacle of the almond blossom billowing upon the banks of the Swan river in Western Australia, write with fascination upon the tragedy of the Hapsburgs and the charm of Vienna some sixty years ago, and describe a quaintly pretty interlude in his vacation work at Freiburg. " It was the custom for colleagues to make a trip into the Black Forest at the week-end. One Saturday two of us climbed the Feldberg for a view of the Alps. We found the hotel near the top full up—food, but no accommodation—and had to make the best of it in a barn nearby, one side packed with newly mown hay, the other occupied by two friendly old horses. We lay just beyond reach of their noses and I had almost dozed off when suddenly in the quiet gloom, broken by the munching of the horses, a soft light swung to and fro as an old peasant entered with his hurricane lamp, set it upon the floor, saw that his horses were comfortable, knelt and told his Rosary, then patting his beasts a final goodnight, left with his lamp a-swinging shadows, while the horses munched beside us in the darkness."

The farm of his birth and boyhood on the banks of the river Don lies within sight of the farms where Sir David Ferrier, a pioneer in cerebral localisation, and Sir Arthur Keith, the anthropologist, were born.

As might be expected from his upbringing he had a great love for the land. His small garden contained a little of everything, and that little was excellent. His lettuces attained the size of cabbages, and his parsley plants almost rivalled kale. Even in the winter months there was always an old-fashioned posy of flowers in his home. He had a boyish delight in excelling his brother, a farmer, with early potatoes, although he would confide to his friends that he did not inform his brother about the precautions he took to protect his plants with sacking against a late frost.

He would talk of his boyhood days on the farm, his friendship with a poacher and the poacher's dog. " When the three of us met the policeman on the road even the dog used to slink past with its ears down, and what a hypocrite I felt because I was good friends with the policeman too."

His research upon the development of the lower jaw is classical— witness the comment of a subsequent investigator: " the work of Low has so thoroughly covered every phase of this problem that I am at a loss to find any further point upon which debate or discussion can profitably be made "; or, again, the remark of the late Ariens Kappers of the Central Institute for Brain Research in Amsterdam—" Your Professor Low, ah yes, of course, I know the name, that is why it is called the Low-er jaw."

For many long years he made careful measurements of children, 450 male and 450 females measured at birth; sixty-six male and sixty female children measured annually from birth to five years of age. These measurements were unique in that they referred to the individual child followed for five years, six periods of measurements. This persistent painstaking work was of great interest to the parents though often the grandmothers would say, " Ah weel, I dinna ken what things are comin' tae; nane o' mine ever needed this ".

His histological technique was exquisite.

The careful precision exercised in his investigations upon the burials of the Short Stone Cist or Beaker People was admirable and, thanks to his enthusiasm in this field, Aberdeen University possesses the finest collection of the skeletal remains. He insisted that one must get to the site of such a discovery immediately, otherwise some teeth were sure to disappear as souvenirs although these would sometimes turn up after his tactful remark that such possessions were sometimes unlucky. On one occasion he arrived to find that the beaker itself, with geranium complete, was already installed in the cottage window.

A connoisseur in the appreciation of a skull, he would show anthropologists one recovered from the North Sea in a trawl net, typical of the Bronze Age, in every respect, and then would point to the disarming evidence of a dental filling.

At an Oslo meeting he was being teased by cultural anthropologists that he could come to no definite decision of the racial origin of the young woman conducting their 'bus tour. " Well," said Professor Low, " one of her parents might be Norse and the other an Aberdonian." There was no answer to the derision evoked but to question the girl herself, who answered, " My father was Norse and my great-grandmother came from Aberdeenshire ".

His reply to an examinee seriously in error was characteristic— " Well, maybe, perhaps, but usually one finds. . . . "

Surely few scientists more worthily fulfilled Wordsworth's demand of the true savant, that he be also a poet in soul and a religionist in heart.

Certainly the students at one of the Final Year Medical Dinners summed his character excellently in the phrase " He will give the devil his due ".

R. D. LOCKHART

Professor Low died in 1950 at the age of eighty-three. The writer of these appreciations, R. D. LOCKHART, *has since 1938 carried on the duties of the Chair of Anatomy in his own inimitable way.*

MEDICINE

JOHN MACROBIN

Professor of Medicine, 1860 (1839)-1875

> The habit of regarding the welfare of the Medical School as the chief business of his life.

As a lecturer Professor Macrobin was not brilliant. His teaching was sound, on the old lines. He took no active part in clinical teaching, nor did he hold public appointments. To what, then, are we to attribute the great influence he wielded for many years, first in Marischal College, and afterwards in the University? It was largely owing to his kindly disposition and goodness of heart, combined with what we can only describe as a passionate devotion to the interests of the medical school. He acted as Dean for many years, and in the exercise of his duties was allowed an amount of discretion inadmissible in these days when the universities are bound hand and foot by ordinances, and when a Dean has ever before his eyes the University Court, or that still more awful tribunal, the General Medical Council. In the good old days when Macrobin reigned he had enormous power. . . . It is no exaggeration to say that all through a student's career a word from the Dean was paramount, and that he exercised this autocratic power with wisdom and discretion. He took especial care of aspirants to a medical degree who had a struggle to meet the necessary expenses. Many a poor youth owed much, not only to the kindly advice, but to the substantial help of Macrobin.

JOHN GRAY MCKENDRICK: *A.B.A.*

JAMES W. F. SMITH-SHAND

Professor of Medicine, 1875-1891

> A placid reflective man, carrying a whole world in his head and not finding it too heavy.

As a teacher, Smith-Shand belonged to the days of minute clinical observation—a faculty apt to lapse in these days of improving objective methods. Experimental medicine was a thing of secondary interest to him. His lectures were the carefully-sifted notions of the great physicians; selected by the action of prolonged experience; cleared of dross by reflection; illuminated by cases from daily practice.

In his classroom, from three to four of the afternoon, a voice was heard reading placidly, without halt or haste, without feeling; pens were scratching in many pitches of sound. Now and again a foot would scrape on the floor—the phrase was repeated. Then the current ran on again. Once more a foot scraped, sometimes many feet—the phrase was repeated, and once more it was pens and a voice. That was Smith-Shand lecturing—the only university medical lecture that was truly a " lecture "—a reading without " demonstrations ". The hour struck; the voice was just ceasing; the professor folded his papers, bowed slightly, and passed back to his room. We, on our part, shut our notebooks, pocketed our inks, undid our pens, and rose to go. And a last classroom point: our class had a foible of singing the Old Hundredth every day just before lecture. Sometimes the professor entered in the middle of the penultimate line. But the music went on; the professor smiled; the ultimate line ended, and work instantly began. I have known professors *look* angry in a similar case; Smith-Shand's smile was alone worth the fee.

In his professional examinations, he was exacting, but sensible. What impresses me now is the amount of detail we acquired unconsciously, and what a worthless thing the peddling little bits of examinations were. As a test of knowledge, they were laughably worthless. As a stimulus to read and re-read and inwardly digest, they were excellent.

Of his place in the school one thing was true; he carried the traditions of the older, exact, clinical medicine well into the scientific era. He was a bridge from old to new. He told us once that he was the first to introduce the clinical thermometer into medical practice in Aberdeen. That was precisely the kind of revolution to expect from the man; a simple, fruitful, far-reaching move—a thing done without advertisement.

W. LESLIE MACKENZIE: A.B.A.

DAVID WHITE FINLAY

Professor of Medicine, 1891-1912

> Serious but pawky, and with a very kind heart.
>
> " Gin ye unnerstan' Typhoid fever, ye unnerstan' the half o' maidsin."
>
> " Ye can sputt in the quadrangle, an' ye can sputt whaur ye like, but ye'll no sputt here."
>
> A keen yachtsman: " If ye see a man wi' pneumonia that's been a soaker, ye may say tae yersel, that man's got his blue Peter up. He'll no stop long here."

Professor Finlay was not only an admirable physician but as Dean of Medicine he showed a power of tactful dealing, acute discrimination and absolute fairness.

Those who have met him in his dealings with the hospital patients well know his warmheartedness towards them, a kindness which, though unostentatious, often takes a very practical form. His interests in the poor extend beyond the hospital walls, for his zeal and ability have led to the founding of at least one notable public institution. At the clinic, too, his lectures—like his class lectures—are characterized by lucidity, a fondness for emphasizing " points " of importance, and a love of the exact peculiarly his own.

He takes a deep interest in social reform, and his tenets on questions anent this need no detailing here.

Alma Mater

ASHLEY MACKINTOSH

Professor of Medicine, 1912-1928

> I really do not think it possible ever to estimate the amount of good Ashley Mackintosh has done to the University.
>
> T. WARDROP GRIFFITH

This brilliant brain had much humour in it and a happy outlook on the world. . . . Two or three years ago he asked me to be the senior " older " man at a dinner to his " old residents " placed in or near London. It was an evening to remember. There were some twenty-eight of them, and I had the privilege of hearing the winged words of these forward-straining young experts and of seeing by their endless shades and delicacies of deference, how they showed their admiration and affection for their happy, boyish, witty, chaffing old Chief and friend. I have known many professors, and I have seen them evoke the generosities of spirit that only youth can show; but I never saw anything like this.

> W. LESLIE MACKENZIE

Ashley Mackintosh was a great humanitarian, a great physician and teacher of medicine, and above all a great friend.

He was proud of the fact that he was born and brought up in a country manse. His father, James Mackintosh, the Parish Minister at Deskford, had graduated M.A. at King's College in 1831, and in view of Ashley's subsequent career it is interesting to note that he also was something of a mathematician. One of Ashley's most treasured possessions was the prize volumes in Mathematics and Natural Philosophy which his father had received as a student.

His education began at the early age of four when he was sent to the local Dame's School and from there to the Parish School, where at the tender age of nine he was awarded a special prize for " General Excellence and Special Proficiency in Mathematics ". It would almost seem that mathematics was in his blood. No wonder that in later years he used to say that study was easy for him and that he always enjoyed examinations.

He entered the University as a 1st Bursar where he had a career of exceptional brilliance in Arts and Medicine, a career which few can have equalled, gaining 1st Class Honours in Classics and Mathematics in Arts and later 1st Class Honours in both his M.B. and M.D. degrees. He was, however, no mere bookworm, taking an active interest in all student activities and a great interest in their welfare. He was an active supporter of the proposed Students' Union and he acted also as President of the Students' Representative Council. This early interest in student welfare he maintained until the end of his life, an interest which was warmly appreciated by the students.

In 1880 he went to King's College, Cambridge, to continue his mathematical studies there and it looked at that time as if he were destined for a brilliant academic career. After a short spell, however, he decided that a don's life was not for him, even if, as he himself said, " I could attain to it ". He had decided to study medicine and in this he was undoubtedly influenced by his elder brother who was eight years his senior and who had graduated in Arts in 1880 and Medicine in 1884. The brothers were devotedly attached to each other and Ashley always looked on his elder brother as " my example and mentor ".

He returned to the University here and completed his medical course in 1893. He then went abroad to study at the clinics and laboratories in Leipzig and Vienna. After his Wanderjahre he came back to London and continued his neurological studies in Queen's Square Hospital and King's College, London. This was the third King's College at which he had studied. There he was attached to David Ferrier (later Sir David) who was the leading neuro-physiologist in this country. Ferrier was a very distinguished Arts graduate of Aberdeen but his medical course had been taken in Edinburgh. This association developed into a warm friendship which was lifelong and of him Ashley said, " He remained my dearest medical friend and master ". Then after some two years, despite the pleading of Ferrier and other friends he decided to return to Aberdeen, which he did in 1896.

There for the first eight years or so he engaged in General Practice, but such were the demands for his special services that he entered consulting practice and rapidly became the Consulting Physician for this part of Scotland. Within six months of his return he was appointed Assistant Physician at the Royal Infirmary and as Assistant and later full Physician he served the hospital for some thirty-three years.

In 1912 he was appointed to the Chair of Medicine and during his period as Professor and largely thanks to his teaching the reputation of the University as a school of clinical medicine was raised to its highest point. No one of his former students can ever forget his clinical ward rounds, the careful history taking, the meticulous physical examination of all the systems of the body, the analysis of the signs present and finally his diagnosis and treatment. Even the dullest student was made to feel that Ashley was not merely demonstrating some case of rare neurological disease but rather that he was dealing with a human being in distress and seeking help.

It was this essentially humanistic outlook which made Ashley the great physician he was. It is of the essence of the humanistic outlook " that the physician must be governed in his actions by a wise regard for the whole welfare of each patient individually ", as was so eloquently stated by F. M. R. Walshe in his Linacre Lecture, and Ashley in his outlook was intensely humanistic. No doubt in these present days we have much more scientific knowledge but we have far less wisdom, much to the detriment of medicine as a whole.

In his early days in practice the laboratory side of medicine had scarcely begun to be developed and throughout his hospital years he was singularly little interested in its findings. Modern medical psychology had not yet been invented and yet he himself was eminently successful in his treatment of the neuroses by the old-fashioned Weir-Mitchell method. Freudian psychology in the beginning was anathema to him and remained so to the end.

In the early 1920's Matthew Hay promulgated the Joint Hospital Scheme. It did not meet with universal approval and even within the University there was considerable opposition, but from its very commencement Ashley was one of its strongest supporters and helpers.

After his retirement from the Chair of Medicine he joined the Board of the Royal Infirmary where his advice in the design and planning of the new hospital was invaluable. He lived long enough to see the scheme almost complete but he did not live to see the opening of the new Medical School.

The University was not deprived of his services as he was almost immediately appointed to the Court as Assessor to the General Council, a position which he held for some seven years.

In all the many Honours which fell to him I am sure none gave him greater pleasure than the fact, of which he must have been well aware even while he held the Chair, that he was never referred to as the Professor by the students but always as Ashley, it was the same with his friends and colleagues, although with them it was " dear old Ashley ".

In all my long experience at the University I can think of no other Professor who was so universally beloved by the students, who knew him to be their most faithful friend.

In his lifetime he was the soul of generosity and it was said of him at the time of the presentation of his portrait, "no one in need, mentally, spiritually or financially was turned away empty-handed by Sir Ashley ". When he was presented with his portrait a fund of £1,000 was raised and this he handed back to the University to help any student in any Faculty who was in difficulty through illness.

His whole life was spent in his work and he had relatively few amusements or hobbies. He did, however, enjoy a round of golf at which he played a very good game. He was a formidable opponent, for his golf like his work was characterized by a deadly accuracy. He was not a hard hitter, his ball did not go far, but it was never off the fairway, never in a bunker, never in the rough. Each deadly accurate shot fell right. A young doctor might think he was an easy mark, but long before the round was finished he discovered his mistake.

17*

Latterly he spent his holidays at his favourite haunts of Edzell and Upper Deeside. There with a few friends as his guests and free from cares and anxieties, he was at his best, overflowing with wit, humour and kindliness. He loved entertaining his friends and was the perfect host; those of us who were so honoured have the happiest memories of these very pleasant occasions.

Aberdeen University has had no more devoted and loyal servant than Ashley Mackintosh and by all who came under his influence he will ever be remembered as The Beloved Physician.

ALEXANDER GREIG ANDERSON

The Chair of Medicine was next filled by LEYBOURNE STANLEY PATRICK DAVIDSON, *Professor of Medicine 1928-38, a brilliant physician who left us all too soon to occupy the parallel Chair in Edinburgh, where he built up a great reputation as an expert on nutrition.*

From 1938 to 1948 the occupant of the Chair was R. S. AITKEN, *who went on to Birmingham University, and the present occupant is* H. W. FULLERTON.

PHYSIOLOGY

GEORGE OGILVIE

Professor of Physiology, 1860-1877

> The students at once made their way to the microscopes, under which were displayed with scrupulous care specimens showing the structure of the lungs, liver, skin or other organs of the body. In those days such specimens were rare and were to be found only in the hands of a few experts, and the ordinary student looked at a section showing Lieberkühn's glands, or at one revealing the sweat ducts of the skin, with feelings deeper than those of mere curiosity.
>
> *A.B.A.*

George Ogilvie came of two good families, the Ogilvies and the Forbeses, and when in 1876 he inherited the estate of Boyndlie, he added Forbes to his name and retired to live the life of a country gentleman. There was a certain nobility about him, a dignity that impressed his students, and that was not unaccompanied by kindliness.

All felt his was a personality that commanded respect; no student ever dared to be forward in his presence; a somewhat cold, almost timid manner effectually prevented anything like undue familiarity.

He never engaged much in original physiological work unless we include in this the cultivation of histology and the use of the microscope. He was an accomplished histologist, as matters stood in his day. . . . The development of research in physiological laboratories, and the practical teaching of students, came after his day. Dr. Ogilvie was much more a naturalist than a physiologist in the modern sense of both words, and, in addition, it was the philosophic aspect of the subject that was always reflected by his thoughts.

Perhaps his most important work, the one with which his name will be associated, is *The Master-Builder's Plan, or the Principles of Organic Architecture as indicated in the Typical Forms of Animals*, which was published in 1858. About this time the doctrine of special types, first enunciated by the mystic Oken, was in favour with biologists, mainly owing to the splendid researches and brilliant powers of generalization of Richard Owen. Ogilvie was greatly attracted to it as affording an explanation of the variety of animal forms and yet the relationship that each form had to a great type. . . . In the concluding chapter he showed the relation of the theory to Natural Theology. . . . All this was written before the appearance of Darwin's *Origin of Species*, but although the point of view has changed, much of Dr. Ogilvie's reasoning appears to me to be sound.

He was not a specialist in the modern sense: he was greater, inasmuch as with clear and calm outlook he faced many of the great problems that perplex the minds of men, and more especially, perhaps, the minds of those who devote their lives to the sciences that deal with life and living things.

JOHN GRAY MCKENDRICK: *A.B.A.*

From 1877 to 1886 the Chair was held by WILLIAM STIRLING.

J. A. MACWILLIAM

Professor of Physiology, 1886-1927

Professor MacWilliam was typical of his Highland ancestry; none who knew him could fail to recognize this fact. His whole bearing, calm, courteous and unassuming, revealed the subtle blend of the scholar and the scientist. Deeply meditative, holding opinion strongly, he possessed the faculty of brevity and clarity of expression. Upon him professional eminence rested lightly; one sensed distinction; but the great attraction lay in those qualities of heart and mind which made him ever the perfect Highland gentleman. To know him in the laboratory was to be impressed by the shrewd observation and critical judgment of the skilled investigator; to visit him in his home at " Inverdee ", Cults, was to discover, in an almost Highland setting, the natural philosopher and to learn with a strange surety that scientific knowledge is a part of our culture.

The Professor was born in Kiltarlity, Inverness-shire and died in Edinburgh in 1937 at the age of eighty. Coming to the University of Aberdeen about the age of eighteen, he swept everything before him, and, as the most distinguished student of his year, graduated M.B., C.M., with 1st Class Honours in 1880. Following upon this brilliant beginning he elected to go to Leipzig to study under Ludwig and then to Berne to work with Krönecker.   While abroad he had been caught up in the new interest which had been awakened concerning the peculiar properties of cardiac muscle, upon which the rhythmic beat of the heart depends.   At this time a prolonged controversy had been raging over such questions as: the origin of the heart beat, was it myogenic or neurogenic?; the influence of ions; the nature of the conducting system and the interpretation of the electrical changes within the beating heart.   Drawn into this field of research and heated discussion were such pioneers as, Bowditch, Krönecker, Gaskell and Marey, and later, Keith and Waller. Into the midst of this galaxy of controversialists the brilliant young graduate from Aberdeen was ushered, destined to make substantial contributions to physiological knowledge.

As a result of his research work in Germany, MacWilliam was awarded the M.D. degree with honours (1882), for a thesis entitled, " The structure of cardiac and diaphragmatic fibres of various animals ". In the same year he was appointed a lecturer in physiology under Sharpey-Schafer at University College, London.   Under the dynamic influence of Sharpey-Schafer (later Sir Edward), MacWilliam, his line of research clearly defined by his recent studies, now entered upon a period of great fruitfulness.   Possessing a strongly comparative outlook upon biological problems, he decided to investigate certain physiological characteristics of the frog's heart—rhythmicity, refractoriness and conductivity—in order to determine whether these factors, which apparently determined the action of the cold-blooded heart, could be regarded as generally applicable to the warm-blooded heart, and, ultimately, to the heart of man.   He selected two types of animal, the fish and the mammal, far enough removed the one from the other, to allow the assumption that, if similar properties were to be found in such widely divergent types, such properties might also prove to be of functional significance in man.   This was the problem in which MacWilliam was engaged when, in 1886, he was appointed Regius Professor of Physiology in the University of Aberdeen.   Research on the heart of the eel having been completed he now continued with his plans for work on the mammalian heart.   Within a few years his most outstanding contribution to physiological knowledge had appeared in several scientific journals. Remembering that these were not the days of the cathode-ray oscillograph, high speed cinematography or even of the electrocardiograph, we are made aware of the many technical problems with which physiologists were then faced.   It was in 1887 that MacWilliam published the original statement concerning the peculiar condition known as fibrillar contraction of the heart, when he wrote: " the muscle fibres instead of contracting and relaxing all at the same time, do so independently of one another, so that the beat comes to be replaced by a delirious unharmonious activity whereby the heart ceases to act as pump and the circulation fails." When by further research he showed that ventricular fibrillation could be produced by faradic stimulation of the heart and also by the inhalation of chloroform, clinicians were aroused to the implications of these findings. That chloroform, if not given with extreme care, could cause fatal stoppage of the heart was contrary to the findings of the Hyderabad Commission, which regarded death under chloroform to be due to a failure in respiration.   Having regard to these early discoveries one can readily imagine with what eager interest MacWilliam would have viewed the recording of electrical potentials within the cardiac cell by means of the almost invisible electrodes of today.   Space does not permit reference to the valuable, if less intriguing, research on cardiac inhibition and the factors which control blood pressure. A comprehensive account of these investigations, of interest both to clinicians and physiologists, appeared in *Physiological Reviews* in 1925.

It may surprise some to know that despite all the work on the heart that was going forward in the Department of Physiology, no personal reference was made to it by the Professor in his lectures.   Only those, and they were few, who glanced occasionally at the Journal of Physiology had the slightest inkling of the extent to which their Professor was involved in building up present-day knowledge.   It is also of interest to learn that the Professor was no believer in taking copious notes.   He left us in no doubt as to the value of listening to the argument, for and against, a point of controversy; and he was most skilled in setting forth the facts as he deemed them important.   He had the gift of a most retentive memory and it is not too much to say that upon the exercise of this gift depended much of his success as a lecturer.   By voice, word and gesture, not to forget the flash of some appropriate reminiscence, he held the attention of his students.   Every lecture was a finished product, clearly related to what had gone before and to what was to follow.   Few who attended his lectures at the somnolent hour of 2 o'clock, could ever forget the slim figure, the rather pale bearded face, the soft, well modulated Highland voice, the slow walk from one end to the other of the long lecture bench and the gentle swing of the arm which led to the final summing up, " and gentlemen, the balance of experimental evidence is . . . "; and the argument was closed succinctly but never dogmatically.

In 1927, after forty-one years of service to his Alma Mater, Professor MacWilliam retired.   His many activities within and without the University were recognized by the award of the LL.D. degree, the highest distinction which the Senatus Academicus can confer upon those whom it seeks to honour. He thus passed quietly from active service, remembered, respected and beloved by all who had the privilege of knowing him.

E. W. H. CRUICKSHANK

J. J. R. MACLEOD

Professor of Physiology, 1928-1935

Professor John James Rickard Macleod was a son of the manse, his father being at one time minister of John Knox United Free Church, Aberdeen. Born at Cluny, near Dunkeld, he received his early education at the Grammar School, Aberdeen, thence he proceeded to the University of Aberdeen, where in 1898 he graduated M.B., CH.B. with honours at the age of twenty-two. Having been awarded the Anderson Travelling Scholarship he spent the first years of his scientific career in Leipzig, returning to London in 1900 on being appointed assistant in physiology at the London Hospital Medical School. Although he obtained the D.P.H. of Cambridge in 1902, his interests were clearly centred upon the investigations into carbohydrate metabolism initiated by v Mering and Minkowski, who had, in 1889, discovered the relation of the pancreas to diabetes mellitus. In 1903 Macleod accepted an invitation to the Chair of Physiology in the Western Reserve University, Cleveland, U.S.A. Here, despite the many unrelated activities into which the First World War drew him, he continued active in the field of research which held his attention. In 1918 he published his text book on *Physiology and Biochemistry in Modern Medicine*, which passed through many editions and is still widely read. It was in 1918 that Macleod went to Toronto as professor of physiology and here entered upon the most fruitful and enlivening pathway of his scientific life. The key to the solution of the problem of the cure of diabetes was still to be found; it was found with dramatic suddenness when, in 1922, Banting and Best, working in Macleod's laboratory in Toronto, extracted from the mammalian pancreas and isolated the anti-diabetic hormone—insulin. Macleod's contribution to this discovery was recognized, in 1923, by his election to the Fellowship of the Royal Society and the joint award, with Banting, of the Nobel Prize in Physiology and Medicine.

It is not unusual in the field of scientific discovery that early, but none the less significant investigations, which presage events, are forgotten in the acclaim given to epoch-making discovery. The work of Dr. Tom Fraser, physician, and of Dr. John Rennie, zoologist, both of Aberdeen University, has fallen into this category; they had discovered, about 1905, that the all-important Islets of Langerhans, which presumably contained the anti-diabetic hormone, were structurally separated from the main body of the pancreas in Teleostean fish, *Lophius piscatorius*. Acting on this they fed raw Islet tissue to, and injected saline extracts into, severely diabetic patients with marked amelioration of the signs and symptoms of the disease. Lack of an adequate supply of material precluded any prolonged investigation, but their results were highly significant; they had shown that the hormone, then unnamed, was to be found in the Islet tissue of the pancreas (*Biochemical Journal*, 1906-7, Vol. 2, p. 7). Some fifteen years later Banting and Best clearly demonstrated how insulin could be obtained from the mammalian pancreas where the intimate structural relation of the Islets to the rest of the gland had been the barrier to its successful extraction.

From Toronto Macleod came to the Regius Chair of Physiology in Aberdeen in 1928; he was fifty-two years of age. His later years in Canada had seen the insidious onset of arthritis which led increasingly to a curtailment of research activity. It did little to hinder a lively interest in and service to the University, the Rowett Research Institute and the General Medical Council. To his great distinction in the world of science were added personal qualities which endeared him to his friends. None can ever forget his charm of manner, his modest bearing and unfailing interest in music and literature. His home was a revelation; pictures there were, large and small, many of them the work of the gracious lady who was his wife; under the eye of such a talented artist "J. J. R." could hardly fail to be knowledgeable in "water and oil". A most striking likeness of Professor Macleod, in black and white, is to be seen in King's College. In this etching one can almost see "those clear blue eyes which conveyed not only a certain boyish innocence, but an integrity which shamed any pretentiousness, evasion or vulgarity".

E. W. H. CRUICKSHANK

The Chair was next filled by the writer of the above appreciations, ERNEST W. H. CRUICKSHANK, *1936-1958, whose interests lay in the scientific side of medicine, and who held Chairs in Peking, Patna and Halifax before returning to Aberdeen. He has also travelled extensively for the World Health Organisation, and as an adviser on Medical Education in Burma, Ceylon, Indonesia and Egypt.*

The present holder of the Chair is JOHN L. MALCOLM.

SURGERY

WILLIAM PIRRIE

Professor of Surgery, 1860(39)-1882

A teacher of the true stamp was William Pirrie, a teacher who loved his work, who looked forward to his lecture hour as the happiest of the twenty-four, and who, when he became acquainted with any new fact, thought first of all " how best he could put it before the students."

The dignity of " Barron ", to which Pirrie's pupils elevated him, is unique. The name was bestowed not as a nickname, but as a complimentary and fitting title. An unusual dignity in Britain, it served to prevent confusion with all others. Who gave him the name or when exactly it was bestowed, is lost in the dim past of the " forties ". The spelling with a double " r " no doubt arose from the fact that his own name was spelt with two " r's ", and it served to increase still further the distinction which his admirers wished to bestow upon him.

As a teacher the one great characteristic he possessed was enthusiasm. It was an infective, bursting enthusiasm, which was wholly irrepressible; it was not his brilliancy as a surgeon, but his zeal as a teacher that held the student spell-bound. The intense desire to " put things nicely ", and, " to have his ideas all arrang't ", was at once his forte and his foible. In supreme attempts at clearness, he not unfrequently misplaced words, and at times became truly aphasic towards the climax, putting " the cart before the horse ", and thereby producing a word-dilemma of which he was wholly unconscious. What if " pus corpuscles " would come as " cus porcuscles "? Pirrie was unconscious of the slip and his audience was all the happier.

One morning Pirrie was lecturing on " cleft palate ", and he had in his hand a dissection of the parts in which he took great pride. Not content with showing the specimen from the lecture table, he walked up through his class, crossing desks and forms, saying, " Do you see, for instance, that now? Isn't it so nice to see the delicate parts themselves before you? It's just knowledge appealing to the eye. See'til the little musclie how nicely it works round the bone." Such an exhibition of enthusiasm in teaching is a thing of the past; it was buried with Pirrie.

Withal he had a peculiar self-consciousness, it can scarcely be styled vanity, but to an onlooker it seemed as though his every act was studied. His very walk betrayed his feelings; but Pirrie never walked—he waacked—a totally different procedure to any one who knew Pirrie; it was a studied, slow, unbending, colossal gait, which after a time became second nature to him. It was as much part of his character and enthusiasm, as the gratified pleasure with which he performed a rapid amputation or wound up a bout of teaching.

As a hospital surgeon he attained great eminence both as an operator and as a consultant. . . . Pirrie's contributions to surgery may be summed up in the one word—acupressure. In pre-Listerian days, there is no doubt that the use of the " pin and wire ", as a means of arresting haemorrhage had a distinct claim to serious consideration. Clean, neat, and in the hands of Pirrie and his colleagues, effective, acupressure stood a fair chance of becoming widely adopted by Aberdeen graduates; but Listerism removed the basis of the useful conception, and the practice of acupressure has become a matter of history.

JAMES CANTLIE: *A.B.A.*

ALEXANDER OGSTON

Professor of Surgery, 1882-1909

> Every single student was impressed by the greatness of his personality and
> his efficiency in his work.   Apart from his handsome appearance he had a
> dignity and created the suggestion of a reserve power which were altogether
> out of the common.
>
> WM. BULLOCH

> Ogston's admissions " are sometimes declared to be the only thing worth
> seeing or hearing at the Hospital.   How his patients like him, to be sure!
> . . . Some people seem to think that patients are simply useful to be treated
> for the surgery of the case, just as a piano is made to be played for the sake
> of the music.   But not so Ogston.   His motto might be: The surgeon is
> made for the patient, not the patient for the surgeon."
>
> *Alma Mater*

In the long history of the University there have been many graduates who
have achieved greatness, and the name of Sir Alexander Ogston, Professor
of Surgery, must be awarded a high place in that list. He was an
Aberdonian born and bred, his father being Professor of Medical Jurisprudence at Marischal College.   Educated at the Grammar School and
the " Gym," he was a member
of the last Bajan class to go to
Marischal College in 1859.   He
continued his studies after the
union of the two colleges in 1860,
and graduated in Medicine with
highest honours in 1865, proceeding to take the M.D. degree a year
later also with highest honours.
During his student days he had
the good fortune to study abroad
at Vienna, Prague, and Berlin.
The names of his teachers ring like
trumpets through the hall of medical fame, Virchow, Von Graefe,
Langenbeck and Hebra.

After graduation he proceeded
to general practice, and held minor
appointments at the Aberdeen Royal Infirmary.   In 1870 he was appointed junior surgeon, and in 1874 full surgeon.   He was one of the earliest
converts to the technique of Lister, stating that he was convinced of the
value of Lister's work after one round of his wards in Glasgow Royal
Infirmary.   He had great difficulty in convincing the staff of the Aberdeen
Royal Infirmary of its importance, and met with indifference if not
actual hostility.   Then, as now, the question of finance arose and the
Infirmary Board were with difficulty persuaded to meet even his moderate
demands for new equipment.   He had the force of character to ensure

that he got his way, and his results were his justification. His enquiring mind led him to try to find the cause of suppuration, which was the curse of the wards at that time. After careful experimental work with what would now be thought very primitive methods, in 1880 he gave to the world his theory that inflammation, suppuration, and abscess formation were due to Micrococci. He found there were two varieties of cocci, the streptococcus, which had already been described by Bilroth, and the staphylococcus, the latter of which keeps his name for ever in medical history, Staphylococcus Aureus Ogstonii. The name was suggested by Professor Geddes (Greek). He delivered a paper on his results to the Aberdeen Branch of the British Medical Association, and it was received with incredulity and ridicule. He went to see Lister, who was interested and appeared satisfied, but Watson Cheyne, Lister's assistant, was very sceptical. Somewhat discouraged he took his work over to Germany and lectured upon it to the Congress of German surgeons in Berlin. They were very enthusiastic and his work was accepted in Germany as valid and proved. Its reception in Britain, however, was a cold one: the editor of the *British Medical Journal* asked scoffingly " Can any good thing come out of Aberdeen ? " The *Journal* refused to publish some of his later papers on this subject following the first report he had sent in. But these rebuffs did not deter him, as, in his own words: "The men who mattered knew!" It is interesting to note that for some years after, all the organisms causing disease were identified by Germans and no British name was associated with a germ until Bruce discovered Bacillus Melitensis.

Ogston was appointed Professor of Surgery at Aberdeen in 1882, and for the next twenty-seven years he was an inspiration to his students and his fame became world-wide. In 1892 he was appointed Surgeon in Ordinary to the Queen in Scotland. As a surgeon he was deft and thorough, and gifted with great powers of observation, combined with a sympathetic consideration of his patients, thus gaining their implicit trust. He must be almost the father of orthopaedic surgery, as his operation for Genu Valgum was the standard one until McEwen of Glasgow improved on it.

He was a man who shunned publicity, but his work in military surgery and its application in the field brought him into the public eye. He served in the Egyptian war of 1884, the South African war, 1899-1900, and the Great War 1914-18. What he saw in the first campaign made him a severe critic of the existing military medical organizations, and he expressed himself very forcibly on the inefficiency of the R.A.M.C. in the South African war. Although he met with strong opposition from the seniors in the Medical Service many of his reforms were gradually adopted. In the Great War, 1914-18, in spite of his being over seventy years of age he saw active service in Serbia and in Italy.

Sir Alexander was a very handsome man, tall and well built, frock-coated, his topper worn at an angle, in later years called the " Beattie tilt ". Such a strong personality as he had led to the formation of strong friendships, and strong antipathies, and many are the stories of academic clashes. Like many surgeons he had a mild good-natured contempt for the art of medicine, well illustrated by the following incident. During a ward round his attention was drawn to one lad who was due for operation but who had " some kind of a rash ". Sir Alexander remarked, " Chicken pox, Russell ". He was about to pass on when Russell asked, " What shall I give him, sir ? ". Ogston quietly said, " Give him a stick of barley sugar".

Another anecdote was told by the late Professor Wardrop Griffith who was one of his dressers, and who Ogston thought should have specialized in surgery. After Griffith had for some years been a consulting physician in Leeds he turned up in the theatre when Ogston was operating. He asked Griffith what he was doing. Griffith replied, " I am practising as a physician ". Sadly Ogston said, " Oh, Griffith, what CAN you do with medicine? " Ogston was not a man who wasted words, and on one occasion he replied to a long letter by sending a post-card on which was written " NO " signed A. O. He was very sparing with his testimonials, and gave them only to students who he thought deserved them. One newly graduated doctor who insisted on a testimonial although he had not been one of the Professor's dressers, received the following: " Mr. James Smith, who has recently acquired the degrees of M.B., C.M., has never distinguished himself in any way so far as I know. A. O., Professor of Surgery."

Professor Ogston was a truly great man, honoured and respected, regarded by his students as one of their greatest teachers. They remembered him as " Sandy " Ogston, and it is only such leaders as he who gain affectionate cognomens. He was a man who did his own thinking.

JAMES F. FRASER

JOHN MARNOCH

Professor of Surgery, 1909-1932

Amongst the great names in surgery in the North East in the early part of this century was that of Sir John Marnoch, who succeeded to the Chair of Surgery on the retiral of Sir Alexander Ogston in 1909, and remained as Head of the Department until ill-health enforced his own resignation in 1932.

The son of James Marnoch of Aberdeen, he was educated at the Grammar School, Old Aberdeen, proceeding to the University where he graduated M.A. in 1888, and M.B., C.M. with highest honours three years later at the age of twenty-four. The medical course was much shorter in those days.

As was usual then, Dr Marnoch started in general practice with a part-time attachment to the University as Assistant to the Professor of Physiology. In 1893 he was appointed Assistant Surgeon to the Aberdeen Royal Infirmary while still remaining in general practice until 1900, when he became full surgeon to the Infirmary at the age of thirty-three.

Experience in general practice provided a sound basis for a more specialized surgical career. His election to the Chair nine years later was the natural sequence. He was already publishing the results of his work in what was then a new field, the treatment of gastric ulcer. He was amongst the first to operate freely in the peritoneal cavity under the new technique of aseptic approach.

He was particularly skilled in appendicectomy and it is reported that he could complete the removal of the appendix within six and a half minutes from his first incision to his final stitch. His skill and experience in this respect were put to good use when Prince Albert (later King George VI) was put ashore at Aberdeen in 1914 with appendicitis and operated upon by Professor Marnoch at the Northern Nursing Home.

During the 1914-18 war he gave his services in the R.A.M.C. and was surgeon to the military hospitals in the area.

Professor Marnoch took a special pleasure in teaching the large number of students who returned to the University after the First World War. Besides set clinics and dresserships, he personally took the class of Operative Surgery, which was at the early hour of 8 a.m. One morning both Sir John and his class were unable to enter the Department as the door on the quadrangle was locked. Presently Booth the attendant was seen to walk in a leisurely manner towards the waiting crowd at the door. " You're late today, Booth ", said Sir John. " Aye, Marnoch ", retorted Boothie, " But I've stoppit rinnin doon the Gallowgate noo! "

In sheer surgical technique and deftness of fingers Sir John Marnoch had few rivals. His operating theatre was a model of orderly routine carried out in an atmosphere of ecclesiastic calm.

He knew his limitations and with some wisdom bowed to the inevitable when further operation was impossible in the face of established malignancy.

Honours came in due course. The c.v.o. in 1915, the k.c.v.o. in 1928, and the ll.d. in 1933.

In his leisure moments he loved the relaxation of the musical quartet of which he was the cello, and of the quiet of the river Spey at Garmouth, casting a fly for finnock or sea trout.

Partial loss of power of hand and foot was a great trial to him and he did not long survive the curtailment of his powers. He was survived for some years by Lady Marnoch who regularly attended the Marnoch Lectures established in his memory. All the medical students of the 1914-30 era remember his tall figure and his quiet smile with real affection.

ALEXANDER LYALL

After Sir John Marnoch, the Chair was held by one of our brilliant birds of passage, J. R. LEARMONTH *(Professor of Surgery, 1932-39), who came to us from Minnesota with a high reputation in neural surgery, and left us for the Edinburgh Chair and further honours, including a knighthood, in 1939. Since then the present holder,* W. C. WILSON, *has been in possession.*

MIDWIFERY

ROBERT DYCE

Professor of Midwifery, 1860-1869

Dr. Dyce was a tall, spare, erect and handsome man, with well-cut features, and a remarkably pleasant and winning manner. A perfect gentleman, he would have scorned to do a mean action, and he was consequently thoroughly trusted by his professional brethren. As a teacher, he was a great favourite with his students; he at once gained their esteem.

It was, perhaps, when he met a student at a case, that his best points and at the same time his little peculiarities of temper were best shown, especially if a student had sent for him needlessly in the middle of the night. He would at once answer the call, but if he found on his arrival that the student had mistaken a simple case for a serious one, his somewhat hasty temper would burst out, and the unfortunate pupil would be soundly abused for his stupidity. This, however, was soon over, the student would be made to do himself all that was required, and after the patient was left, and as teacher and taught walked together through the deserted streets, the Professor would inculcate the lessons to be learned from the case, and when they parted with a hearty shake of the hand, and probably a jocular remark on the night's experiences, the pupil would feel that he had got beyond the somewhat stately manner of the Professor, and found behind the warm-hearted kindness of the man.

ANGUS FRASER: *A.B.A.*

From 1869 to 1875 the Chair was held by ANDREW INGLIS.

WILLIAM STEPHENSON

Professor of Midwifery, 1875-1912

> The star joker of the University.
>
> Of fine presence, kindly face, with dark brown hair, he looks pre-eminently a lady's doctor.
>
> Dr. Stephenson has done a good deal of original work and he does not hesitate, in defence of his own views, to differ from, or even to stand out alone against, some of the biggest authorities on his subject. . . . A feature of the lectures is the stories. They are mainly instances of that pawky humour which is so characteristic of Scotland, and told as they are in such inimitable style, seldom fail to bring down the house.
>
> *Alma Mater*

In 1875 William Stephenson was appointed by the Crown to the Chair of Midwifery at the University of Aberdeen. This was indeed a fortunate choice, not only for the University but also for the City of Aberdeen, since it provided for the former a first-class obstetrician, teacher and administrator and for the latter a public-spirited citizen who rendered valuable service and made lasting contributions to the well-being of the community of North-East Scotland.

Stephenson, who was of Northumbrian extraction, was born in Edinburgh in 1837 and received his early education in that city. He entered the Medical School of Edinburgh University in 1857 and graduated M.D. in 1861. For the next thirteen years he practised in Edinburgh, acting as physician to the Sick Children's Hospital and to the Public Dispensary. In addition he lectured on diseases of children to the medical students at the Extra-mural Medical School in the city.

William Stephenson was considered one of the best teachers of obstetrics and gynaecology in the country. He did not provide his students with a systematic view of his subject, referring them to the available textbooks for such a presentation. His lectures were essentially practical in nature and although the real value of this practical teaching was not realized by all his students at the time, it was fully appreciated by them later in the course of their professional careers when the notes they had taken in his class were found to be of great value and sound guides in their every-day work. He spoke with a pleasant Scots accent and made apt use of the Doric when the occasion arose, to the great delight of his class. His illustrations were drawn from his own wide clinical experience and important points in his lectures were driven home and stamped indelibly in the memory of his listeners by the recounting of many a well-told tale. Indeed the Professor of Midwifery came to be regarded by many as a second Dean Ramsay. On one occasion it is related that a story told by Stephenson so convulsed both teacher and students that the class had to be dismissed some twenty minutes before the hour! There can be little doubt that his lectures arrested the attention of his hearers by virtue not only of their manner of delivery but also of the interest of their content. This latter point is evidenced by the report that in the course of an hour's lecture on gynaecology the Professor gave a dissertation on the making of gruel, touched on the vexed question of ladies' dress, enlarged on the advantages under certain circumstances of ale on draught to children and wound up his lecture by showing that school teachers by becoming Sunday School teachers thereby pursued their daily calling and were therefore guilty of breaking the Sabbath.

For ten years Stephenson was Dean of the Faculty of Medicine and gave valuable and much appreciated service to the University. This duty he carried out in a pleasant and efficient way and the medical students regarded him as a friend accessible at all times of difficulty and doubt. Indeed his sound advice and kindly good-natured disposition gained him the respect and affection of all with whom he came in contact.

The services rendered by Stephenson were not confined to the University, and the contributions which he made to the enrichment of the lives of his fellow-citizens of Aberdeen must not be forgotten. It is to his initiative and persistence that we owe the origin of the Hospital for Sick Children in Aberdeen. There was no special hospital for the treatment of the ailing child in 1875 when the new Professor of Midwifery arrived in the city. He knew, however, the value of, if not the necessity for, such an institution and in 1876 he issued an appeal for the establishment of a hospital for children. Quickly he rallied the support of a number of citizens in Aberdeen with the result that it was found possible to open a Children's Hospital with fourteen cots, in a house in Castle Terrace in September 1877. For a period of twenty years Stephenson acted as physician to this important institution.

The establishment of the Aberdeen Maternity Hospital also resulted from the promptings and encouragement of Stephenson. In 1872 a small Maternity Hospital had been commenced in connection with the Dispensary but for one reason or another it ceased operation in 1874. Stephenson wrote to the Managers of the Dispensary in 1890 urging them to set up a Maternity Hospital. This they did in 1894 in a house adjoining the Dispensary and placed it under the charge of the Professor of Midwifery. The undertaking prospered and indeed it was so successful that its accommodation soon became inadequate and in 1900 it had to be moved to more commodious premises.

Throughout his long career Stephenson was regarded as one of the foremost obstetricians and gynaecologists in the country by virtue of the high quality of his work and his many valuable contributions to medical literature. Although his professional attainments were appreciated by his colleagues, students and fellow citizens it was his fine personal qualities, his uprightness and unselfishness, his kindliness and friendliness which accounted for the affection and esteem with which he was regarded, both within and without the University.

IAN A. PORTER

ROBERT GORDON McKERRON

Professor of Midwifery, 1912-1936

Robert Gordon McKerron was a son of the manse, his father having been Parish minister of Auchindoir. McKerron was a typical product of the North-East and of the University of Aberdeen. He had in a marked degree the physical toughness and mental alertness of this part of the country.

After graduating in the University in both Arts and Medicine he went to Dingwall as an assistant in general practice, but soon returned to Aberdeen and commenced practice. From the beginning his main interests were in midwifery and the diseases of children.

"Here's a How-dy-do"

He built up a large practice and soon became assistant to Professor Stephenson of the Chair of Midwifery and also physician to the Sick Children's Hospital. In addition to his general practice he had a wide consulting practice and became the authority in the North-East on midwifery and children's diseases. He also was physician to the Maternity Hospital.

He was beloved by his patients and his clinical shrewdness and cheerfulness were a comfort to many. In his work he was conservative and dogmatic and he had to be convinced before he accepted new theories or methods.

In 1912 he was appointed to the Chair of Midwifery and held the post until 1936. He was the last general practitioner to occupy a medical chair in the University. He became one of the notable triumvirate who occupied the Chairs of Surgery, Medicine and Midwifery in the nineteen-tens, twenties and part of the thirties.

He was a great favourite with the students and his instruction was practical and to the point. His lectures were clear and easily followed.

Apart from his teaching, his greatest interest was in the sporting side of university life. He never missed a Rugby football match at King's College and was always a great inspiration to the University team. He knew them all personally and also their strengths and weaknesses. Cricket was an equal interest and I well remember, when the M.C.C. were playing test matches in Australia, his first words on leaving the lecture room were " What's the score? "

He was also a keen golfer and a brilliant if somewhat unorthodox card player and, almost needless to say, he was a staunch Tory.

As long as any of his students are alive he will be remembered with affection. He was a unique figure of a type that is now disappearing with the ironing out of so many characteristics.

He died in March 1937 on a visit to Edinburgh to see the Rugby International.

ROBERT SEMPLE

The present holder of the Chair of Midwifery, Professor DUGALD BAIRD, *1937, is widely known (and has received the honour of knighthood) for his work on pre-natal and sociological influences on child-birth. He is Director of the new Obstetric Medicine Research Unit, one of the most advanced in the country.*

MATERIA MEDICA

ALEXANDER HARVEY

Professor of Materia Medica, 1860-1878

Son of the founder of the Aberdeen Medical Society, Professor Harvey contributed a variety of works to medical literature: *First Lines of Therapeutics, On the Remarkable Effect of Cross-breeding, Man's Place and Bread Unique in Nature, and his Pedigree Human, not Simian, Trees and their Nature, or the Bud and its attributes*—the titles suggest the variety of his interests and the probing curiosity that led him further and further into the mysteries of nature.

As illustrating his thirst for originality we may refer to the eager way with which he used to take up any new remedies, which, in his day—as compared to our own—were very few and far between. During the time he was physician to the Infirmary the bromide of potassium first came into notice, and it is hardly exaggerating to say that, in order to test its virtues, he tried it upon every case which came under his care, a circumstance humorously referred to by Dr. (then Mr.) Philpots in the original song he gave at the medical students' supper in 1867, which ran thus:

> The bromide of potassium, there can't be any doubt,
> Cures ague, typhus, measles, croup, small-pox, rheumatic gout.

He was always anxious for his students personally to experiment upon any new drugs which came under his notice, and the writers of this article both took overdoses of cannabis indica, in order to relate their experiences to him, which resulted in one of them attacking an imaginary tiger seated on the hearth-rug of his sitting-room, an attack which was associated with a general " smash up " of the fender, and the contents of the mantleshelf, with the poker. The other exhibited the peculiarity of his delirium to the public, for on his way up Union Street he sat down on the brass plate of a fashionable millinery establishment, and amused the passers-by with a series of ludicrous antics and yells, which soon collected a crowd, and he would no doubt have been promptly " run in " by a policeman who happened to be near, had it not been that some of his fellow-students, who were passing, explained that what appeared to be at first sight the result of an overdose of " Glenlivet ", was a state brought about by a poisonous dose of " a new drug ". This little incident came vividly before the writer when, years afterwards, he prescribed the drug in physiological doses in a case of hydrophobia, with markedly good effects.

E. P. PHILPOTS and JOHN RUXTON: *A.B.A.*

ALEXANDER DYCE DAVIDSON

Professor of Materia Medica, 1878-1886

> A student: " Dycy's orals were quite friendly and conversational—although I am bound to say that in my case the conversation was somewhat one-sided."

As a University lecturer he was unambitious. He had a due sense of proportion, an important qualification in the professor of a subject which consists largely of judicious skipping.

Dr. Davidson was a man who aged very fast. His earlier career gave brilliant promise. He was a man of keen insight and very acute intellect. He heartily enjoyed an argument, and if you had any weak point in your armour you were pretty sure to have it punctured in any contest of wits with him. Owing, however, to frequent and painful illness he failed to maintain that promise. He suffered severely from gout (" I have it in all my joints except my jaws ", he used to say), and had sometimes on this account to be carried into his classroom on Peter Robb's back. This affected his mental powers so much that he lost to some extent concentration and acuteness. He was, however, a man who possessed the knack of attracting to himself and retaining the friendship of many extra-professional men of ability or even genius in literature, art and science. Robertson Smith, Niven, Philip were among his intimate friends.

Poor " Dycy " had a most tragic and picturesque end, and the mention of his name must, first of all, call up in the minds of his students that wintry afternoon when the news of his death was first spread among us. And that death became him well. Struggling still to lecture while the fatal haemorrhage was pouring into the *pons varolii*, uttering, as his last words just as the black shadow of unconsciousness finally gathered down upon him, the exclamation, " Monday, at four o'clock! " as an indication to the students of his determination to resume punctually at that hour, there we see the lover of his work dying honourably in harness. Young, handsome, good-natured, quick-witted, and genuine to the core—a hater of all cant and sham, we mourned him deeply.

A. T. G. BEVERIDGE: *A.B.A.*

JOHN THEODORE CASH

Professor of Materia Medica, 1886-1919

Professor Cash exerted an abiding and highly beneficial influence upon the early development of the science of Pharmacology.

Prior to 1886 were begun his elaborate and careful researches upon the series of aconitines—the poisonous principles of the monkshoods—and his sustained endeavours to establish, through investigations upon the substituted ammonias and benzene compounds, co-ordination between chemical structure and pharmacological action . . . pioneer work which laid the foundations of a relationship between the chemical constitution of organic compounds and their effects upon the body; this research indicated to workers in synthetic chemistry paths which led towards the discovery of many new remedies.

At Aberdeen he continued to advance knowledge upon many of his previous subjects, and also investigated, among other problems, the effects of caffeine, theine and lead upon muscle, the variable actions of opium, the relative reduction of blood pressure caused by nitrites of the paraffin series, and the causes of the dermatitis produced on workers by an East Indian satinwood. Mention of this last recalls to memory that he frequently experimented upon himself, and on one morning he arrived to deliver his morning lecture with both arms inflamed and a face so red and swollen that one hesitated before inquiring the cause.

As an experimentalist Cash displayed extraordinary dexterity and mechanical ingenuity; he laid great stress on the axiom that experimental work in pharmacology, if it is to be of value, must be done with a minimum disturbance of the tissues, so that their typical responses to drugs can be anticipated. Much of the elaborate apparatus he evolved to achieve this practical ideal remains almost unknown, because he rarely published the means but only the results he gained.

Apart from his researches, Cash became notable as a highly skilled angler for salmon and trout and as an expert on diseases of the salmon; one could always date the opening of the salmon fishing season by his sudden disappearance from the laboratory after months of close devotion to research. A day spent with him on the river bank of Dee or Don was an education in the art of angling, in which he displayed superb accuracy and judgment. His reputation as an angler will be preserved by the composite hairlug and woodcock salmon-fly which bears his name.

W. J. DILLING: A.U.R. 1931

CHARLES ROBERTSHAW MARSHALL

Professor of Materia Medica, 1919-1930

> Professor Marshall has burst upon us as quite a new thing in Medical Professors. There is about him a fraternity that is distinctive. Both his geniality and his dignity have an individual touch as if Dame Nature had decided for once to make a daring experiment in the matter of her Professor creation. And, to put it briefly, the experiment was a success.
>
> Alma Mater

His was a pleasant personality, complex only to those who did not see below the surface. He was always anxious to help and advise his students and he never spared himself. Undoubtedly, the most outstanding characteristic was his versatility. Most of us endeavour, in vain, to know everything of something, and something of everything. Professor Marshall knew everything of many things, and a lot about everything else.   Nothing seemed outside his ken.   In his own subject the very numerous references to his work bear evidence of his prominence.   He would discuss the intricacies of the benzene ring with the chemist, the velocity of beta-particles with the physicist, or the Hylozoistic theory with the philosopher. His knowledge of fine arts was outstanding, and oft-times he would find relaxation in music.

Our University and hospitals are the richer for his being here.   Into his lectures he put the greatest care, his whole course was modelled on very definite lines.   He sought to teach things which he knew would be of use to his students, and he taught well.   In Materia Medica and Thera-peutics his teaching was essentially utilitarian.   He selected the significant and let the insignificant go.   It was not required that his students should learn the sources of drugs, or the botanical classification of crude vegetable medicines, or that the memory be burdened with the knowledge of drugs which have no bearing on toxicology or therapeutics.   He limited the scope of his subject to knowledge which would be of use in the treatment of disease.   He made important changes in the system of teaching, which must add much to the value of medical education in our University.

As a member of the Board of Directors of our Infirmary he did an enormous amount of very useful work.   The new Hospital Scheme was dear to him, and he worked very hard, and with considerable success, to bring about co-operation between the various corporations that constitute our medical school.

A. W. HENDRY: *A.U.R.* 1930

The next holder of the Chair was DAVID CAMPBELL, *1930-1959, Dean of the Faculty, assessor to the University Court and representative of the University of Aberdeen on the General Medical Council, of which he has been President for more than ten years.   He was Dean during the transfer of medical departments to Foresterhill, through the 1939-45 war and during the inception of the National Health Service, and the University valued his wise and courageous guidance.   He has received the honour of Knighthood.*

The present holder of the Chair is ALASTAIR G. MACGREGOR.

FORENSIC MEDICINE

FRANCIS OGSTON

Professor of Forensic Medicine, 1860(57)-1883

Francis Ogston acted as police surgeon and medical officer of health to the city for nearly half a century.   He began to lecture on medical jurisprudence in 1839 and when the lectureship was raised into a Chair (through the bounty of Alexander Henderson of Caskieben), Dr. Ogston became the first holder.

Dr. Ogston was not only a medical jurist. His chair also included the subject of medical logic. So far as I am aware, the University of Aberdeen alone devoted special attention to this subject. The course consisted of a number of lectures on what might be called Applied Logic; that is to say, the students were instructed in the laws of reasoning and in the various methods employed in the investigation of phenomena, while the illustrations were culled from medical literature. . . . Dr. Ogston took a great interest in this part of his course, and, by apt illustrations, he endeavoured to fix the attention of his hearers. It was delightful to observe the pleasure he took in exploding some of the fallacies that have too often crept into medicine, more especially in the Department of Therapeutics. Over-worked as the student of medicine now is, my opinion has always been that he might profitably dispense with more than one of the courses of instruction now forced upon him, and that a few lectures on medical logic would develop his powers of independent thinking. By our present methods, his absorptive capacities are strained to the uttermost, while there is no time and scarcely any faculty for reflection.

JOHN GRAY MCKENDRICK: *A.B.A.*

MATTHEW HAY

Professor of Forensic Medicine, 1883-1926

> This very great man who will stand out as one of the greatest benefactors of our City and of our University.

The portrait by Charles Sim, R.A., gives an excellent impression of Matthew Hay as he was in his later and declining years, but there is something far more than a mere portrait; the genius of the artist has placed upon his canvas a remarkable and unforgettable interpretation of the inward spirit of the man—that upward tilt of the chin, the somewhat sad and sombre expression of the eyes and his gaze peering as it were into the future —the picture of the man of dreams, of the man of vision. In some ways the expression is very similar to that in the etching of the late Lord Lister by Appleby, and one sees the same brooding expression and the forward seeing of his eyes.

My first contact with Matthew Hay was as a student in the class of Forensic Medicine and Public Health. Of his subject I remember little or nothing except that he was a brilliant lecturer, and an even more abiding memory that it was one of the horrid classes which were held at 8 o'clock on a summer morning. I did not see him again until many years had passed, when he was already nearing his retirement and his health was beginning to cause some anxiety. As a patient I do not remember that he was any more difficult than the average medical man when he is ill. For one, however, who was a trained pharmacologist he had one amusing foible in that he had an inordinate faith in drugs, and his bedside table was generally littered with the numerous medical samples with which we are daily drenched by the manufacturers. He tried them all not only successively but simultaneously no matter whether they were sedatives or stimulants—but always with a charming and somewhat apologetic smile as if he were ashamed of one of his few weaknesses. Fortunately, as far as I could see, they did neither good nor ill.

In 1883 at the early age of twenty-seven he was appointed to the Chair of Forensic Medicine. Already he had a well established reputation as a brilliant research worker in Pharmacology and Physiology, and his earlier work is quoted to this day—on the sulphates, the nitrates and the bile salts. In 1884 he was appointed to the Chair of Materia Medica in the newly founded Johns Hopkins University in Baltimore, but this appointment he was for family reasons never able to take up. In 1887, on the sudden death of Dyce Davidson, he took over the duties of the Chair of Materia Medica in Aberdeen until a successor was appointed. Of how many men nowadays could it be said that at the age of thirty they had been appointed to two Chairs and had carried on the duties of a third? He had henceforward little opportunity for active research, but he stimulated the enthusiasm for it in many of his pupils. In his own words: " Research is the well-spring of a University, without which the field of work would remain as arid as the sands of the Sahara."

His services to University and town were manifold. He represented the University on the General Medical Council and the Medical Research Committee: indeed he was pressed to become the first secretary of the latter, but felt himself too old and his health too precarious to accept. His services to the town lay in what is now known as Social Medicine—housing, wages, nutrition, maternity and child welfare, mental welfare, particularly of the mental defective—and in his study of these problems he was his own social worker, visiting the people in their own homes, and in this, as in so many of his activities, he was very far ahead indeed of his time. When he became Medical Officer of Health the City Hospital, or Cunningarhill (ominous name), had an unsavoury reputation and patients would agree to go there only under duress; but from this he built up one of the leading infectious diseases hospitals of the country.

Through all these activities he gave much time and thought to the future development of the medical services. In 1916 he committed himself to the idea that a " single communal or State Health and Medical Service would give the best results for the health of the community—to make available for everyone the full resources of the most skilled and specialised medical treatment—and to take a much larger part in preventive medicine ".

His crowning achievement—the Joint Hospitals Scheme—was announced in the twenties and received the unanimous approbation of the various bodies concerned. Many, however, considered that to throw over the existing hospitals and rebuild completely on a new site was Utopian, and that the money for such a scheme could never be raised.

But Matthew Hay's faith never wavered. He walked every highway and byway within a radius of five miles looking for a suitable site. The foundation stone of the new Infirmary at Foresterhill was laid in 1928, and he lived long enough to see the building fairly well advanced.

Intellectually Matthew Hay was one of the ablest men of his generation, with an extraordinary range of knowledge. He was in the front rank of forensic pleaders and his assistance was sought in many important criminal cases. All his work in this sphere was marked by his inherent passion for truth and justice.

The main driving force in all that he was and all that he was able to do was his abounding charity. He was much interested in the fate of prisoners: " I have spent many hours in talks with the inmates of prison cells, and the more I know and the more I have seen of such cases, the more I am inclined to say that apart from heredity and environment in their broadest sense, there go many of us." He had a deep and abiding sympathy with the poor and the needy, the under-privileged and the underdog. He saw always the good that was in man, never the bad. In the words of Sir T. Browne: " He allowed one eye for what was laudable in them."

It is my hope that one day an adequate memorial will be put up to him where it ought to stand, at Foresterhill, and that it will bear the inscription: *Si monumentum requiris, circumspice.*

ALEXANDER GREIG ANDERSON

When Professor Matthew Hay retired, his Chair went out of being. Originally instituted for the teaching of Medical Logic as well as Forensic Medicine, it had ceased to concern itself with the former and to the latter had added a good deal of what came to be called Public Health. It seemed desirable to separate these two. Forensic Medicine, not in itself sufficient for a Chair, became a lectureship in the hands of DR. ROBERT RICHARDS.

PATHOLOGY

DAVID JAMES HAMILTON

Professor of Pathology, 1882-1908

" Prove all things, use your senses, and above all the common sense that God has given you."

Excellent to listen to, but a terror when questioning. " Lord bless you, Mr. ——, I never heard such nonsense! "

In the pathological class Professor Hamilton deftly makes disease discourse on itself. The lecture table is littered with actual preparations of disease; there are also models, made by himself, on the walls is a profusion of diagrams, all drawn from actual preparations. Sometimes they are so

profuse that the walls are hid from view; and it is said that a Dundee
painter on holiday once mistook them for an expensive wallpaper of elaborate design, and refused to be comforted till told the price per yard.

Alma Mater

*In the new Chair of Pathology, there worked a man whose reputation was world-
wide. He had discovered the causes of two diseases in sheep (Braxy and " loupin'
ill ") and worked steadily all through his years of teaching in discovering and
combating the organisms that were responsible for disease.*

Professor Hamilton is a peripatetic. We have never seen him but moving.
In his laboratory, in his lecture-room, in the mortuary, everywhere he
knows no halting. When he speaks he looks away into space, and stalks

up and down like an impatient
watchman ; or he stands, handling
a specimen or with his fingers in his
waistcoat pockets, pushing against
the table, looking up, looking down,
twitching his upper lip, and blink-
ing so that his very spectacles seem
to move.

You see from his walk that he
has decided views about this Universe and his relation to it. He has
no doubt about what he does and
he does it as if he had none.

Professor Hamilton has a very
clear idea of what a lecture ought
to be. . . . " And take notes—take
notes of everything. What's the use
of my coming here to talk to you if you don't take notes ? You can read
a book at home. Take notes ! " . . . In every lecture he has an idea or
part of an idea to set forth; his facts are never an unrelated series; they
have always an explicit meaning and purpose. What is thus true of the
lecture is true of the whole discourse. Pathology is not naked-eye or
microscopic examination of morbid changes; it is the working up of
all such to one end—the causation of disease. It is this that makes
pathology a science.

But the lecture is not all pathology: the professor has ideas on other
subjects. This, for example, on anatomy: " Not know where the pul-
monary artery lies ? You never know any anatomy till you come to me;
I didn't know that myself when I was a third year student. You learn
all about everything that's of no use—all about pisiform bones—pisiform
bones !—why, it's knowledge a man wouldn't be found dead with ! "

But come now into the laboratory for a little. . . . That sliding
apparatus is the brain-cutter, which produces the beautiful sections of the
whole brain that you see on those innumerable glass plates on the shelves.

There are hundreds of them and competent men say they are the finest sections of the brain ever made. Then those tubes—they are culture-tubes of bacteria.[1] Here you have in bondage the active agents of disease and death; there is more danger in these tubes than in gunpowder or dynamite. Our modern pathologist governs and directs disease; he is Jupiter, holding in his hand a bunch of thunder-bolts.

This is where Professor Hamilton works. He is always working. When he teaches, it is as if his sole end in life were to teach; when he works, it is not different.

Alma Mater, 1887

GEORGE DEAN

Professor of Pathology, 1908-1914

Professor Dean's brief tenure of the Chair was marred by ill-health. Angina pectoris forced him out of active life (" Excuse me, I'll be back ", one of his former students remembers his saying as a spasm of pain interrupted the last lecture he gave) and he died some time after. But he came to Aberdeen with a high reputation.

The more one knows him the more one realizes, what is rare enough in these days, that his scientific reputation is a perfect reflex of his personal character.

In Berlin he came under the influence of Virchow and his school of Pathology, but to the eager enquirer the new school of Bacteriology offered the more attractive study. The enormous improvement in bacteriologic technique had led to the discovery of the infective agents in many diseases. Now the products of bacteriological action were being enthusiastically studied and the foundations of the science of Immunity were being laid. It was only to be expected, then, that Dr. Dean would throw himself into the study of Bacteriology and the bearing of Immunity theory on serum and vaccine therapy.

In 1906 he was appointed to the new post of Chief Bacteriologist to the Lister Institute. As a supervisor of research he possessed valuable qualities. He was widely read, he was cautious—perhaps too cautious for young enthusiasts—but at the same time he would not readily discourage the working out of any suggestion that might seem unpromising or even fanciful. The humanity in him was always uppermost.

Alma Mater

---

[1] In *The Arches of the Years* Halliday Sutherland recounts the blast of wrath that fell on a nervous student who spilt a culture of cholera germs and mopped it up with his handkerchief. . . . Professor Hamilton, says the author, was called The Bull—" he charges like a bull, he bellows like a bull, and he stands no damned nonsense."

THEODORE SHENNAN

Professor of Pathology, 1914-1936

Recollections, even of such august personages as our old professors, fade after nearly forty years, but there is one tall, handsome figure in a white coat and little black skull cap, quiet voiced, sitting at his microscope in the old Pathology Department at Marischal College, that is as clear to me as if it were yesterday.   Professor Shennan had an air of well turned out elegance that impressed and sometimes frightened us, but, I am told, attracted the lady students.

Before coming to Aberdeen in 1914 he held high posts in the Edinburgh school of pathology which at the beginning of the century was pre-eminent in Britain.   If his translation to Aberdeen was like a transfusion of fresh blood it was not without its febrile reaction, for his attempts to introduce the Edinburgh tutorial system spread dismay.   Weekly essays in pathology were regarded by the students as an interference with their time-honoured liberty to defer studies till the weeks preceding examinations, and went by default.

In the long run he was well out of the reading of essays, because that brilliant unforgettable summer of 1914 was soon to crash into a winter of war followed by four dark years, when, almost single-handed, he had to reorganize a department that had been for months without a director. But he took it all in his imperturbable stride and in the year following his appointment he also took on the deanship of the medical faculty.

There was never a more sympathetic dean, and many a veteran of the war had reason to be grateful for his leniency and understanding of the problems of readjustment to civilian life.   He instituted the mid-week half holiday for athletics and the Dean's Medal for the best athlete of the year, and if he showed a little pique on hearing that members of his class played solo in the Union on fine Wednesday afternoons it was excusable. Aberdeen students were not easy to understand, but neither were reforming professors.

How wrong students can be in the assessment of their teachers.   One had to work as his assistant for some time to know Shennan for the kindly man he was.   Shy, retiring and sometimes apparently distant in manner, he was nevertheless easily approachable and always ready to help.   For some he was the ideal chief because he would set a job, show how it should be done and leave one to get on with it.   He could moreover discuss scientific problems on equal terms with his juniors and in a way that was far in advance of that age when authority was the key note in medical education.   With those who won his confidence he would sometimes lay bare the ideals which animated his working life, and they were ideals that any young man would wish to emulate.

I believe that something of this side of his personality did get across to us as students for, although he was a dull lecturer, we recognized the sincerity of his teaching. We knew that what he taught was worth knowing and needed no dramatic emphasis. He scorned showmanship; to him the fitting out of young men for a gentle profession was a solemn mission and in his teaching he set an example of quiet dignity and restraint.

In writing of our old professors it is usual to recount little incidents that reveal their personalities but in this instance it would be out of character because Shennan's personality did not reveal itself in trivial episodes. He was a morbid anatomist of the old order, painstaking, methodical and unhurried in his work, taking his subject with the gravity that befitted a discipline modelled on the German schools. Nevertheless he had a sense of humour that sometimes bubbled up unexpectedly. Like some others amongst his Scottish colleagues he had a sneaking attraction for medico-legal problems and would sometimes find himself giving evidence for the Crown, but crimes of violence were rare in the North, which was fortunate for him, because he lacked the instincts of the sleuth.

He was refined and quiet in tastes, a lover of music and old furniture. He took golf seriously, never missing a staff versus students match or the annual match between the Glasgow and Aberdeen University Senates. I saw little of him in his last ten years as professor but I know that the death of his first wife after a long illness left him lonely and dispirited and that his second marriage to his assistant Dr. Ann Thomson restored his happiness. But what a whispering there was in the corridors at Marischal when it was known that he was walking out with his assistant. I saw him in retirement which was a happy period because it gave him leisure to enjoy the society of his adored young daughter. Shennan never aspired to be a prominent figure, but he tried to do a good job for the science of pathology which he loved, and in his quiet way he succeeded.

JOHN B. DUGUID

JOHN STIRLING YOUNG, *Professor of Pathology, 1937, continues to hold the Chair.*

After the First World War, a lectureship in Bacteriology *was instituted and made into a Professorship in 1925. The holder was* JOHN CRUICKSHANK, *1926-54. A Glasgow man, small in stature but of immense vitality, with a passionate conviction that science held the key to the future, he built up from the foundations an admirable Department, which is now in the hands of* ALEXANDER MACDONALD, *Professor of Bacteriology, 1954.*

In 1938 another new development came with the appointment of DOUGLAS R. MACCALMAN *as Lecturer in* Psychopathology. *Eight years later the Crombie-Ross Chair of* Mental Health *was instituted.*

DOUGLAS R. MACCALMAN

Lecturer in Psychopathology, 1938-1946
Professor of Mental Health, 1946-1948

> In his addresses to the Association of Psychiatric Social Workers, he gave full measure of his rich, literary, artistic, humanistic self—brilliant and bright—renewing us. It is this quality of renewing, this therapeutic personality, which I feel was his peculiar gift as a psychiatrist; and I recall the many patients, simple and sophisticated alike, who have spoken of this.
>
> MARION WHYTE

When Douglas MacCalman came to Aberdeen in 1938, there were no facilities other than the mental hospitals for psychiatric treatment. In appointing a lecturer in psychopathology, the University acted in conjunction with the voluntary hospitals and the local authorities, and part of the work was that of building up a comprehensive mental health service. Close co-operation with the Maternity Hospital, the Maternity and Child Welfare organization, the School Medical Service, the Juvenile Courts and Youth Organizations, helped to build up a comprehensive Child Guidance service. An adult out-patient clinic was also formed for the diagnosis of mental illness and the treatment of neuroses and early psychoses. In 1948 Professor MacCalman left us to become Professor of Psychiatry in Leeds University, but his career was cut short by illness and early death. We are privileged to reprint part of the tribute written of him by Professor Meredith of Leeds:

Douglas Robert MacCalman was born in 1903, a son of the Manse, and, after a life of rich achievement, was struck down at the height of his powers by arthritis in 1952. After over four years of gallant and uncomplaining struggle he died on 31 January 1957. The following brief tribute can provide little conception of the complex, creative, subtle and lovable personality whose loss is so widely mourned.

In the thick of our over-urbanised civilization the boy from the Highlands retained, as an intact living experience, a core of absorbed communion with wild nature. This core provided the unchallengeable standard by which were judged both the follies and neuroses of our modern way of life and the prescriptions and panaceas offered by way of remedy. A sort of secret inner reference to this enduring standard gave many of his words a hint of mysticism. I doubt if his ultimate beliefs were ever formulated—even to himself. They did not need to be: they were feelings rather than propositions, and they gave assurance, though not optimism. Yet he was a thinker, though not an intellectual in the current sense of the word. He was too vividly aware of the disturbing forces underlying the specious rationalisations in what so frequently passes for intellect. For these forces were the uneasy matter of his daily work.

His strength in work came not only from assured feeling but also from skill. His boyhood contact with nature was no mere passive contemplation but gifted attainment. With an oar, a gun, a rod, a golf-club, a trowel, he had the kind of hand which always excels. Transmute that into the touch which transforms human relations and you have a clue to his work both as a psychiatrist and as a creative administrator. There is an odd synthesis in his deadly marksmanship. Shooting is not to everyone's taste but I think he accepted man for what he is, and himself as a man, yet even as a boy with a hunter's instinct he hated to see suffering or to inflict it, and so perfected his aim as to hit a duck through the head at 100 yards. (The fact that it turned out to be a favourite tame duck, not a wild one, led to complications!)

Rather late starting school at Glasgow Academy, and apparently destined for the ministry, he silenced a persuasive tutor with the words " Sir, do you realize how much suffering there is in the world? I think I can help." And hence a medical career at Glasgow University, graduating M.B., CH.B. in 1929 and winning the Hunter medal in pathology. His course was now set for his future in psychological medicine, and already in his graduation year appears his first publication " Group Personality in Neurotics " in the *Journal of Neurology and Psychopathology*. He was not yet twenty-six but this study of neurotics in a mental hospital reveals not only a gift for precise observation but astonishingly mature powers of observation and independent judgment, and a capacity to use theory without being dominated by it. It also shows a profound sympathy for the nameless sufferings of the mental patient.

Two years in the U.S.A. opened his eyes to the perplexing panorama of American life. One senses that in this period the seeds were sown which later ripened into his mature conceptions of the international functions and implications of organized psychiatry.

Returning to Britain in 1932 he was appointed Medical Director of the Notre Dame Child Guidance Clinic, Glasgow. Here were laid the foundations on which his later authority in the field of child psychiatry and infant development so firmly rested.

About this time the Child Guidance movement, already well-established in the United States, was gathering momentum in this country. For the position of General Secretary to the newly-founded Child Guidance Council in London MacCalman was the obvious and ideal choice. From the handful of scattered voluntary clinics of the thirties to the nation-wide service of today was a journey of organizational triumphs which, of itself, would be sufficient of a memorial.

Scotland claimed him again in 1938 as Lecturer in Psychopathology in the University of Aberdeen, and elevated him to a professorship in 1946. Here, through the war years, he threw himself with all his gifts and his humanity into vast tasks and performed prodigies of psychiatric, organizational and educational achievement to which justice can be done only by those who witnessed it.

The fifth step brought him to Leeds as Nuffield Professor of Psychiatry in 1948. Add to this that from 1929 almost up to the day of his death, there flowed from his pen a growing stream of publications revealing not

19

only the physician, the teacher and the administrator but also the man of letters, the artist, the traveller, the social reformer, the visionary and the philosopher. All these, and above all the guide and companion, we have lost, and the world has lost a builder who was humble, wise and good.

G. PATRICK MEREDITH

1948 saw Child Health *given the importance it merited.* JOHN CRAIG *became the first Professor in the new Chair, and still holds it in a highly acceptable way.*

In 1949 the Chair of Biological Chemistry *was founded, and* W. O. KERMACK *became Professor and with eyes in his fingers (for he is blind) directs much important research.*

Finally in 1958 the new Chair of Social Medicine *brought* E. MAURICE BACKETT *into our midst, to carry on and develop the work already done as an outgrowth from Public Health by such men as Douglas Berry and Ian Richardson.*

JOHN PARLANE KINLOCH *was lecturer in* Public Health *from 1914 and Reader from 1923. Other lectureships covered Clinical Chemistry, Radiology, Tropical Medicine and Parasitology; while eye, ear, throat and nose had their specialists.*

The fragmentation of medicine, as each new science is brought to bear on the processes of the human body, troubles some of the older men. One of the finest physicians of our day, a consultant and clinical teacher of rare acumen, still happily with us though not professionally active and therefore not to be portrayed in this gallery, Sir Alexander Greig Anderson, " A. G." to the elite, insists always that a patient is a man, not a sum of measurable reactions; and that a man must cure him when he is sick. Whole man to whole man is the necessary relation of doctor to patient. Let us conclude this survey of our medical personalities by one or two of those who, teaching in the presence of the patient, have left vivid memories in the minds of those they taught.

GEORGE DUNCAN

Lecturer in Clinical Pathology, 1914-1933

" Daddy Duncan "

George Duncan probably never talked about our fashionable phrase: " co-operation between the clinician and the medical scientist "—first because he took it for granted and was too busy practising it, and second because he was too modest to think of himself as a medical scientist— although he was a first-class one. " Laddie ", he would say to a new resident, " this is just plain common sense! Give me a decent sample from your patient and I'll tell you his story—past, present, and future—as well as I can." How well he told the stories is one of the clearest memories I have of Woolmanhill between 1927 and 1932. He had a benign and shining appearance; a characteristic stotting walk; an enveloping white coat that reached the ground; a quip and a laugh; an ironical word for folly, of which he met plenty; and that instinctively right judgment of what really mattered which made his work so highly esteemed.

As a student, I found his fifth-year class in clinical pathology just what was needed to make the third-year teaching of pathology and bacteriology mean something about patients and be a mighty aid in the finals. Later, as a young graduate venturing into his subject, I enjoyed his confidences, his jokes, and his ability to select what mattered and let the remainder go hang. " The one thing that matters about a vaccine is that the bugs in it should be dead." " I don't know what this tumour will be called next year or the one after; I'm not sure what it's best called now—but this I know: it won't come back. Let's report it ' Nil malignant '. "

Reports of his bearing these reassuring words meant much to many doctors, patients, and relatives in the North-East. So did his suggestions for what to examine next when the diagnosis remained obscure. He always wanted to help. He nearly always could. And if he could not help he knew it and said so squarely. A modest man, a great servant of his profession, a worthy pupil of the great Professor Hamilton, an encouraging, cheery fellow with a fine sense of what was right—that was " Daddy Duncan ". Like many another, I was much the better for knowing him.

J. W. HOWIE

GEORGE HERBERT COLT

Lecturer in Clinical Surgery, 1912-1935

Amongst the teachers in the clinical medical subjects in the years after the first war, few will be better remembered than Mr. Colt. He possessed that unusual combination of genius and idiosyncrasy which always makes a big impact on the student body.

He never quite understood the Scottish character, and his own brand of humour was quite alien to the North. He came to Aberdeen as assistant in the Department of Surgery and assistant surgeon to the Royal Infirmary in 1910. He had already a reputation for invention, and had to his credit the Colt coiled spring and insertor for aortic aneurysm.

He also had a fine academic record with a 1st Class Natural Tripos of Cambridge and a medical qualification from St. Bartholomew's Hospital.

He was secretary of the Section of Surgery at the meeting of the B.M.A. in 1914 in Aberdeen, and the outbreak of war in that year found Colt mobilized with the 1st Scottish General Hospital, with beds at the

High School for Girls and Oldmill Hospital, where the earliest casualties from the Mons fighting were received.

Colt went abroad as O.C. Surgical Division of the 43rd General Hospital to Salonica and latterly to Constantinople. He had weird stories to tell of the insufferable state of the drains in his hospital. He sent an S.O.S. to the G.O.C. when the waste rose to the third floor!

He returned to Aberdeen in 1923 and was made surgeon in charge of wards. He was most conscientious about attending hospital for emergency admissions at any time of the day or night. He made a specialty of the treatment of varicose veins either by extraction or injection, and could record the number of miles of veins he had removed. He was well known for his publications in surgical centres in Europe. Colt and Low were the two Aberdonians whose names were familiar in Copenhagen.

Amongst his collateral activities was his love of medical literature, and he saw through the press the catalogue of the Historical Works in the possession of the Aberdeen Medico-Chirurgical Society by Miss Mabel D. Allardyce.

He took a great interest in horticulture and the layout of gardens. He was a collector of antiques and an entertaining raconteur. He was much in demand at re-union dinners even until his latter years in London.

Colt is remembered with affection as one who took a useful share in the education of students of the first post-war era.

ALEXANDER LYALL

WILLIAM ANDERSON

Lecturer in Clinical Surgery 1922-1949

William, or Willie as he was affectionately called by all, was a man who made you glad that you had chosen a medical career. In those days, when there was much more freedom allowed in attending out-patient clinics, William's " out-patients " was invariably packed with enthusiastic students of both sexes. He was lucid, concise, extremely practical, and had the faculty of " putting over " the essential facts of general surgery. Without all the present aids to diagnosis, a good surgeon had to be a good clinician, and William Anderson was a first-class clinician. He made it clear to us that the care of the patient was the first duty of every doctor, and it was a real joy to see how he could set patients at their ease, so that many of them actually enjoyed what, for most people, is a rather terrifying ordeal.

In his ward he made everyone feel they were part of a team, encouraging, but also telling them in no uncertain terms if work was not properly done. In these days at Woolmanhill, when there were only two surgeons attached to each ward, Mr. Anderson was responsible for all the emergencies admitted on his receiving nights. Then you could see William at his best. His rare clinical judgment, his common-sense approach, his reasoned decisions and his perfect technique taught his house surgeons something for which they were eternally grateful.

To the general practitioner he was a tower of strength. William would come to see an emergency, day or night, if the practitioner found himself in trouble; and many a weary night he spent travelling long distances to see a patient or even to operate in some country hospital, returning to Aberdeen for a full day's work, having had little or no sleep.

HUGH G. SMITH

ALEXANDER MITCHELL

Lecturer on Surgical Diseases of Children, 1928-1946

Throughout his undergraduate days and during a long spell of a very active professional career in Aberdeen, Mr. Alexander Mitchell was known to his colleagues and medical students as " Sandy " and any reference to his surname was deemed unnecessary. This fact in itself bears testimony to his universal popularity and established the hallmark of his integrity and honesty. An apparent brusqueness of speech and manner concealed a highly erudite mind, a most kindly disposition, and a keen sense of humour.

His upbringing was in continual contact with medicine, his father, Patrick Mitchell, M.A., M.D., practising at Sandy's birthplace in Old Rayne, Insch, for many years. Following in his father's footsteps he graduated in Arts in 1901, in Medicine in 1905, and obtained the CH.M. in 1907, the highest surgical qualification which his University could grant. It was to the old family house in Old Rayne that Sandy retired to enjoy his beloved countryside and to dispense highland hospitality to his frequent visitors.

Like many in the early decades of this century, he broadened his experience of medicine and of human nature by carrying on a large general practice. His natural leaning was towards surgery however, and at first he devoted much of his time to gynaecology. Children's surgery attracted him early and he became assistant to the late Sir Henry Gray at the Royal Hospital for Sick Children before the 1914-18 war.

During the First World War he freely gave his services as a surgical specialist to the First Scottish General Hospital in Aberdeen and, in spite of a physical disability, insisted upon doing a period of relief duty for a sick colleague in a hospital at Rouen. His contribution to the service of his country was completed in the Second World War when he was appointed consulting orthopaedic surgeon to the Emergency Medical Service, which position he held with merit until the cessation of hostilities.

Eventually in 1928 he was appointed Lecturer in the University on the Surgical Diseases of Children and was senior surgeon to the Royal Hospital for Sick Children until his retirement.

Orthopaedic surgery constitutes a large part of children's work and it was to this branch that he devoted much of his energy. Upon the establishment of an Orthopaedic Department at the Royal Infirmary he became the first orthopaedic surgeon to that unit. Skilled in the specialty of orthopaedics as he was, his greatest love remained for the Royal Hospital for Sick Children and for a considerable period before his death in 1953 he acted as Chairman of the Board of Management of the special hospitals group.

He was a regular attender at the meetings of the British Orthopaedic Association at home and abroad and in 1950-51 was honoured by his fellow members by being elected Vice-President of that scientific body.

His teaching was simple and direct and had the great advantage of reinforcement by a vast clinical experience which made his delivery and his clichés remembered.

Sandy was a great countryman and during his few leisure hours in a busy life and in his retirement his greatest delight was to go for long rides on his pony. He was loved by all who knew him and his familiar figure will be long remembered, whether riding to the Aberdeenshire Hunt or hacking on the wonderful terrain of the lower slopes of Bennachie.

ANDREW FOWLER

SCIENCE

Mathematics and Natural Philosophy have already been dealt with under Arts.

NATURAL HISTORY:
ZOOLOGY AND GEOLOGY

JAMES NICOL

Professor of Natural History, 1860(53)-1878

> Leaving time and the unchanging mountains to confirm or refute.
>
> *Memorial in Geology Department*

> His tall gaunt figure, large brow, honest gentle countenance (only once so far as I remember seen in anger, when a student's hat was found upon the skull of a skeleton monkey) . . . .
>
> *Alma Mater*

Large of bone, spare of flesh yet not lean, erect in figure and firm in gait, he looked a man in hard condition, unused to luxury and capable of physical endurance. Time had made his head bare from the crown to the broad sloping brow, but the fringe of hair on the temples and occiput had not quite lost the luxuriance and the brown hue of earlier manhood. The eyes shone with undiminished brightness under the level eyebrows, if the crow-feet at their angles and the weathering of the face betokened years of exposure to the storm and stress incidental to a life spent much out of doors. The nose straight and refined; the upper lip clean-shaved, in contrast with the untrained luxuriance of the whitening beard and whiskers. A kindly man, withal, to look at; but something in the firm straight mouth told of a possible dourness it were better not to provoke.

In dress he had long ceased to follow the vagaries of fashion; he was not even careful of his appearance in his old-fashioned way; sometimes his waistcoat would be buttoned awry, and then a whispered query would pass round the class whether the mistake should be geologically described as a " fault " or a " slip ".

Looking back on his teaching, one is impressed with the idea that he had acquired his knowledge of zoology laboriously and without enthusiasm in order to fulfil the duties of his chair. When the subject touched upon his favourite geology his interest in it rose; that antediluvian-looking monster, the king-crab of the Moluccas, he handled with affection as the nearest surviving representative of the fossil trilobites; the chambered nautilus interested him on account of its extinct congeners the ammonites; and the fossil gryphaea, " strange old-world oyster ", as he called it, was an especial favourite. But of the modern marine fauna, cast ashore in abundance in Aberdeen Bay after any winter storm, no fresh specimen found its way to his lecture-room, and no dissection by his own hand was ever shown in demonstration of the structures he described.

When he came to lecture on the geological part of the course the difference in his tone was markedly apparent. He spoke from the fullness of his knowledge, and his living interest in the subject was undisguised. If he did not search the lines of Torry fishermen for waifs and strays of the marine fauna, he would describe with animation what rock structure we would meet with in a walk to Cove; or would tell us in what road-side dykes we might discover travelled boulders scored by glaciers in the days when the ice-floe filled the North Sea, and the Tap of Benachie was a lonely rock peering through the ice-cap of a frozen land. He spoke with the earnestness of one who tells what is worth knowing as he expounded the mineralogy of our native granite and pointed out that, adamantine though it seems, it could by slow process of time and weathering be re-solved into the elements of a not unfertile soil. It came as a surprise to us when he expressed doubt as to the durability of the polish that can be imparted to its surface. " It remains to be seen ", he said, " whether it will stand the test of time "—his thoughts carrying him away from his classroom and the polishing yards of Aberdeen to the wild corries of the Cairngorms, where he had seen, as we then had not, how the granite crags are rotted by wind and rain and frost into fantastic unstable pinnacles like tottering towers of Cyclopean masonry.

But chiefly he loved to dwell on the geology of the West Highlands. " Oban in the West Highlands ", " The Basalt of Staffa and the Scuir of Eigg ", " Torridon Sandstones ", " The Quartzites of Sutherland ", " Hebridean Gneiss ", and " Durness Limestones ", were catchwords among his students. Upon the stratigraphy of those rocks the great controversy of his life turned. At a meeting of the British Association in Aberdeen in 1859 he brought forward proofs that the quartzites should be geologically considered as overlying the metamorphic rocks of Eastern Scotland. In this he was opposed by Murchison, who argued that the Eastern metamorphic rock was really superimposed on the quartzite. Nothing could well be simpler than the point at issue; but the available evidence was scanty, and the argument turned on the interpretation of a fault-riven rock section requiring much technical knowledge and scientific acumen to unravel. Nicol failed to carry opinion with him; but he knew he was right. The British Association met again in Aberdeen in 1885, and his views were declared to be completely verified. Alas, he had not lived to see the day.

WILLIAM BANNERMAN: *A.B.A.*

From 1878 to 1882 the Chair was held by J. COSSAR EWART, *who left on appointment to the corresponding Chair in Edinburgh.*

HENRY ALLEYNE NICHOLSON

Professor of Natural History, 1882-1899

> He did a day's work and a man's work.
>
> *Inscription on Memorial in Geology Department*

> He has no spice of the schoolmaster about him and treats his subject in a quiet conversational manner, as if to men who have come to years of discretion; as a natural consequence he presides over the most orderly and attentive class in the University.
>
> *Alma Mater*

Henry Alleyne Nicholson was born at Penrith. He spent his boyhood among the hills of Westmorland and Cumberland, which he learned so much to love, and whose character in after years he did much to elucidate. He received his early education in Appleby Grammar School, but nature herself was his great teacher. Nothing could have more impressed those who had the privilege of actually visiting his native ground on those memorable Geological excursions than his close familiarity with every nook and corner in that country. Though one of the most difficult parts of the British Isles to understand from a geological point of view, it was through long and patient study very largely unravelled and read by Professor Nicholson.

In the lecture room, Professor Nicholson commanded the eager attention of his students. As he guided them in the most fascinating manner through the mazes of his subject, he was deeply interesting, lucid and attractive. . . . The lecture hour passed away all too quickly.

His frankness, companionableness and easy outflow of sympathy bound his students to him. Outside the walls of the College in those delightful excursions to the Lake District, he was as joyous, free and fresh as the mountain air he so loved to breathe—the generous instincts of youth were blended with the knowledge of age.

Notwithstanding his activities as a teacher, he found time to engage in numerous researches and in the publication of many textbooks for the use of students, e.g. *Manual of Zoology*, *Manual of Palaeontology*. The latter was his particular study as an original investigator.

> *Alma Mater*, 1899

J. ARTHUR THOMSON

Professor of Natural History, 1899-1930

> The attention is riveted by the clear-cut face, the high-pitched pleasing voice, the thoughtful march to and fro behind the long table, and the gentle brushing aside of that wayward lock.
>
> *Alma Mater*

> I have heard him, too, raise the imagination of a large audience by his "Drama of life". We felt as if we were present at great moments of evolution.
>
> W. LESLIE MACKENZIE

The charming personality of Sir John Arthur Thomson, the Prince of Lecturers, the master of the exquisite and telling phrase. . .

First tapping back one cuff and then the other, he would walk across the rostrum announcing " and the worm is a nocturnal animal, those which you see in the daytime are diseased; indeed, it is not the early bird which catches the early worm but the worm which would not go home till morning ". And " all the chimpanzees were kept together for a chimpanzee by itself is no longer a chimpanzee. Bananas were strung up out of reach of the animals, but one of them piled boxes one on top of the other and so gained the fruit—a great advance—it has learned to put two and two together."

Once he lectured upon the Thinking Horses of Eberfeldt, and how a little Shetland pony called Hans could extract the square root of a number that would keep a mathematician busy for hours. Thereafter one never passed a Shetland pony without raising one's hat to it!

R. D. LOCKHART

John Arthur Thomson was born in East Lothian in 1861, attended country schools and studied at the Universities of Edinburgh, Jena and Berlin: for a time, after graduating in Arts, he had been a divinity student at New College, Edinburgh, before finally deciding on science. In 1886 he became an extra-mural lecturer on zoology in Edinburgh, at times teaching also in Glasgow and Dublin. From 1899 until 1930 he held the Chair in Aberdeen. On his retirement in the latter year he received the honour of knighthood; he was also an honorary LL.D. of Edinburgh, California, McGill and Aberdeen; and he had been a Vice-President of the Royal Society of Edinburgh. He died in 1933 at Limpsfield, Surrey, where his grave lies by that of Delius.

These are the bare facts of his career; but it is germane—be it a matter of inheritance or tradition—that he came of a family in which a love of nature and an interest in science ran, and still runs, strong. His maternal grandfather, the Rev. Dr. David Landsborough of Saltcoats (*Dictionary of National Biography*, vol. xxxii), was a naturalist of repute, author of works on zoophytes and seaweeds and on the natural history of Arran. One of his uncles, also David Landsborough and an Ayrshire minister, had similar interests; another, William Landsborough (*D.N.B.* xxxii), was an explorer who is commemorated by several place-names in Australia and New Zealand. His father, the Rev. Arthur Thomson of Saltoun, was a keen field-botanist; and his own younger brother, James, became like himself a professional zoologist. His wife Margaret (died 1953), daughter of the Rev. John Stewart of Pitlochry, shared his interests and was his constant helper and constructive critic. Their children, three sons and a daughter, all followed science as a profession in some form; and a grandson, bearing his name in full, is a zoologist in Canada.

Thomson was pre-eminently a teacher; his gifts were those of the interpreter rather than of the discoverer; he devoted himself largely to exposition and undertook relatively little research. He had, nevertheless, made a special study of Alcyonarians and was a recognized authority on that group of coral-like animals; this was systematic work in the Linnaean tradition, and the material entrusted to him from marine expeditions in all parts of the world enabled him to describe and classify many new species in a long series of scientific papers and monographs. Apart from this intensive study, he constantly refreshed himself by observation in the field and in the laboratory, as well as by wide reading, so that he possessed a very extensive mastery of the facts of natural history. This gave a breadth to his teaching which he could not easily have attained had he occupied himself to a greater extent as a specialist.

Another essential characteristic was that he regarded it as part of his function to spread an appreciation of nature and a knowledge of science among the general public, as well as to instruct his own students, and thus his activity ranged over a wide field of popular education. He was in great demand as a lecturer throughout the British Isles—also making three visits to America and one to South Africa; he was a prolific writer; and the advent of broadcasting gave him a further opportunity which he eagerly accepted.

As a teacher, Thomson strove first to understand, by submitting the facts to critical analysis. He had the scientific passion for truth; one must not palter with the strictly ascertained facts or attempt any evasion of the logical conclusions. His mind always remained open to new findings and fresh ideas, gladly assimilating these into the matter of his instruction.

Next, he strove especially to make things clear to his hearers or readers. He possessed a notable gift of lucidity, with great facility and felicity of expression both in the spoken and in the written word. He concentrated on essentials, making his points distinctly, marshalling them in due order and building them into the structure of the main generalization. He made a practice of summing up.

In addition, he strove to make things vivid, not despising the better arts of showmanship. To this task he brought imagination, a poetic touch and flashes of humour. His was a gentle personality in private life; yet at the lecture-table he quickly dominated his audience, and the fire of his enthusiasm kindled a receptive glow. Even his ordinary classes were acknowledged by critical undergraduates to be of outstanding interest, and his opening lecture each session attracted crowds of former students.

Of these things there is no abiding record, but only memories among those who were students more than thirty years ago. In his many books, however, his words may still be found as evidence of what, and how, Thomson sought to teach. Some of these were frankly popular in appeal, calculated to arouse and feed the interest of the general reader; others were more serious expositions for the earnest student; others, again, were contributions to scientific thought.

One may discern three different tendencies. Firstly, there is a romantic—sometimes almost mystical—attitude towards nature. That was the poet in him. The ideas of beauty, of wonder, of drama and of infinite complexity, constantly recur. The very titles of his books suggest this—*Secrets of Animal Life*, *The Wonder of Life*, *The Biology of the Seasons*, *The Haunts of Life*.

Secondly, there is a desire to promote knowledge and understanding. That was the scientist. He passionately wished to make the facts of science known and to explain scientific theories. Again there are indicative titles—*The Study of Animal Life*, *The Science of Life*, *Darwinism and Human Life*, *The Biology of Birds*, *Biology for Everyman;* his *Outlines of Zoology* was a textbook widely used, through a succession of editions, in the universities. Some other books were written jointly with Patrick Geddes.

Thirdly, there is the probing into the inner meaning of things, and the attempt to link science at its highest level with other branches of human thought. That was the philosopher. His *magnum opus*—addressed to the learned—was *The System of Animate Nature*, comprising the Gifford Lectures which he delivered in the University of St. Andrews in 1915-16. In this all the facets of his teaching are displayed, for it is a synthesis of his whole philosophy as naturalist and zoologist, as an evolutionary biologist of the vitalist school, and as a man reverently seeking knowledge and always moved by a profound impulse to impart his vision of the truth.

A. LANDSBOROUGH THOMSON

The three holders of this Chair after Sir J. Arthur Thomson passed fairly quickly to other posts. JAMES RITCHIE (*1930-36*), *an Aberdeen graduate and an Aberdeenshire man, went to the corresponding Chair in Edinburgh. He was a Zoologist in the old natural history tradition, with interests wide rather than specialized. Already in Aberdeen he had shown a deep interest in the relationship between the animal kingdom and man, and his publications have been on such themes as* The Influence of Man upon Animal Life in Scotland *and* Beasts and Birds as Farm Pests. *He was a member of the Scottish Office Advisory Committee on Wild Birds' Protection, and of the Sanctuaries Committee for Royal Parks. While in Aberdeen he took a leading part in the formation of the Aberdeen Regional Museum, and from 1954 till his death in 1958 he was President of the Royal Society of Edinburgh.*

He was succeeded by LANCELOT HOGBEN (*1937-42*) *the scintillating genius who wrote* Mathematics for the Million *while recuperating from an illness, and translated Dr. Dahlberg's book on human genetics while waiting in Uppsala (having been caught in Oslo by the German invasion) for a chance to return home via Moscow and Vladivostock. That he had also broadcast in Swedish (a talk on Aberdeen University), delivered part of his Oslo lecture in Norwegian and given a journalist an interview in Danish, shows how many-faceted was this dynamic man who occupied our Chair of Natural History for less than five years. In these years he had stimulated and guided research and reorganized the Department. Principal Sir William Hamilton Fyfe said of him that he " combined, like Socrates, the best features of the midwife and the gadfly."*

His successor was A. C. HARDY (*1942-46*), *now Sir Alister Hardy, Professor of Zoology and Comparative Anatomy in the University of Oxford, widely known for his research into the nature and movement of plankton. The instrument of his investigation, which he invented and designed himself, he first used on the voyage of the* Discovery *to the Antarctic in 1925-27. Coming to Aberdeen as he did in the middle of a war, he was involved in investigations into the possibility of using plankton as a food. His oceanographic researches have now led him to the belief that in the course of his evolution man spent a period as a denizen of the shallow shore waters.*

Since 1946 the Chair has been held by Professor V. C. WYNNE-EDWARDS.

The study of Geology was separated from that of Zoology in 1898.

ALFRED W. GIBB

Lecturer in Geology, 1898-1922, Professor, 1922-36

Memory conjures up the somewhat old-world figure—dignified and erect as a lancer—the characteristic moustache, the kindly eyes beneath the rather bushy eyebrows: a figure familiar to many students during the first three decades of the century. Dr. Gibb was known and loved by the many students who passed through his classes, but not so well known to the general public, for his was a retiring, shy and gentle disposition. He had the somewhat aloof shyness which was characteristic of the Scottish scholars of his day, with a quiet, unobtrusive refinement of feeling.

He was a most competent head of a department which he ran with quiet efficiency. A teacher of the old school—not a researcher in the modern sense—he preferred the continental, authoritarian approach, explaining and proclaiming the facts of his subject, to the more modern teaching by discussion group. He was not an inspirer of research, but he was a very fine teacher, with a flair for beautiful language and vivid description—aided by an enviable gift for blackboard illustration. These gifts shone in a particular way in his lectures to his first year classes: these were big classes, including Arts, Science and Agricultural students, and he held the interest of the students with ease and skill.

He lectured with a studied elegance of phrase: an unusual twist would stamp a detail indelibly in the minds of his students, as would one of his well-timed studied jokes. For example, when dealing with one of the many geological controversies, he would say, in his whimsical way: " Even at the time of the flood there were two schools of thought—there were the diluvians, who were for the flood, and the antediluvians, who were against it! "

There was an old-world pleasing formality in all he did: everything was done according to plan, and precisely on time, without haste and with a satisfying smoothness. His quiet influence pervaded every section of his department. Nothing was done, either by himself or his staff, in slovenly fashion—everything was carefully prepared and well in hand. His laboratory attendants attended to the setting out of the material for his lectures, but the finished lay-out of specimens, diagrams, etc., was always carefully scrutinised: he would remove a specimen here, add another there, and perhaps bring a cherished specimen from his sanctum to illustrate a special point.

He put a great deal of thought into the setting of his examination questions, and put them in a form which permitted of two ways of treatment, as far as was practicable: they could be fairly simply and straightforwardly answered, thus giving the average student a fair chance—but also they were often open to a more elaborate and complex treatment, allowing the good students to show their paces. His testimonials very often had a quaint and whimsical turn of phrase which was telling. His students were his first consideration, and he gave them of his best. His relations with his staff were always pleasant: he was never careless himself, and he expected the same maintenance of high standards in his staff. He was very generous in his dealings with them, and was a man big enough to be able to delegate a considerable amount of responsibility to his assistants—and, by virtue of his endearing personality, he got from them happy co-operation and loyal service. His one piece of advice to a young assistant was: "Never try to bluff your students. No one can be expected to be able to answer all their questions off-hand, but make sure you are able to tell them how and where to get the information they want."

His class excursions were eagerly looked forward to by the students: one felt that here he was in his element. At first he would walk shyly on ahead, but soon the shyness disappeared as the students clustered round him, asking questions and imbibing the knowledge he was ever ready and willing to impart.

It gave great pleasure to his friends, most of all perhaps to his assistants, when, after having served the department for many years as Lecturer-in-charge, he became Aberdeen's first Professor of Geology, when in 1922 a Chair of Geology was established.

In private life he was intensely shy and reserved, and his quiet manner, allied to an attractive old-world courtesy, gave him a dignity which was unassailable: but, beneath the almost insurmountable shyness he was very human—simple and delightful, full of quiet whimsical humour. He was not a " public man " in the accepted sense—but he was a born teacher, and his students and his staff remember him with gratitude and affection.

MARGARET CURRIE

Since 1937 the Chair of Geology has been held by THOMAS C. PHEMISTER, *who is thus one of our Professors of longest service.*

BOTANY

In 1860 the study of Botany belonged to the Medical Faculty and was allied to Materia Medica. The first Professor began life as a physician and a teacher of Materia Medica, but was progressively enthralled by the pure study of Botany as a subject in itself.

GEORGE DICKIE

Professor of Botany, 1860-1877

> " The garden, when I knew it best, was filled with plants gathered from very various sources, most of them being of botanical rather than of horticultural interest; for Dr. Dickie was a botanist first and a gardener afterwards."
>
> GEORGE KING

Dr. Dickie first practised as a doctor and taught Materia Medica and Botany at King's College. In 1849 he became Professor of Botany in Belfast, and in 1860 received the same appointment in Aberdeen.

Well do I remember the first appearance of Dr. Dickie when, at 8 o'clock on a cold morning early in May 1860, he delivered his introductory lecture as professor in the old botanical class theatre at Marischal College. The earnest gentle manner and quiet dignity of the man, the singular picturesqueness of his face, and his homely manner of speech very soon subdued the tendency to make a disturbance which existed pretty strongly amongst those of the students whose sympathies were with Marischal College, and who were disposed to resent the appointment to the new chair of a quondam lecturer at King's. And, long before the lecture ended, every student was attentive and silent because his heart had been won by the new teacher.

It was as a systematic botanist, and especially as an expert in the group of *Algae*, that Dr. Dickie had chiefly made his own reputation. He had collected extensively and carefully in the North of Scotland, and he knew the flora, both phanerogamic and cryptogamic, familiarly and accurately. . . . He fully recognized that botany plays but an ancillary part in the curriculum of medical education; and his chief effort in teaching it was to utilize it as a means of quickening and training his students in the arts of observing natural phenomena with truthfulness, and of drawing conclusions from their observations with accuracy.

In 1860 Dr. Dickie published his *Botanists' Guide to the Counties of Aberdeen, Banff and Kincardine*—a book based largely on his own collections. This was followed in 1864 by a similar volume on the *Flora of Ulster*, also based on his own work.

After the conclusion of the class session of 1860 he took a party of his students on a botanical tour to Ben Macdhui and Cairngorm. [Although this was not repeated because of a break in his own health, it shows that from the first the Botanical Department understood and practised field work.]

GEORGE KING: *A.B.A.*

JAMES W. H. TRAIL

Professor of Botany, 1877-1919

In the early years of the century the lad starting a science course at Marischal College would meet, in his first year, three formidable men then coming to the last phase of their careers. Niven, Japp and Trail were of the real stuff of the Scottish professoriate, old style. The botanist would be the first encountered. From the Gallowgate a bicycle with outsize frame would wheel into the quadrangle and, prompt on the stroke of eight but with no margin, Trail would walk into his classroom. Doors locked, latecomers must wait in limbo till after roll-call; no serious fate overtook the casual laggard. Tall, spare, bearded, buttoned into an old surtout, the professor talked for his hour to a hundred men and women of arts, science and medicine. In 1906—perhaps as marking the quater-centenary, though the active cause was never known—the famous beard came off, and the rounded profile of the Memorial Volume gave way to the resolute chin of the Memorial Tablet.

The Trail family came from the Mearns and Aberdeenshire but James William Helenus was born in the Manse of Birsay and there spent his early boyhood; we always thought him an Orcadian. His love of natural history started in Orkney and, until much later, was devoted to animals—insects, spiders, birds and mammals. In Aberdeen, at the Old Town Grammar School and the University, he went on with his collecting and observations and added plants to his interests. He soon set his heart on a naturalist's career, on a post abroad, on a journey to the Amazon. Meanwhile his father, an able but indolent man, had in 1867 won appointment to the Chair of Systematic Theology, as the result of a competitive examination; thenceforward the fortunes of the family were linked to the University. After James's appointment to the Chair of Botany in 1877 father and son sat for some years together in Senate.

He resisted his father's endeavours to make him train for the ministry, even though—or perhaps because—the bait of presentation to an important living was held out. Yet, after taking the Degree of M.A. with honours in natural science, he studied divinity for a year to show his good will. Only then did he get reluctant permission to start the course in medicine. During these years he had come under the influence of Dickie and Nicol. He did a great deal of work for the latter in arranging the natural history museum and his tastes still leant to the animal side. He had made a deep impression on both these men and through their influence he realized his first ambition. When half-way through his medical course he was offered the post of botanist and medical adviser to an expedition to the Amazon. He was fond of telling how, on a walking tour, his boots gave out forcing him to return home early and in time to accept the offer which had come by telegram. We fostered the legend that the sole of one of these boots was preserved in the botanical museum to show a growth of Penicillium.

The 15,000 miles on the Amazon made him. His collections were extensive and exceedingly well prepared. Many of the groups were worked over by others but he himself dealt with the palms in a series of important papers which won the approval of Sir Joseph Hooker and, later, the fellowship of the Royal Society. After three years he came home, a bearded stranger, to finish his medical course. Only a year after graduating, and at the age of twenty-six, he was appointed to the Chair which he occupied till his death in 1919. Of the many duties he assumed during these forty-six years one deserves special mention. He was happy and proud in his long chairmanship of the Library Committee; and the Librarian was fortunate in a Chairman who supported him in setting the library on a course to meet modern needs.

In the long list of his papers the insects and spiders continued to make an appearance. He did important work on the fungi and was an authority on plant galls. But his interest settled more and more on the flowering plants of Scotland. His mind was not of the cast for making generalizations. His interest in nature was Linnean—in identification, classification and distribution. He spent endless time in gathering facts on the distribution in detail of the flowering plants and devised methods for systematically recording his data. Only in the last few years has there been a real attempt to make such a survey for the whole kingdom. Trail was doing the work for the counties round Aberdeen at the turn of the century. In this, and in his attitude to the teaching of botany, he was, as Professor F. O. Bower once said to me, a very far-seeing man.

As a teacher he was painstaking. His lectures were dry. But the evident care he took to make things clear and orderly earned respect. And the dryness was an astringent which inculcated love of work for work's sake and for the sake of the subject. This was the major influence which Jimmie Trail had on his science students. The diminutive showed that respect was tinged with affection. It was a rather awed affection, for he was not a very easy man to approach—except on matters scientific. An awkward shyness masked a kind nature; and he abjured the socially ameliorating influence of wine and tobacco.

The excursions helped. They were an essential part of his teaching; and in the informal atmosphere out-of-doors we got closer to him. He strode along, pausing now and then surrounded by a crowd peppering him with questions to which the answers never failed. There were evenings at Scotstoun Moor and the Links, mornings on the Dee, days at Cruden Bay and St. Cyrus. The pictures I hold clearest in mind are of the tall, trim figure, umbrella in hand, cap on head, a vasculum over one shoulder and the portfolio of records over the other, perched on a rock at the Bay of Nigg surrounded by students with seaweed offerings; or seated eating his oat cake and apple, relaxed and talking at large on the Pinkie Braes.

MACGREGOR SKENE

20

WILLIAM GRANT CRAIB

Professor of Botany, 1920-1933

Professor Craib was an authority on Systematic Botany and spent many of his vacations at Kew, working on the Siamese flora. (This part of his work has been continued by Dr. Euphemia C. Barnett.) Born in Banffshire, he graduated at Aberdeen with special distinction in Botany, but after graduating he turned for a time to marine engineering; turning again, he resumed his study of Botany, acted as assistant in the Botanical Gardens of Calcutta and carried out research in tropical plants under the Indian Government. In 1909 he was transferred to the Royal Botanic Gardens at Kew, where his particular branch of study was Indian trees. His next step was to the Royal Botanic Gardens of Edinburgh, his special interest going with him and finding scope in lectures on Indian forest trees to the Forestry Department. In 1920 he came to Aberdeen, but the following year he sustained a serious accident which involved the amputation of a foot and curtailed his subsequent activity. All through his years in Aberdeen, in addition to teaching and acting as Curator of the Cruickshank Botanic Garden, he continued to follow his interest in Asiatic flora, and was engaged in work on it at Kew when he was struck down by illness and died at the age of fifty-one.

J. R. MATTHEWS

Professor of Botany, 1934-1959

A Professor's life may be a happy one—it is certainly not an easy one! Those of us who have had the privilege of working with Professor Matthews in the Botany Department are in no doubt of the happiness but find it difficult to believe that so much could have been accomplished in a mere quarter of a century.

As a lecturer and teacher Professor Matthews is outstanding. His many students—some now scattered to the ends of the earth—owe him a deep debt of gratitude. But large as was his share in teaching he devoted much time to reorganizing his department to cope with the ever increasing number of students and the ever widening scope of his subject. A new Herbarium in the Cruickshank Building took shape to house the large collection of plants—some 55,000. These are mostly from the British Flora, many from Professor Trail's collection from Aberdeen and the adjacent parishes, and a large collection from Thailand. The Cruickshank Gardens were quite transformed; the sunk garden, ruined during the war by the erection of that ugliest of buildings—an air raid shelter—was converted into a wonderfully beautiful rock garden.

But Professor Matthews saw further than his own department. He worked hard to establish a friendly and close relationship with other departments and with the Research Institutes and the North of Scotland College of Agriculture. He was Chairman of the Committee of the Macaulay Institute for Soil Research and was largely responsible for the foundation of the Department of Microbiology which was housed in the Cruickshank Building until suitable accommodation was available at the Institute. He was a member of the Governing Body of the College of Agriculture and for many years Convenor of the Staff and Research Committee.

As a member of the University Court for some years and as Dean of the Faculty of Science during the war years he did yeoman service on many committees. He represented the University at the 7th and 8th International Botanical Congresses at Stockholm (1950) and Paris (1954) and at the Jubilee Celebrations of the Long Ashton Research Station (1953). When in 1953 the University acquired the Tillycorthie Estate Professor Matthews was appointed to the Committee to consider the uses and management of the estate. Less erudite work also fell to his share. A court minute records the expression of thanks to Professor Matthews and others for " their most excellent assistance in organizing fire-watching for students ".

In 1952 the Secretary of State, with the approval of the Court, appointed Professor Matthews Chairman of the Governing Body of the Scottish Horticultural Institute at Mylnefield, Perthshire.

Professor Matthews' services to outside Bodies—the Nature Conservancy for Great Britain, of which he is an original member and Chairman of the Scottish Committee, the Botanical Society of Edinburgh and others, have been recorded in a previous number. The university and his many friends rejoice with him in his award of C.B.E. (1956), the Veitch Memorial Medal in Horticulture (1958) and the degree of LL.D. by the University (1960).

E. C. BARNETT

The present holder of the Chair is PAUL E. WEATHERLEY. *A notable member of the Department through the last forty years was* DR. DOROTHY DOWNIE, *latterly a Reader, who with the exception of three years spent in Chicago worked all through that period in teaching and research, her special subject being Mycology.*

CHEMISTRY

FROM RETORT TO GRID—1860-1960

" The erection of the present-day edifice of Chemistry is a great human achievement." So wrote Professor Findlay in *A Hundred Years of Chemistry* published in 1937, and during the hundred years since the union of Marischal and King's the Chemistry Department has kept pace with this development; it has grown from " a circular bench round which the students took their stand " at Marischal College in 1860 to the magnificent but already over-crowded building at King's College, opened by Sir Robert Robinson, O.M., in 1952; from a staff consisting of an invalid professor, his deputy (later appointed professor), and William Creyk, M.B., assistant to the professor and later Surgeon Lieutenant-Colonel in the Army Medical Staff, to the present staff under Professor G. M. Burnett, consisting of a reader, twelve lecturers and six assistants. This year, on the eve of a further great expansion in student numbers, Aberdeen celebrates the hundredth anniversary of the fusion of two universities into one and of two chemistry departments into one, but the time may not be far distant when in view of the continual growth of the Department the University will have to consider some form of sub-division with, it may be, the appointment of an additional professor.

When the two Universities were united it was decided that only one Chair of Chemistry should be retained. Professor Clark (Marischal College) was superannuated and his apparatus purchased for the sum of £78 4s. 2d. Professor Fyfe (King's College) was appointed to the new Chair, the purchase of his apparatus costing the University £80. These expenditures would appear to provide a precedent for the present-day large transfer fees when scientific professors and their apparatus migrate from University to University. Although of little eminence as a chemist Fyfe had proved himself " a good enough teacher "; he was popular with his students who called him " Fifie " as a term of endearment, although they did not always behave correspondingly in the classroom.

JAMES SMITH BRAZIER

Professor of Chemistry, 1861-1888

Fyfe, however, was unable to take up his professional duties, for in 1860 his health broke down and James Smith Brazier, who had been assistant to Professor Clark at Marischal College, was appointed to act as deputy. On Fyfe's death at the end of 1861 Brazier was appointed to the chair. Before coming to Aberdeen he worked under Professor A. W. Hofmann in London and Professor T. Andrews at Belfast; affectionately known as " Jimmy " he " had a great human heart and cheery kindly face "; his

" laugh so lightsome and characteristic brightens up the chemistry class-room ". Professor William Bulloch, F.R.S., writes of him:

" He was tall and portly—his silvered hair parted carefully and his beard neatly trimmed. His whole toilet seemed to be performed with the same neatness and care which characterised his lecture table. Precision and exactitude were evidently important things with him. Every student in trouble found him a good adviser and a perfect gentleman." When he retired they presented him with his portrait in crayon by F. Anderson. " If only a fair lecturer, he was a superb technician. Of the many practical teachers I have seen he was by far the greatest. All his experiments seemed to come off. On one occasion only do I remember an experimental failure. It was dramatic. A combustion of two gases was to take place in a heated glass tube. The professor leaned against the bench, gave his puff (he had some respiratory or circulatory affliction) and said, ' I have never done this experiment in my class before '. He lighted the bunsen, bang went the tube in a thousand pieces and he added with perfect presence of mind ' and I shall never do it again '." Each year, during the elementary lecture course, Brazier, to illustrate the action of hydrofluoric acid on glass, etched some note of historical in-terest on a glass plate. This interesting collection dating from 1855 survives, with a few exceptions, and forms a valuable link with the past. One such record relevant at this time may be quoted:

" 1860. Bon-Accord Chemistry University of Aberdeen."

THOMAS CARNELLEY

Professor of Chemistry, 1888-1890

In 1888, Professor Brazier was forced, through illness, to resign and Thomas Carnelley who had studied at Manchester, Bonn and Heidelberg was appointed to succeed him. Prior to coming to Aberdeen, he had been for three years the first professor of Chemistry in the Firth College, Sheffield, and for six years the first professor of Chemistry in the then recently established University College, Dundee, where he played an important part in the promotion of technical education. He was an excellent lecturer, " as a demonstrator in the laboratory he has few his equal " and by his numerous investigations, he actively contributed to the advancement of chemical knowledge. On his death in 1890, Sir Henry Roscoe and Professor Bedson wrote: " Of a retiring, modest, unselfish and deeply religious nature, his earnest enthusiasm served not only to create in all a sincere regard for him but to make him beloved by those who were privileged, whether as teachers or students, to become intimately ac-quainted with him." He was a man of wide vision who was deeply aware of the ever-increasing importance of chemistry in everyday life and " in the curricula of a great university ". In his inaugural address he said:

" The function of a university is two-fold; to distribute knowledge by successful teaching and to extend it by research work. If it lacks in either of these it is one-sided and imperfectly developed." " Such was the key-note, the manifesto so to speak of the remarkable inaugural address of our new professor of chemistry and such has been the key-note of his achievements in the world of science " (*Alma Mater*). During his brief period in the Chair, Professor Carnelley persuaded the Court to approve the institution of degrees in Science. Professor Carnelley died during the summer vacation, 1890.

FRANCIS ROBERT JAPP

Professor of Chemistry, 1890-1914

Francis Robert Japp was appointed in October 1890 to succeed Carnelley. A member of a family of Dutch origin, Japp graduated in Arts at St. Andrews University before proceeding to study law at Edinburgh; unfortunately his health broke down, necessitating a period of convalescence abroad and it was during this time that he became interested in chemistry. After studying under Bunsen at Heidelberg and under Kekulé at Bonn he was appointed head of the Research Laboratory at the Royal School of Mines in South Kensington. Of Japp in Aberdeen, Professor Findlay writes:

" Unskilled in the art of self-advertisement and indifferent to the world's estimates of eminence or wisdom, Japp looked upon the general activities of the world and the impatient hurrying of men with a certain Olympian detachment and philosophic calm; and the petty annoyances which were laid upon him by the jealousies or inconsiderations of lesser minds he bore with amiable resignation. A lover of literature and of art, a linguist of ability and a musician of cultivated taste, Japp looked on life through many windows and to know him was itself a liberal education."

Japp's interests were almost entirely centred on the classical organic chemistry of the period and as a lecturer on that theme to his advanced students he was at his best. " He did not, however, lecture freely and was rather too much addicted to reading from his lecture notes." Nevertheless his lectures were not altogether uninteresting and were sometimes punctuated with anecdotes. " One, told in connection with the use of magnesium in photography, did service for a number of years. It was a story told of a lady lion-tamer who was to be photographed with her head in the lion's mouth and ended with the words: ' At the flash of the magnesium light, the jaws closed.' "

" As a lecturer to young Scottish students, Japp fell somewhat short of achieving complete success." He had little interest in their out-of-class activities. Although the majority of his first-year students were

" medicals ", the context of the course was largely for science students. His lectures—even his inaugural address—were greeted by noisy behaviour on the part of the students, behaviour which was frequently aggravated by the sarcasm with which Japp on occasion protested. On one occasion during his first year he interjected: " I have been accustomed to address my class as gentlemen; I can see that some hardly feel at home in the part."

It was, however, in the research laboratory that Japp excelled and during his tenure of the chair at Aberdeen upwards of forty papers were published by him in collaboration with his private assistants or research students.

James Strachan, H.M.C.I.S., writes of Japp: " He was highly respected, though one would hardly call him a popular figure. He wore spectacles with very thick lenses, being very short-sighted, and he carried a large

Japp and his laboratory assistant

pear-shaped head on top of an inverted pear-shaped body. In spite of the dyspepsia from which he habitually suffered, he expounded, with a steady flow of well-chosen language, chemical theory and demonstrated experiments which were always carefully devised. Some share in his success he would have been the first to acknowledge was due to his patient laboratory assistant, James Taylor, a white-faced little man with a sandy beard who sat on a stool in a corner and promptly responded to the careful briefing of the part he had to play. James was himself no mean chemist and his superior knowledge acquired through many years of service was readily placed at the disposal of the worried students in the labs."

The smooth running of a scientific department depends upon the ready and efficient co-operation of technical and other staff and the Chemistry Department has indeed been fortunate in this respect. James Taylor joined the staff in 1877 and for forty years served the Department quietly and efficiently. In 1909 he was joined on the staff by William Laing who since that date, apart from six years spent at McGill University, has continued to serve the Department with skill and devotion. Laing, who now enjoys the status of chief technician and is the most senior technician in the University, has, with his sound knowledge and wide experience, played an important part in the growth of the department. It was with the greatest of pleasure that all members of the Department learned that the Senatus on 8 June 1960, decided to confer an honorary degree of B.SC. on Mr. Laing.

FREDERICK SODDY

Professor of Chemistry, 1914-1919

Professor Japp resigned at the end of session 1913-14 and in July 1914 the Court appointed Frederick Soddy, F.R.S., to the Chair. A graduate of the University College of Wales, Aberystwyth, and of Oxford, Soddy had, with Rutherford, with whom he was working in the University of Montreal during 1901-3, advanced the fundamental theory of radio-active disintegration. Shortly afterwards Soddy went to work with Ramsay in London and once again his work led to important advances in the field of radio-activity. During both these periods of research Soddy was working with well-known, already established investigators. When appointed lecturer in Glasgow University, Soddy devoted himself to the study of the chemical behaviour of radio-active substances and, in much of his work, he was assisted by a young man, A. Fleck, who was later to become Chairman of I.C.I. Their work was a significant contribution to the understanding of isotopy. It was anticipated in the world of science that Soddy, when appointed to the Chair of Chemistry at Aberdeen, would build up a strong school of radiochemistry. But no such event took place. True, the war interrupted the normal trend of his researches in Aberdeen but even after he was called in 1919 to the Dr. Lee's Chair at Oxford (which he held until 1936) little scientific work emerged from his laboratories. In 1921 he was awarded the Nobel Prize in Chemistry, the first English-born scientist to receive this honour. How can this unfortunate change be explained? It was not a result of the war but rather of the man's outstanding—sometimes difficult—personality. He resented the dominant role that physics had assumed in radioactive research. Further, he was gifted in too many ways. A brilliant writer of prose, he found it all too easy to barb his articles with vehemence and sarcasm. He had a sincere interest in social questions and he fought hard on behalf of any whom he considered to be suffering from an injustice. He tried hard to introduce changes in the social structure, even in the structure of Oxford University; he took a deep interest in political economy and wrote several articles on the theory of money. As Professor Panneth wrote: " A brilliant intellect, an experimenter second to none among the founders of radiochemistry and an uncompromising champion of his ideals."

On 27 May 1960, Dr. J. A. Cranston, formerly Principal Lecturer in Physical Chemistry, Royal College of Science and Technology, Glasgow, who had worked with Soddy both in Glasgow and Aberdeen, delivered, under the auspices of the Soddy Memorial Trust, a lecture entitled " Frederick Soddy—The Pioneer ". Dr. Cranston gave his own ideas on Professor Soddy's switch into the field of Economics. Quoting from the lecture:

" During his sojourn in Aberdeen, 1914-19, I am not aware of any other work done by Soddy in the field of radioactivity—apart from supervising the completion of some work by his research student, Miss Hitchins, on the growth of radium from uranium. Some explanation of this is called for. *I* believe it was due to the outbreak of War. To a man of Soddy's idealism; to a man who saw how the immense developments in science could be used to benefit humanity; to a man who had speculated on the enormous powers that would accrue to mankind when the energy of the atom became available for his use; to a man of international outlook, who must have been dreaming of the approach of world government; to such a man, the outbreak of war between civilized European nations seemed an act of incredible folly.

" Soddy's first duty in Aberdeen was to deliver his Inaugural Address, and this was done on 16th October, 1914. Anyone knowing Soddy, and listening to that address, as I did, could not have failed to observe the change in him. Instead of being his usual buoyant self, confident in proclaiming the scientific outlook, of which he was proud,—instead of that—he was a grim figure, declaiming against the morality of a civilization that was prostituting for evil ends, the power for good that science was revealing. Soddy felt so strongly on this matter of the unfitness of society to be entrusted with scientific discoveries that he stated he would publish no more in that field. He set himself, with ever-increasing application, to discover the root causes of war, and he decided that they lay in the field of economics. His first essay in the subject led him to a description of the nature of wealth. Tracing the ultimate source of all material wealth as the energy we get from the sun, he applied the laws of thermodynamics to show that wealth had the nature of a flow, which, although it could be used as it passed, could not be hoarded.

" I am completely incompetent to assess the value of Soddy's contributions to the study of economics, nor to say what influence, if any, his views have had on the more modern outlook on the subject. What I can say is, that his approach to the subject, via thermodynamics, was almost certain to be incomprehensible to orthodox economists (if there are such beings), and was thereby ignored by them. Nevertheless, Soddy's investigation went on for the remainder of his life, leading him to examine such questions as the nature of money itself—and the effect of the convention that money should earn interest. In particular, he traced the development of the modern system of credits, and showed how the banks were empowered to create and destroy money at will, and as he said, for their own profit."

ALEXANDER FINDLAY

Professor of Chemistry, 1919-1943

To succeed Soddy, the University Court appointed Alexander Findlay, a graduate of the University in Arts and Science, who had worked with Ostwald in Leipzig. After holding lectureships in the Universities of

St. Andrews and Birmingham, he became in 1911 Professor of Chemistry in the University College of Wales, Aberystwyth. Clarity of thought and expression are necessary attributes of a lecturer and these Findlay had in high degree. He was a stimulating teacher. Meticulous in everything he did, he took infinite care in the preparation not merely of a lecture but also of the lecture-table experiments; no experiment failed through lack of rehearsal and every drop of chemistry was wrung from it. Discipline even with large post-war classes was quietly yet firmly maintained. His accuracy and lucidity of expression are also evidenced in his many publications. As soon as the re-organization of the department allowed, Findlay resumed his phase-rule studies and also opened up new fields of research.

It is odd to note that the major changes in the teaching of science within the university have emanated from the Chemistry Department. Carnelley had been largely responsible for the introduction of the B.SC. degree. Findlay realized the limitations of this degree in a world of rapidly expanding chemical industry; a progressive school of research, he argued, could not be built up in Aberdeen until an Honours degree in Science was instituted and until the University encouraged post-graduate research by the award of a research degree. In 1921 he was instrumental in getting his colleagues to approve regulations for the Honours B.SC. and for the PH.D. degrees. As the new degrees attracted students in increasing numbers, the accommodation within the Department proved inadequate and Findlay persuaded the Court to give a new Chemistry Department high priority in its building programme. As plans gradually took shape and in order that his successor might be consulted, Findlay announced in May 1939 his resignation as from 30 September 1940. Before any appointment was made, however, the Second World War broke out and Findlay consented to remain in office. Ultimately Dr. H. W. Melville was appointed to the Chair but as he was engaged on war work he was unable to take up duties until the beginning of session 1943-44.

H. W. MELVILLE

Professor of Chemistry, 1943-1949

Melville, who was a graduate of both Edinburgh and Cambridge Universities, was elected a Fellow of the Royal Society just after his appointment to the Aberdeen Chair. He was Assistant Director of the Colloid Science Laboratory from 1938 to 1940 when he went to the Ministry of Supply. Even after taking up duties in Aberdeen Melville continued his work with the Radar Research Station and this necessitated much railway travel. His tremendous energy and unruffled personality, however, enabled him to overcome the discomfort and inconvenience of war-time travel, to overtake the duties of the chair and to build up a strong research school; in addition much of the detailed planning of the new department had to be tackled.

When, in 1949, Melville was appointed Mason Professor of Chemistry in the University of Birmingham, the Court appointed to the Chair RICHARD MALING BARRER, a graduate of New Zealand and Cambridge who had already held appointments at Bradford Technical College and in the University of London.   On the year in which Barrer was appointed excavations began for the new department and he had many urgent problems to deal with.   On 17 September 1952 the magnificent new department was formally opened by Sir Robert Robinson, O.M., F.R.S.—a building which it was anticipated would provide adequate accommodation for many years to come.   In 1954 Barrer was appointed to Imperial College, to be succeeded by GEORGE MURRAY BURNETT, one of our own graduates who had been on Professor Melville's staff in Birmingham. Already Burnett is tackling the problem of overcrowding in the department at both undergraduate and postgraduate levels, a problem which threatens to get progressively greater as the student population increases.

R. B. STRATHDEE

DR. STRATHDEE, *Reader in Chemistry, who has written the above survey of the Department, has himself been on its staff for thirty-three years.*

AGRICULTURE

PIONEERS IN AGRICULTURAL
EDUCATION AND RESEARCH AT ABERDEEN

Agricultural education in the University dates back to 1790 when Dr. Fordyce, a distinguished medical graduate left a bequest to found a lectureship in " Agriculture in connection with Chemistry and Natural History ".   It was not until 1840, however, that the first Fordyce Lecturer, John Shier, was appointed.   At the time of the fusion of King's and Marischal Colleges, the Fordyce Lecturer was James Smith Brazier (later appointed to the chair of Chemistry) and he was followed by Thomas F. Jamieson, a farmer who was also something of a geologist. Curiously enough, his successor was also a Thomas Jamieson, the city analyst of Aberdeen and a man of great enterprise and enthusiasm.   He organized a Research Association, carried out field experiments and, with the help of some members of the University staff, started courses in agricultural science for school teachers.   He had his own experimental station at his home at Glasterberry, Milltimber, and, although he got considerable support from landowners and farmers, much of the work was done at his own expense.   He was regarded in many quarters as a crank but that is a common fate amongst prophets and pioneers.   His science was weak in places but his work on fertilizers and particularly on phosphates was widely enough known for him to be appointed a Chevalier (Agricultural Order) of the French Legion of Honour.

In 1895 a B.Sc. course in Agriculture was instituted and the Fordyce lectureship became a full-time lectureship in Principles of Agriculture. A University diploma in agriculture was also started which was continued until the 1920's when it was replaced by a College of Agriculture diploma.

James Wilson was the first of the full-time Fordyce lecturers and the early graduates included W. R. Buttenshaw (1898), J. G. Stewart who became a prominent official in the Ministry of Agriculture, W. A. Davie, later director of agriculture in the Sudan and W. J. Profeit. The first diploma was awarded to Alexander Pardy in 1897.

James Wilson was succeeded in 1903 by R. B. Greig (later Sir Robert), a very able teacher and administrator who became head of the Department of Agriculture for Scotland. He did much for agricultural education and took a leading part in establishing the chain of agricultural research institutes in Scotland. Greig left his mark on the Agriculture Department of the University for, during his eight years in Aberdeen, with William M. Findlay as his assistant, he started small-plot experiments at the Cruickshank Botanic Gardens and field experimental work on farms over the north of Scotland. This brought much good-will from the farming community and later led to Findlay's outstanding work at Craibstone becoming the focus of wide attention.

After Greig, J. M. Caie, a graduate in Arts, Law and Agriculture of the University, was Fordyce lecturer for two years until 1912, when he followed Greig to the Board of Agriculture for Scotland where he had a distinguished career as an administrator.

JAMES HENDRICK

Professor of Agriculture, 1912-1942

In 1911, thanks to the generosity of Lord Strathcona, the Strathcona-Fordyce chair of Agriculture was founded and James Hendrick, who had been University lecturer in Agricultural Chemistry since 1896, was appointed professor. The foundation of the Chair and Hendrick's appointment opened up a new era in the development of a school of agricultural science in Aberdeen. The close connection with the North of Scotland College of Agriculture (founded in 1904) continued and diploma as well as degree students had the inspiration of being taught personally by such well known science professors as J. W. H. Trail and J. Arthur Thomson.

Hendrick continued to teach agricultural chemistry and the choice of senior lecturer in Principles of Agriculture fell on W. J. PROFEIT who occupied the post until 1935. Profeit's approach to agricultural science was historical and philosophical. He had been disciplined in classics and philosophy before he studied science and the logic of his argument cut through many an apparently well founded " scientific truth ". He was a scholar of distinction and a great teacher. He had a deep influence on Findlay and helped to bring the Craibstone work to wider than local notice.

Of all the " Founders " of this modern school of agriculture, however, the most memorable will undoubtedly be Hendrick. He was recognized throughout the country and even further afield as one of the leading agricultural scientists and his students, when they went out into the world and measured themselves against others, discovered that they knew a bit more chemistry and had been more thoroughly trained than most. He was director of studies and research in the College of Agriculture and saw where advances were desirable and necessary. No sooner had the Development Commission been set up with funds available for agricultural research, than he put forward proposals on behalf of the University and the College of Agriculture for research in Animal Nutrition and Soils at Aberdeen. He secured the sympathy and support of the Commissioners and work was started in 1913 in a basement laboratory in his Department. The facilities were meagre—a bench for Animal Nutrition, another for Soils and one experimental animal, a goat—but from these small beginnings arose the Rowett Institute in 1919 and the Macaulay Institute in 1930.*

Hendrick made personal contributions to soil research. In 1912 he arranged for the construction at Craibstone of a set of lysimeters, blocks of soil enclosed in situ, for the study of soil drainage. They were the first of their kind with a rotation of crops grown on them and they yielded valuable results.

After Hendrick's retirement in 1942 the Strathcona Fordyce chair was occupied for three years by J. B. ORR (later Lord Boyd Orr) and since then by T. L. BYWATER (1946-53), A. B. STEWART (1954-58) and J. R. RAEBURN (1959).

The University of Aberdeen, through the work of the early builders, stands as one of the first centres in this country, and, indeed, in the world, to have fostered research and education in agriculture.

WILLIAM G. OGG
GEORGE DONALD

FORESTRY

Forestry was taught in the University from 1908, when a lectureship was instituted. In 1913 the degree of B.Sc. in Forestry was first given and new lectureships were formed in Forest Botany and Forest Soil Science. The first Forestry lecturer, William Dawson, had travelled extensively and had first-hand knowledge of continental forests. When in 1926 the Forestry Chair was inaugurated, Principal Sir George Adam Smith said: " This is the culmination of a long series of efforts

---

* [The first research officers in Animal Nutrition and in Soil Science became the first Directors of the Institutes. They were J. B. Orr, now Lord Boyd Orr of Brechin and W. G. Ogg, now Sir William Ogg.]

to secure a properly equipped Department of Forestry in this region of the United Kingdom most natural for the establishment of a scientific and practical forestry school." The Forestry Commission entrusted to Aberdeen the duty of carrying out on scientific lines investigations concerning the best methods to be employed in the afforestation of peat areas, which they regarded as one of the most important problems to be solved in the development of British forestry.

ALBERT WILLIAM BORTHWICK

Professor of Forestry, 1926-1937

The choice which the University made in 1926, when the Chair of Forestry was instituted, could not have been more fortunate. Borthwick was one of the few men in the country who by training, experience and mentality was qualified to undertake the organization of a Department designed for the training of young men in a highly specialized branch of applied science. A master of the detail of his subject, he had also the breadth of view which enabled him to grasp scientific problems as a whole and gave weight and authority to his opinion. In spite of his years—or perhaps because of his years—he was eminently fitted to be the first occupant of the new Chair. When he was good-naturedly twitted about being rather old to assume professorial duties, his reply was apt: " My father is still alive and well at ninety-four." But the son did not live to enjoy such length of years.

He came of an old and distinguished Border family. . . . Even to his more intimate friends Borthwick remained reticent about an interesting lineage. He was by nature shy and reserved; modesty and simplicity combined to make a personality of quiet dignity and charm. If he lived a somewhat detached life, nevertheless he found life full of interest and he certainly got a great deal of pleasure out of it. He was excellent company and had a fund of unsuspected humour.

After graduating at St. Andrews he spent three years at Munich in the study of continental methods of Forestry and in laying the foundations of a knowledge of systematic forestry and forest tree pathology which he made peculiarly his own. Seventeen years spent in the service of Edinburgh University were a period of active teaching and scientific investigation. He became President of the Edinburgh Botanical Society and the Royal Scottish Arboricultural Society and a Fellow of the Royal Society of Edinburgh. But an honour which he treasured more highly than these was the award by the Arboricultural Society of a gold medal for a collection of normal and pathological specimens of trees. The collection formed the beginning of what became probably one of the finest private collections of its kind, an invaluable aid to teaching which was brought into use at both Edinburgh and Aberdeen. During and after the First World War he rendered valuable service to the nation in connection with home-grown timber.

J. R. MATTHEWS: *A.U.R.* 1937

In 1938 HENRY MARSHALL STEVEN *became Professor of Forestry and still holds the Chair. During the Second World War courses were provided by the Department for men of the Canadian Forestry Corps on leave.*

ENGINEERING

WILLIAM BLACKADDER

Professor of Engineering, 1924-1940

In 1924 the University founded a Chair and Degree in Engineering. To found is one thing, to organize and operate a new Department is quite another. The new venture required as its head a scientist and a teacher, but it needed more,—someone able to formulate curricula, to equip laboratories, but above all, to attain and preserve a liaison between the University and Robert Gordon's College, alike essential to the success of the scheme. It seemed as if the University Court, seeking for a man with all the necessary qualities, had a well-nigh impossible task. In selecting Blackadder, the Court chose perhaps better than it knew. The son of a notable engineer, he had received his early education in a famous provincial seminary, the High School of Dundee. He was a Bachelor and Doctor of Science, and a Vans Dunlop Scholar in Engineering of Edinburgh University. Moreover, he had been for a number of years a Lecturer in Civil Engineering and Applied Mechanics in that most highly equipped of all extra-mural schools, the Royal Technical College of Glasgow. All this, with practical and responsible experience in harbour and railway engineering in Aberdeen, Glasgow and elsewhere, left no doubt of his fitness on the academic and practical sides. But what of his capacity to solve the initial and recurring problems inherent in an undertaking so complex? He quickly gave the answer. For he threw himself into the work of making the new Department ready in every particular with a quiet, unobtrusive, self-forgetful devotion which won general admiration. No detail seemed too unimportant if it contributed to the completeness of the whole. And his is the credit for the fact that the Engineering Department in Aberdeen University soon bore comparison with far older and richer schools. This also must be remembered: Blackadder himself was a Civil Engineer. His Department included Engineering, both electrical and mechanical, taught chiefly in the laboratories of Gordon's College by members of the College staff. On him alone rested the responsibility for that co-ordination of effort so essential to success. And yet, during the sixteen years of his tenure of the Chair, there was no whisper of friction anywhere. To his beneficent influence this tribute is due.

Nevertheless, it would be an error to suggest that Blackadder's only line must have been the line of least resistance. It was not so. He espoused causes in which he believed with persistence and courage.   No one could truthfully say of him that he had the gift of fluent, verbal persuasion, but he had a more effective gift.   The psychology of his persuasion was unselfconscious.   His power lay in the transparent simplicity and sincerity of his conviction, and in the fact that he never sought merely his own.   Without realizing it, he made those whom he desired to influence really want to do what Blackadder wanted done.   Sometimes in conversation he might say something which one less sincere would have said otherwise, or even something which sounded for the moment a little unkind, but offence against him was an impossibility, for he had made enmity to himself as unthinkable as enmity in him to other folk.

Blackadder loved the wide open spaces and all the joy of life.   In his long last illness he never quite gave up hope of sharing in it again.

A. C. MORRISON: *A.U.R.* 1940

Professor Blackadder died after a long illness in the early part of the Second World War.   Principal Sir W. H. Fyfe said, " While engineers are scarce no steps will be taken to fill Professor Blackadder's Chair ", and it was not until 1946 that his successor, who is still the holder, Professor JACK ALLEN, *was appointed.*

Of new developments in Science, mention must be made of a Diploma in Statistics, (in which there had been a lectureship since 1906, held by J. F. TOCHER, *1911-1940: the present holder is* D. J. FINNEY, *since 1954 a Reader) and a Readership in the History and Philosophy of Science, held by* WILLIAM P. D. WIGHTMAN *(Lecturer 1951, Reader 1955).*

THE LIBRARY

To those who know the Library of today, with its immense (but never immense enough) resources, the books of 1860, stored in galleries in the ante-chapel, and only (it would seem) sparingly used, would have appeared poor indeed. It was Professor Fyfe, who filled the post of Librarian till he was appointed in 1877 to the Chair of Moral Philosophy, who had the books moved to the present building: the late Sir Alexander Hosie told how, as an impecunious student, he was engaged by Dr. Fyfe to assist in removing the books. Dr. Fyfe was followed by Dr. Robert Walker.

ROBERT WALKER

Librarian and Registrar, 1877-1893

Registrar, 1893-1918

When the Librarianship was detached from the other office in 1893, he chose to remain Registrar. This post he filled till 1918 and, on his demitting office, the University Court resolved that he be retained on the list of the staff with the title of Emeritus-Registrar. He died in 1920.

The memory of him will not easily fade—the outlines are too clear and sharp; but while it is at its freshest we would gather up some fragments of recollection of his long useful life, and put on record the debt that the University owes to him. It is not a slight one. He served her as Assistant Professor, as Examiner, as Librarian, as Registrar, as Secretary of the University Court, as Clerk of the General Council; and in each case served her well and truly, and with meticulous conscientiousness.

It was as assistant to Professor Fuller that he received his nickname of " Function ", and this had a curious development, unique probably in the annals of nicknames. He was called " Function " because of his frequent use in class of the phrase " function x ", $[f(x)]$; and after he had broken his connection with the University, left Aberdeen, and again returned, the name still clung to him, in spite of a blank in the students' minds as to any particular reason for it. Finally, in their natural abhorrence of a void, they evolved an improvement, and he became " Functions "—one who played many parts in University life. Among these was the collecting of fees, over which he presided as Registrar, holding his court in one of the Library side-rooms; and on entrance to the University, students signed their names in the Album which was kept by him with most scrupulous accuracy. One of these old students, remembering the days gone by and the loving care with which that volume was treated, exclaimed with affectionate humour on the evening of his death: " I can fancy him even now, crying out to the Heavenly Registrar, about to use blotting paper, ' Stop, stop!—let the ink dry '."

Of his four academic posts, the Librarianship was least congenial to him, his mind being more satisfied with records that could be kept absolutely correct and spotless, than with books which may go amissing or be mishandled or grow unsightly. As a matter of course he carried out the duties of the office conscientiously; and he did good work in inducing the Government to extend the King's College Library hall in 1882. . . . But when in 1893 the post of Librarian was separated from that of Secretary, no one was surprised when he elected to retain the latter and devote himself to the business of the University Court and the General Council.

He might have stepped straight out of a page of Dickens. Boythorn, roaring anathemas against an objectionable neighbour, while he gently feeds the canary perched upon his shoulder, is but one remove from Dr. Walker shouting through the telephone vigorous objurgations against some " scoundrel and villain ", and in almost the same breath addressing dulcet tones of punctilious courtesy to the girl at the Exchange. He would worry the life out of the clerks working for him on the General Council Register, denouncing their inaccuracy, raging at their " incredible stupendous carelessness "—and in the midst of all there would arrive hot soup and delicious sandwiches, sent by his orders from Tillydrone, to revive their drooping spirits. Who could help laughing at his irascibility? Who could help loving him for it?

P. J. ANDERSON: *A.U.R.* 1920

PETER JOHN ANDERSON

Librarian, 1894-1926

> " I am bound to my University by no ordinary affection. . . . ' I take pleasure in her stones and favour the dust thereof '."

> " Naebody kens onything about thae new Ordinances except God Almichty and P. J. Anderson."
>
> DR. DAVID RENNET

When Mr. P. J. Anderson took charge of the University Library, he brought to his task, among other qualifications for the post, what Professor Masson once described as a greater and more loving knowledge of the intellectual history of the North-East of Scotland than anyone else had ever possessed. Mr. Anderson's knowledge of intellectual history was, of course, not bounded by geographical limits, nor could he have known the story of our special area without knowing much that lies beyond it. He was familiar with the problems of University origins all over Europe and with the various forms of academic constitutions, and the wide range of his studies, in the mathematical sciences, in law, and in literature and history, made him a fitting interpreter of the records of learning, invention and thought in many ages and many countries. But, wide and varied as was his knowledge, the University of Aberdeen, with the district of Scotland which it serves, was always his intellectual home.

Mr. Anderson's learning, his powers of mind, his capacity for organisation, his remarkable faculty of exposition, and the dignity and charm of his personality could not have failed to bring him name and fame in the great world beyond the quadrangle of King's: but such quests were not for him.

> Linked to the story and aim of the Crown,
> Bound by unbreakable tie—

the lines of his friend Dr. Bulloch are not less appropriate to the life of " P. J." than they were to the career of Sir William Geddes, in whose honour they were written.   In a sense in which I can never apply the words to anyone else—and I have known many lovers of Aberdeen—Mr. Anderson " was the University ".   His knowledge of its history has been partly embodied in the works which he has left behind him, but only those who have been his pupils can tell how intimate that knowledge was.   As a raw youth, ignorant of everything beyond Aberdeen and of most things in Aberdeen, I undertook to write a history of the University.   There was no official instruction in History, but I found my Master, and it is of a Master that I am thinking today.   A busy man, immersed in the reconstruction of the Library, he found time to give me my first lesson in palaeography, in heraldry, in historical method.   There was nothing, as it seemed to me then, that he did not know, no question that he could not answer or to which he could not show me how to find the answer.   Thirty years have passed and have increased rather than diminished my respect for his knowledge and his critical power, and, at all events with regard to our own University, I feel now as strongly as I felt then that he did indeed know everything that can be known, both the great things and the small things.

ROBERT S. RAIT: *A.U.R.* 1926

To appreciate the services that Mr. Anderson has rendered to the Library, we must try to realize the conditions that he inherited.   Before he took over its control, it was more a storehouse of books than a workshop for students, and greater consideration seems to have been given to the security of the books than their use by the students.   When I knew it first, the part most frequented was the fireplace, and the books most thumbed were the volumes of examination papers that had tested our predecessors.   It was open about three hours a day; there was but one assistant at the bar, and he himself merely a student, who could be but little service to his fellows in directing them to suitable literature in the discussion of a topic or the preparation of an essay.   The cases were kept locked and there was no opportunity of handling the books and allowing them to make their own appeal.   Recent additions were not easily discovered.   In recounting these disabilities, there is no suggestion of slackness or reproach against those responsible for the conduct or the supervision of the Library.   The income available was small, and the richer opportunities of today have come only with the ampler means

provided through additional Government grants and the aid of the Carnegie Trust.   When Mr. Anderson came, the key of his policy was the
use of the books;   all the organization of the Library must be made to
encourage students to use the books and to aid them in the easy discovery
of material that would assist them in their studies, and from that cardinal
purpose have grown the many facilities of today.   The Librarian was
proud of his office, but his pride was based neither on the beauty of the
Library, much as he liked and praised it, nor on the quarter of a million
volumes of which he was in charge, but on the relatively large number of
students who frequented it, and were found busy in its reading-rooms.

It is not possible to measure the services of Mr. Anderson, for he lived
and worked without regard to measure.

JAMES GILROY: *A.U.R.* 1926

To most boys the first taste of independence and of College camaraderie
is sweet; but to this one, who had never left home alone before and had
had no brother or intimate companion with whom to share his thoughts,
the life was enchanting.   He was poor, quite poor—even a share of his
first bursary instalment must be sent home—but poverty was so common
among the general run of students at that time, that it was scarcely
recognized as a hardship, and only added zest to the rare joy of a pit seat
in the New Town theatre, or the dissipation of mild beer from the old
brewery.   As one session followed another, there awoke in him a sober
passion for the place as a whole which, as he felt, not only brought him
gaiety and happiness, but evoked in him the best of which he was capable.

Before he had actually left College, there had risen in his mind the
ambition to do something towards reducing the chaotic condition of the
University records; and for many years after, he toiled away in all his
spare time to produce his tribute—a more complete list of officers, graduates and alumni, than is possessed by any other University in Scotland.

In accepting the post of Librarian to the University he lost from the
pecuniary point of view—and this was necessarily a very important point
for him—but he gained immeasurably every other way, for he had come
back to his natural home.   It was only when he was definitely installed
in the University, when he settled down finally to give all his energies
to her service, that peace and real contentment came to him.   From
thenceforth his work, his love, his happiness, were all concentrated round
the spot which, even in student days, had appealed to him more strongly
than any other, which had called to him through the intervening years,
and which now offered him a happier field of work than any he had dared
to hope for.

It was in the Library that his greatest work was done for the University—excepting always the editing of her records, which by this time was
almost completed.   With an enthusiastic and sympathetic Curator in
Professor Trail, he went steadily to work to remould not only the organisation but the spirit of the place.   So quietly the change came about, that

it was only those who had suffered under the former restrictions who recognised what a transformation had been accomplished.

One of his great desires was that the Library should be not only of use to its readers, but a pleasure to them; that the atmosphere should be one of goodwill and friendliness. He did much to attain this end, and it was a real satisfaction to him when former professors as well as students testified, as many did, that the time they had spent in the College Library was their happiest recollection of King's College.

MAUD S. BEST: *A.U.R.* 1926

Under the present Librarian, W. DOUGLAS SIMPSON, *whose knowledge, pressed down and running over, is so freely put at the disposal of all who seek it, the Library has continued to expand and to extend its services and its resources.*

ADMINISTRATION

As perforce must happen, administration increases in complexity as numbers grow. It was therefore a wise thing for the University to do when in 1894 the Court appointed one man as Secretary of the University, combining the offices of Secretary of the Court, Secretary of the Senatus and Faculties, and Factor and Treasurer of the University. That man was DONALDSON ROSE THOM, *a man of great dignity of carriage and mastery of detail. The Principal in whose time he died (1920) said of him:*

I never knew him to neglect what he undertook to do, or to grumble, or even to talk, about the heavy aggravation of his duties [during the war]. In my hearing he never said a harsh word of anybody else, and till he was forced by the state of his health to ask leave to resign I never knew him to seek anything for himself.

GEORGE ADAM SMITH

In 1919 the duties of the Secretaryship were taken over by HENRY JACKSON BUTCHART.

Aberdeen has had many distinguished sons whom Alma Mater has delighted to honour, but none who has rendered more filial, devoted and continuous service to his own University than has Colonel Butchart. The past three decades have seen tremendous changes and developments in the Universities of this country, and to cope with them administrators of the highest order were essential. This University has been outstandingly fortunate in its Secretary, upon whom the great daily burden of administration falls. Those qualities apparent in his many and varied interests were happily blended to make the ideal Secretary of this University. He has the skill of the lawyer, the enthusiasm and sociability of the sportsman, the loyalty and determination—and might one add the ' ferocity '—of the soldier; the selfless devotion of a son for Alma Mater. There is no aspect of University life upon which Colonel Butchart does not hold firm views, and none lies outside the range of his astonishing and tireless activity.

T. B. SMITH in a Graduation Laureation

Perhaps Colonel Butchart's greatest service to the University lay in his foreseeing the need for the huge expansion programmes we are at present engaged upon, and his advising and achieving the purchase of property and ground in the Old Town. The University is therefore in a position to go ahead with its building programmes on land of which it is already possessed. Although he resigned the Secretaryship in 1952, he remains Law Agent to the University. His other activities—mountaineering, ski-ing, soldiering—help to make him the warm, vital personality he is. After a distinguished career in the pre-1914 Volunteers and in the 1914-19 war, he was appointed in 1925 to command the Aberdeen University O.T.C., and in 1951 he became Honorary Colonel of the Contingent.

The quality of leadership has been defined as the influence exercised by an officer over his command when shorn of the authority of Military Law. This quality Harry Butchart possesses in full measure. He is a genial companion in and out of the Mess, emphatic in debate, fair and efficient in the fulfilment of his duties, with a tremendous reserve of energy. Enthusiastic in everything he undertakes, his enthusiasm is infectious and spreads to all who come into contact with him. It was his practice to know that little bit more, to be able to perform a task that little bit better, than the men he commanded. " What you can do, I can do better " was his motto. He was what Field-Marshal Alexander referred to as " that rare being, a first class staff officer who is also a first class commander ".

When General Montgomery took over command of the Eighth Army in North Africa he emphasized to all ranks the value of physical fitness. Butchart has long upheld this idea. In June 1908, with four companions, he climbed the six highest Cairngorm peaks within nineteen hours. Mr. John N. Milne, in lauding Colonel Butchart to the June Statutory Meeting of the General Council, recalled how in 1915 Captain Butchart, training amid the hills of Perthshire, " was always ahead of his men showing, by example, what was expected of them ". Twenty years later, in command of the University Contingent of the O.T.C., he was at his happiest when, amid the hills of Aberdeenshire, Perthshire, or the Borders, he was reconnoitring or participating in a training exercise. His beloved hills seem to catalyse, if this is possible, his activity.

R. B. STRATHDEE: *A.U.R.* 1953

The present Secretary, WILLIAM S. ANGUS (1953) is a grandson of Professor Stephenson.

Other officers of the University unknown to the earlier part of the century are the Director of Physical Education, ARTHUR W. BROCKS, (1927-1958) who with his assistant EILEEN M. CAMPBELL (1927-1938) made a vigorous impact on the student body. Mrs. Campbell in 1938 became the first official Adviser to women students, a post held after her too-early death in 1946 by MRS. MARGARET E. CLARKE, daughter of Sir George Adam Smith. New also was the Health Service for Students (ALEXANDER H. MACKLIN, 1947-1959) and the Chaplaincy (A. ALLAN MCARTHUR, 1947-1952, IAN R. PITT-WATSON, 1952-1958, and ALAN O. ROBERTSON, 1958). Many others we should like to include, but there is not room. We conclude with a handful of the best-loved and most vividly remembered Sacrists and Servitors.

21**

SACRISTS AND SERVITORS

JOHN COLVIN

Sacrist, 1860(43)-1872, Marischal
1872-1891, King's

Born at Stonehaven, he entered Marischal College in 1843 in his late twenties, and for nine and forty years he clung to each college in turn with a curious tenacity until he became one of the landmarks of our Alma Mater. During the last twenty years of his tenure he served King's College as sacrist, jingling his keys year in year out with the optimism which really gave him his eighty long years of life; meeting the grandsons of men whom he had known as beardless boys at Marischal College in the old days; and welcoming all who crossed his path.

" John " had seen great things in his time, boisterous crushes—which became less boisterous I think in consideration of his years; rectorial exploits, and as much pease-meal as would have fed the whole Aulton for a year. He had come to welcome as professors learned scholars whom he had known as bajans; and thus it was he never became the mere servant, for the professors of the eighties saw him with the eyes of bajans in the sixties or earlier.

J. M. BULLOCH: Alma Mater

John was an essential part of the Institution in all my time, and he was in a sense the real Principal or Dean at Marischal. . . . The recollections of John were often more vivid than the recollections of professors themselves.

SIR JOHN STRUTHERS

Minto regarded him as " a part of the place ". The feeling was mutual, and he viewed with a pleased smile the spectacle of the old man closing the door of the logic classroom and genially blowing a kiss to all within.

W. KEITH LEASK: I.B.

CHARLES HENRY BATH DANKESTER

Sacrist at King's, 1891-1918

" What will Dankey and the other members of the Royal Family say to this? "

Alma Mater

Dan . . . " goes up and down
To scourge abuses shadowed by the Crown."

Alma Mater

The " Lex Dankestris ".

Alma Mater

When I came as a Bajan to King's,
I heard some most horrible things:
    They told me that Dankey
    Was a pal of old Sankey
    And wrote quite the most of the hymns.

WALTER INKSTER

The remarkable thing about Dankester was the way in which he got into
the very soul of the University, and had assimilated its spirit.   The
Cornishman has always a greater sense of country pride than almost any
other type of Englishman, and this love of tradition, this pride of place,
had been accentuated in Dankester by the force of tradition which is
cultivated in the Army, especially in such an historic arm as the Gunners,
to whom he belonged.   But if the army gave Dankester the sense of
tradition, it did not turn him, as it very well might have done, into a
military martinet, for barrack yard discipline would be useless in tackling
the youth of a northern University.   Nor did it destroy that resourcefulness
which life in the army, unlike that of the navy, frequently induces.

From the time that he entered the service of the University Dankester
made himself thoroughly at home with us; he was absolutely one of
ourselves.   If he had been a graduate and had had generations of kinship
with the University, and sons being educated there, he could not have been
prouder of the place.   He had the spirit of " Ours " in his very blood.

J. M. BULLOCH: *A.U.R.* 1918

*Dan's sanctum was lined—tiered almost—with photographs of the students who
had been his friends—and who wasn't?   We learned there wisdoms that our
Professors didn't teach us and insights that we have not forgotten.*

JOHN BOOTH

Attendant in Surgery, Medicine and Midwifery, 1881-1932

" Boothie " *was a character remembered by all medical students through more
than half a century.   The famous tale, " Me and Ashley managed it a' oorsels ",
sets him securely beside the old-time " minister's man ".   Born in 1854 he entered
the University's service in 1881, and until 1932 his forthrightness, his energy and
particular knowledge in his own sphere, and the short work he made of pretension,
endeared him to the men whom he bullied and served.   Stories about him are legion:*

I recollect the occasion when along with some others, I went to the
Surgery Department at Marischal to look over the " Instruments "—a
collection of archaic tools, the uses of which I think Boothie alone knew.
I asked him if Sir Ashley Mackintosh and Sir John Marnoch were just
bursting with knowledge or as anxious as we were when they came to

their finals. Boothie replied: " Ach, Johnnie Marnoch and Ashley Mackintosh used to come to me an' spier ' What's this and what's that '; they were just as stupid as ye are yersel."

A. M. HENDRY

During an altercation: " Professor, when I tell lies I like to mak' the facts of it."

Just prior to the appointment of a successor to Professor Marnoch, Mr. Wm. Anderson was crossing the Quad when Boothie met him and asked, " Here, Anderson, are ye guan tae get the Chair ? " Mr. Anderson replied, " That remains to be seen; why ? " To which Boothie answered, " Weel gin ye get it, I'll hae tae bide on, cause ye dinna ken onything aboot the diagrams; but gin the ither chiel gets it, weel, he can jiest scutter awa himsel."

A self-assurance that touches the sublime and that went hand in hand with a very real efficiency.

JOHN HARVEY

Fireman at Marischal, 1906-1907

Assistant-Sacrist, 1907-1934

> If Harvey kept a plot
> With sweet forget-me-not
> And succulent shallot,
> 'Twould be a fragrant spot:
> But clearly he could not,
> No, clearly he could not;
> He'd have to bend a lot
> To cultivate his plot—
> He'd have to bend a lot—
> No, *clearly* he could not.

JAMES SUTHERLAND

> When all the Quad is hard and froze
> And Harvey's face looks red and raw . . . .

Alma Mater

Memories of Harvey are plenty as blackberries—and occasionally as ripe—of Harvey walking a girl-student down the Quad with his arm around her shoulder; of Harvey finding that the mouthpiece of a new telephone in the S.R.C. room was broken—and then mysteriously wasn't broken—of Harvey knowing every class, time-table, examination list, professor and lecturer and student—but the classic tale of Harvey is of the day when H.M. Queen Mary arrived for her Honorary Graduation, and the car swept into the Quadrangle a few minutes before it was expected, while the reception party was hastily struggling into its gowns. Imperturbably Harvey took out his watch and held it towards the Queen, and said: "Ye're ower seen, Yer Majesty." The academic horologe. . .

WILLIAM CHRISTIE

Attendant at New King's, 1913-1936

Crest: A handbell *agitato*.

Alma Mater

What does gloomy Christie say
In his bed at break of day?
" Gau'n to rain," says gloomy Christie,
" Ay, it's gau'n to pour the day."
Christie, it will surely brighten,
Sullen skies at length will lighten—
Christie only lights his pipe an'
Then repeats his prophecy.

JAMES SUTHERLAND

Long, gaunt, morose, Christie in the years between the wars exercised a harsh but stimulating educative force on the young men who frequented New King's. " Those were days of fierce political antipathies and I rather think ", says Ralph Walker, " Christie despised as a villain or a fool anyone who did not openly declare himself a socialist." But brusque and grumpy though he might be, he was meticulous in his care for the college lawns (Christie's mower was one of the perennial summer sounds) and meticulous in his regard for time (Christie's bell—a large handbell—was one of the perennial sounds summer and winter.) Between him and Professor Jack there was a deep mutual respect. The Professor visited him on his death-bed, and reported the last words, so right and so convincing, as he fumbled for a watch that wasn't there: " Fat's the time? "

What then is the time? It is 1960, and our survey is ended. We may name but not portray the present holders of office. It is for the future to record them and for them to create the future that will be recorded.

O Christie, though the cold grey sea
Between us flows, yet still to me
Clatters thy mower in memory!
The Bishop stirs within his tomb
Lapped in the Chapel's stained gloom,
And swears, " Now, by Saint Jeromy,
That's Christie's mower," and drowsily
Sleeps on another century.

JAMES SUTHERLAND

But it will not be a century for sleeping through.

INDEX NOMINUM